Communism in Hollywood

The Moral Paradoxes of Testimony, Silence, and Betrayal

Alan Casty

THE SCARECROW PRESS, INC.
Lanham • Toronto • Plymouth, UK
2009

Published by Scarecrow Press, Inc.
A wholly owned subsidary of The Rowman & Littlefield Publishing Group, Inc.
4501 Forbes Boulevard, Suite 200, Lanham, Maryland 20706
http://www.scarecrowpress.com

Estover Road, Plymouth PL6 7PY, United Kingdom

Copyright © 2009 by Alan Casty

British Library Cataloguing in Publication Information Available

Library of Congress Cataloging-in-Publication Data
Casty, Alan.
  Communism in Hollywood : the moral paradoxes of testimony, silence, and
betrayal / Alan Casty.
      p. cm.
  Includes bibliographical references and index.
  ISBN 978-0-8108-6948-6 (hardback : alk. paper) — ISBN 978-0-8108-6949-3
(ebook)
  1. Motion picture industry—Political aspects—United States—History—20th
century. 2. Communism and motion pictures—United States. 3. Blacklisting
of entertainers—United States—History. 4. Blacklisting of authors—United
States—History. 5. Screenwriters—United States—Political activity. 6. Motion
picture producers and directors—United States—Political activity. 7. United States.
Congress. House. Committee on Un-American Activities. 8. Communism—United
States—History. I. Title.
  PN1993.5.U6C347 2009
  384'.8097309045—dc22
                                                          2009015438

⊚™ The paper used in this publication meets the minimum requirements of
American National Standard for Information Sciences—Permanence of Paper
for Printed Library Materials, ANSI/NISO Z39.48-1992.

Printed in the United States of America

For Jill

In gratitude to Sue Rossen
and in memory of Steve Rossen,
who lit the fire

Contents

Part I

BEFORE THE CONGRESSIONAL HEARINGS: THE SHAPING OF A CULTURE OF IDEOLOGY, ART, AND CONFLICT

1

Emblems of Righteous Ideology: The "Trials" of Albert Maltz and Robert Rossen

In early 1946, screenwriter Albert Maltz was at the peak of his career. In his successful recent screenplays, he had structured the material to embody in them some of the idealistic principles of his political beliefs, at that time regularly proclaimed as the principles of the American Communist Party. In February—enthused by the seeming prospect of idealism that could be acted on in the postwar world, but wary of the doctrinaire rigidity that could stifle it—he had published an article in the party organ *New Masses*, "What Shall We Ask of Our Writers?" In it, he proclaimed the need for a writer to freely follow his calling and ideals. It did not take long for him to be summoned before a night-long tribunal of his Communist Party comrades, indicted and "convicted" for his sinning against the party's code of discipline, for violating its ideological principles for the role of writers.

Three years later, in 1949, Robert Rossen had reached an imposing position of status and power in Hollywood. The former screenwriter was working on the final stages of his third film as a director, the powerful political film *All the King's Men* (1949), which was to go on to be one of the most honored films of its time. It was a film that embodied the very principles that were the basis for many of the party's avowed crusades and of its criticisms of the capitalist system and the American government. Yet Rossen was summoned before a night-long tribunal of his Communist Party comrades, berated for the deviations from party doctrine that his notable film allegedly contained.

At a second tribunal, Maltz relented and confessed his sins. At *his* inquisition, Rossen finally walked out.

One "trial" before and one after the first hearings into Communism in Hollywood by the House Un-American Activities Committee (HUAC)—the two, in their similarities and significant differences, are focused dramatic emblems of the moral, artistic, and political conflicts with which Hollywood was riven in the twenty-five years of active and influential Communist life in the movie world, 1935–1960. The paradoxes that were the moral maze, the unhealing wound, through those two and a half decades and even the decades since can be epitomized and defined in the levels of implication provided by the two meetings and by their protagonists and the strikingly contrasting aftermaths of their lives and cinematic and political careers.

These meetings—and others like them through the years—reveal the elemental distorting discrepancy between idealistic beliefs and goals and the realities of the Communist world. The rhetoric of idealism, a golden crusade, was distorted into destructive ideological rigidity, into deceit and denial of fact and truth. The trials encapsulate the obedience of Communist parties and their members to the definition of principles, issues, and judgments, to the forceful insistent control of all parties and their members by the Soviet Union and by the Comintern and its successor, the Cominform, the Soviet organization in control of worldwide Communist parties and movements. In this constant interaction, discipline and the rule of doctrine deny the nature of art, of human complexity. They distort idealism itself. Those who crusaded for free speech submitted to censorship, accepted the denial of the very freedom of speech that was the core of their political protests. In turn, they enforced that thought control on others, to the ultimate point of personal vilification of those who dared to disagree.

Even the differences in the two trials reveal the precise nature of this control and obedience. In 1946, the dominant issue for the Soviets in the new postwar world was the reassertion of hard-line principles and necessary measures to enforce discipline in parties worldwide after the strategies and allowances during World War II, as had been exemplified in America by the wartime dominance of Earl Browder and Browderism. By 1949, as the Cold War strategies took more specific shape, so did the programs, often murderously so, for discipline, for peace crusades, and for the actual *content* of art, literature, and film. The attack on Rossen's *All the King's Men* applied the doctrines of Zhdanovism as it enunciated the requirements for progressive art as part of the battle within the crisis posed by the hostile capitalist world.

The two central figures were in different circumstances in relation to the party at the time of their sessions. Those differences, however, were minor compared to the significant and exemplary differences that their two responses prefigured—Maltz capitulated, Rossen walked out. As the anti-Communist and blacklist period developed—and its aftermath continued through the decades—the two men can serve as the ultimate representatives, the epitomes of those at the extreme opposite poles of actions and consequences along the tortured spectrum of belief and action of the era. Maltz, who refused to testify, was blacklisted and subsequently honored as an idealistic hero; but he continued to remain silent about the monstrous evils of the Soviet Union that he continued to defend. Rossen, who eventually did testify and did name names, did begin to work again, but he stood up against the party and the Soviets, and was subsequently castigated vehemently as a betrayer.

In the five years before his two party trials, five of Maltz's screenplays had been produced; two—*Destination Tokyo* (1943) and *Pride of the Marines* (1945)—had been praised both for their wartime patriotism and humanistic idealism and their technical skill. He had also been praised for a World War II documentary honoring the wartime struggle of the Soviet Union, *Moscow Strikes Back* (1942), and a postwar documentary calling for multiracial equality, *The House I Live In* (1945; theme song performed by Frank Sinatra). He thought he could express that kind of mixture of idealism and ideology in a public Communist Party forum. He was wrong. In his article in the February 12, 1946, issue of *New Masses*, he advocated that the standard for the writer's role in the progressive struggle should be reviewed, and that less restrictive approaches be considered. As for himself, he said, "I have come to believe that the accepted understanding of art as a weapon is not a useful guide but a straight jacket. . . . In order to write at all, it has long since become necessary for me to repudiate it and abandon it."[1]

The attacks on such a claim for freedom of speech were quick to arrive and brutal. In fact, the attacks had likely been arranged in advance: at least half a dozen counter-articles in *New Masses* and the *Daily Worker*, as well as numerous letters to the editor, suddenly appeared. It had been odd for the *New Masses* to print Maltz's article in the first place. The article was clearly being used as a ploy in the main American Communist Party (CPUSA) internal campaign at the time, the broader battle to completely destroy the traces of undisciplined "Browderism" in the CPUSA, and to instill in the American party the demands of the new directives that the international body had mandated for its national subsidiaries. At a meeting of the national committee, still in February 1946, the new ideological czar Eugene Dennis echoed the terms of the current Comintern campaign being officially promulgated by its leader, Andrei Zhdanov. Dennis rebuked the *New Masses* editors for this example of a "bourgeois-intellectual and semi-Trotskyite article." The chief editors, Joseph North and A. B. Magil, immediately published their mea culpas and attacked Maltz, whose article was defined, and used, as a dangerous lingering vestige of the "soft" united-front wartime policies of longtime leader Earl Browder (Browder had already been expelled from the party a week before the Maltz article was published). The article was seen as dangerous to Communism and the

Soviet Union in this new time of American imperialist aggressiveness. It was no time for such declarations of renegade independence.

A few months later, in a speech to the Soviet Central Committee in August of 1946, Zhdanov defined in more complete terms the details of the "necessary measures" that the party had already initiated and acted upon in earlier directives. He called for continuing and constant vigilance so that "our comrades, both as leaders in literary affairs and as writers, be guided by the vital force of the Soviet order—its politics."[2]

New Masses literary critic Samuel Sillen, William Z. Foster, Joseph North, and Mike Gold, among others, took this political approach in their condemnation of Maltz's proposal. Gold, a longtime friend and one-time colleague of Maltz in the left-wing theater of the early thirties, set the exaggerated apocalyptic context in four of his *Daily Worker* columns in February and March: "We are entering the greatest crises of American history. The capitalists are plotting (and the big strikes are the first example) to establish an American fascism as a prelude to an American conquest of the world." And so Maltz, as what he called a "veteran," should realize the necessity of rejecting "Browderism, when Marxism was being liquidated. . . . All that was truly Communist and rooted in the masses was being skillfully wrecked by the champions of 'breadth' and Browderism." Sillen published a series of six articles in the *Daily Worker*, all in February. In one of Gold's articles, he admonishes Maltz to heed the conclusion of Sillen's "searching analysis": that Maltz's thesis is a dangerous example of broader evils—"a retreat from Marxism . . . a denial of the social role of the artist . . . a veiled attack on the Communist movement [that] lays a new basis for conciliating Trotskyism . . . [that] defends the liquidation of leftwing literature."[3]

As usual, the pattern of doctrine was new—for example, in yoking Browderism together with Trotskyism—and yet not new at all. In the *Daily Worker* of October 20, 1937, party literary czar V. J. Jerome had echoed the traditional line as he cautioned against "scribblers and unskilled intellectuals in the literary field who have sneaked back to the bourgeosie through the gateway of Trotskyism." He condemned "the too common notion . . . that the literary battle is a thing apart from the political struggle."[4]

In 1946 in his *New Masses* contribution, novelist Howard Fast rebuked Maltz "for *liquidation* [emphasis added] not only of Marxist creative writing, but of all creative writing which bases itself on progressive currents in America."[5]

Screenwriter Alvah Bessie joined in: Maltz should realize that "we need writers who will joyfully impose on themselves the discipline of understanding and acting upon working-class theory." As did John Howard Lawson, the dominant Hollywood party member, in a subsequent, chapter-ending article in *New Masses*, "Art Is a Weapon" in the March 19, 1946, issue.[6]

In February, the word had gone out to the Hollywood comrades, and Maltz was called to a fraction meeting of more than fifty people, loosely presided over by Lawson, held at Abe Polonsky's house (or, as some remembered, across the street from Polonsky's house at Morris Carnovsky's). Among several others, Sillen had come from New York to ensure party discipline. Los Angeles party boss Nemmy Sparks was there. Writer Leopold Atlas was there, and in later testimony before the HUAC remembered Sparks' "sneering look of contempt . . . the personification of the commissar." Atlas recounted that when Maltz rose to defend himself, "almost instantly all sorts of howls went up in protest against it." Any attempt to defend him was "literally shouted down." Atlas recalled Bessie's "bitter vituperation and venom," and the voice of Herbert Biberman, "his every accent dripping with hatred. Others from every part of the room jumped in on the kill. . . . They worked him over with every verbal fang and claw. . . . They evidently were past masters at this sort of intellectual cannibalism."[7] Writer George Beck remembered that the "trial" had lasted through the night.

A week later at a second meeting, Atlas was again present as "the hyena attack continued . . . with a rising snarl of triumph, and made him crawl and recant." Dalton Trumbo, however, afterward found something moral in Maltz's surrender. "It was a measure of himself, a sign of belief, a sign of loyalty, and there is a virtue in that."[8]

Atlas saw it differently: "Maltz's martyrdom, if that what it was, was false, sterile, destructive."[9]

In the *New Masses* of April 9, 1946, Maltz made public the confession of his mistakes in "Moving Forward." He criticized himself for publishing harmful personal impressions, for a "one-sided non-dialectical treatment of complex issues." In his first article Maltz had used novelist James T. Farrell as a positive example; in his second he attacked him. With eerie, unrecognized irony, he now said he realized that "Farrell's history and work are the best example I know of the manner in which a poisoned ideology and an increasing sick soul can sap the talent and wreck the living fibre of a man's work." He repeated the terms of his recantation when paraded out at a public meeting at the Embassy Auditorium in Los Angeles, a meeting pointedly entitled "Art—Weapon for the People." Sillen again came out from New York for the meeting. In his speech, he stressed the meeting's theme: "If the term 'weapon' seems crude, remember the struggle is grim." Lawson and Trumbo also spoke. This time Sillen praised the three—Maltz, Lawson, and Trumbo. All three, Sillen said, represent "the advance consciousness of the artist."[10]

At the HUAC hearings in October of 1947, Maltz was one of the "Hollywood Ten" who testified but refused to testify; Robert Rossen had been called to Washington as one of the original Nineteen, but he and the rest were not asked to testify at that time.

In the thirties and forties, Rossen had been active in the Communist Party in Hollywood, more of a participant in party organizations and major activities than Maltz. During World War II, for example, he was chairman of the party's single most important wartime organization and public event, the Hollywood Writers Mobilization. As the Cold War set in, however, his beliefs began to weaken, his doubts to strengthen. His rebellion against party discipline increased.

Beginning with *They Won't Forget* and *Marked Woman*, both in 1937, thirteen of Rossen's screenplays had been produced, and he had then directed three films, including *Johnny O'Clock* (1947) and *Body and Soul* (1947). In 1949 *All the King's Men*—the first on which he had acted as writer, director, and producer—was not seen at the time in its full implications, yet received great immediate public and critical acclaim and some thirty awards. Among them were the Academy Award for Best Picture, Best Actor (Broderick Crawford), and Best Supporting Actress (Mercedes McCambridge); the *Look* Achievement Award for best screenwriting; the Screen Directors Guild Award for best directing; and the Foreign Language Press Film Critics Circle Award for best film, best screenwriting, best direction, and best production.[11]

More significant than its awards were the film's political and psychological themes, and the visceral impact of its style and visual verve. It was in its time the strongest, most direct critique of the uses and abuses of political power in American film. It retains its power today as a dramatization of the corruptions arising from greed and betrayal, the destructive consequences of the complicity of money and politics, of the excesses of capitalism itself. On a personal level, it was the first major example of the themes of corruption and betrayal—betrayal of community, of ideals, of others, of oneself—that would become so central in Rossen's films.

He had produced a film with stronger and more meaningful social content than anything created by his fellow Communist Party writers and directors. There was little likelihood that a party meeting could produce any changes in the film. Nonetheless, the critique—the attack—was called, a matter more of purifying the spirit and repenting, of admitting one's errors and promising to do better in the future. At the meeting were many of those who had, like Rossen, been among the Nineteen called to Washington in 1947. By 1949, the Hollywood Ten had subsequently been convicted of contempt of Congress and were all facing imprisonment (which began after legal appeals were denied in mid-1950). All in attendance were suffering through the first stages of the blacklist, and so were understandably even more emotional than usual in the meeting's typical mix of ideology and personal feelings.

However, in addition to the added tensions generated by HUAC investigations, this particular meeting was fueled by two other volatile areas of emotion and belief. On the one hand—in contrast to the strictly ideological attack on Maltz—there was the personal resentment over Rossen's wavering about his party membership and loyalty (not "paying" his dues, for example) combined with his rise in the industry (a three-movie contract with Columbia as a producer, for example). For many, this was a clear signal of his impending sellout. And for some it was certainly tinged with an unfaced envy.

But still, the meeting was in the main another example of the CPUSA and Hollywood party obedience to current doctrines and strategies of the Soviet Union.

Once again the latest formulation of the international cultural line had been produced under the auspices of Andrei Zhdanov, influential member of the Soviet Central Committee and longtime culture commissar. The new principles of "Zhdanovschina"—and the necessity for their enforcement—had first been enunciated at a so-called peace conference, the World Congress of Intellectuals, in Wroclaw (Breslau) Poland in August 1948 (attended by some thirty Americans, including Donald Ogden Stewart and Howard Fast). These principles were then defined in directives sent to the leaders and culture czars of Communist parties throughout the world; they were emphasized particularly in major conferences throughout the Soviet-controlled areas of Europe. Zhdanov's speeches and articles through this period were also translated and quickly published in book form. The principles set forth how "the writer must educate the people and arm them ideologically." The result, as philosopher Sidney Hook noted, was "the intensification of cultural and political terror during the Zhdanov period, when the Central Committee of the Communist Party of the Soviet Union laid down the Party line in every discipline from art to zoology."[12]

The political and human consequences went far beyond the literary field—destructive of both art and life as they were in that realm. As was consistently the case, this cultural Zhdanovschina reflected, was indeed a part of, a broader strategic orchestration of the aggressive, antagonistic postwar political program of the Soviet Union.[13] The definitive form of the political program had been set in September 1947 in Poland at the organizing meeting of the Cominform.[14] At this meeting it was Zhdanov who presented the basic principles of this Cold War strategy, ostensibly, as he claimed, to defend the peace (and the Soviet Union) against the alleged aggressions of American imperialism. The world, he proclaimed, was divided "into two main camps—the imperialist and anti-democratic camp on the one hand and the anti-imperialist and democratic camp on the other. The main, leading force of the imperialist camp is the U.S.A. . . . The anti-imperialist and antifascist forces constitute the other camp. The U.S.S.R. and the countries of the new democracy [e.g., Eastern Europe] constitute the mainstay of that camp."[15]

The cultural principles within the political program were defined in a speech by V. I. Pudovkin, the legendary Soviet director, at the International Film Conference in Perugia, Italy, early in 1949. It was translated and distributed to party organs worldwide.[16] In general terms, however, the principles and demands of Zhdanovism had first been expressed by V. I. Lenin many years earlier, in 1905. Years before he could implement his principles in the new Soviet state, Lenin had proclaimed, "Down with non-partisan writers! Down with literary supermen! Literature must become a part of the common cause of the proletariat, a 'cog and a screw' of one single great Social-Democratic mechanism set in motion by the entire politically conscious vanguard of the entire working class!"[17]

As Pudovkin stressed in his 1949 speech, for the film medium (as well as all art) content was supreme. Film must be used in the struggle against capitalism; it must create "positive heroes," embodying "the people's" fight for freedom. "One of the main tasks of the cinema," he said, "is to bring to the screen the characters of positive people and to show them as an example to follow." To be avoided were the "bourgeois and cosmopolitan" artistic evils of formalism, pessimism, subjectivism, and insufficient social commitment. Interestingly, the Italian Communist Party itself, also using Zhdanov's speeches as a virtual manual, had the year before adopted two resolutions (one of the fascinating titles: "Against Imperialist and Clerical Obscurantism") calling for an art that served political goals and embodied most of these same principles.[18]

In America, the party line, as often was the case, was promoted and brought down to local levels by V. J. Jerome. In the American Communist Party, Jerome was a rather amorphous figure, a man who wore many, and changeable, hats. He was ostensibly the culture czar, and from the mid-1930s on, he had attempted, not always successfully, to enforce the party's interests and strategies among the Hollywood filmmakers. Through this period his chief conduit in Hollywood and loyal aide in maintaining discipline was Lawson—playwright, drama theorist, longtime screenwriter, one of the founders of the Screen Writers Guild, de facto leader of the Hollywood Reds. Lawson was the fervent, abrasive enforcer of party lines, as well as abstract Marxist theory, among the Hollywood CPUSA members and their close followers. Dorothy Healey, the longtime leader of the Communist Party of Los Angeles (LA) County, felt that Lawson "was a tragic figure. He was a man of talent and ability but he was struggling so hard to prove he was not a petty-bourgeois intellectual." Others, like fellow party member Paul Jarrico, had a less kindly view: "he was, in Party terms, and certainly in my eyes, an infantile leftist, a sectarian sonofabitch."[19]

Late in life, in his memoir *Being Red*, Howard Fast struck a lighter, wry note in his criticism of what he called Lawson's "puritanical lunacy." His anger dissipated by the years, he recounted a favorite party members' anecdote regarding Lawson's repeated and insistent critiques of the "antihuman lust for brutality" of Fast's novel (and subsequently movie) *Spartacus*. At various social events Lawson even demanded that his reluctant listeners consider calling for Fast's expulsion from the Communist Party. In response, Fast recalled, "certain people put up signs in their homes: THERE WILL BE NO DISCUSSION OF SPARTACUS HERE TONIGHT."[20]

Lawson himself was to go through the rigors of party discipline and repression in the fifties. After he had loyally served his time in prison for contempt of Congress, in 1951 he was ousted from his leadership position by a members' revolt, primarily led by Jarrico and screenwriter Michael Wilson. However, Sparks, the LA County Communist Party leader, stepped in and reinstated Lawson with the new title of liaison between the county party and the Hollywood Communists. He soldiered on; with that party support, he still maintained a good deal of power, especially in the face of government and industry attacks on Communist Party members.[21]

It was Lawson who called and chaired the meeting for Rossen. The chief complaints directly followed the terms of the Zhdanov directives, but the levels of vituperation and emotion were strictly Hollywood.

The Rossen tribunal early in 1949 was held at Maltz's house. Despite what he had gone through, or maybe because of it, Maltz was ardent in his attacks on Rossen at the new meeting. But as Edward Dmytryk, who was at the meeting and was one of the original Ten, remembered, he was outdone by others:

> *Censure* is too flabby a word. Rossen's *excoriation* took place during a meeting for the Ten held at Maltz's home. Thoroughly bewildered, he was, for the better part of the evening, pilloried by Lawson and those two acid-tongued specialists in the party's disciplinary procedures, [Herbert] Biberman and [Alvah] Bessie, three men who, lumped together, had not one-tenth of Bob's talent. . . .
>
> Bob did his best to fight back, but he was outnumbered, and there was no meeting ground. Eventually, he had more than enough. "Stick the whole Party up your ass!" he said and walked out of the house. And out of the Party.[22]

In his memoir, Ring Lardner Jr., another member of the Hollywood Ten, commented that "the result of the discussion [*sic*] was to drive Rossen out of the Party."[23] Lardner, among others, did not want to admit that there were other very important reasons that made someone want to leave the party; but the "discussion"—and what it revealed—certainly did contribute to Rossen's final break with the party. Beyond the emotions, what were the substantive issues at the meeting? What did they find so flagrantly wrong in the admirable *All the King's Men*? The problem was that it *was* a serious film of political criticism, and so, it was felt, it was more essential that it have the right ideological approach—especially as that had been redefined by Zhdanov. From this perspective, Rossen's film did not have the proper emphasis upon and "analysis" of the economic structures that should have been seen as the underlying causes of the corruption of Willie Stark's state government. Willie's violations were too personal, too unconnected to these basic capitalist structures. This plodding analysis did not allow for Rossen's more sophisticated development of Willy as *embodying* these capitalist evils, as dramatized by many details in the film. For another "flaw," the people were passive, complicit in their own enslavement. There was no proletarian uprising. And worst of all, that was part of a general lack of positive elements, the absence of positive proletarian heroes (a central emphasis in the Zhdanov program). The only positive action is taken (and at the last minute) by two weak bourgeois intellectuals!

Dmytryk's interpretation of the basis of the attack was more jaundiced. The film, he wrote, exposed "the evils of dictatorship," and the group knew, but could never admit, that dictatorship was "the rock on which the Communist Party was founded."[24]

In January of 1953, while thinking deeply about his past, his beliefs, and his present course of action, Rossen composed a letter to the *New York Times*. He apparently decided not to submit it. While the letter focused mainly on his desire to expose the destructive duplicity of the Soviets toward the Jews (which he talked about at some length when he testified in May of 1953), he did refer to the 1949 meeting. He commented on the response of "certain sections of the extreme left" to *All the King's Men*. "I was told by them," he wrote, "that the leading character of the film would be likened to Stalin and its theme to the Soviet regime, and to this degree, I was fanning the flames of World War III." He goes on: "In the light of history their apprehension was well grounded."[25]

In the days and years of turmoil and moral testing that followed these similar party sessions of ideological discipline, Maltz and Rossen took two strikingly divergent paths. They represent two emblematic extremes of action, consequences, and moral judgments. The consequences can be defined in two stages: (1) the immediate effects of their actions on their lives and careers and (2) the long-term moral paradoxes revealed in their actions and the enduring moral and character judgments based on their actions, shaped by the power of ideology and unrelenting feelings of betrayal.

Maltz epitomizes one form of the moral paradoxes engendered in the period. On the one hand, he refused to testify or relent. In this, he courageously and honorably stood up against the infringements of the HUAC and the industry blacklist. He served a short term in prison and was blacklisted. For what he believed in, he sacrificed years of a major career that was reaching its highest level. He suffered emotionally and economically—although, he like others, did manage, through much scrambling, to continue to get some work through "fronts" and other devices, at a much lower level of payment and status. When he was able to work under his own name again, his career could not regain the momentum or accomplishment of his pre-blacklist days.

Through the years of travail that followed, however, and despite some later doubts and party disputes, he remained a loyal believer in the ideals of the Communist Party, in the "magnificent things" accomplished by the CPUSA and the "extremely significant accomplishments" of the Soviet Union. He remained a persistent and often distorting critic of the policies and actions of the United States. In this he illustrates the other side of the moral moonscape, the contrasting aspect of the moral paradox. For what he believed in, he was one representative, and adamant, voice in what was really a "silence." In the silence of this kind of testimony, he denied the consequences of the actions, campaigns, and policies of the Soviet Union. As will be developed throughout the text, Maltz evaded the immensity of its assaults on humanity. Even when, much later, he admitted with obfuscation and limitation some degree of belated recognition, he expressed no regrets, saw no personal moral flaw in himself or his comrades for so belated a recognition of evil so long evaded and denied, allowed no recognition of any consequences of those years of active "silence."

Rossen had broken with the Communist Party by the time he was called before the HUAC during the second round of hearings in 1951. When called, he, as well as some others, took what was called "the Diminished Fifth"—stating he was not then a member of the Communist Party but refusing to discuss any possible prior membership or participation of himself or others. For two years he was blacklisted. In 1953, for what he then believed in—and certainly for the sake of the work he wanted to do—he testified fully. Much has been made of his naming names; little has been said of the thorough, thoughtful statements of principle and the detailed criticism of international Communism and the Soviet Union in his testimony. He did begin to work again, first in Europe, and then in Hollywood productions. But he never returned to Hollywood again.

For Maltz, then, the immediate consequence was loss of work and eventual return to work, but with less opportunity and fulfillment. The long-term consequence, however, was that in reputation he was glorified as a courageous martyr to the cause of free speech; in a key term of Victor Navasky, a "moral exemplar." During and after the blacklist period, he was also one of the most assertive of the righteousness of his cause and action, clamorous, often vicious in his denunciations of those who strayed, mainly those like Edward Dmytryk, Elia Kazan, or Robert Rossen, who betrayed by testifying. At times Maltz even found fault with a fellow loyalist like Dalton Trumbo, who in a speech in 1970 "erred" in allowing publicly that in those troubled times there were "only victims." Maltz's work, as has been the case for the work of many who were blacklisted, has been praised beyond its actual sturdy, workmanlike value, interpreted as having a profundity beyond its actual content of characters, structures, themes. In much of the writing about the period and its protagonists, he, again like others, has been given embellished and exaggerated credit for the major "writing" of films on which, within the Hollywood system, he did do some initial work; for example, such landmark films as *It's a Wonderful Life* (1946), *Broken Arrow* (1950), and *The Robe* (1953).

For Rossen, the consequences were strikingly opposite, the pain and turmoil like a reversed mirror image. He did work after his testimony, but not without struggle all the way. Early in this stage of his career he wrote, directed, and produced the monumental but flawed *Alexander the Great* (1956), then worked within the system on films he did not control until regaining the power to have total control over his final personal and complex films, *The Hustler* (1961) and *Lilith* (1964). He died at the age of fifty-eight in 1964. Through the years, in the conventional left-oriented treatment of Rossen's work in film criticism and history, the characteristics and themes of his work, its significance, are disputed, distorted, or merely ignored.

But there is more than this denial of the value of his work, more that is closer to the bone—and the heart. As has been the case for other key figures who testified, for more than half a century, the volatile mix of righteous anger and ideology has produced vituperative personal attacks on him as a man, not only as a filmmaker.

There are too many vulgar and disturbing examples; among them Walter Bernstein's rant to Paul Buhle in the interview anthology *Tender Comrades* (1999). After complaining about Rossen's mistreatment of him when Rossen supposedly reneged on a deal to hire him in 1949, Bernstein says, "I felt there was something essentially corrupt about him on a personal level. . . . You could tell that there was something slippery about him." Or Jules Dassin, whose resentment was unabated years later, despite the success he had found in Europe with such films as *Rififi* (1955), *Topkapi* (1964), and *Never on Sunday* (1960), and his marriage to Melina Mercouri: "His kids had to live with what he did." It was a note sounded by others as well about a number of people.[26]

These judgments of Rossen and his work typify an important level of truth and fairness that is denied within the orthodox interpretations and judgments of the period and its principals. In his way, Rossen, too, like others, stood up for what he believed, felt should be done—principles allowed no credence by the standard leftist critiques. He also did act out of personal need. Where, then, is the moral balance point between these needs and desires in the intricate dynamics of motive? Does the latter motive cancel out the first, deny it any credence? How does one judge this combination of motive and action in a man? Rossen turned against the international Communist Party and its actions, testified to what he saw as the truth. But in doing so, he and others named names and thus cooperated in a process that affected and damaged the lives of others. The agreement under pressure to naming names has another aspect of moral paradox. By the early fifties, the ritual had no practical use. All those who were going to be named had already been a part of many lists—whether the lists were accurate, distorted, unjust, or unwarranted. And so within the situation that did exist, it was rare that someone's livelihood was any longer actually threatened because of his or her name being spoken by a witness, checked off from a list provided. On a broader issue, cooperation with the Central Committee, it has been claimed, contributed to the ability of right-wing McCarthyite anti-Communists to infringe on people's rights, and lives.

In contrast, Maltz, and others, refused to cooperate and thus did not name names. But in their own complex mix of personal needs and beliefs, they remained silent in ways that were lies. Through many years and in many ways they defended and supported, often directly denying, monumental evil. Indirect as it might be, through their silence they cooperated in a process that was slaughtering and imprisoning millions of people.

Yevgeni Yevtushenko, the Russia poet of protest, passion, and moral honesty, has written about this unspoken defense of human violation, "When the truth is replaced by silence, the silence can be a lie."[27]

The contrast between Maltz and Rossen and between their places in the history of the period, its mythology, is a point of focus for another iconic moralistic phrase, again used by Navasky, "behave decently." Confined within the absolute dualism of the conventional wisdom, it is only Rossen and others who testified who did not behave decently, are nothing beyond the namer of names, the informer, the betrayer.[28]

But are there not many forms of, many paths to betrayal—in ways not faced and allowed in the decades of moral judgments of the painful drama of the period and its protagonists? What is it to testify, or not? What is one's full testimony, testament? Just what is it to behave decently? As a character in a Flannery O'Connor story memorably said, "It ain't easy in this here life"—and not without wreckage along the way.

2

The Moral Equation Redefined: Testimony and Silence, Decency and Betrayal

The hearings conducted from 1947 to 1953 were not the first congressional investigations of Communism in Hollywood, but no others had anywhere near their impact—on lives and careers, on the continuing narrative of film history and American history. No others resulted in a blacklist, which was accelerated by 1951 and was not ended for more than a decade; for some, it never ended. The intense momentum of these hearings and the extremity of their consequences, the vehemence of the responses from all sides—then and ever since—rose, in part, from the intensity of this stage of the Cold War between the United States and Soviet Russia. The Cold War conflicts and tensions fueled the power and influence of right-wing demagogues and the acceleration of the terms of protest by the Left. But the tragic, shattering human impact of the hearings was also the final volcanic explosion of more than a decade of rabid and cumulative battles in Hollywood between the radicals and the conservatives. And caught between—pulled back and forth like children emotionally tugged between neurotically warring parents—were the moderates and liberals.

By the end of 1953, many had refused to testify to one degree or another in the sequence of hearings; many had been blacklisted without being called to testify. And many had testified. A few examples of their reasons can define the direction of their thinking. Among his reasons, Robert Rossen, for example, referred to his previous action (in not testifying fully) as "what I considered to be a position of individual conscience. . . . I did a lot of thinking. I don't think, after two years of thinking, that any one individual can ever indulge himself in the luxury of individual morality or pit it against what I feel today very strongly is the security and safety of this nation." Among the things he realized was that in the Com-

16

munist Party, "none of the things that you believe in were being fought for in terms of the ideal itself. They were merely being instruments for some other end in itself."[1]

Among *his* reasons for testifying, Elia Kazan listed his similar belief that "we must never let the Communists get away with the pretense that they stand for the very things that they kill in their own countries."[2]

After serving his sentence for contempt as a member of the Hollywood Ten, Edward Dmytryk testified. "Defending the Communist Party," he had decided, "was something worse than naming names. I did not want to remain a martyr to something that I absolutely believed was immoral and wrong."[3]

As screenwriter Leo Townsend said when he testified, "Several years ago all of us fought with all our might against German and Italian fascism. Today there is a section of people who shut their eyes to Soviet fascism. I think it is time that they open them. If what I say here and if what this committee does here can help these people, I think that this will show a large measure of success."[4]

We will look again at the reasoning, statements of principles, and motives of those who testified and the reasoning and responses of those who did not. It is always instructive, though, to keep in mind the words that Jean Renoir had Octave (played by Renoir himself) say with both skepticism and rueful sympathy, in his great film of 1939 *Le Regle du Jour* (*The Rules of the Game*): "Because you see, on this earth, there is one thing which is terrible, and that is that everyone has their own good reasons."

The established history of this era of congressional investigations and blacklisting does not, however, allow for this sympathetic and rueful view of human complexity, of human possibilities and limitations. It posits, instead, an utter mythic duality of biblical dimensions and righteousness, an absolute moral dichotomy. It enshrines pure heroes and martyrs who did not testify versus totally irredeemable, untouchable informers, scoundrels, and betrayers who did—and named names. And never the twain shall meet in the complex paradoxes, the all too human ambiguities of acting on one's ideology and political beliefs—or on one's tangle of personal feelings and needs. There is a kind of political Gnosticism at work here—the forces of light against the forces of darkness—that has been accepted by now as the conventional wisdom about the period, unexamined and unrelenting.

The relentless, scornful flavor, the fervent religiosity, of this crusade is captured in the biblical allusions used by Victor Navasky in the introduction to his iconic *Naming Names* (1980), a book with a major influence on generations of responses to the issues and conflicts of the period. "The Aramaic word for informer as found in the Book of Daniel is *Akhal Kurtza*, whose literal translation is 'to eat the flesh of someone else.' The so-called Minean curse, which was introduced as the twelfth benediction to the daily

Amidah prayer, says 'And for the informer may there be no hope.' . . . Penalties for the informer range from flogging and imprisonment to branding
the forehead, cutting out the tongue, cutting off the hand, banishment, and,
most frequently, death."[5]

Writing about this period of intense anti-Communism and the equally
strong backlash against it, the noted critic Lionel Trilling commented on
"that dark and bloody crossroads where literature [we can certainly say all
art] and politics meet." He caught the painfully fraught mixture of personal
intensity and righteous ideology that carries artists and intellectuals not
only to defenses of extreme intellectual positions, but to defenses of literal
bloodshed as well.

Yevgeni Yevtushenko's eloquently wrought insight—"When the truth is
replaced by silence, the silence can be a lie"[6]—points the way to the path we
can take in reviewing and rethinking the moral dimensions of "testifying"
or not, of staying silent. The moral flaws of those who testified have been
written about, filmed, taught extensively. There were those who testified
who responded in fear, anxiety, and selfishness solely because of the pressures of being denied work or being liable to public exposure of personal
foibles or secrets. But there were those who testified who acted on principle
and belief—including, to be sure, those who acted on an intricate mix of
motives, but whose statements of principle were not, as is so often claimed,
merely a ruse and masquerade. The moral issues among those who did not
testify have received far less attention. For those who were, or had been,
members of the Communist Party and those who stayed close to its line
and activities through the years *stayed silent* about much more than the
party memberships of themselves and their colleagues.

In the introduction of the monumental *The Black Book of Communism*,
its chief editor Stéphane Courtois cogently defined the issue: "Most of the
time, however, the witness statements and the work carried out by independent commissions . . . have been buried beneath an avalanche of Communist propaganda, aided and abetted by a silence born of cowardliness
or indifference. . . . Regrettably, it was most tenacious in Western societies
whenever the phenomenon of Communism came under the microscope.
Until now they have refused to face the reality that the Communist system,
albeit in varying degrees, possessed fundamentally criminal underpinnings.
By refusing to acknowledge this, they were co-conspirators in 'the lie.'"[7]

From the earliest stages of the Soviet state, V. I. Lenin proudly proclaimed
these "fundamentally criminal underpinnings" and their necessity. Citing
Engels, he insisted that "in reality the state is nothing but a machine for the
suppression of one class by another. . . . Dictatorship is rule based directly
on force and unrestricted by any laws. The revolutionary dictatorship of the
proletariat is rule won and maintained through the use of violence by the
proletariat against the bourgeoisie, rule that is unrestricted by any laws."[8]

A major influential presence in the study of Communist terror, Robert Conquest was more forceful in extending this accusation to non-Communist commentators who defended and promulgated Soviet terror, as in their response to the "Great Terror" of the thirties: "In particular, the trials would not be so significant had they not received the blessing of some 'independent' foreign commentators. These pundits should be held accountable as accomplices in the bloody politics of the purges."[9]

One limited two-part program of the bloody Soviet horror show can serve here to capture symbolically the full import of the depredations of international Communism that were given this "blessing." In 1937 the politburo issued Order 00447. It instituted a quota system for regions and cities, establishing exact numbers for those to be arrested, within ten days of the assigning of each quota, on two levels—to be shot and to be deported, including whole families of the individuals selected. As the system proceeded, zealous regional officials (the great majority of whom were later executed or became major powers in the government, or, of course, both) almost always exceeded the assigned quota. Some even asked Moscow for permission to raise the quota level for their region. In addition, leaders at various levels of power were sent out into the regions to conduct the campaigns. Among the most notable:

- In the south, Lavrenti Beria exceeded his quota of 268,950 (such precise numbers were given) arrests and 75,950 executions.
- In Leningrad, in one of his other loyal roles—one destructive of lives, not art—Andrei Zhdanov arrested 68,000, executing most of them, before being assigned to conduct massive purges in the Ural Mountains and middle Volga regions.
- Future Premier Georgi Malenkov, it is estimated, was responsible for 150,000 deaths in Armenia and Belorussia.
- Future Premier Nikita Khrushchev, then party chief of the Moscow area, had 55,741 shot when the quota was 50,000. A year later when he was the Ukrainian "viceroy," he had 106,119 people arrested, to be either executed or sent to the Gulag.

Soviet records show that the system under Order 00447 produced 767,397 arrests and 386,798 executions in the general anti-Soviet category and 350,000 sentenced and 247,157 shot in the "national" category.

In conjunction, there was Order 00485. Under it, quotas were established for what were called "national contingents," because of their potential as "diversionists and espionage groups," or in the much-used terminology, potential "wreckers." The overall quota was 350,000 arrested, with special emphasis on Poles—144,000. Of those arrested, 246,157 were to be shot (and more were), including 110,000 Poles.

In less than one year, the two orders together produced about 1.5 million arrests and 700,000 executions.[10]

Many on the Hollywood Left could only see such reality through their ideology darkly. The creator of wonderful silent comedies Charles Chaplin did not, unfortunately, remain silent during speeches at rallies in support of Russia during World War II: "We are no longer shocked by the Russian purges. They liquidated their Quislings and Lavals, and it was too bad that Norway, Hungary, and other countries didn't do the same."[11]

Years later, Albert Maltz, with no recognition given to the historical context of his glowing phrases, could still regularly rhapsodize about "the Party experience. It actuated a passion for social justice which cultivated one's own innate passion and decency."[12]

And then there was the corollary, the ubiquitous cry that it was America and the West's fault. As for what caused what seemed to be the "cruelties of Stalin [not, of course, the system]," Lester Cole, in his autobiography *Hollywood Red*, many years later still insisted, "To me, the context was crucial: for decades, the Soviet Union was surrounded by military forces which had vowed to destroy the first Socialist revolution." Similarly, in *his* autobiography, even though he believes he has left "dogma or the unthinking obedience to the Soviet Union" behind, Walter Bernstein still insists on understanding the "suffering" of the Soviet Union (not of the people), "their terrible struggle to build the first socialist state in a world that had tried from the beginning to destroy them."[13]

As symbolized by this briefest of samplings, what must be considered is the meaningful juxtaposition of the "real world" of the Soviet Union and international Communism with such statements and beliefs as these by Maltz, Cole, Bernstein, and others and by the Communist Party policies and actions they followed and supported. This counterpoint provides the context for a reexamination of the established moral equation of the world of Hollywood at the time of the blacklist, and the reevaluation of the character and even the work of writers and directors who testified.

The moral complexity of the conflicts of the era, its paradoxes, were captured nicely in 1976 in a *New York Times* piece by Hilton Kramer. There were, to be sure, he wrote, those for whom "informing became a career in itself, and innocent people *were* smeared and even destroyed by false accusations." But, he insisted, there were "other villains of the tale—the many wealthy Communists in the industry . . . who denied their true commitment and beliefs, and thereby created an atmosphere of havoc and hazard for the truly innocent." Kramer's essay was written in response to the publication of Lillian Hellman's memoir *Scoundrel Time*. In his response to the same political memoir, William Phillips widened the scope of the betrayals, indirect as they were, by Communist writers who were "apologists for the arrest and torture of countless dissident writers in the Soviet Union."[14]

In the Hollywood film industry, the several hundred people who were blacklisted (a meaningful counterpoint to the millions on millions of victims of international Communism) were more of a mixed bag than is depicted in the conventional mythology, the tragic romance of the era.

At the center of this sad and wide web of damage and loss were the party members who did not testify and people who were as close to the party and its shifting lines as the actual members. They railed against the evil of the infringement on their freedom and of the blacklisting of the hundreds who suffered the loss of their jobs and substantial incomes; they proclaimed their rights under the First and Fifth Amendments. They had faced hardships and suffered losses. They had acted on principle, taken a moral stand in refusing to cooperate. But how they refused, and within what ideological context, had its consequences, and these consequences must be balanced against their losses in determining the moral equation. They denied and in some instances justified the espionage and subversive activities of the Soviets, denied absolutely the participation of the Communist Party of the United States in any of these activities, denied the control of the American Communist Party by the Comintern and Soviet Union. In ways that may have been small and indirect, but meaningful, they actually contributed to the implementation of Soviet foreign policy strategies and the continuation of Soviet tyrannies by their fund-raising and participation in—and often organization of—strategically orchestrated propaganda campaigns. These were the Communist-controlled rallies, conferences, organizations and committees, speeches, marches, open letters, books, articles, pamphlets, and so forth that were, through the decades, the smiling mask for Soviet intentions and destructive actions, both inside and outside of the Soviet Union. Even years later when the immensities penetrated the righteous armor of some, they found the path of evasion in such obfuscations and euphemisms as only the *madness* of Stalin, debatable *methods* and *techniques*, *unfortunate mistakes*. In later years, the frequent euphemism for their evading the recognition of any complicity was being *politically active*.

Whatever the hardships and the injustices that were endured, these varying degrees of loyal "moral silence" can also be seen as making them morally complicit in the ultimate, even if far-removed, consequences of what they defended and supported. As was summarized by Thomas H. Pauly in his recent study *American Odyssey*, "The reluctance to speak out on Communism increased its current threat." And by Irving Kristol in *Commentary* in 1952, defining the central destructive moral rationalization of this self-righteous silence: "[Their] belief that one is guiltless of the crimes that Communism has committed so long as he was moved to this association by a generous idealism."[15]

In 1973, in response to an article by the left-wing historian E. P. Thompson, who was still insisting on defending the value of their "utopian energies

Chapter 2

within the socialist [*sic*] tradition," the eminent scholar of Marxism Leszek Kolakowski wrote to his old friend and comrade: "O blessed Innocence! You and I, we were both active in our respective Communist Parties in the 40s and 50s, which means that, whatever our noble intentions and our charming ignorance (or refusal to get rid of ignorance) were, we supported, within our modest means, a regime based on mass slave labor and police terror of the worst kind in human history."[16]

Budd Schulberg, who wrote *On the Waterfront* (1954) and *A Face in the Crowd* (1957) after he testified, is, of course, not an objective commentator. But a mocking pithy phrase of his is a nice counterpoint to Yevtushenko's: "They question our talking. I question their silence."[17]

The actions and statements of the core of true believers had direct consequences in Hollywood. As Richard Schickel commented some years ago, this self-righteous zeal produced a kind of collaboration with their very enemies, the committees and the Hollywood Right and business power structure. It built further suspicions in the general public and fueled the demands and actions of their extremist counterparts. Schickel pointed out that this ideological rigidity continued to affect the defining and judging of those who opposed them. What became an "inarguable gospel" was a "tragic and ludicrous attempt retroactively to impose their mind-set, and the strategies that it proposed, on people who had broken with them, often with a great bitterness, and had every reason to distrust and deplore them." It "permitted no deviation from the stark dialectic" it enforced.[18]

A case can be made that the loud raucous silence of the zealous crusading Left stifled the possibilities for opposing and limiting the zealous crusade in Hollywood that the Right was mounting against them and the specter of Communism, real and imagined. And in the nation, these highly publicized provocations had an impact on a broader span of public opinion, providing more credence to the ranting and distorting of the Hearst press and other reactionary forces.

More specifically, remaining silent created an atmosphere of confusion that blurred the important distinctions between defense of liberal beliefs and dissent, on the one hand, and support of authoritarian ideological conformity and active subversion, on the other. While supporting teachers' rights "to reach *any* conclusion—no matter how heretical, even Communist and Fascist," the philosopher Sidney Hook, an indefatigable fighter for a liberal viewpoint in these battles over civil liberties, "sharply distinguished this right (to avow heresy) from conspiracy, which I defined as playing outside the rules of the game or participating in the organized preparation to do so." As he defined the issue succinctly, "the central distinction [is] between 'heresy' whose defense is integral to a free society and 'conspiracy' whose secrecy is inimical to it." In another context, Hook regretted the failure of members of the party to "seize the opportunity to plead their cause openly and honestly as earlier generations of radical Americans had done. . . . Instead, they acted like conspirators rather than like heretics, refusing to tell the truth or defy with dignity those who they believed should be defied." Thus, from this viewpoint, they betrayed the cause of the battle for freedom of speech and contributed to the power of those who infringed on it.[19]

The true party loyalists added a lesser level of their betrayal of the human rights of others. The strategy, the strident righteous antagonism and rhetoric in the statements and actions of the Communists at the first hearings and for years after, had detrimental consequences for the lives of others in Hollywood.

The larger and more eclectic number of those who were called and refused to testify, or were otherwise faced with career dilemmas, were generally at some distance from those at the party core, and from their beliefs and actions. In the widening web of zealous, and frightened, intimidation, these people were influenced by the narrow, rigid moral ground rules set from the start by the Left, the vehement either-or positions taken at the first hearings and "marketed" and insisted upon afterward. In this crusade— speeches and articles orchestrated by the Communist Party, for example, as the Ten were trotted out for appearances for years—any middle ground, any *cooperation*, was defined as *collaboration* with incipient *Fascism* (a term and its variants frequently hurled about). Those caught in the middle were placed in greater jeopardy than they would have been if the issues had been more clearly and honestly drawn. Those caught between were misled into accepting a restricted definition of the moral dilemmas they faced and the spectrum of possible moral options available to them. They were even swept into defending and contributing to some of the Soviet-oriented propagandistic positions and distortions that were being equated with the important defense of personal freedoms. A false unity and equality of all victims was created and has endured in the conventional history and interpretation of the period.

But at the time a more direct consequence of the actions of the Hollywood Reds and the American Communist Part was the destruction—as had often been the case in preceding years and conflicts—of any alliance with liberals that could have been a force to challenge the extreme pressures from the Right. While weakening the liberal Left, the actions of the Reds and their acolytes supplied ammunition and justification for the propagandistic claims of the Right.

Veteran screenwriter Philip Dunne was an active and staunch supporter of liberal causes and a leader in the early defense of the civil rights of the Hollywood Nineteen and then the Ten. But as he later wrote, he began to recognize the consequences for others that the conduct of the party members produced: "It remains my firm conviction that [the blacklist] could not have been imposed if a few misguided souls had not provided the witch-hunters with that fatal linkage. Those who joined the Communist Party, and faithfully followed its twisting line, cannot escape their share of responsibility for the broken careers and bankruptcies, the ruin of reputations, the sleepless nights and heartaches the many had to endure because of the [selfish] folly of the few." Dunne saw, too, that the strategies and activities of the Hollywood Reds in the fifties had important political repercussions in abetting the repression of freedom of speech: "It was primarily their conformity to the twists and turns in the party line dictated by the exigencies of Soviet foreign policy and their tacit support of repression in the Soviet Union itself that provided McCarthy, Nixon [and the others] with enough credibility to destroy the reputations and livelihoods of Communists and non-Communists alike."[20]

Some years afterward, in 1958, screenwriter Dalton Trumbo, one of the Ten and arguably the party's most effective pamphleteer, had painfully come to a similar conclusion. In an article that the party press refused to publish, he criticized the party's demand of secrecy and the accompanying stance of extreme confrontation. "For the blacklistees, he wrote, "all we can be certain of is that secret membership did destroy them." And he admitted the destructive impact on those not at the core of the Party, whose "quality of choice was radically changed for the worse . . . [who] were never given an opportunity to face the first and real choice." Whether "informers" or not, they were given "no realistic moment of choice."[21]

In a full-page ad in the *New York Times* that he placed at the time of his testimony, Elia Kazan linked several of the aspects of the betrayal involved in remaining silent: "Secrecy serves the Communists. At the other pole, it serves those who are interested in silencing Liberal voices. The employment of a lot of good liberals is threatened because they allowed themselves to become associated with or silenced by the Communists."[22]

At the time of the hearings, novelist and independent Socialist thinker James T. Farrell took a modulated position about the legality of the hearings, but not about the testimony of the Communists at the hearings. It was "shameful . . . to belong to such a totalitarian party," but it was not "*legally* a crime." And so he defended their right to remain silent about their affiliation with the party, but not their silence about "the millions of slave laborers who are rotting in the concentration camps" or the "trials which will end in death sentences, in bullets shot in the back of broken victims in Lubianka prison."[23]

It is interesting—and one can hope instructive—to wonder, What if? What if the major players in this passion play had chosen or been allowed to free themselves from the hidden agendas and authoritarian doctrine? What might they have done? There are several directions for our conjectures about alternatives. One option could have been to say, "Yes, I am a member of the Communist Party, I do defend the Soviet Union, and you have no right to do anything about it because . . ."

A second option could have been to say, "Yes, I am a member of the Communist Party, but I do not defend the Soviet Union or any conspiratorial activities. But you have no right to question my political activities because . . ."

Or, since behaving decently is such an important issue, the decent thing to say could have been, "On the basis of my first amendment rights, I refuse to state whether I am a member of the Communist Party, but on the basis of human rights, I do want to state that I realize the Soviet Union has committed . . . And is . . . And that the American Communist Party is . . . and has . . . I also know that both have participated in espionage against this country, which I don't approve of; but this is not the right way to deal with that espionage."

Of course, it might be said that the result of doing any of those would have been to be blacklisted; but then, the result of not doing so was the same, and had less moral stature and more destructive consequences for others. Similarly, it has often been said that any testimony would have led to the demand that one name names, and that once one testified, one could not then escape legally by taking the First or Fifth Amendment; and so that was a justification for not testifying at all.

Whatever the Communist Party and party members did, the attacks on Hollywood by the emotional and political tornado of demagogic anti-Communism would not have stopped. But for many who were not party members or that close to it, a less hostile climate in the industry, a different set of premises of what would be allowed by both sides, could well have made a difference in their lives. By the early fifties, and particularly by 1953, diverse negotiating procedures were conducted (and, typically, criticized) for allowing people to continue their careers, despite the loud continuing demands of right-wing, and often commercially venal, publications and organizations. Even the Congressional Committee had changed its approach—citations for contempt, for example, were infrequent. But the ritual naming of names was still held onto, like a rote catechism. It was, most of the time, still required as a public display to prove one's loyalty— no matter how much a person was testifying out of a principled opposition to Communism. By this time, however, any strong unified campaign by a liberal-left coalition had been impeded and basically destroyed by the adversarial extremes of the Communists. If such a coalition had lasted and flourished, it might well have influenced public opinion. A more favorable body of public opinion would have forced a softening of the rigid position of the anti-Communists—as the pressure of public opinion influenced the downfall of Senator Joseph McCarthy himself. The iconic demand of "naming names" would not have maintained its symbolic power. Legally—and, of course, hypothetically—if there had been a less adversarial stance by earlier witnesses and a less extreme adversarial climate, open and truthful answers would be far less likely to result in a citation for contempt, even if one answered some questions but still refused to answer others.

In his memoir of 1980, Dunne continued to support this position. "I cannot be shaken in my belief," he wrote, "that if the Ten had confined themselves to the simple and dignified statement we had proposed, Congress might have found it much more difficult to cite them for contempt, juries to convict them . . . and the Supreme Court to refuse to hear their cases."[24]

In the more than half century since the hearings, more attention in the media and in libraries is regularly given to hagiographic books by and about the blacklisted martyrs than to solidly documented studies of worldwide and U.S.-based Communism by such writers as Harvey Klehr and John Haynes or Ronald Radosh. Two branches of a typical small local library (mine) have six books by Paul Buhle and his collaborators in sanctification—because they are on the recommended list of a librarians' association—and none of the important and authoritative Klehr-Haynes series on Communism.

These communication filters—from the books and interviews of the protagonists to the articles, courses, programs, books of intellectuals and academics, to the unexamined assumptions of the popular press and media—have restricted and distorted the viewing of film history and the understanding, and even knowledge, of the works of individual film artists.

Within this orthodox viewing, the awkward, retrograde, and pedantic *Salt of the Earth* (1954)—still a constant in showings in courses, festivals, and lectures—is claimed by some as the "masterpiece" of social films of the time, while Edward Dmytryk's probing and humane, far superior *Salt to the Devil* (1949) is consigned to oblivion. In the first decade of the twenty-first century, workmanlike (at best) filmmaker Herbert Biberman is glorified as a martyred major artist in a movie about him and his work on the production of *Salt of the Earth*—while Rossen and Kazan are ignored, when not being reviled; while Kazan and Budd Schulberg's masterwork *On the Waterfront* is mocked as merely a self-serving apologia. Some historians of the Left have even claimed that in the film Terry Malloy testifies against his *friends*. Terry, of course, testifies against the totalitarian gangster union leaders who are oppressing his friends, who have in fear remained silent. In 2003 the ubiquitous Communist pamphleteer and prolific script and letter writer Dalton Trumbo received the idolatry of a factually distorting and evasive play about him as a witty moral exemplar—*Trumbo, Red, White and Blacklisted*. He is charmingly played by Nathan Lane at its premier and by more than a dozen other charming stars in theaters across the country ever since. In 2008 *Trumbo: The Movie* magnifies on the big screen the play's reverential myth of pure martyrs and utter scoundrels. In its review, the

New York Times opined it could "finally put to rest the hunt for good guys and bad." In contrast, the worst spiteful personal vituperations about Rossen, Kazan, Dmytryk, and others are perpetuated from one current book to another. In a passing anecdote in her book *Hellman and Hammett*, for example, Joan Mellen, no ideologue herself, picks up and passes on the jargon: "One day as [a group of people] were chatting about the Korean War on the Rosen porch, filmmaker Robert Rossen, a *government informer* [emphasis added], appeared."[25]

It is indicative and probably inevitable that a conflict between Albert Maltz and Trumbo provides a dramatic late summary of the entrenched dogma of absolute good and evil. Trumbo was the most successful screenwriter of the Hollywood Ten; he was also the most articulate and rhetorically, even ornately, polished of the defenders of their cause. Still, at times he was paradoxically independent and unpredictable. In a speech before the Writers Guild in 1970, upon being presented with the Laurel Award, he had allowed that in that troubling and terrible time, when you looked back, you could understand that there were in some ways not heroes and villains, but "only victims."

Maltz protested, insisting on the utter dichotomy. There *were* heroes who refused to testify and villains who testified and named names. In an exchange of letters Trumbo responded both with anger at Maltz's extremism and with some amendments and refinements of his original statement. Maltz was unrelenting and even vituperative; in a long letter, Trumbo finally broke off the exchange. But he also redefined further what he *really* meant to say about heroes and villains. He still defended his original phrase because one needed to recognize the difficulty of coping with personal pressures, but his final position was quite different from his speech. This last word has been ignored in the usual conventional references to the humane magnanimity of his phrase "only victims." In his final restatement of his position, Trumbo still reaffirmed the standard moral dualism:

> They [The Ten and the others] were, quite simply, the men who chose in that particular moment and situation . . . to behave with honor; and who in the face of enormous oppositions, have had the courage to remain honorable in that aspect of their lives to this day.
>
> They [the informers] were people who chose in that particular moment and situation . . . to abandon honor and become informers. So be it. They have lived with that terrible knowledge of themselves for over two decades, just as—even more terribly—their children have lived in such knowledge of their parents.[26]

But is it really so simple and easy, so moral, to name the names of the betrayers? If there are those who sinned to some degree or other by testifying, are there not those who sinned, to what greater or lesser degree, by *not* testifying, by keeping silent on a whole system of totalitarian terror and extensive espionage—before, during, and after the period of the blacklist?

Posing this question, and the implied ambiguity of its answer, does not defend the blacklist or *all* anti-Communist investigations, does not defend all that which is *rightly* called "McCarthyism." However, the filtering down of this dualistic dogma about the blacklist and its spreading into accepted conventional wisdom have developed within the context—ideological or unexamined assumption—of the use of *McCarthyism* as a meaningful definition of *all* the anti-Communism of the period. Within this defining premise, there was no justification for *any* anti-Communist activity or investigations. In this view, it was all—as Arthur Miller's *Crucible* so neatly encapsulates—a witch hunt.

Historian Thomas Powers points out that the distortion continues today at all levels of the academic world: "History texts routinely held up Joseph McCarthy to symbolize the full meaning and meanness of all American anti-communism." And Sidney Hook states that "future criticism of Communist thought and practice was not infrequently dismissed without consideration as merely a manifestation of McCarthyism."[27]

In the *New Republic*, in 1998, Michael Ybarra concluded, "But the government's effort to bolster internal security—however horrendously flawed—was a response to a genuine Soviet threat. Yes, most of the original blacklistees did suffer. But they did so in support of a cause that was neither benign nor remotely 'progressive.' It is in on-balance judgments such as these, not in moral absolutes retailed by today's ostentatiously repentant Hollywood, or by the media, that the real lessons of the blacklist are to be found."[28]

David Horowitz and Peter Collier define an interesting, if rhetorically exaggerated, connection between the blacklistees and McCarthyism: "Again . . . if self-styled 'progressives' like [Lillian] Hellman had not earlier apologized for Stalinism or maintained a disgraceful silence about its homicidal nature, there would not have been a field on which a McCarthy could have played."[29]

In his book *Reds*, Ted Morgan impressively shows that contrary to repeated claims of Nazi-like (the epithet "Soviet-like" was never used) depredations against civil liberties, "there was never a wholesale purge, either in universities or in the entertainment world." Klehr and Haynes nicely summarize the issue of McCarthyism in understanding the nature of the Communist penetration and the necessary security measures to combat it: "To recognize the excesses, mistakes, and injustices of McCarthy's anti-communist crusade is not to accept the distorted view that anti-communism was irrational and indefensible persecution of a group of American reformers or that it was impossible for the CPUSA to have been engaged in nefarious activities." Morgan documents and provides a striking summary of the basis for justifying investigations and security measures in the forties and fifties. Soviet espionage in the United States during and after World War I was "without historical precedent. Never did one country steal so many political, diplomatic, scientific and military secrets from another."[30]

Soviet intelligence officials themselves attest to the fact that many of the various investigations and governmental programs *were* effective in curtailing real Soviet espionage in the United States. Sergei Savchencho was at the time head of a Soviet intelligence department. A sample passage from his March 1950 report on the collapse of the Soviet's spy network in America indicates the Soviet understanding of the reasons for this collapse: "American intelligence intensifying their work against us, managing to inflict serious blows to our Agent network in the U.S. . . . . The most tangible blow to our work was inflicted by the defection of our former group-leading agent [Elizabeth Bentley], who gave away more than 40 most valuable agents to American authorities. The majority of agents betrayed by [Bentley] worked at key posts in leading state institutions: the State Department, . . . American intelligence, the Treasury Department, etc."[31]

Still, Communist espionage in the United States was the lesser of the horrifying dark truths that the idealists were silent about. Eugene Genovese, Marxist historian and former Communist, captures indelibly the nature of this kind of betrayal by silence, a betrayal by "admitting nothing, explaining nothing and apologizing for nothing." He concludes, "In a noble effort to liberate the human race from violence and oppression we broke all records for mass slaughter . . . we have a disquieting number of corpses to account for."[32]

The era of the blacklist was a period in which most movies were in black and white. It is time to revisit the politics and morality, the conflicts and crusades—and some of the films—of the period and what led up to it to see beyond the black-and-white dualism of moral judgments that has itself become an intellectual blacklisting and to arrive at a clearer and fuller view of the complex world of ideology, passions, art—and betrayal—that was the world of Communism in Hollywood.

3

The Birth of the Hollywood Party: The Establishment of Comintern Control

The Hollywood branch of the Communist Party that hundreds joined in the thirties was officially formed in 1935. Its formation at that time was a direct consequence of the international "Popular Front" policy being promulgated by the Soviet Union and the Comintern. The birth of the Hollywood branch and the early stages of its life set the pattern of deep, organized control by the national and international Communist Party, the ideological control that was the reality beneath the idealism and passion—and also the duplicity—of its members and followers.

Yet, at the House Un-American Activities Committee's (HUAC's) Hearings on the Communist Infiltration of the Hollywood Motion Picture Industry in October of 1947, one word was almost totally absent from all the testimony given by those who began proudly to bear the name, like an Arthurian knight's banner, the Hollywood Ten. For no matter what the content of the question posed, responses evaded the word *Communism*—or any variation thereof, particularly *Communist* Party (except for one significant use and a minor passing facetious reference or two). More than the word was missing, unfaced, unadmitted—as evidence in the legal sense, as a crucial element to be considered in a moral sense—was the reality of the Communist parties of the world, of the Communist Party of the United States of America, and of its branch in the motion picture industry. Denying this reality at the hearings—and their responsibility in being a part of it and its consequences—was the first morally questionable instance of the years of silence.

The nature of these hearings and of the blacklist that followed was not sui generis, arising fully formed out of nowhere. The strong tensions and conflicts in the world in 1947 were certainly part of the context for the extent and political velocity of the hearings. It was a time, and particularly a year, of crises—and of fears, justified and not—in the postwar Cold War confrontation of the Soviet Union and the West. Nonetheless, it was the swirling whirlpool of conflicts produced by the formation and history of the Communist Party in Hollywood—the antagonisms and accelerating power struggles of that history as the Hollywood group followed the dictates of the Soviets—that generated the intensity of the passions and ideological disputes, the virulent fanaticism of the hearings, that fueled the destructive excesses of the blacklist.

In 1932 a fledgling organization—more accurately dis-organization—a precursor, conducted sporadic study groups, mainly involving recent arrivals after their connection to left-wing causes and groups in New York City. By 1937–1938, however, the full-fledged, tightly organized Hollywood branch had several hundred members, and a wide range, rippling outward, of front organizations and fellow travelers. The change was not measured, gradual. It was fostered in 1935 and 1936—the crucial years when significant people and events, policies and strategies conjoined to form the Hollywood branch or section of the Communist Party of the United States (CPUSA). In testimony before the HUAC in 1952, Martin Berkeley described a meeting at his house in June of 1937 where, he believed, "the Hollywood section of the Communist Party was first organized."[1] The comment, and the dating, are self-promoting. By that date, the party had already established detailed organization and procedures, had already conducted many events and activities, and was already drawing in large numbers of supporters for its causes.

By 1937 meetings such as those described by Berkeley were regularly held to "organize" activities and subgroups of the party, not to form the party itself. As membership grew, branches were set up to group twenty or thirty members, and these were sometimes referred to as sections. Then there were fractions, which were smaller groups, whether within a branch or not.

Sam Ornitz, later the father figure within the Hollywood Ten, was instrumental in organizing those earliest study groups in the first years of the decade. On one of *his* trips to Hollywood in the early thirties, John Howard Lawson attended one. Known on the Left as a "Marxist scholar," Ornitz was a rigid party loyalist, but a quiet, bespectacled, rabbi-like proselytizer. He was a "true believer" and a born spreader of the gospel. During the early thirties he lectured at a variety of events in his pedagogical manner. At one he spoke, along with Lincoln Steffens (accompanied by his wife, Ella Winter) and novelist Theodore Dreiser, at a meeting at the Longshoreman's Amphitheater in San Francisco to support Tom Mooney. In prison for allegedly taking part in a bombing in San Francisco in 1916, Mooney was later pardoned. A few years later, Ornitz was in a group that went to Kentucky to protest the treatment of miners in Harlan County. His play *In New Kentucky* praised the role of the Communist Party in radicalizing the miners, leading them to a Marxist understanding of the power structure of the world.[2]

Ornitz was as fervent about Judaism as he was about Marxism. Before coming to Hollywood in the early days of talking pictures, he had written several novels about Jewish life in New York City, including the well-received *Haunch, Paunch, and Jowl* in 1923. So entangled were his two faiths that even into the fifties he could not admit, or believe, that there was any anti-Semitism or any anti-Jewish pogroms in the Soviet Union. He continued to passionately insist on this "fact" before many Jewish audiences. In 1956, he was deeply crushed by the very limited Khrushchev revelations.[3] Ornitz worked at several studios, from the mid-thirties on, mainly at Republic Pictures, a small studio that specialized in minor Westerns and other light entertainments. In the forties he worked on few scripts; he had no screen credits for several years before the hearings.[4]

Screenwriter John Bright—blacklisted though not called to testify—accompanied Ornitz to the Mooney meeting, as he did to other meetings and study groups in those years. Bright was a prolific and successful Warner Bros. writer in the early sound period. His seven coscripting projects (with two uncredited contributions in 1931 and 1932) included several for Jimmy Cagney, including the landmark *The Public Enemy* (1931), Bright's very first screen credit. In 1933 he coscripted *She Done Him Wrong* for Mae West. In an interview in 1983, Bright described, with a good deal of self-romanticizing, how he was one of the "secret four," the first four members of the Hollywood section of the party in the transition period before its formal organization in 1935. Bright was known as a rebel within the party. He rebelled against its over-insistence on conformity; however, as he commented years later, he believed that the CPUSA had not been radical enough in its policies. It had, he insisted, betrayed revolutionary ideals in joining with British and American "imperialism" in World War II and in pursuing its Popular Front Browderism.[5]

In describing the organization of the party in Hollywood, Bright referred to Stanley Lawrence as a major influence on his joining.[6] Others also have described Lawrence's active role in the early stages, even their actual recruitment by him. Budd Schulberg and Maurice Rapf describe his authority, even sending them to work with others in organizing farmers in the San Joaquin Valley. For this and other "mistakes," Lawrence was chastised and removed from Hollywood, eventually ending up working for the party in the Spanish Civil War. He was killed in Spain, but the circumstances remain mysterious. Schulberg told Victor Navasky that he had seen a reference "in the *Worker* that he [Lawrence] had been shot as a traitor." Lawrence was one of the people, on several levels of activity and organization, who were part of the synergy, the ideological excitement—and the tight control of the CPUSA—that produced the Hollywood branch.[7]

In Hollywood already were the pioneers like Ornitz and Bright, as well as some newer activists and eager potential, left-tilting recruits like Donald Ogden Stewart. From New York came John Howard Lawson (not for the first time), Francis Faragoh, and Herbert Biberman. Soon they were joined by such celebrity figures as Dorothy Parker, Lillian Hellman, and Dashiell Hammett. While the relationship between the Communist Party and these "notables" was kept more ambiguous (which served the party more effectively), they were involved in as many, if not more, organizations and events, open letters and calls, conferences and committees, and fund-raisers as any of the more official members.

Though a recent arrival, Biberman early on was applying the organizing energies, skills, and unceasing crusading that would be a valuable component of the party's conduct through the years. Fellow Hollywood Ten member Lester Cole praised Biberman's work in leading the rapid growth of the Hollywood Anti-Nazi League from 1936 on. In 1947, before the first hearing, it was Biberman who organized the first strategy meeting of the Nineteen and their legal team within hours of the delivery of the first subpoenas, Biberman who went on to organize support groups and fund-raising events. A fervent and aggressive ideologue, Biberman was described by Alvah Bessie (also of the Ten) as "a pain in the ass, but he is our pain in the ass." In New York in the thirties he had been a stage manager for the Theater Guild, impressive as well as obnoxious for many as an indefatigable pontificator about the "movement"—during rehearsals at the Theater Guild, at meetings and workshops at the Actors Lab. In New York he directed, for the guild's Studio Project, two plays by Soviet playwrights: *Red Rust* (at the opening of which the *Internationale* was sung before the curtain went up) and *Roar, China,* in which the townspeople of a Chinese farming village, oppressed by British military imperialists, unite and rebel against their oppressors. While finding the play not much as a work of art, critic Richard Lockridge admitted, "It makes me want to fight oppression."[8]

In Hollywood, through the years, Biberman directed minor films and then, after being blacklisted, directed the Hollywood Ten's film *Salt of the Earth* (1954).

Stewart, in contrast, was affable and stylish, a former playboy of the literary world. In the twenties he had shared the revels of the lost generation with Hemingway, taking in the bullrunning and bullfighting fiesta in Pamplona in 1924, the basis for *The Sun Also Rises.* "Excited, drunk, hot, hungover," he wrote, he stood in the bullring as the bulls entered. Knocked over twice, he earned a big clap on the back from Ernest. After his conversion, he served on many committees. Even when a board member or chairman, he was not really an organizer. More the public enthusiast, Stewart was often a master of ceremonies, a gracious host. At a reading of Irwin Shaw's one-act antiwar play *Bury the Dead* at the Hollywood Women's Club, for example, he introduced the performance and called on Hollywood to take a positive part in the struggle to preserve democracy in the world.[9]

Stewart was an eminently successful and skillful screenwriter; in the deep depression years of the mid-thirties he was making up to $5,200 a week. He wrote numerous screenplays, some in collaboration, including sophisticated comedies like *Dinner at Eight* (1933), *Holiday* (1938), and *The Philadelphia Story* (1940). His talent for winning sentimentality, still controlled and accented by the wit of polished dialogue, was typified in the successful *Love Affair* (1939) with Irene Dunne and Charles Boyer.

When Stanley Lawrence was sent to Hollywood in 1935, he had just returned from international party work in Austria. His appearance in Hollywood at this time was not accidental. As directed by the Comintern, party headquarters (the Central Committee) in New York sent out "Culture Commissar" V. J. Jerome and his representatives in the field, including Lawrence and John Leech, who was later to break with the party and testify before the Dies Committee in 1940. And directly from the Comintern there magically appeared the legendary Otto Katz, known in Hollywood as Rudolph Breda. Katz, in one of his many roles and disguises, was under the direct instructions of Georgi Dimitrov, secretary general of the Comintern, or the Communist International.[10]

The Comintern had been created in 1919, but took its final, and powerful, form at a congress in the summer of 1920. It was then defined as the "headquarters for world revolution." Its manifesto announced, "The Communist International is the international party for insurrection and proletarian dictatorship." That 1920 Congress first set the twenty-one conditions that had to be met by all associated groups and parties in the world, conditions that centralized control and discipline for all associated organizations in the Soviet Union and its international operating arm, the Comintern. Through the years, these conditions of control and discipline were toughened and strengthened.[11]

Katz was an associate of, indeed the prime operator for, the Comintern's chief of public relations, propaganda, and proselytizing, the fabulous Willi Munzenberg. One of Katz's allies on the scene in Hollywood was the notable spreader of Marxist enthusiasm, ideals, and ubiquitous social events Ella Winter—who was soon to be the widow of the muckraking author Lincoln Steffens, and soon to be the wife of her new husband, Donald Ogden Stewart.

Locally, there was impetus for this confluence and its consequences from the battle over the establishment of the Screen Writers Guild as the accepted voice of the screenwriters. Just coming up over the chronological horizon was the beginning of the Spanish Civil War; it would provide an emotional and (seemingly) unarguable cause to spread the word and the generally hidden Marxist cause. The civil war would accelerate the momentum not only of increasing party membership, but of drawing in fellow travelers and liberal allies and creating party-controlled organizations and events.

The major impetus for the formation, however, was the new strategy of the Popular Front policy just instituted by the Comintern, and managed at the highest levels worldwide by Munzenberg. Chief among the applications of the Popular Front policy were anti-Nazi subsidiaries such as the Joint Anti-Nazi League that many Hollywood Reds and followers joined and financially supported.

Why in 1935? Why just then? This fascinating and significant confluence of people, issues, and strategies was not mere serendipity. The earliest strands of the political design that created the Hollywood party as part of the worldwide Popular Front can be found in Paris and the complex manipulations in the world of Willi Munzenberg. For a decade from the late twenties to the late thirties, Munzenberg had, in the apt phrase of Francois Furet, "during the anti-fascist shift served the Comintern as a kind of clandestine minister of world propaganda."[12] He was not only gifted with a pioneering talent for political publicity, manipulation of words, of images in the broadest sense, not only willing and eager to work almost ceaselessly; he was also an instinctive manipulator of people, individually and in groups. He lavished his charm on those who apparently never could dislike him, even when they might have realized how he had manipulated and even deceived them.

Author and playwright (*Darkness at Noon*) Arthur Koestler, a one-time believer and then a longtime critic of Communism, saw Munzenberg as the inventor of modern propaganda devices—protest marches, peace conferences, writers congresses, mock trials, committees, and letterheads. Munzenberg, Koestler said, "produced committees as a conjuror produces rabbits out of his hat." In her biography of him, his longtime companion Babette Gross said she learned that "[Munzenberg] left nothing to chance, particularly not the manipulation of fellow travelers." Munzenberg himself summed up his goals in a speech to Comintern associates: "We must organize the intellectuals. . . . We must avoid being a purely communist organization. We must bring in other names, other groups, to make persecution more difficult."[13]

In the early thirties, Munzenberg's main project, as determined by Moscow and the Comintern, was a combined peace and anti-Nazi campaign. By the mid-thirties all this was contained within the campaign for the Popular Front. Both campaigns, which became intertwined, had the same motivations: fear of Germany and the Nazis, fear of an alliance between Germany and the West, but also the masking of events in the Soviet Union and the popularizing of Communist causes and policies.

A number of organizations and conferences that yoked together peace, pacifism, and anti-Nazism went through a mystifying sequence of name changes, but maintained their agendas. The basic agenda used the popularity of a call for peace to promote Soviet criticism not only of the Nazis and their threat to peace but also of the deceitful, hidden aggressive policies of the Western nations and *their* threat to peace. Again to quote the French historian Francois Furet from his seminal book *The Passing of an Illusion*, "The fight 'against Fascism and war' had remained above all a war against bourgeois pacifism and the chauvinistic anti-Fascism of the affluent powers." And further, "During the worst phase of the Kremlin's bloody dictatorship, only the Comintern militants could provide the appearance of anti-Fascism that would help win democratic hearts."[14]

Two of the chief "Munzenberg Men" (as they were called) in these operations, in fact his two main emissaries, were Otto Katz and Louis Gibarti. Both were also associated with the Soviet secret service, the NKVD, but it is not clear if Munzenberg was aware of any specific hidden assignments. By, 1932, however, it *was* definite that "infighting among the various services was ended by a simple change that united the Comintern with the secret services under the control of the head of the CPSU [Communist Party of the Soviet Union], making them directly accountable to Stalin himself for their actions." Katz and Gibarti were involved in Munzenberg's major operations in Europe, and then were sent to America to extend his operations there. In his special assignment in Hollywood, Katz charmingly glittered like an émigré movie star himself.[15]

Gibarti was more involved than Katz in the direct management of the various organizations and congresses—the glowing causes that were the lure for the idealism of the new true believers. His World Committee for the Relief of the Victims of German Fascism not only generated strong responses among young idealists; it was also a useful tool for the Soviet secret service. Elizabeth Bentley told how her first contacts with the NKVD were through that organization. Kim Philby was sent to Paris and then to Vienna for that organization, leading to his major espionage career.[16]

In addition to exuding charm, Katz's major talent was writing in several languages. This talent was used in the two most influential single attacks on the Nazis in the early thirties. According to Koestler, Katz was the closest to Munzenberg of all of his men and the author of most of *The Brown Book on the Hitler Terror and the Burning of the Reichstag*, which Koestler called "the bible of the Anti-Fascist Crusade." It was published by Gibarti's World Committee in August of 1933 and quickly translated into twenty languages. In true Munzenberg style, Albert Einstein was cited as the president of the World Committee and "wrote" an introduction. When asked if he was or did, Einstein said no, but since it was for a good cause, "it does not matter."[17]

During the night of February 27, 1933, the German parliament, the Reichstag, had burned. The Nazis had been quick to blame the Communists and to claim that Marinus van der Lubbe, the only one of the suspected arsonists who was caught, was a Soviet agent. Consequently they rounded up every Communist still in sight. *The Brown Book* reversed the Nazis claim: With manufactured evidence and clever arguments that tied this false data to credible and accurate information about Nazi terror in general, the book accused the Nazis of setting the fire themselves and of using van der Lubbe as their tool and scapegoat. It was convincing for the good people of the world who were ready to be convinced; later it was Katz's chief calling card in Hollywood. So successful was the book and the campaign around it, that Katz and Munzenberg then organized a "legal inquiry," an unofficial but highly publicized counter-trial to be conducted in London in September of 1933. A number of prominent English and Continental figures took part. Katz organized and developed its every stage, but stayed behind the scenes so that the mock trial was given great respectability.[18]

The trial and the other anti-Nazi campaigns, designed to reach out to as wide as possible a circle of respondents and participants, were a prelude to the new policy and strategy taking shape in Moscow in the fight to protect the Soviet Union from Germany and from any alliance between the Germans and the West. This policy was the turn to the Popular Front, and at its center was Georgi Dimitrov. Because of his bravery in Germany at the time of the Reichstag fire (commemorated in plays and poems), Dimitrov had become a hero—almost the symbol—of anti-Fascism. On his return to Moscow, he became the organizer of a new united front strategy as the best means to combat the Nazis and at the same time disguise the parallel strategy of calling all adversaries of the Communist Party, particularly Leon Trotsky and his followers, "Fascists." Thus, the two simultaneous faces of the new strategy were the smiles and handshakes of the Popular Front and the brutal imprisonments and killings of the new purges and terror. The first helped to direct attention toward the Nazis and away from the second! Named as general secretary of the Comintern, Dimitrov worked at carrying out both phases of the new policy, while maintaining as well the basic goal of world revolution among the Communist parties of the world.[19]

The first direct trial run, on a limited scale, of the new approach to a united front was in France in February of 1934. By mid-1935, the campaign was in full operation. In a speech in August of 1935, Dimitrov, however, defined the two levels of policy. In his report to the Seventh World Congress of the Communist International, he announced the importance of "a broad people's anti-fascist front," but he strongly stressed that such a coalition was temporary, a tactic to allow the defeat of fascism. It must still help to promote the broader goal, "the revolutionary training of the masses. . . . We state frankly to the masses: Final salvation this [Popular Front] government cannot bring. . . . Consequently it is necessary to prepare for the socialist revolution! Soviet power and only Soviet power can bring such salvation!"[20]

And so, as Dimitrov emphasized, Communism and its heart, the Soviet Union, must continue to maintain control. Parties around the world must still act with an appropriate reserve in their dealings with capitalist nations, and with organizations and individuals in that sphere.

Munzenberg was busy spreading the surface ideals and phrases of the new doctrine. Probably the most famous instance of his invention of a parade of writers, artists, and intellectuals in a "congress" took place in June 1935 in Paris. This kind of public forum was a parallel operation to the actual organizing of "intellectuals" into far less publicized party organizations. The Paris congress took place while Communist operatives were working on organizing the artists, and especially the writers, of Hollywood; while with great panache Otto Katz arrived and was feted; and while, as Furet summed up, "in 1935, the Soviet Union was subject to the most widespread state terror ever imposed." In Paris the mood was only praise and hope, as Munzenberg brought together an "A-list" of European writers—the kind of intellectuals he loved to "organize," and manipulate—in the Congress of Writers for the Defense of Culture, also known as the Congres de la Mutualite.[21]

The Comintern-Munzenberg speciality of a two-level, two-pronged campaign of developing general organizations for political causes and more defined organizations for intellectuals, particularly writers, was carried out in the American campaign. While the Communist Party, along with its satellite organizations, was being developed in Hollywood, work was underway to create a nationwide writers' organization that would proceed on a parallel track, promoting the Soviets' ideas and drawing in as many liberals and idealists as possible. Thus, at a large dinner arranged at the home of Lillian Hellman in 1935, with many of the core players present, V. J. Jerome presented the plan for a cosmetic revamping and reorganizing of the "Congress of American Revolutionary Writers," as it had been called in a first presentation in the *Daily Worker* in January of 1935. That phrasing would never do; therefore, soon after, the first call went out to hold a congress to found the League of American Writers. Among the initial sponsors were Hellman and Hammett. When the First American Writers' Congress convened on April 26, its proclamations echoed the terms of the Comintern's version of anti-Fascism.[22]

The popularity of the anti-Fascist, peace-loving Popular Front was instrumental in spreading the gospel in Hollywood and elsewhere in America. To promote and celebrate the strategy, Earl Browder's CPUSA coined the slogan "Communism Is Twentieth Century Americanism." At first the Soviets approved, but several years later Browder was accused of "tailism" (too much imitation and praise of President Roosevelt's policies) and the slogan was eliminated. But that was later. In 1935, that was the message: just another version of American democracy.[23]

The combination of manipulating cultural elites through the strategy of the anti-Nazi Popular Front and still maintaining Soviet control was the basis of the mandate given to Otto Katz and Louis Gibarti when they were sent to America in March of 1934. Mandates—the *mandat*—were an actual organizational tool, a written order given to local Communist officials requiring full cooperation, even obedience. On his arrival in New York, Gibarti presented such a *mandat* to Browder. Legend, or fact, has it that it was written on silk so that it could be hidden or disguised more readily. The responsibility for carrying out the cultural activities required by the *mandat* of the Comintern was passed on to V. J. Jerome, who went on to the West Coast ahead of Katz.[24]

It is probable that Munzenberg was not aware that his pair of emissaries were also sent to carry out NKVD tasks. While on the East Coast late in 1935—and later again in 1936—they established contact with John Herrman, who was a courier for Soviet sources in Washington during the decade, and with Gardner Jackson, a charming Munzenberg group front man from the Sacco Vanzetti campaign on, who was then working in Washington.[25]

Katz's entry into the Hollywood world was eased by the presence there of the anti-Fascist crusader and refugee Prince Hubertus zu Lowenstein, who had allied himself with Munzenberg's campaigns in his fight against Hitler.[26] In Hollywood, Katz assumed his other charming, old-world manner. Babette Gross describes how "in Hollywood he charmed German émigré actors, directors and writers. Katz had an extraordinary fascination for women, a quality that greatly helped him in organizing committees and campaigns." Koestler saw him as "a smooth and slick operator . . . dark and handsome, with a somewhat seedy charm." As Breda, the anti-Nazi freedom fighter and author of *The Brown Book*, Katz overwhelmed eager new recruits like Donald Ogden Stewart. At the one-hundred-dollar-a-plate fund-raising dinner for German refugees that introduced Katz to his movie-world fans, Stewart, as the master of ceremonies, sat next to "Breda" on the dais. "It was one of the happiest evenings in my life," Stewart wrote in his memoir. "Herr Breda gave his moving description of the Nazi Terror, the details of which he had been able to collect only by repeatedly risking his own life. I was proud to be sitting beside him, proud to be on his side in the fight." Later, tears in his eyes, his voice choked, Stewart asked, "What can *I* do?"[27]

After Katz's stay in Hollywood, Lillian Hellman was with him on a number of occasions, political and personal, in New York and Paris. She told friends how he had inspired her to go to Spain during its civil war. She was so enthralled by the man and the myth that she based the heroic anti-Fascist Kurt Muller in her play *Watch on the Rhine* (1943) on her idealized view of him. In what was a typical Hellman mixture of fact and fantasy, in her memoir, *An Unfinished Woman*, she tells a fanciful tale of how Katz "stayed in Spain until the very last days of the Franco victory, when, in New York, a few of us found the bail to buy him out and to send him on to Mexico." Katz was not in Spain at that time. He had been in Paris working for the Loyalists (and Communists) and then went on to New York. While Katz was in New York, there was an auction by the Exiled Writers Committee to assist anti-Nazi writers. Hellman did take part in that event, and Katz did go on to Mexico during World War II.[28]

In Hollywood, Katz was assisted in spreading the glow by Ella Winter, at that time still married to Lincoln Steffens, whom she had so molded as a Stalinist sympathizer that even while dying in April of 1936 he stoutly defended the truth of the Moscow purge trials.[29] When she married Stewart, she shaped his enthusiasm into productive propagandistic doctrine. Winters had been a true believer since her student days at Oxford and had been part of the Comintern apparatus since the early thirties. Gibarti had nurtured her "career" when she was in his World Committee for the Relief of the Victims of German Fascism when she then worked in turn with its American branch. He called her "one of the most trusted Party agents for the West Coast." In context, by *agent* he did not mean espionage, but rather recruitment, influence, propaganda. A term often used was "agent of influence." For the faithful at rallies, she was introduced as "our beloved Ella." For Ernest Hemingway, in a foul-mouthed letter to Ezra Pound in 1926, she was "a 19-year-old Bloomsbury kike intellectual [who had, to Hemingway's disgust] corralled Steffens [into marriage]. . . . Last chapter in the book of revolution."[30]

While Katz and Winter were raising fervent hopes and money, Jerome and his men in the field were doing the official work of organizing the party branch itself—and ensuring the control and direction of Moscow and the Comintern. Early on, Jerome's assistants in the field, in addition to Stanley Lawrence, were Henry Carlisle; John Leech; Lou Harris; Mike Pell, also known as Matt Pell; and Max Appleman, whose actual name was Matt Pellman. John Bright remembers that in this formative period Jerome "came out to *advise* us [emphasis added]."[31]

Jerome was a devout believer, untiring in his efforts all over the country (imagine all the time he spent on trains) to have others truly believe as well. In a 1943 article in the *New Masses*, "The Individual in History," he professed his faith in Stalin as "the true forward-looking son of his epoch . . . the individually gifted and socially endowed fighter for freedom." Jerome's function, and his calling, was to define the proper form of proletarian literature and other forms of art, according to Soviet and Comintern doctrine at a given time—such as the implementation of Zhdanovism in the forties—and to enforce loyalty (or obedience) to that doctrine and forbid deviations. He found failure to live up to Marxist ideals everywhere, often finding in a specific instance a grand abstract danger and evil. In 1950, in *Political Affairs*, in "The Negro in Hollywood," he found that despite some advances, "it would be even more unrealistic not to see . . . a new mode—more dangerous because more subtle—through which the fascist ruling class of our country is today re-asserting its strategic ideology of 'white supremacy' on the Hollywood screen."[32]

Jerome seemed to have eyes (and spies) everywhere. He conducted an endless round of meetings, year after year, whether he actually attended or managed from a distance, including the well-known attack meetings. Budd Schulberg tells of having such a meeting in 1940 with Lawson, who sharply criticized him and then sent him on to a group meeting headed by Jerome.[33]

His control of the Hollywood branch continued for years after the formative period, often with Lawson as his chief spokesman and enforcer (or attempted enforcer). Jerome's strong influence on Lawson produced what Dorothy Healey, longtime Los Angeles (LA) County party official, called a counterproductive "cultural sectarianism," damaging to the party and its members. Jerome felt a special connection with his Hollywood charges, yet thought of them as difficult, as a parent would feel about a precocious but intransigent child who needed special treatment. He felt that "their academic training, their aloof habits of work and thought, their instilled, illusory ambitions retard their alliance with the working class for common struggle."[34]

Insistent as he was on his own authority, Jerome was slavish in following the variations, the twists and turns of Comintern policy. As enforced and acted upon in Hollywood, this double level of conformity and its consequences was a strong source of friction, resentment, and antagonism both within the Communist Party and between the party members and the rest of Hollywood's politically active people. This ongoing friction added to the intensity of the passions of the blacklist period.

Visits by Jerome and friends were, of course, only one, occasional, way of enforcing party policies and discipline, but they are indicative, and symbolic, of the constant attention the party paid to its Hollywood charges. Here's a sampling of some of the reported "sightings," the presence of Jerome or his emissaries at meetings in Hollywood through these years:

- Through the early stage, during visits in 1935 and 1936, Jerome, with others like John Leech, even conducted indoctrination retreats for small groups. John Bright remembers spending a fortnight of lectures with a group in San Bernardino.
- Leech was a constant presence, focusing particularly on forming and developing the Hollywood Anti-Nazi League. (Some years later he was expelled from the Party.)

- After Lawrence went off to fight in the Spanish Civil War (though there are rumors that he had to because he was found embezzling funds), Carlisle assumed the task of regular classes for members and new recruits.
- In 1937, Jerome and several aides lectured to a large group at a party at the home of Martin Berkeley, while in town for days of meetings and study groups.
- A party at the home of Frank Tuttle featured Jerome lecturing on the dangers of Trotskyism and the necessary means to combat it.
- At a meeting at Tuttle's, Jerome introduced Harry Bridges, head of the West Coast Longshoreman's Union, to the group.
- At a meeting at the home of Lionel Stander, Jerome prescribed positions to take in some conflicts within the Screen Actors Guild.
- Marc Lawrence described a series of ten or twelve meetings in 1938, some of which included lectures by Jerome or by an aide from the Central Committee, Harold J. Ashe.
- Dinners and parties at Salka Viertel's, and other *salon* hosts and hostesses, featured rousing, often fund-raising, speeches by visiting "dignitaries," including Jerome.[35]

During World War II much of the control of the Hollywood party passed to the local LA County party. Then in the postwar period, when it was beset by a barrage of actions by the government, the CPUSA had less time and effort to devote to shepherding its Hollywood flock. Even the LA chapter had other, more serious concerns. Its leadership, too, was under fire, and in 1948, county chairman Nemmy Sparks left LA, "with secret orders to set up a nationwide underground organization for the Party."[36]

John Stapp was one of Sparks' men in the field to deal with movie people. Sterling Hayden, for example, testified that in 1945, after a meeting with Jerome himself, he was sent to meet with Stapp at Victor's on Sunset Boulevard and was quizzed about his background and his reasons for wanting to join the party. In 1946, Abe Burrows was asked to meet with Stapp and Abe Polonsky. Polonsky questioned him about why he was not more active in the party, while Stapp, he testified, mainly gave him hard, intimidating stares: He'd better mend his ways.[37]

Long after the HUAC hearings, many still denied this control and manipulation, seeing themselves as free-acting idealists. Half a century later, Paul Jarrico was typical of what Robert Conquest called the "brain blindfolds" of the Left in avoiding any contemplation of the consequences of their ideological fervor: "The Communist Party was not a revolutionary organization, not in the period when I was in it. It was a reformist organization, and for most of the years I was in it, it was the tail of the liberal-Democratic kite."[38] There is an unintentional ironic revelation here in Jarrico's use of decades-old party terminology. Back in 1935, it was exactly this liberal-democratic claim that was the basis for the temporary Browder-based version of the Popular Front. After World War II, however, William Z. Foster attacked this version and called it reactionary "tailism." The Comintern took up the issue. As they replied in controlling and settling the dispute, "Comrade Foster was not correct in accusing the Party leadership of tailism in respect to movements and organizations adhering to Roosevelt, but the danger of tailism undoubtedly exists in connection with the Party's mass policy and the Central Committee in its documents must warn the Party of this."[39]

4

The Hollywood Party in Peace and War: Idealism, Discipline, and Reality

Many of the conflicts generated by the Communist Party in Hollywood, the intramural disputes and the public battles, had to do with chameleon changes in the definition of peace and war, war and peace. From the Hollywood party's beginnings, these issues and shifts (along, of course, with others) reflected the consistent subservience to the discipline of the Comintern and the policies of the Soviet Union. The consequence for members and close followers was a knotted mixture of idealism about just causes and evasion and duplicity about the real goals of the Communist campaigns. In turn, the statements, activities, and campaigns of the Hollywood Reds early on began to build tensions between party members and the liberals who joined them, at least temporarily, in the decade's campaigns for peace and justice.

In 1936, the elusive, enigmatic, and charismatic Otto Katz did more than stir the hearts and souls of the Hollywood elite. He had been assigned the specific task of founding and getting funds and followers for the Hollywood Anti-Nazi League within the parameters established by Willi Munzenberg's campaigns in Europe—his leagues, congresses, committees.[1]

The American sequence of Communist-controlled organizations that (at least in name) merged the constantly linked terms of peace and anti-Fascism was fostered by the World Congress against Imperialist War, which had met in Amsterdam in August 1932 as so carefully organized by Munzenberg. The first step in America was the American Committee for Struggle against War. Its first congress was held on September 29, 1933. At that first American congress, in line with the major emphasis of the Comintern at that time, its name was changed to the American League against War and Fascism. In December Earl Browder proudly told an executive committee of the Comintern, "The Congress from the beginning was led by our Party quite openly but without in any way infringing upon its broad non-Party character." At the same time, the original manifesto of the congress was modified to include a recent resolution of the Comintern that emphasized that "the masses" must not be confused by "pacifist swindlers" but must "join the revolutionary united front in the struggle against war."[2]

In turn, the Hollywood Anti-Nazi League and its subsidiaries became the most significant left organization of the period in Hollywood, a magnet for attracting idealistic non-Communists to its causes. Donald Ogden Stewart recalled that Jack Warner offered his assistance in fighting Hitler, even, he said, if they *were* Reds. Until the Nazi-Soviet Pact destroyed the Popular Front alliance of liberals and Communists, the league's publicizing of the threat of Nazi Germany allowed it to serve as the center of Communist influence, recruiting, and pro-Soviet propaganda in Hollywood. At the organizing meeting for the Hollywood Anti-Nazi League at the Wilshire Ebell Theater, Stewart was named chairman by acclamation, with Dorothy Parker, one of its most fervent publicized organizers, as honorary chairman. Herbert Biberman was once again a tireless hands-on, voice-on promoter. One of the earliest members and financial supporters was Charlie Chaplin.[3]

After an early career of acerbic stories and poems, Parker had made a lot of money and accomplished little of significance in her long intermittent stay in Hollywood and bouts of heavy drinking. Edmund Wilson, himself a one-time believer in the deadly Communist utopian fantasy, was later to comment on her suffering "one of the dooms of her generation." She has gone out to Hollywood, he wrote, and in turn "succumbed to the expiatory mania that has become epidemic with film-writers and was making earnest appeals on behalf of those organizations which talked about being 'progressive' and succeeded in convincing their followers that they were working for the social revolution, though they really had no other purpose than to promote the foreign policy of the Soviet Union."[4]

One of the league's first major events was a mass meeting at the Shrine Auditorium in October 1936, its ostensible topic "The Menace of Hitler in America." Sponsors of the event included Rossen, Faragoh, Lardner, Bright, and Biberman. A subsequent rally was held at the Philharmonic Auditorium.[5]

With the start of the Spanish Civil War on July 17, 1936, the activities of the Hollywood Anti-Nazi League often took the form of activities for the defense of the Spanish Republic. This campaign was the party's most popular and successful of the decade—with a subsequent increase in participation and a significant widening of the political spectrum of the participants. These activities included rallies, films, fund-raisers large and small, radio broadcasts, publications, public relations appearances and campaigns, and interviews.

In the summer of 1937, for example, the Ernest Hemingway–Joris Ivens film *The Spanish Earth* had four money-raising, spirit-raising showings—at the homes of Fredric March and Salka Viertel, at the Ambassador Hotel, and at the Philharmonic Auditorium. At the dinner at the home of Fredric and Florence March, Stewart raised thirteen thousand dollars, besides his own contribution, when he presented the Hemingway film with his old drinking and bull-running buddy present. The French novelist, Loyalist supporter, and pilot Andre Malraux came to town to raise money. He gave two public speeches and was hosted at a dinner at Lillian Hellman's home. Actor Lionel Stander hosted a party at which Andre Malraux was the guest speaker, introduced in glowing heroic terms by Clifford Odets, who was then on an early sojourn in Hollywood. Stewart introduced Malraux at a private dinner at the home of Viertel, the émigré's and Left's favorite hostess. He again introduced Malraux at a giant rally for the Loyalists at the Shrine Auditorium. At the end of his speech, Malraux gave the raised-hand, clenched-fist Communist salute and shouted, "No Pasaron!"—the phrase made famous by the publicized heroic woman known as La Pasionaria. The audience rose, echoing his cry and returning the salute. As Salka Viertel commented, "Ladies in mink rising and clenching their bejeweled hands."[6] *No Pasaron!*

Malraux also spoke at several fund-raising functions on the East Coast. At one, he created a furor even among the Left by proclaiming, "Trotsky is a moral force in the world, but Stalin has lent dignity to mankind; and just as the Inquisition did not detract from the fundamental dignity of Christianity, so the Moscow trials do not detract from the fundamental dignity of Communism."[7]

Donald Ogden Stewart was so impassioned by the speeches of the visitors and himself that he found a way to get to Spain, meet La Pasionaria, and send back several glowing articles for *New Masses*. John O'Hara, typically acerbic, wrote to F. Scott Fitzgerald after a visit to Hollywood in 1936, "Don Stewart, who is full of shit, has converted himself to radical thought . . . he is such a horse's ass."[8]

Among the most fervent in their response to the cause of Spain was Dorothy Parker, who was moved to declare that this was no time for humor: "I know that there are things that never have been funny, and never will be." She went to Spain in 1937 and wrote several reports for the party's *New Masses*, in one describing the bombing of Valencia by Fascist aircraft, in another exaggerating the quality of a Communist center for children, proclaiming it to be "as good as American children at a progressive school" receive. On her return, at a fund-raising party in Washington, she wept openly. In line with the Luce press mocking of her "conversion," *Life* magazine ran a picture of her weeping over the plight of Spanish children while wearing a fur jacket.[9]

Without fail, the Spanish Civil War programs of the Communist Party of America (CPUSA) and its Hollywood devotees followed the detailed protocols that had been established in 1936 by the ECCI, the Executive Committee of the Comintern. The exact activities were, in turn, the result of the elaborate, meticulously detailed, worldwide nine-point public relations campaign that had been devised and organized by Willi Munzenberg—as assigned by the Comintern. Spanish Civil War historian Stanley Payne calls Munzenberg "undoubtedly the leading propagandist of the Spanish Civil War."[10]

In Hollywood, party members and followers were able to attract a wide swath of sympathizers—and generous donations—for the proclaimed humane and democratic purposes of such organizations as the Motion Picture Artists Committee to Aid Republican Spain (for which Parker was recruited to act as a cofounder), North American Committee to Aid Spanish Democracy, American Friends of Spanish Democracy, American Society for Technical Aid for Spanish Democracy (which in one of its public letters called for recruits for the International Brigades), American Committee for Spanish Freedom, United Americans Spanish Aid Committee, Spanish Refugee Relief Appeal, Joint Anti-Fascist Refugee Committee.[11]

However, this Comintern campaign for an idealistic cause once again was a mask for the Soviets' increasingly dictatorial actions in Spain, even while they aided the Republican fight against the attack by Francisco Franco's dictatorial Fascist forces, supported by Germany and Italy. The campaign provided the justification for the necessary measures taken against the factions and individuals in Loyalist Spain that were labeled—in terms that went all the way back to Lenin—left-wing deviationists, social Fascists, infantile leftists, and so on. All were "counterproductive" for the conduct of the war—and, of course, for the long-range plans of the Soviet Union—and so needed to be eliminated. While they proclaimed their democratic goals, the Soviets began to implement and steadily increase their control of the defense of the republic through diplomatic promises, economic rewards and pressures, and through Soviet-style terror, orchestrated from Moscow. As Soviet military historians Oleg Sarin and Lev Dvoretsky commented in 1997, "For example, late in 1937 when the Spanish situation was discussed at a Politburo meeting, a comprehensive directive to the Spaniards was approved. It covered among other things that it was necessary to remove all saboteurs and traitors from the army, to develop measures to mobilize industry for military production, and to clear rear areas of Fascist spies and agents." Even during the heroic defense of Madrid in the early stages of the war—when La Pasionaria, one of the most zealous advocates of brutal Comintern tactics, famously proclaimed "No Pasaron"—the terror, the purges, the executions had begun. While the battle raged on, between two thousand and three thousand prisoners, many of them army officers who could have helped in the struggle, were taken from jails in and around the city and executed. Within the various factions in the nationalist army, summary trials, imprisonment and torture, and executions continued and increased as the war went on.[12]

Spanish anarchists and similar extreme left groups were more frequently the target than any so-called reactionary factions. Early in the war, Andre Marty, the French Communist in charge of Soviet security in Spain, wrote to the secretariat of the ECCI and to General Vorishilov in Moscow, explaining his delay in moving against the anarchist forces. They could use their support at the moment, but they will deal with them later, he said, and "after the war we will get even with them, all the more since at that time we will have a strong army."[13] As it turned out, Marty did not wait until after the war, and the attacks accelerated, culminating in the destruction of left-wing factions, the battles, betrayals, and executions in Barcelona that George Orwell wrote about, soon after the events, in *Homage to Catalonia* (1938). As the "blood bath" throughout the Loyalist zone intensified, Marty himself was personally responsible for the issuing of some five hundred execution orders. At one point he complained in a note that "I am also not at all happy that spies and fascists whom I sent to Valencia to be liquidated are being sent back to me here in Albacete. You know very well that the International Brigades cannot do this themselves here in Albacete." One knowledgeable conclusion, by Katia Landau, is that by war's end fifteen thousand prisoners had been executed.[14]

As the facts about Spain were revealed (including the purposes, nature, and consequences of the Soviets' military strategies), the party loyalists disputed, belittled, and denied them, despite the revelations of Orwell and other writers, some of whom had fought in Spain. Far from the battlefield, the deniers played their part in the betrayal of the people of Spain. Typically, Lillian Hellman in the late seventies still insisted to friends that Orwell's book *Homage to Catalonia* was "a load of crap."[15]

As the revelations increased, these disputes over what the Communists were really doing in Spain were one more instance of the eruptions that began to split Hollywood liberals from the Reds and the devout. These disputes began to build distrust and foment the intense resentments and antagonisms that exploded in the forties and fifties.

With far greater impact and consequences, another crucial stage of this repeated pattern of alliance and subsequent resentful disillusionment was produced by the Nazi-Soviet Pact of August 23, 1939. Instantly, the Hollywood Anti-Nazi League became the American Peace Mobilization—as did other organizations all across the nation and within the Communist constellation. The Comintern's instructions were explicit. As Dimitrov summed up at the end of a long, detailed analysis and set of directives in a telegram to Earl Browder in late September 1939, "At the present stage of the war [the start of World War II] the Communists' task is to boldly, as befits Bolsheviks, fight against the war . . . to expose the bourgeoisie as profiteers and marauders of war."[16]

While the Comintern led this "struggle against war" (for the duration of the pact), Hitler went on to invade and conquer Poland, Denmark, Norway, the Netherlands, Belgium, and France. Russia invaded and appropriated half of Poland, appropriated the three Baltic States—Latvia, Estonia, and Lithuania—and invaded Finland

In response, Hellman made one of her most egregious outbursts, "Finland? I've been there, and it looks like a pro-Nazi little republic to me."[17]

Dalton Trumbo, too, could find no sympathy for Finland; more important was the principle of neutrality: "But, I am, in the interest of American neutrality, obliged to ask, 'Why [this concern only for] only Finland?" And on another occasion, "This, of course, is all changed. We know that our enemy is Germany. We know that Finland is allied with Germany."[18]

Lester Cole said, "How could it be made clear that the open fascist, Baron Mannerheim, head of the Finnish government, would open another major avenue of invasion of the USSR similar to Czechoslavakia."[19]

In November 1939 in the *Daily Worker*, an "Open Letter to President Roosevelt" by leading artists, intellectuals, and Hollywood people even demanded that the United States declare war against Finland after the Soviets (in "self-defense") invaded it. The time was awash with open letters and calls, regularly signed by many of the same names from Hollywood and the other arts. In the *New York Times* a one-person open letter from Hellman proclaimed, "Theatrical benefits for Finnish Relief would give a dangerous impetus to the war spirit in this country." Even the American Youth Congress published a statement attacking President Roosevelt for referring to "valiant Finland."[20]

Albert Maltz had been an advocate for peace throughout the thirties, especially when, as defined by the prevailing Communist ideology, war was seen as a result of capitalist aggression and imperialism. In *Peace on Earth*, an agitprop play written with George Sklar in 1933, one of the characters (with a typical uneven mixture of editorial rhetoric and colloquial slang) protests, "The bosses in Wall Street and Washington build up war fever—in the newspapers, in the movies, over the radio—build up hate, build up hysteria. . . . No, when we go out to fight it's not gonna be for the bosses. It's gonna be for a new world—for a world where there won't be any wars."

While he could maintain this position during the pact period, Maltz did need a further rationale to defend the refusal to fight the Nazis when the war went far beyond Poland, and, like the others, to ignore what the Soviets were doing. He found it with this rather righteously tortured logic: "Those of us who had been ant-fascist since the rise of Hitler had gone through a period of enormous bitterness because we now saw Hitler beginning the dismemberment of Europe with the assistance of the English and French governments. England had not been interested whatsoever in stopping fascism. . . . To go and support England now, in the face of her whole record during the thirties, is something that we do not think is merited."[21]

Screenwriter Maurice Rapf was unswerving in his devotion to every aspect of Soviet policy since his visit to Russia in the early thirties. As far as he was concerned, they deserved each other—Germany, France, England. "World War II," he continued to believe, even years later, "started as an imperialist war . . . it was intended to be a war against the Soviet Union, but got turned around. I still believe that." Donald Ogden Stewart's blinkered naïveté was typical in that after his immediate misgivings, he had to believe that "only Stalin had the correct Marxist understanding of the situation."[22]

Not without their share of doubts, tensions, inner conflicts, and some defections, the Hollywood Reds responded to the words, not the invasions and depredations. They betrayed their own idealism with the twisted logic of the Soviets' rationales. The American Peace Mobilization was the main umbrella organization, but there were many subvarieties, such as the American Peace Crusade. In the film world, the Hollywood Peace Forum was a central focus for action, with its own subsidiaries, such as the Hollywood Peace Council and even the Mother's Day Peace Council.

In the year before the pact, the Motion Picture Democratic Committee (MPDC) had been established. It was the last Popular Front alliance between liberals and the Reds. As the Communist faction pushed their claims for "peace" in 1939, the usual dissension developed within the group. The conflict reached its climax when the Communists mounted a campaign to oppose President Roosevelt in the California primary of 1940 with a "Keep America Out of War" program. This opposition to Roosevelt was one bridge too far for the liberals in the MPDC. Furious, they quit en masse. Liberal committee leaders Philip Dunne and Melvyn and Helen Douglas called the party loyalists "the same wrecking crew, as all over town the industrious Communist tail wagged the lazy liberal dog." In *their* MPDC newsletter in May, the party-controlled remnant proclaimed the Roosevelt administration "exploited" the actions of the Nazis "to force a peaceful people into slaughter." In the presidential election, they supported Earl Browder for president as he ran with the slogan "The Yanks Are Not Coming."[23]

During this period of fervent cries for peace, the Hollywood Peace Forum held a series of lectures at the First Unitarian Church. Biberman, the organizing dynamo, was the group's chairman, John Wexley and Guy Endore among its officers. Speakers included Biberman, Sam Ornitz, and Endore. Endore wrote the bulk of the group's pamphlet *Let's Skip the Next War*. It had the subtitle "No War for the USA but a House and Lot for Everyone." "A Living Newspaper for Peace," written by Michael Blankfort, Gordon Kahn, and others, was performed at a number of events, including a large

"America Declares Peace" rally at the Olympic Auditorium on April 6, 1940. A popular song at these meetings had as its central refrain, "Let God Save the King/The Yanks Are Not Coming."[24]

Decades later, Cole summed up their intentions: "How to make it clear that this Non-Aggression Pact was not a military alliance, that it was necessary for the USSR to buy time, since it was now clear that the Western allies were trying to turn Hitler against their common enemy."[25]

The path of Dalton Trumbo through these crucial moments for the party, and of course the world, was typically busy and hectic, and a useful reflection of the flavor and actions of the peace crusade—and then its sudden denouement. Trumbo completed his devastating antiwar novel *Johnny Got His Gun*, which the *Daily Worker* began to publish in serial form in April 1940. He participated in the lecture series at the First Unitarian Church. He spoke at a meeting of the Hollywood Peace Forum, the speech reprinted in the *Sunday Worker* of February 11, 1940. He spoke at a rally for peace at the Hollywood Legion Stadium. He gave the keynote speech, entitled "America Declares Peace," at a rally at the Olympic Auditorium sponsored by the MPDC, and subsequently published as a pamphlet by them. He spoke at a forum organized by the Hollywood Chamber of Commerce in July of 1940 to present both sides of the issue. After speeches by Trumbo, Carey McWilliams and novelist Theodore Dreiser defended the cause of peace, and screenwriter Howard Emmet Rogers responded that he had heard much denunciation of the "perfidy" of Great Britain, France, and Poland, but none of the perfidy of Adolf Hitler. Trumbo was a featured speaker at a mass meeting of the American Peace Crusade, organized by the American Peace Mobilization, at the Shrine Auditorium on April 24, 1941. In that speech he went even further; he called for action to *defeat* the government's proposals for a lend-lease program to send aid to Britain in its fight against the Nazis![26]

Later—after more than a year and after a cataclysm—on September 14, 1942, Trumbo spoke at the Philharmonic Auditorium. This time, however, the rally was organized by the Citizens for Victory Committee. This time he advocated the immediate initiation of the Second Front to fight the Nazis. The committee now issued this speech as a pamphlet, *An Open Letter to the American People*. On October 7, 1942, Trumbo spoke as a founding sponsor of the American Artists Front to Win the War. Another founding sponsor was John Howard Lawson. Earlier, Lawson had been a cochairman and speaker at an American Artists for Peace meeting in New York City, on April 5 and 6, 1941, sponsored by the American Peace Mobilization. Now he, too, as did many others, had to make an abrupt about-face.[27]

For in the meantime, on June 22, 1941, Germany had invaded Russia.

On June 28 the CPUSA published its new campaign: "The People's Program of Struggle for the Defeat of Hitler and Hitlerism." By July, the CPUSA had turned the American Peace Mobilization into the American People's Mobilization—to support the war effort and defend the Soviet Union.[28]

Trumbo's obedience to the new party line had a more personal dimension as well. He took back the actual printing plates for *Johnny Got His Gun* and let it go out of print. When he still received letters asking where the book could be purchased, he turned over the letters to the FBI because, he said, these people must have been isolationist and Fascist sympathizers, dangerous to the security of the nation.[29]

After the German invasion, the MPDC was also no longer concerned with keeping America out of the capitalist war. As a member of its executive board, along with others of the Hollywood Reds, Lawson was instrumental in shaping its rebirth as the Hollywood Democratic Committee. With its new name and new pro-war programs, it once again attracted liberals and non-Communist progressives. It issued its pro-war newsletter *Target for Tonight* and conducted rallies and publicity campaigns for encouraging and supporting America's entry into the war.

Suddenly, even going to war was not enough. The new party line came down: The consistent point of emphasis of the new "war crusade" became the call for an immediate opening of a *second front* on the European continent. Joseph Losey, who had organized several events calling for peace, now produced three extravaganzas to support the war and Russian war relief: at Madison Square Garden, Boston Arena, and Constitution Hall in Washington, D.C. At the Washington event, the British ambassador, Lord Halifax, was booed. Shouts and banners proclaimed, "Open Up the Western Front!" Losey agreed, believing that the British were planning it so "that the Russians would be defeated by the Germans." Albert Maltz, now with a war he could support, created the commentary and edited footage of fighting in Russia taken by Soviet cameramen. Called *Moscow Fights Back,* the resulting documentary was distributed by a satellite of the Hollywood Democratic Committee. Lawson wrote a statement for the *Daily Worker* calling for a campaign to demand a second front. Even Writers Clinic conferences and workshops concluded with a call for a second front.[30]

One of the largest rallies of this campaign was held at Madison Square Garden on July 22, 1942, with the keynote statement (stretching both logic and fact) "Support the President, Rally for a Second Front Now." A featured speaker at the rally was Charles (Charlie) Chaplin. It was not his first speech promoting a second front, nor his last. In early spring he had been at one of the first such rallies, held in San Francisco.

He began, "Thank you, Dear Comrades, and yes, I do mean Comrades. When one sees the magnificent fight the Russian people are putting up, it is a pleasure and a privilege to use the word Comrade." In a similar fashion, on May 25, he had addressed the crowd (when the standing ovation for him had subsided) at the Shrine Auditorium in Los Angeles. In October, he called for a second front at an American Artists Front to Win the War rally at Carnegie Hall in New York, at which a number of Hollywood party members spoke. In December, when Chaplin spoke at a Russian War Relief fund-raising banquet in New York City, he was honored by the Soviet literary spokesman Ilya Ehrenberg on behalf of Joseph Stalin and the people of the Soviet Union.[31]

In previous years—even years in which he did not speak on the screen—Chaplin had spoken in support of Communist Party positions, defending the Moscow trials in extreme terms, defending the Nazi-Soviet Pact, and of course calling for America to stay out of the war in Europe. In later years, while he was in Europe, his passport was revoked and he was not to return to the United States for many years, and then only briefly.[32]

Whether Chaplin was ever a party member has been debated, to no conclusive decision, though it is not likely that he was. What is definite, however, is that he had been drawn into the orbit of the Hollywood party and a reading of the classical Marxist texts by his own predilections and the sway of friends. In the mid-thirties they became his guides and, to the degree that his independent spirit allowed, his mentors. From his difficult, underprivileged childhood on, and despite his success and wealth, Chaplin had always been—under his offscreen charm and on-screen plaintiveness—a rebel, resentful of those who had power and wealth, whether in terms of society or his own personal life. This natural sense of alliance with the working class and opposition to the "bosses" (which principles, it often seemed, were a justification for his own dictatorial behavior), these basic attitudes were given sharper definition by the texts he read and the people he met. Through the circle of Salka Viertel, he had become friends of Ella Winter and Donald Ogden Stewart, enthusiastic convert extraordinaire. He had met with Egon Kisch during his ventures into Hollywood and had been won over completely by the European charm and progressive ideas of Otto Katz during *his* visit.[33]

While Charlie, the Tramp, was always in generic conflict with people of money and power and in *Modern Times* (1936) with the "means" of mass production, Charles Chaplin's only direct dramatization and enunciation of the ideology he embraced was *Monsieur Verdoux* (1947). Despite his concluding polemics, it remains a masterpiece of ironically structured criticism of capitalism. For Verdoux is a nice man who wants to do well for his dear wife and family, but he is willing to quietly do whatever his *business* requires—seduce and kill wealthy women. At the end, however, Chaplin is impelled to speak in his own voice to make clear and direct—too clear and direct—the significance of his metaphor. He insists that the capitalist system that convicts and executes Verdoux for killing to produce profits has no right to do so. For the sake of the profits of *its* businesses, capitalism produces munitions, goes to war and kills on a much larger scale. Despite the nature of the war just concluded—and his earlier support of it—Chaplin is back in the ideological world of his prewar antiwar crusade and in the new propagandistic world of the beginning of the postwar peace campaigns.

Through the war and early postwar period, Chaplin's fervor as an ideologue intensified; among many others in Hollywood, however, it was distrust and antagonism that were building in intensity. Repeated conflicts of ideology and political action were fomenting painful and lasting feelings of betrayal.

And where—in this time of tumultuous change and devastation, of ideological loyalty and betrayal—were the men who had been able to inspire such fervent beliefs in so many? Willi Munzenberg was dead, victim of the relentless brutality of the Soviet system he had for years helped to disguise with his propaganda campaigns. Caught in the far-flung purges of the later thirties, Munzenberg managed to dodge the consequences until June of 1940. Still in France, by then he knew the Soviet executioners were after him, and now the Nazis and even the French. The latter placed him in an internment camp in May of 1940 because he was a German. To flee before the Nazis arrived, he escaped, probably attempting to get to Switzerland. His escape was undoubtedly assisted by Soviet people, and was short-lived. He was found hanging in a tree in the woods in southeast France. It was claimed that he had somehow acrobatically managed to kill himself! Some have wondered if his old aide Otto Katz had something to do with his assassination.[34]

Katz, after leaving Los Angeles, in late 1936, had returned to New York and then, before being expelled, went on to Mexico City and then back to Europe. During the Spanish Civil War, Katz was first in Madrid as a Comintern agent of influence and by some accounts an aide to Alexander Orlov in enforcing Communist discipline, even through executions. Then, back in Paris, using the name Andre Simone, he was director of the Soviet-controlled Loyalist propaganda agency Agencia Espagnola. He spent much of World War II in Mexico doing the work of the Comintern and NKVD in Mexico, the Caribbean, and Latin America. He is said to have attempted to recruit, with substantial offers, Cuban dictator Fulgencio Batista into the Sovier orbit. By 1943 he was reunited with his earlier Comintern associate and Munzenberg Man Egon Kisch. Ostensibly a roving reporter, Kisch was also connected to both the Comintern and the NKVD. According to an FBI report, he was instrumental in organizing "Stalinists immigration into Mexico."[35]

Kisch eventually returned to Czechoslovakia with Katz when, after the war, Katz was assigned to infiltrate the new government of Edward Beneš and Jan Masaryk in his native country. Katz was useful in preparations for their overthrow and the takeover by the Communist government of Klement Gottwald in 1948. At first he was rewarded with the editorship of the government organ *Rude Pravo*. But as the new wave of purges swept through the Eastern European satellites in 1951 and 1952, he too was betrayed by the cause to which he had devoted his life, energy, and devious and dangerous charm. He was arrested during the infamous Slansky Trial, the first and most important of a series of trials in Czechoslovakia. Many of those who had been involved in the Stalinist strategy of domination during the Spanish Civil War were executed during these purges, and that may be the reason for Katz's arrest. On December 2, 1952, he was hanged with ten other prominent Czech communists, including Rudolf Slansky, former general secretary of the Communist Party in Czechoslovakia. Most were Jews.[36]

Eugen Lobl was one of the two Communist officials who were sentenced to life imprisonment instead of death. (All, including the dead men, were "rehabilitated" in 1968.) Katz had confessed and *named* Lobl and others as traitors. Most were then executed. Years later, when Lobl was asked if Katz had been tortured so that he would confess, Lobl sardonically replied, "He confessed in the elevator." At the trial, Katz gave that one last measure of devotion to the illusion that betrayed him. He confessed that he had been a Trotskyite, a Zionist agent, a Titoist, "an enemy of the Czech people in the service of American Imperialism." But again and again, clearly shaping his emphasis to fit within the context of the then current Soviet anti-Zionist campaign, he stated that he was an "agent of capitalist Jewry." He reached a dramatic peroration: "I have joined the U.S., British and French anti-semites against the Soviet Union. Therein lies my crime. I am a writer, supposedly an architect of the soul. What sort of architect have I been, I who have poisoned people's souls? Such an architect of the soul belongs to the gallows. The only service I can still render is to warn all who, by origin or character, are in danger of following the same path to hell."[37]

What role in the high drama that he lived as his life was he playing here? Was he still the true believer or was he still the dramatist of a strangely romantic self? Was there irony in this florid mea culpa or merely one more task performed?

On the morning of his death in a last letter to his wife, Lobl wrote, "I have had enough time to think about the future, and I saw in it all its glory."[38]

5

A Climate of Hostilities and Betrayals: Writers Wars, Street Battles, and Broken Alliances

In the immediate postwar period, three areas of conflict in Hollywood intensified the accumulated antagonism, the searing, scarring power struggles of the Communists and their close followers with liberals and conservatives alike. One conflict, in the Screen Writers Guild, had been emerging and reemerging for years. The other two—the industry strikes and the new political alliances—had a new intense focus, but also rose from years of earlier hostilities. In the forties these battles were the final stage of the consequences of the ideological conformity of the Hollywood party. These ideologically fostered conflicts exacerbated the passions and tensions of the blacklist period, helped fuel the flagrant attacks by the Right, alienated the liberal Left, and blocked any effective counterthrust by a unified alliance.

In the early thirties the struggle to form the Screen Writers Guild (SWG) had drawn many into the orbit of the Communist Party. It would seem inevitable that sixteen of the first nineteen to be subpoenaed in 1947 were screenwriters. It was equally inevitable, within the plot of the ideological drama that would develop and intensify through the years, that John Howard Lawson was one of the SWG's chief organizers in 1933 and its first president. For he became the weathervane, the seismic gauge of the political, economic, and personal conflicts that developed through the decades; he was often the most crucial and psychologically fascinating actor in this real-life Hollywood melodrama.

Historians of the subject—on one side or the other—agree that Lawson was the leader of the Hollywood Communists for some fifteen years. But why? Was it the strength of his beliefs, the forcefulness of his personality? That was certainly part of it. But within the context of all that occurred, it was clearly the result of more than that. Lawson—an obsessive true believer—was the choice of the American Communist Party leadership; he was maintained by the party leadership as their instrument of control in the film community.

As the crucial force behind the formation of the SWG, Lawson worked with people with a broad spectrum of political beliefs, or even disinterest, who had practical, realistic, and just goals. He believed in those goals, but he was now a true believer in the goals of Marxism. The motives for his activities with the SWG were filtered through the dynamics of the development of his own personally intense political persona. In 1933 he was not yet a member of the party, and thus some historians have declared him one of the non-Communist organizers of the guild. But that is far too simplified an appraisal. For many years before his formal membership in November 1934—as his plays and other writings show—he was already a believer, though in turmoil intellectually, emotionally, and ideologically over what to do with his beliefs. Like all religious conversions (and it had that kind of emotional intensity), the progress was gradual and erratic, yet like Augustine's on his road to Damascus, finally fated and inevitable when it came to pass.

From the mid- to late twenties on, Lawson had practically commuted between New York and Hollywood. In 1931–1932 he had met with Sam Ornitz, John Bright, and others at their Marxist study groups. When a group of ten writers met to discuss a writers' group at the Hollywood Knickerbocker Hotel on February 3, 1933, present were Lawson, Ornitz, Bright, and Lester Cole, three of them part of the later Ten; Bright, not one of the Ten, was as ardent a believer as the others.

Until 1933, writers who worked within the highly splintered procedures of silent screenplays (stories, treatments, shot scenarios, dialogue subtitles, descriptive subtitles, etc.) had created the Writers Club, more of a cultural, social, and drinking club than a bargaining agent. Its president was Rupert Hughes, who continued on for some time as a conservative force in the new Writers Guild. James M. Cain once called Hughes, the uncle of Howard Hughes, "one of the goddamnedest boring writers in history—I could fall asleep over one paragraph of his prose." In 1932–1933, when salary cuts were being threatened at the studios, the Writers Club was obviously not enough. At the February 3 meeting, an organizing committee was formed; it included Ornitz and Bright, as well as Hughes and other moderates. Its agenda and program were still strongly influenced by Lawson. His colleague from left-wing New York theater groups, Francis Faragoh, was also influential in these early days of the SWG and continued to be a strong and radical activist within the group. Faragoh was a forceful member of the executive board during the crucial 1935–1936 battles with the studios and within the guild. By 1933, he had already written three minor talkies, but he is best known for his screenplay for *Becky Sharp* (1935), the first full-length color film, directed by Rouben Mamoulian. However, from 1936 to 1943, Faragoh was without a major screen credit, "punished," he felt, for his role in the SWG. The drought was broken with *My Friend Flicka* (clearly without any danger of propaganda) in 1943.[1]

Richard Collins remembered these formative days of the guild during his testimony in 1951: A major influence behind the scenes, as well as in the development of the party in Hollywood, was V. J. Jerome, who Collins testified was in Hollywood at the time of the February organizing meeting. The SWG, Collins said, was organized and promoted mainly "because of the efforts of the Communist Party. . . . John Howard Lawson took V. J. Jerome's place . . . at eight or nine meetings."[2]

Known Communists continued to play a major role in the SWG until 1947. They contributed to valuable bargaining results, but also to destructive radical stands and proposals, pro-Soviet campaigning, severe conflicts—and to an eventual final split in the power structure that resulted in their defeat. Estimates vary, but the most likely number of Communists in the SWG was between 150 and 200, not necessarily all at the same time. On the executive board they regularly played a major role (many felt a dominating, manipulating role). Lawson was on the board for only one year after his stint as president; but even with his time-consuming and life-consuming role of leader of the Communist Party, he was still a driving force in the SWG. Faragoh, while continuing to be active, was on the board only once more, as treasurer in 1942–1943. Robert Rossen was most active during the war years: secretary of the 1941–1942 slate, on the board in 1945, and chairman of the Hollywood Writers Mobilization, which the guild had initially sponsored. In the years until 1947, Communist Party members had between four and eight seats on the executive board, with a high of eight in 1941 and then eight again on the 1945–1946 board. When, however, the next board was elected, there were none.[3]

By April 6, 1933, the SWG was a reality, though still affiliated with the Authors League of America, with Lawson elected as its first president. There were soon 173 charter members and more than 750 members by the end of 1934.[4]

As the membership swelled quickly in 1934, the leaders of the new guild, and especially Lawson, were busy attempting to establish effective bargaining procedures and collective contracts with the studios. The producers balked at every stage, even stalling on SWG attempts to have *initial* negotiating sessions to establish the ground rules for negotiating collective bargaining agreements. Conflicts developed as well within the SWG, particularly over the proposed nature of the organization itself. Lawson defined his and the radical position. He saw the fight with the producers in Marxist terms. "The founding of the Guild in 1933," he later said, "made it inevitable that there be a struggle with big business to control the new forms of communication." The guild, he insisted, needed to act accordingly—as a *workers'* union. "We of the SWG wanted to be regarded as both writers and workers," Lawson said. He wanted the SWG, as well as the Dramatists Guild and Authors League of America, to be included in the new National Recovery Administration as a standard union. Many in the guild disagreed. In its decision, the National Labor Relations Board (NLRB) did not recognize the guild as a union; the attempt by Lawson and the radicals only added to this first stage of more than ten years of conflicts within the SWG.[5]

Lawson did not run for reelection as president in the fall of 1934. Later, he claimed that "reactionaries" insisted he be thrown out and that for the sake of the SWG he withdrew formally while continuing to work for what he felt was the guild's best future.[6] After a fight over the California gubernatorial election of that year, Lawson was fired by Columbia Pictures.[7] His next actual screenplay credit was the successful *Algiers*, a vehicle for Charles Boyer and Hedy Lamarr, which he worked on in 1937 and was released early in 1938, though it seems that he did work on scripts in the time between. The decade between 1937 and 1947 *was* Lawson's most successful writing period with credited work on nine screenplays, several as sole screenplay credits.

In 1934, in the midst of the hectic political and organizational activities of that year, Lawson had gone through the final stages of his conversion to Communism. In an article in *New Theatre* in November, he announced his membership in the Communist Party and declared that "I do not hesitate to say that it is my aim to present the Communist position, and to do so in the most specific manner." He did through the years go on to present that "position," with great dogmatism and scrupulous exegesis of Communist doctrine, but not in the movies.[8]

The personal drama of the conversion that so reshaped his own life and so affected the life of writers in Hollywood was the dramatic core of half a dozen plays that he wrote in the twenties and early thirties. In his case it is a dramatic development from being a man torn and doubting—too aware of ambiguities; of multiple philosophies; of mysticism, art, or politics, yet yearning to *believe*—to being a man of intellectual action, with a rigid controlling vision of personality, belief, and action. The plays dealt with characters who were caught between—between conflicting beliefs, between emotional possibilities.

In *Roger Bloomer* (1923), Roger sees the evils of materialism and capitalism, the masses as "servants of death and time, hungry, moaning for bread!" He rebels against the conformities of society, but his quest is mainly and vaguely spiritual and even sexual. He cannot take the necessary step to revolution. In *Processional* (1925), there is again a central seeker who cannot make up his mind to act. As in several of Lawson's plays, in *Roger Bloomer* there is a woman who tries to lead him on the right, righteous, and revolutionary path. After two further attempts to work out these political and inner paradoxes, Lawson's *The Internationale* (1928) tries to synthesize the demands of the inner life and the demands of Marxist history with the Marxist criticism of his previous work. The *people* of an Asian, oil-rich country are terrorized by stereotypical imperialist, capitalist force and brutality and do revolt. The voices of the rebellion chant, "At your door crowds are singing, soldiers are dragging machine guns. . . . Which side, then, WHICH SIDE?" The tormented, isolated progressive intellectual, David, knows he should stay with the revolution, but cannot choose and act, and seeks escape in love. Poignantly reflecting Lawson's own passionate dilemma, David says at play's end, "How do I get home? Christ, for the love o' pity, where do I go home?" Two further plays, both with very short runs, carried on this inner and outer battle. In *Gentlewoman* (1934), for example, Rudy does see the nature of capitalist evil, but fears that it may be too late for him to choose and act, to surmount the despair that the bourgeois world has instilled in him.

None of this was enough for Mike Gold, up from the docks himself to become an influential rough-hewn voice of the people in columns, literary and drama reviews, and plays and novels of his own. He was a friend, colleague, and mentor of Lawson, founder with him and Faragoh of the left-wing Playwrights Company in 1927 and even earlier in the formation of the Workers Drama League. After *Gentlewoman*, Gold demanded that Lawson become a true radical and write like one, in an article in *New Masses* on April 10, 1934, "A Bourgeois Hamlet for Our Time." "He is still lost," Gold found, "like Hamlet in his inner conflict"; still asking "where do I belong in the warring world of two classes."[9]

Lawson responded, and continued to respond throughout 1934. A week after Gold's complaint, his own article in *New Masses* was called "Inner Conflict and Proletarian Art." While he admits that his "work to date is utterly unsatisfactory in its political orientation," he does argue that writing about capitalist "decay" doesn't mean an acceptance of or involvement with that decay. It was a valuable literary principle that he would later reject. Accepting Gold's terms, Lawson tries to show how his work *has* been advancing in terms of revolutionary consciousness: "I believe *Gentlewoman*, in spite of faults, shows a considerable ideological advance. . . . It is a play about a dying bourgeois class . . . on Marxian lines." In what he called "a Reckless Preface" for a book that included his two 1934 plays, Lawson did not equivocate: "The only answer is to turn resolutely to the building of the revolutionary theatre."[10]

In June the very title of Lawson's article in *New Theatre* said it all: "Toward a Revolutionary Theatre—The Artist Must Take Sides." In the July 23, 1934, issue of the *Daily Worker*, Lawson's article "Play on Dimitroff" attacked the play (about Georgi Dimitroff and his courage) for "not giving us the Marxian attack or the Proletarian vitality which we (workers in all branches of the theater trying to solve the difficulties of a revolutionary approach) need so desperately . . . the detailed reality of economics and politics."[11]

In the November article in which he pledged his new total allegiance, Lawson defined his new catechism for dramatic technique, with examples. While allowing that Albert Maltz's *Peace on Earth* and Paul Peters and George Sklar's *Stevedore* were honorable efforts, he opined (in his new tutorial manner), "Is it not correct to say that these plays would have been more effective *aesthetically* [emphasis added] if the political line had been hammered out more clearly." On the other hand he praised Sam Ornitz's play *In New Kentucky*, about Harlan County miners' strike, for Ornitz's "terrific job in presenting the specific role of the Communist Party in the Kentucky situation. Ornitz shows that the radicalization of the miners led them to a Communist position,"[12] as Ornitz, as director, was to insist on in directing the film *Salt of the Earth* twenty years later.

Lawson's final play, *Marching Song* (1937), struck Harold Clurman of the Group Theater as "cold, artificial, mechanical—a creature of the author's will." When Lawson protested, "Don't you think proletarian plays should be written at this time?" Clurman answered, "Perhaps. But not by you." Nevertheless, Nathaniel Buchwald in the *Daily Worker* found it the "finest labor play . . . the most eloquent and poetic dramatization of the class struggle in our time."[13] In its Soviet-style epic form, *Marching Song* encompasses all the ideological precepts for authentic proletarian art that Lawson had absorbed and transmuted as his own. It includes practically every element, device, symbol, caricature, narrative pattern, cliché that the genre partakes of. Sadistic gangsters are brought in to break the strike of the electrical workers. While there are individual symbolic characters, the real hero is the group. When one of their leaders is tortured to death by the company thugs, the workers, carrying his body proudly, are inspired (a la Eisenstein's film *Battleship Potemkin* [1925], which Lawson analyzed in one of his books) to make their heroic and triumphant revolution against their oppressors. An indecisive worker is finally converted to the union's struggle; a strong wife energizes her wavering husband. All end up as a marching chorus singing the song that Lawson had predicted ever since *Roger Bloomer*, that Pete Seeger would later make popular: "Step by step the longest march can be won, can be won; single stones will form an arch, one by one, one by one."

Once fully committed, Lawson was tireless and dogmatic, imperial. He had found the one pure grail and been able to accept its call—and the discipline it required, the discipline that he would demand of others again and again. Even his personality, in a sense his image of himself, was changed. Few in the subsequent years would recognize the fellow in John Dos Passos' description of him at the time of their attempt to join an ambulance corps during the First World War. As Dos Passos remembered him, Lawson was an "extraordinarily diverting fellow . . . with bright brown eyes, untidy hair and a great beak of a nose that made you think of Cyrano de Bergerac. . . . He was a voluble and comical talker." Dos Passos also said, however, that "he had drastic ideas on every subject under the sun."[14]

One new drastic idea was at the core of a major battle between the SWG and the producers; it was also the cause of the eruption of a civil war within the ranks of the guild. Even when he was in New York or Washington, Lawson was in constant communication with party stalwarts, including Faragoh, and his positions were a strong influence during the organized "fraction meetings" held by party members in the SWG. As Leo Townsend explained during his appearance before the House Un-American Activities Committee (HUAC), party members would meet "to set a plan of operation at the membership meetings of the Guild. . . . [Besides general strategy] sometimes it would be decided who would speak, who would make a speech on a certain issue, and who would follow him. Especially if electioneering. This fraction was effective because it had a chance to push candidates for the board who were members of the Communist Party, because each of us was given a list of 10 or 15 noncommunist members of the guild and directed to campaign with them."[15]

Since its founding, the SWG had increased its membership dramatically, but it had not been able to obtain appropriate recognition and bargaining rights from the producers. In 1936, the drastic idea was to solve all this—or so the Progressive bloc claimed. The SWG would affiliate with the New York–based Authors League of America and its subsidiary, the Dramatists Guild, and thus increase its power to force the studios to accept the SWG's demands. This was a strange program for the Left leaders to promote; it was seen by many within the SWG as merely a troublemaking bluff, a temporary strategic ploy to obtain leverage in negotiations with the studios. As Laurence Beilinson, the SWG's own lawyer, said, "I was opposed to the attempt to *force* [emphasis added] Article 12 and the affiliation from the beginning. . . . I always felt the attempt would end in disaster, as it did."[16]

During this controversy, the issue of Communists in the SWG, and Communist control, arose and took its first form and had its first consequences. In 1936 the *Hollywood Reporter* ran several articles on Reds moving west and seeking control. The trade paper was not alone in seeing the move toward affiliation with New York guilds as a move toward affiliation with New York Communists, and Moscow.[17]

The conservatives used the internal conflicts over Article 12 to attack the power of the progressives. Led by Rupert Hughes, they promoted a series of massive resignations, formed their own guild, the Screen Playwrights. The SWG was decimated, lost its charter, and a kind of "graylist" (as it was later called) hit the more prominent activists. The remnants continued to meet unofficially and regularly in members' homes, and it was remarked by several both in and out of the loyalist group that at times it was hard to remember if one was going to a Communist Party meeting or an SWG meeting.

When, however, the new Screen Playwrights also ran into the recalcitrance of the producers and when tempers began to subside, writers began to return. The first new open meeting was held June 11, 1937, and the SWG was officially reinstituted with a mixture of radicals, mainly Communist Party members, and conservatives on the board, a mixture that produced constant disagreements and growing hostilities. The guild could now claim approximately 75 percent of the writers in its organization, but it still had to contend with the diminished Screen Playwrights and still made little headway with the studios.[18]

When the Soviets and the Nazis signed their pact, the three-way conflicts intensified. The Communists in SWG wanted the guild to declare its support for the antiwar peace organizations the party had formed. This was seen by the majority of members as the most flagrant attempt yet to pressure the SWG to follow a Communist policy. They soundly defeated the proposal.[19] This new flaming of antagonism was to be calmed only with the patriotic unity of World War II, when all sides agreed to work together for victory, though not necessarily for the same reasons. The Hollywood Writers Mobilization was one result.

As the war ended, that harmony was shattered when a major strike erupted. It was the most extreme and violent of a series of labor disputes that were another major source of the long-seething antagonism between the studios and the "progressives," and between the conservatives in Hollywood and in the SWG and the Communist Party. In the postwar labor battle, the radicals (read: Communist Party members) played a prominent role. There were a number of forces and influences in these battles.

Labor disputes had begun early in the movie industry, but a general period of stability had been established by the consolidation of most craft and labor groups into the International Alliance of Theatrical Stage Employees (IATSE). In the depths of the depression in the thirties, however, the IATSE had allied itself with Al Capone's mob in Chicago. A strike in the spring of 1937 was a direct foreshadowing of the postwar strike. The reign of the IATSE was challenged by a new coalition of some rebellious craft unions. Progressives in both the SWG and the Screen Actors Guild found they could widen the support of their own guilds by standing against the power of the bosses and their IATSE "Fascist" collaborators. Party functionaries in the Congress of Industrial Organizations (CIO) sent out Jeff Kibre, one of the most radical of their union organizers, to try to break the control of the IATSE. Fred Rinaldo, a longtime screenwriter and onetime Communist Party member, called Kibre "the official communist in the Hollywood trade union movement." Documentation has substantiated his membership. The party press joined the fray with articles in the *Daily Worker*; the *New Masses* ran feature articles in its May 11 and May 18, 1937, issues. Rallies were organized, fund-raising dinners and parties were held, a major, celebrity-sprinkled May rally held at the much-used Hollywood Legion Stadium.[20]

That strike was broken. Before being forced to leave the Hollywood soundstages, however, in September of 1938, Kibre was the first to break the silence and file a complaint with the NLRB—openly accusing the IATSE and it mob-affiliated leader Willie Bioff of racketeering. The Left joined in enthusiastically. Years of legal maneuvering followed, but eventually Willie Bioff, George Browne, and producer Joseph M. Schenck of Twentieth Century-Fox were sent to prison. But another seedbed of hostility had been planted.[21]

The much more important postwar sequel was led by Herbert (Herb) L. Sorrell. He was a stocky, burly, pugnacious man, broken nose and all, who looked more like a longshoreman than a Hollywood painter. He did in fact have close ties with Harry Bridges and his West Coast longshoreman's union, but not because he had worked on the docks. While the party membership of both Sorrell and Bridges was long disputed and denied, documentation has since supported the claim of their membership. Members or not, their alliance with party strategies and programs was consistent—except when they chose to disagree on matters involving their own personal crusades. For both were rebels to the core, Sorrell more impulsively, less strategically.

In the late thirties, during the period of the Nazi-Soviet Pact, Sorrell was president of the Painters Union and was elected president of the California Labor Non-Partisan League, which was organized to oppose Roosevelt in the Democratic primary of 1940. A key member of this league was Harry Bridges. The group—a short-lived and a rather abstract fund-raising (read: pressuring on union members) entity—flourished the party slogan "The Yanks Are Not Coming." In the words of Sorrell, the war was "just another imperialist struggle." Following the invasion of Russia, he, of course, was now loud in his demands for U.S. intervention; during the war, he was equally fervent in joining the Hollywood chorus in demanding a second front. Sorrell, with a new coalition called the Conference of Studio Unions (CSU), supported the drafting of workers in key industries, which the party was then supporting and both the CIO and American Federation of Labor opposing.[22]

By 1945, the CSU had thousands of members. Sorrell's radical positions and party connections—and the threatening workers' power that the strength of his conference had created—produced a strong reaction from the producers. One result, on the union front, was to use the power of the reformed IATSE, and its new president, Richard Walsh, a bona fide union man. He sent Roy Brewer to Hollywood as his representative. Brewer became one of the major figures, if not *the* major figure, in the union, and in the economic and ideological wars that followed. His unprepossessing appearance and quiet, polite manner belied his aggressive zeal, the insistent certitude of his methodical, effective mode of action. He was a small man, pudgy rather than burly and barrel-chested like Sorrell. But his soft, precise speech carried just as much intense belief in his cause. As he later told Dan E. Moldea, "The truth is, [the Communists] had this town in the palm of their hands; they were calling the shots."[23]

On the political front, Brewer soon forged an alliance between the IATSE unions and the producers as a means of fighting the Communist Party influence in all the unions and the industry. In 1944 the producers had already joined with sympathetic filmmakers to form the Motion Picture Alliance for the Preservation of American Ideals. Its purpose was far broader than a union struggle. In its "Statement of Principles" the group declared, "We refuse to permit the effort of Communist, Fascist, and other totalitarian-minded groups to pervert the powerful medium into an instrument for the dissemination of un-American ideals and beliefs." Its main, indeed only real, concern was Communist groups, and it became the leading anticommunist force during the investigation and blacklist period. Director Sam Wood, one of the organizers, was the alliance's first president. Brewer soon joined the alliance and eventually became its active and directly controlling chairman of the executive board, while John Wayne became its president. As a leading conservative in the alliance, James McGuiness told an audience in 1946, "To know the nature of your enemy, you must realize that Communism is a complete conspiratorial movement, dedicated to the overthrow of our form of government for the benefit of a foreign power and an alien ideology." As early as 1944, the alliance had used its influence to bring the investigating committee of Representative Martin Dies to Hollywood to conduct a brief and unfocused investigation. On October 11, 1944, there had been a meeting at Lawson's house for those subpoenaed for those hearings.[24]

The radical CSU strike that Sorrell declared in March 1945 actually strengthened the crusade of the conservative Motion Picture Alliance—his and the Communist Party's arch enemy then and for years. This was a typical paradox and frequent consequence of activities of the party and its followers. Even Ben Margolis, later the leading attorney for the Nineteen and the Ten, was disturbed by the destructive consequences of Sorrell's persistence: "The strike nourished the Motion Picture Alliance and made it more powerful. The Alliance was largely responsible for what Congress did. It was a stimulant to HUAC."[25] The strike's primary purpose was jurisdictional, a continuation of the power struggle between the CSU and the IATSE. The producers and the Motion Picture Alliance supported the IATSE. The Left supported the CSU, but the nature of the support at first got entangled with the shift in the Moscow-Comintern policy at the close of the war. The first party position, promoted by Lawson, was to *not* support the strike because the war had not yet ended. Within the Comintern's wartime policy of a united front against the Germans, the party had supported labor's pledge not to strike, and so it did not initially condone the strike. A *People's World* headline about Sorrell proclaimed, "A Good Guy Gone Wrong." Another on April 19: "For National Unity—End the Strike." This created confusion and dissension among the Hollywood Left. Within months, however, the situation changed. The war ended. The Duclos letter announced the new hard-line international policy of the Soviet Union. Earl Browder and the soft united front were out; William Z. Foster, always tightly in step with the toughest Comintern line, was in. On a nationwide tour, Foster visited Hollywood, laid down the new decalogue at a meeting at Lawson's house. The party now favored strikes, any and all strikes. The Hollywood party, along with the *People's World*, now officially supported the CSU strike.[26]

Within the SWG, the battle line over the strike was set. Lawson and the Left called for total support of the strike; the moderates and Right called for adherence to the SWG's policy of not taking part in labor disputes. Citing a no-strike clause in its current contract, the SWG refused the CSU's request to respect the picket lines (as had the Screen Actors Guild). However, individual members and groups continued to demand that this request be accepted. Typical of the infighting, a compromise was reached and the SWG officially called for the reinstatement of all strikers who had been fired.[27]

A striking confluence of Communist Party icons powered a rally at the Hollywood Legion Stadium on October 7. Harry Bridges brought the usual symbolic "greetings" and the support of the longshoremen. Dalton Trumbo wrote a witty and impassioned speech for Herb Sorrell. John Howard Lawson, Larry Parks, and others spoke. Paul Robeson sang. (Pete Seeger was busy elsewhere.) A pamphlet prepared by party members in the SWG was passed out for further distribution, telling how bosses had locked workers out of their jobs and announcing a weekly schedule of meetings. As usual, organizations were created, such as the Citizens Committee for Motion Picture Strikers and the Hollywood Welfare Fund. Regular Sunday meetings of support were held at the Hollywood Legion Stadium.[28]

By October the strike had turned vicious. Warner Bros. had been chosen for a mass picket line. Beginning on October 5, the picket line was more a daily march and demonstration; many rushed in to take to the streets. On the 8th, violence, and arrests, erupted on the streets outside Warner Bros. Autos were overturned, a variety of missiles hurled, batons swung by the sheriff's riot squad. And accusations were hurled as wildly as the bricks and rocks. Brewer claimed that Bridges had sent in longshoremen goons to precipitate the violence, that strike leaders were carrying lead pipes wrapped in rolled-up newspapers. Lawson wired Jack Warner, protesting against the Fascist brutality of the police and strikebreaking goons, telling him he was responsible for injuries if he didn't do something. Warner responded by getting Harry Cohn to cancel Lawson's contract.[29]

In testimony later, Brewer took a broader view of the consequences: "injuries of the Reds who started the trouble were nothing compared to injuries sustained by thousands of innocent persons who were thrown out of jobs by the strikes fomented by the Communists."[30]

A week after the picketing began, the NLRB ruled in favor of the CSU and its local affiliates. The strike was officially over, but the producers stalled.

This time the SWG protested against the producers' violation of labor law, even threatening a writers' strike. The producers continued to stall. The SWG issued protests, but did not strike.[31]

But in 1946 Sorrell and the CSU did again go out on strike. It was more than coincidence that State Senator Jack Tenney began another of his scattershot investigations of Communism at this time. And this time pickets were set up at eight studios, at which some fifty movies were in various stages of production. At Columbia 1,500 strikers practically laid siege to the studio. When it all became violent again, *Time* magazine, with its inimitable dramatic style of bias, reported that strikers "scattered tacks in the path of movie stars' automobiles, threw coffee in the faces of picket-line crossers, stoned bus-loads of AF of L workers convoyed through their jeering, milling ranks." It did not report the baton-swinging and the excessive number of arrests. Although the SWG voted down the resolution to strike, leftist screenwriters refused to cross the picket lines. Some joined the picket lines. John Bright rather romantically remembers acting as chauffeur for Sorrell, who it was believed was in danger of being beaten, even killed. Bright was fired by MGM. Others were threatened with dismissal, some were fired. Ironically, the highest-paid writers had work-at-home clauses in their contracts, so people like Donald Ogden Stewart, Dorothy Parker, and Alan Campbell could show their solidarity and not cross the picket line by just staying home.[32]

Party members and others on the Left remained steadfast when the strike dragged on, but other support began to dwindle. Criticism of Sorrell's intransigence increased. Sorrell wouldn't back down, and his stubborn crusade produced a new heightening of hostility in the SWG. The party caucus in the guild continued their crusade in supporting him, forcing a showdown in executive board elections. The broader issue had become clear: The strike had become a focus point for the beginning of the campaign to crush the influence of the Communist Left within the SWG.[33]

A similar pattern was taking shape in the Screen Actors Guild (SAG). On the Left, the Hollywood party worked at getting SAG members under its influence to influence other actors to support the strike—and thus support the goals of the Communist Party. Joint meetings were held for party members in the SWG and party members who were actors. In his testimony in 1951, Sterling Hayden, who was in the party for a short period in 1946, discussed his attendance at several meetings in which members were instructed to support the strike at SAG meetings. His group of eight presented such a proposal to the SAG board on November 11, 1946. As part of the fund-raising procedures, he made out a three-hundred-dollar check to Abe Polonsky, at whose house several meetings were held.[34] After an attempt to mediate, the SAG mediation delegation, led by Ronald Reagan, issued a "Screen Actors Guild Report to the Motion Picture Industry," stating that "the Guild board reluctantly has been forced to the conclusion that certain of the leaders of the CSU do not want the strike settled." A petition by several hundred members called for a review of the SAG executive board's position on the strike, and the leadership called for a mass meeting at the Hollywood Legion Stadium, everyone's venue of choice. At the meeting, Reagan was the main defender of the board's antistrike position. The speech undoubtedly contributed to his winning the election three months later for president of the SAG. After the meeting, a referendum by mail was conducted, and the board's position received the strong endorsement of the membership. The SAG had made a major turn toward a strong anti-Communist position.[35]

Sorrell and the CSU held on and on, disrupting many lives and careers; they lost, struck again, until they and other progressive unions were destroyed. Sorrell was eventually expelled by the international headquarters of the painters union for associating with "groups which subscribe to the doctrines of the Communist parties."[36]

Whatever their initial validity as labor actions, the strikes ended up strengthening the Motion Picture Alliance, the ideological wing of the producers' power structure. The battles over the strikes and the Communists' actions during them hit harder, more personally than the conflicts over more abstract political issues like the Nazi-Soviet Pact or the second front. They left all sides—Reds, labor, liberals, bosses, conservatives—with raw wounds of emotional, as well as ideological, hostility that were definitely carried over into the extreme antagonisms of the blacklist period. The producers continued to use the strikes as one of the key justifications for taking an aggressive stance against the influence of Communists in Hollywood. For some, this interpretation was seen as an excuse for trying to break the power of the unions. For Brewer, however, the devastation of the strikes showed "the capacity of the Communists to destroy things. . . . Things will not grow naturally with he Communists in the picture. . . . I don't mind opposition—I like opposition—because sometimes I'm wrong, but I don't want a guy telling me something that he isn't, especially when he's attached to an organization that's trying to destroy the world."[37] Many saw this as a reasonable position, but the consequences were often as unreasonable as the actions they believed they were defending against.

Reagan and Brewer were also actors in the later stages of the third area of conflict that fueled the intense antagonisms and extreme consequences of the hearings and the blacklist. This was the formation and shifting, ever-splintering alliances of directly political organizations. The fate of what was known as HICCASP (Hollywood Independent Citizens Committee of Arts, Sciences, and Professions) was indicative as it evolved from the wartime Hollywood Democratic Committee (HDC), attracted a broad spectrum of supporters, splintered, and faded.

During World War II the HDC had grown to nearly a thousand members. Party members on the executive board and major committees in the brief span of the group's existence included Lawson, Robert Rossen, Sidney Buchman, Edward Dmytryk, Lester Cole, and Paul Jarrico, among others. Lyricist E. Y. "Yip" Harburg was vice chairman. The HDC backed Franklin Delano Roosevelt in his reelection campaign in 1944, roused to a rush of activities by Communist Party forecasts of the dire consequences of a Thomas Dewey victory in November. Party members addressed organizational groups with such warnings as John Howard Lawson's of a nation in a crisis "so freighted with the possibility of danger" to our democratic system, and Dalton Trumbo's of a "situation so desperate" that our democratic rights could be lost (his speech was also printed in the *New Masses*).[38]

As the war ended, party stalwarts were prime movers in having the HDC affiliate with a new national organization called the Independent Citizens Committee of the Arts, Sciences, and Professions (ICCASP) and then in changing its name to the Hollywood version of that unwieldy title, HICCASP. The terminology of the new name, echoing the phrases of party-line organizations of the thirties, should have been fair warning for the liberals. With the Soviet and Comintern turn to the Cold War hard line, the national organization ICCASP followed the new Communist Party line. The Communists in HICCASP insisted it play the same chord as the national group: attacking Harry Truman and every one of his policies while supporting those of the Soviet Union. A December 1945 ICCASP rally in Madison Square Garden set the tone. A resolution was endorsed "denouncing" the Truman administration's "departures from the Roosevelt foreign policy . . . based on unity of the Big Three."[39]

Hollywood voices joined in. Dalton Trumbo, in April of 1946, addressed a meeting of the Mobilization for Democracy, an offshoot of ICCASP, and, as the *Daily Worker* reported, attacked American imperialism abroad and the rise of American Fascists at home. In a speech at a forum sponsored by the *People's World*, held at the Embassy Auditorium, Trumbo's subject was "Art—Weapon of the People"—in the fight for peace and against capitalist imperialism.[40]

The dedicated stridency of the Communist Party members finally brought on the dissolution of HICCASP within an atmosphere of acrimony and spleen typical of these pre-blacklist conflicts. It was another impetus to the campaign to crush the influence of the Communists in Hollywood. Party members and followers such as Joan LaCoeur Scott (a prolific screenwriter and the wife of Adrian Scott) believed that the liberal flight was occurring because "the red-baiting had reached such a pitch." Producer Milton Sperling saw it differently: "The Communist hard core began to run things openly and to dictate policy. They drove out the middle road [members], they drove out the liberals, by hewing to a very straight line and by organizing everything their own way." In one example, following the new line, the Los Angeles County party, led by Nemmy Sparks, demanded that the Hollywood branch of the party "restore discipline." Reds in HICCASP were instructed to lead the organization to support Ellis Patterson against the liberal Will Rogers Jr. in the California Senate race. The organization did. Patterson lost; the split widened.[41]

A special committee was formed, across the political spectrum—Lawson and Trumbo, Reagan and Don Hartman, Linus Pauling and James Roosevelt. Screenwriter True Boardman was chairman. Its resulting statement was platitudinous, vague, and unconvincing. During revision by the executive board, liberals—led by Melvyn Douglas, Philip Dunne, and Roosevelt—called for an explicit statement to approve the American democratic system and free market economy and to reject Communism "as a desirable form of government for the USA." When that was blocked by the Left, resignations of major figures flowed, including Reagan, with attendant publicity. Years later, Reagan recalled that Lawson and Trumbo had led the fight against the statement approving the American system. In one version, he recounted how someone on the Left had even recited provisions from the Soviet constitution to prove Russia was more democratic than the United States. In another statement, Reagan recalled that Artie Shaw had offered to recite the provisions to prove the point. Reagan told the FBI on April 10, 1947, that at SAG meetings "there are two 'cliques' of members, one headed by [name deleted] and [name deleted] which on all questions of policy that confront the Guild follow the Communist Party line."[42]

After the first spate of resignations, Lawson, a board member, declared that no more announcements of resignations would be allowed. Announced or not, the resignations continued, and soon (as in the case of the HDC), only the hard core was left. By 1947, before it faded away completely, HICCASP's prime activity was defending the Hollywood Nineteen and subsequently the Hollywood Ten. In *The Power and the Glitter*, Ronald Brownstein looked back at the controversies: "But in retrospect it appears clear that HICCASP's disputes with Truman were driven less by emotional need or differing interpretations of liberalism than by the group's Communist contingent—which was, in turn, influenced, if not precisely guided, by the foreign policy agenda of the Soviet Union."[43]

The dissolution of the Hollywood Writers Mobilization (HWM) followed a similar course. It had been created (as shaped by the Hollywood Reds) as a broad coalition of filmmakers to contribute to the war effort. Its high point had been the 1944 conference held at UCLA, but once the war was over and the party line changed, the HWM changed. As the war ended, the radicalization and eventual demise of the HWM coincided with, and was one of the sources of, heightened conflicts within the SWG, which was the chief source of funds for the HWM. With the war over, the SWG executive board debated whether to continue the funding and its public affiliation with the HWM. Radical members, led by Lawson, insisted that the HWM still had an important function and that the move to terminate the funding was a result of "red-baiting." Moderates, led by Emmett Lavery and Allen Rivkin, saw the organization as obsolete and a threat to the SWG's reputation. The subsidy to the HWM was terminated.

Radicals kept the HWM going for almost two more years, its activities becoming more openly pro Soviet: a series of forums (and pamphlets) called "Counter-Attack: Against the Plot to Control America's Thinking"; cultural exchanges with the Soviet Union; benefit screenings of Russian films to aid Russian medical facilities and to protest the termination of American economic aid to Russia; discussions with visiting Soviet filmmakers. Richard Collins testified about a project to meet with scientists at Cal Tech to get information and support for a campaign to publicize the horrors of the atomic bomb.[44]

The dispute over the HWM was but one of the sources of tension and growing personal hostilities that led to the final battle for control of the SWG in the period leading up to the first HUAC hearings in the fall of 1947. In 1946, despite the increase in political controversies, five Communists were still elected as members of the executive committee. This roused their opponents to direct action. An All-Guild Committee was formed by moderates like Leonard Spiegelgass and Rivkin, along with former party member Martin Berkeley. "We were determined, the moderates in the Guild," Spiegelgass said, "that we would finally clean it up once and for all, and that we would do it by letting the membership vote between one slate that was clearly non-left and one group that was clearly left. That's why we formed the All-Guild Slate." Gordon Stuhlberg, later the SWG counsel, remembered, "Spiegelgass told me his group hated the communists. They'd pushed them around in the war, and they felt they had to ally themselves with the Right to create an opposing force to the CP in the Guild."[45]

Throughout 1947, while strategies for the Nineteen's appearance before the HUAC were being shaped, the All-Guild Slate strengthened its position and was attacked in turn by the Progressives. In the SWG election in November 1947—immediately after the first hearings and, for many, in great part because of the conduct of the Ten at the hearings—the All-Guild Slate easily triumphed. No Communists or non–Communist Party radicals were elected to the Board. The battle was over. But only in the Screen Writers Guild.[46]

6

Robert Rossen: A Life in the Party and in the Movies

Robert Rossen's life in the Communist Party began shortly after he arrived in Hollywood. His life in the party and his career in Hollywood provide a unique and significant case study, a quintessential narrative of a central figure's journey through these dynamic and crusading, idealistic and righteously deluded, tumultuous and troubled times. It illuminates on a personal level what it was like to participate in the events, developments, changes, and conflicts of an active party member and be a prolific and major filmmaker at the same time. And all within the hovering irony and scarring dilemmas of his eventual break with the party and his testifying.

Rossen is the preeminent representative among those who testified, the key figure in capturing the paradoxes of the moral choices of the period. For both among those who testified and those who had not, from the mid-thirties to the early postwar period, he was among the most active and prominent members in organizing and participating in party organizations, strategies, and campaigns, was among the Nineteen first called to the HUAC (House Un-American Activities Committee) hearings. He was a member longer than other major figures who testified, such as Elia Kazan (who was only in the party for a short period in the mid-thirties). Rossen then played a major and controversial role in the period of turmoil and dissent, debated and disputed actions, antagonism and destructive consequences. His course through this stage personifies the complexities of moving from being an active Communist to being an outspoken anti-Communist, of the jagged dilemmas and anguished choices involved in breaking with the party, being blacklisted, and then finally deciding to testify.

His testimony was thoughtful and principled, but the consequences of his testifying, in turn, had their own paradoxes. They allowed him to work again, to create several of the most valuable films of the period; but they resulted as well in decades of moral judgments and personal vilification. The nature and degree of the attacks on him as a man and treatment of him as a filmmaker again make him a most representative figure, painfully so. The standard version of Robert Rossen the informer in the conventional history and moral judgments of the time captures the essence of the distortions of the impact of ideology, and of lingering resentment, on the establishing of a view of the past and its meanings. This orthodoxy has created a distorting moral dualism of pure heroes and utter villains that has been promulgated ever since.

Among those who were in the party for a significant period of time—in his case from the mid-thirties into the early postwar period—Rossen was the most successful, even powerful, filmmaker. As writer, director, and producer, Rossen and his films illuminated their time in American in a way unmatched by any save possibly Kazan, and yet his films are rarely acknowledged in the conventional historical and critical narratives of the period that are passed from generation to generation. No other filmmaker of the Left (or the Right, for that matter) created this full and meaningful a body of work that—from the perspective of the Left, even the ideals and ideology of Communism—dramatized the conflicts and paradoxes of American society, of capitalism itself.

This body of work—although never about Hollywood or the blacklist directly—reflected more than the films of any others, even more than Rossen had ever consciously intended, the conflicts and dilemmas, the ambiguities of motive and betrayal, the psychological wounds of the period of the Hollywood blacklist. And in a more universal sense, the dilemmas of choice and action, the pervasive consequences of betrayal—of ideals, of others, of self.

In 1935, Rossen's one produced play in New York—*The Body Beautiful*—had attracted the interest of Hollywood director Mervyn LeRoy. After the brief run of *The Body Beautiful*, LeRoy paved the way for Rossen to begin his career as a screenwriter. By mid-1936 he had a personal contract with LeRoy and then was under contract at Warner Bros., where he remained until the mid-forties. By the spring of 1937, Rossen was a member of the Communist Party.[1]

Rossen had arrived in Hollywood during the heated battles between the studios and the writers over the attempt to unionize and form the Screen Writers Guild. As Rossen later recalled, "The most active people in that fight—it was highly organized and most effective—were . . . members of the Communist Party . . . in retrospect, the most capable; and, naturally, I was drawn toward these people, both from the point of view of their dedication to what they were doing and from the point of view of their prestige and their standing as screenwriters."[2] These motives do seem to fit his temperament and the situation of a young, inexperienced arrival; but these dedicated and prestigious people did also represent ideological positions and ideals that he had brought west with him.

As he looked back years later, Rossen recalled the broader, deeper ideals that membership in the party at that time seemed to support. Echoing the statements of many others, he emphasized the idealism of his commit-ment: "I joined out of a deep conviction that the party was leading the fight against those forces, both here and abroad, which were trying to smash the forward march of the people towards a fuller, a richer and happier life. And I also felt with as deep a conviction that the answer lay in Socialism. I wanted people to live with dignity and not as debased and craven creatures, and this search for dignity is the constantly recurring theme of my work, for I have known what it is to be without it."[3]

As he reflected on the past, he had thought a lot about the intellectual at-mosphere of the twenties, when he grew up, and then the depression years of the thirties, feeling that

> it was a period of great cynicism, disillusionment; it was a period in which I think most young men who were interested in ideas accepted the premise that the system of government . . . that we had grown up under had failed . . . there weren't any more horizons; there weren't any more promises; we had pretty much reached the apex of a pretty materialistic society. . . . We felt that we were looking—I felt that I was looking—for new horizons, a new kind of society, something I could believe in and become a part of. . . . You felt that . . . the Communist Party was the medium through which this could be effected. . . . It offered every possible kind of thing to you at that time which could fulfill your sense of idealism . . . anything that tends toward the realization of the inner man.[4]

It was even stimulating and fulfilling, for some time at least, when that idealism was turned into conforming with the practicalities and regimen of party membership. Even in Hollywood, the system was not as loose and casual as has often been claimed. The first step for an initiate like Rossen was attendance at a Marxist study group for several months with instruc-tors from the Los Angeles County Communist Party. He then moved on to a new members class and was then assigned to a group as a full-fledged member. At first Rossen's branches were based on one's residential area, but later the system evolved into groups, cells, or fractions based on profession and even status.

Payment of dues began immediately—based primarily on a percentage of net income. Rossen estimated that over the ten-year period of his mem-bership he had paid about twenty thousand dollars directly to the party, almost all of which was dues forwarded to the National Committee in New

York. He estimated another twenty thousand dollars given to various Communist controlled organizations, campaigns, and events.

Dues were only one aspect of the demands made by party membership. There were constant rounds of meetings, organizations, "cause" parties, campaigns, statements, and the ubiquitous "calls." As was typical of those in the party, Rossen's life became a life of the party—time-consuming, intellectually controlling, socially determining.[5]

Nonetheless, he did find time to almost instantly become one of the most prolific and influential screenwriters of the years of the studio system. His nine screenplays while under contract were instrumental in developing what became known as the Warners style: fast-paced, fast-talking, hard-hitting, with high-contrasted black-and-white imagery and narrative patterns shaped by standard genres such as the gangster film. In turn, the patterns, formulas, and iconography of these genre films were often developed to at least imply certain points of social criticism, as did more standard social problem films. But from the start of his career, Rossen extended the boundaries of Warners' established genres, drawing psychological and social implications beyond the usual formulas. His later work, culminating in The Hustler (1961) and Lilith (1964), probed more deeply into the complexities of motive, the often destructive interaction of the corrupting forces of society and the internal drives and needs of individuals, the often tragic ambiguities and consequences of why people do what they do—but even within his genre scripts there are early traces of what became his central interests and dramatic concerns.

In an article in Show magazine, Rossen commented that his favorite Shakespeare play was Macbeth, for in it he found a "dramatization of the ambiguity of the human condition"; Macbeth, like contemporary man, was "reaching for the symbols of his identity, rather than the reality, destroying yet finding himself in the tragic process."[6] Seeking these illusory symbols of the self, Rossen's typical protagonists, his searchers also reach for power, through status and money, violence and domination, even love twisted into violation. The destructive consequence is often betrayal—of others, of ideals and values, even of oneself and one's own inner force. It is striking to note that some form of betrayal is present as one destructive aspect of his themes from his earliest scripts, long before the crisis and dilemma of testifying or remaining silent, although the theme is not probed with all its human ambiguities and tragic results until the final works of his life.

While Rossen contributed to the establishment of the genre conventions in the films of the thirties and forties, even his first two screenplays show an almost instant, instinctive adeptness at grasping and using the genre formulas and yet going beyond them. In Marked Woman (1937), for example, the structure of the standard gangster genre (and its basis in real-life events) pits the crusading district attorney (Humphrey Bogart) against the powerful racketeer who controls night clubs, gambling, and prostitution (in the shorthand of censorship, the women are nightclub hostesses). As is frequent in the films of this genre in the thirties written by left-wingers, the gangster-racketeer is seen as an implied symbol of the excesses of greed and the unjust power of money—a shorthand for capitalism.

But the screenplay shifts the expected narrative pattern to a dramatic emphasis on the women and their lives. They are seen not merely as adjuncts to the case and the lives of the men, but as entrapped, the victims of men and society's struggle between the law and the lawless. The district attorney will do anything, betray them, to get the women to testify; the gangster will do anything, beat, slash, even kill, to keep them from testifying.

There is a strange, almost eerie, prophecy in the film's focus on testifying or not. Here, in the first film that Rossen wrote, Mary (Bette Davis) is pressured into testifying by the government and then shamed; yet she knows that she is testifying against what she believes (and rightly so) is wrong, evil. As a result, she is marked by it (the gangster has literally cut an X on her cheek), scarred for the rest of her life.

They Won't Forget (1937), actually written after *Marked Woman* and directed by LeRoy, was released first. Based loosely on a true case, it depicts a corrupt society and system of justice with a cynicism far beyond the usual movie treatment. A power-seeking district attorney (Claude Rains) chooses to prosecute a newcomer to a southern town for the murder of a schoolgirl on the flimsiest of evidence and conjecture. He's chosen this northern interloper over the usual suspect, a Negro janitor, because it will make a more newsworthy case for his campaign for governor. To the end he is not really sure the young man is guilty. The judge, jury, and courtroom audience during the mockery of a trial betray the principles of justice, their passions fueled by the sensation-seeking press. It is a mob—the masses, the southern "proletariat," the people—who commit the final betrayal, the ultimate violation of human life. They take "justice," as they see it and violate it, in their own hands. When the teacher is put on a train to be taken to prison, the mob drags him from the train, carrying him off to be lynched. In a great parallel visual metaphor for the brutality of the act, a speeding train comes roaring down the track, extinguishing the screams of the crowd. As it sweeps by the station, with a jarring clunk, it snatches a sack of mail hanging from its yardarm, its gallows, like a lynched body.

In *Racket Busters* (1938), Rossen's development of a similar structure to *Marked Woman* echoes more closely the patterns and themes of the left-wing and Communist social plays of the thirties. This time the gangster (Bogart) seeking control of labor unions threatens workers to keep them from testifying when a crusading district attorney has brought a case against him. A murder and the protest of women lead the chief driver to his moment of recognition, and he then leads the men to stand up to the gangsters and testify, for he now knows, "We've got to stick together." This narrative structure of raising the consciousness of men to join together and fight injustice was becoming the political emblem of so much literature, drama, and film of the Left.

Rossen's script for the 1939 film *Dust Be My Destiny*, with John Garfield in a typical role, was a more direct but limited foreshadowing of Rossen's later films—and of the screen image given greater force and grit in Garfield's best films, and especially *Body and Soul* (1947). Garfield is a young man of the slums in the depression. He has that innate kind of rude raw energy of the central characters in the later Rossen films. Here, although he has been driven by the corrupt forces of the times to express his energies in the wrong direction, his transgressions are minor and explained away by the plot. Unjustly sent to a prison camp, he runs away with the farm director's daughter, is allowed to find true love. On the road, they encounter unjust treatment but are helped by working-class people. Rossen wanted a tragic ending (which did not actually fit the softness of the treatment of the material), but the studio insisted on setting all right in the world.

The film was the first of four films Rossen and Garfield worked on together, in which Garfield did his best early work as an actor, work that defined the screen image he was to build his career on.

Rossen, in addition, was one of the people who introduced John Garfield to many of the people, the groups, the ideas, the causes of the Left in Hollywood.

While Rossen and Garfield were finishing *Dust Be My Destiny*, the destiny of Spain for half a century would be determined. Gen. Francisco Franco's Falangist forces were victorious in the Spanish Civil War, the armistice coming on April 1, 1939. Campaigns concerning the war were a major focus for actions of party members—as well as an attractive publicity campaign for drawing new people to the cause. During this war Rossen and Garfield were typical of a wide spectrum of liberals and Communist Party stalwarts who were active in organizations and events such as the Motion Picture Artists Committee to Aid Republican Spain. Both were among many who sent telegrams to President Roosevelt in March of 1938, urging him to demand that France open her borders to allow the Loyalists to purchase and receive supplies. To raise money for such supplies (supplied by the Soviets and by others, clandestinely), the committee sponsored a myriad of events: a revue called *Sticks and Stones*, which included satires on domestic Fascists as well as foreign; presentation of films such as Ernest Hemingway's and Joris Ivens' documentary *The Spanish Earth* (in the summer of 1937); a fund-raiser for exhibitions of Pablo Picasso's *Guernica*; various dinners and cause parties; the usual splinter group offshoots such as the Freedom of the Screen Committee. The Hollywood organizations then became part of the national organization Joint Anti-Fascist Refugee Committee. Since the Fascists referred to were the Spanish, not the German, and since it focused on aiding refugees, this organization lasted longer than most of the groups of the period; later it widened its scope to include all refugees, including those who were victims of racism. So Rossen, for example, like many others could sponsor and attend a dinner for war refugees at the Beverly Hills Hotel in 1942, with Paul Robeson as the honored guest, and then attend a dinner for victims of racism at the Ambassador Hotel in 1945, at which John Garfield introduced the honored guest, Paul Robeson.[7]

During his first year in the party, Rossen had begun to take part in the activities of the Hollywood Anti-Nazi League. With the signing of the Nazi-Soviet Pact in August of 1939, he was caught in the whirling merry-go-round of party-line shifts and went through the first serious crisis of faith. In this instance, he was one of those who entertained doubts, but managed to stay among the faithful. It was not until years later that he could see that the party always provided what he then called *rationales*. A key rationale for Rossen at this point was the claim in party publications and statements that the Soviets had, at least in part, signed the pact and invaded Poland to save the Jews of Poland from the Nazis. Still, he soldiered on.[8]

Like others, Rossen still also had time to write more movies. His were more significant than the work of his party colleagues. *The Roaring Twenties*, also released in 1939, was written with Jerry Wald and Richard Macaulay. They had promoted the project, but it was Rossen who supplied the expertise in the structure and characterizations of the gangster film and the final approach, pattern, and detail of the film. *The Roaring Twenties* is like a summing up, almost a eulogy for a passing era—in the country and in the film genre of the gangster film. Eddie Bartlett (James Cagney) is a young veteran blocked by society. He turns to crime, bootlegging, and proceeds to betray his bosses, dominate all those around him, and violate his own inner life force and a kind of deep down goodness. The world changes and he meets his comeuppance, while his former partner, the truly bad gangster (Bogart) thrives. To help the young woman he has always loved, he stands up to Bogart and both are killed. The final sequence of shots is an iconic summation of the first era of the gangster film. Eddie dies on the broad stone steps of a church, in the arms, pietà-like, of his old friend Panama. When a cop, standing over them, asks who this guy is and what was his business, she replies, "He used to be a big shot."

During the period of the pact, Rossen wrote two screenplays—*A Child Is Born* (1939) and *Blues in the Night* (1941)—that are not central to the development of his oevre. But it was two further films that starred Garfield (in contrasting roles) that in the early forties more fully and integrally transformed some personal experiences and beliefs into the basis of the works' power and significance. In both, the sadistic power of the corrupt and domineering antagonists takes on the coloration of, and contains significant allusions to, the Nazis. After the Germans had invaded Russia in June 1941, literally overnight, the Communist party line had changed, and the word was quickly spread: Start to defend the war, promote the fight against the Fascists.

The Sea Wolf, based on the Jack London novel, was released late in 1941. Work on it had already begun before the Nazi invasion, but the sudden change in the international scene fostered new allusions to the sadism and brutality, the threat to humanity of Fascist Germany. John Mosher in the *New Yorker* called the ship's captain, Wolf Larsen (Edward G. Robinson), a "Hitlerian egomaniac."[9]

Garfield's character, Leach, develops from a cynical loner, out only for his self-survival in an animal world, to become the forceful leader of the resistance against the Gestapo-like Larsen and his henchmen. Leach's growth of consciousness energizes the alienated intellectual, Van Leyden, who actually sacrifices himself in a direct final confrontation with Larsen. Both go down with the ship, while the others escape.

The next screenplay, *Out of the Fog,* also released in 1941, had an unusual charm and flavor, however flawed. Based on an overtly "poetic" play by Irwin Shaw, *The Gentle People,* it is a parable of the tyrannical oppression of good people by a brutal gangster.[10] The play was written before the Nazi-Soviet Pact; the film was completed after the invasion. And so both versions have a double level of implication: the gangster-capitalist symbol oppressing the common man, the masses; the gangster representing the forces of Fascism, whether in Spain or in Germany. By the time of the screen version, the latter symbolism, the parallel to the Nazis, could be given greater emphasis. But the broader moral issue still reflects the tradition of thirties left-wing drama that is central in Rossen's work. The gangster is still also the extravagant extrapolation of the worst tendencies of business and the capitalist economic system—the impact of the economic value system on a cross-section of the common, gentle people.

This time Garfield is no young rebel leading these gentle people in Brooklyn to rise up, as they finally do, against the tyrannical gangster. Garfield plays against type as the gangster-capitalist-Fascist Goff; with a strong but controlled performance—the petty, egotistical gangster as satanic force of evil. Rather, it is two elderly men who are impelled to act, who in rather confused, even comical, fashion stand up to the gangster, plan to kill him, can't quite get it done, but have it happen partly through accident. In a further variation on a central Rossen theme, Goff seduces and almost manages to corrupt the young woman (Ida Lupino), who is the shifting moral center of the film, the volatile unformed seeker of something more, of herself, in the false lures of the excitement and money of the big world out there, Goff's gangster-capitalist world.

From 1941 through 1945 Rossen's production was imposing. He wrote six major screenplays that were filmed. Still, these wartime years were also the period of his most active involvement in Communist Party activities. These activities included the usual public organizations, campaigns, events, and parties, but they also involved more practical workaday—and often hidden—Communist Party functions. The latter indicated both Rossen's deep involvement in the cause and his status in the local party, while they illustrate, as well, the relationship of the Hollywood party to the CPUSA (Communist Party of America), of a Hollywood Communist to the international Communist movement.

In May of 1942, for example, the ubiquitous but elusive J. Peters came to Hollywood, and Rossen attended two of the meetings Hollywood members had with him. Peters was an active official in the surface national Communist Party, but he was also an active—though often denied—actor in more clandestine activities, including espionage. Peters had come to town to organize some events and to raise money for the campaign to get party leader Earl Browder released from his short prison term. Peters had a series of meetings: with Herbert Biberman and Waldo Salt; with Rossen, Paul Jarrico, and Hyman Knight; with John Howard Lawson, Biberman, and others; with Lawson, Lester Cole, Rossen, Madeline Ruthven, and others; with Salt, Ruthven, and Lawson. Before departing, Peters went into the safe deposit vault room of a bank with Biberman.[11]

The public campaigns in which Rossen participated, especially during the World War II alliance with the Soviet Union, were designed to draw people across the spectrum of liberal and left-wing politics into a revivification of the Popular Front. In this area, Rossen's two major participations were with the Hollywood Democratic Committee (HDC) through its changes in name and organization through the years, and the Hollywood Writers Mobilization and its subsidiaries. As the HDC went through its typical rise and fall, eventually being reincarnated as part of the broader organization HICCASP (Hollywood Independent Citizens Committee of Arts, Sciences, and Professions), the party attempted to control the organizations by creating majorities on their executive boards. During these new configurations and maneuvers, Rossen was a member of the executive board. He was involved in a speakers bureau and with such rallies as the Shrine Auditorium benefit for Russian War Relief in 1942, Leopold Stokowski conducting Dimitri Shostakovich's Seventh (War) Symphony; and with "United We Stand," tying the war effort to the call for abolishing racism, at the Shrine Auditorium in 1944.

Then there were the ubiquitous fund-raising parties for various related causes: for one, there was the Halloween party for Russian War Relief at the Bob Rossens' in 1942, attended by, among numerous others, many from the regular cast—Ben Barzman, Gordon Kahn, Paul Jarrico, Ring Lardner

Jr., John Garfield, Karen Morley, Herbert Biberman, Gale Sondergaard, Lionel Stander, Gene Kelly, and Betsy Blair. At the party, as they had at many others and mass meetings, Jay Gorney and Henry Myers presented a song honoring the Soviets, fitting such passages as this to music: "the hopes of civilization rest on the worthy banners of the courageous Russian Army." With much more wit and spark, Gorney and Meyers wrote the successful and lively satirical review and celebration of the common man, *Meet the People*. In the late forties, they furnished songs for meetings and rallies to protest against the HUAC and support the Hollywood Ten.[12]

Typically, the Rossens were frequently among the guests at "cause" parties at the homes of others: such as the party to benefit the *People's World* at the home of E. Y. "Yip" Harburg, at which the admission ticket (before the raffle and the call for donations) was ten dollars; the party to support left-wing "cultural" activities at the Hugo Butlers' on January 3,1945; the party at the Frank Tuttles' on June 8,1945, to raise funds for the *New Masses*, beset by the party earthquakes created by the Duclos letter of May 20, 1945.[13]

During the war, Rossen wrote two screenplays that dealt directly with the conflict with the Nazis, but unlike the films by some other party members—including *Mission to Moscow* (1943), *Song of Russia* (1944), and *The North Star* (1943)—they did not idealize the Soviet Union. *Edge of Darkness* (1943) was the first of three films he made with director Lewis Milestone. The second war film, *A Walk in the Sun* (1946), was not released until after the war ended. One of the most successful films of 1943 at the box office, *Edge of Darkness*, maintains the narrative structures and motifs of the basic left-wing social dramas and films of the thirties. Two young Norwegian freedom fighters (Errol Flynn and Ann Sheridan) must raise the consciousness of their downtrodden and indecisive townspeople to act in solidarity to rise up and fight the Nazi oppressors. Their communal moment of truth, their coming together as a "people," is captured in a striking pattern of images through a crucial sequence in the town square: The people flow into the square from different directions, form a circle around the Germans who are tormenting the local schoolmaster, defy them, and, singing, march out as one. These are people who will not remain silent in inaction; they are *testifying* by risking their lives to stand up against that which they think is wrong, hatefully oppressive, and should be stopped.

At this time, Rossen's main participation in party activities was as chairman of the Hollywood Writers Mobilization (HWM). In Rossen's recollection, the HWM was created in the days immediately following the Japanese bombing of Pearl Harbor on December 7, 1941—"quite spontaneously" he claimed—at a meeting of the executive board of the Screen Writers Guild to consider the contribution the writers could make to the war effort. While the board at that time did contain a cross-section of people with varying political points of views, it was the Communist members who were strategically organized and dominant, the most resolutely active. In effect, they controlled the board and the organization, development, and conduct of the HWM. Nevertheless, many who were active in the HWM had no connection to the Communist Party or even any inkling of its involvement, let alone its control. Michael Kanin, who organized and helped edit a HWM newsletter called *Communique*, along with party member Ring Lardner Jr., later remarked, "The communists in Hollywood at the time of the war were very active in the HWM, but then everybody was." During the years of this shared activity, the Communists averaged about 40 percent of the members and were the most active members of the HWM Steering Committee.[14]

The HWM became a typically effective Popular Front action. It promoted wartime unity, patriotic wartime activities to help win the war, and idealistic wartime goals for writers and intellectuals. It used that unity and the accompanying support of the Soviet Union to promote positions dear to the heart of the CPUSA and Comintern and stimulate belief in the goals and intentions of the party and the Soviets.

It is certainly significant that from the start and through its major period, Francis Faragoh, one of the earlier party activists in Hollywood, was its first acting chairman, and Pauline Lauber Finn, also a party activist, its executive secretary. Subsequently, Robert Rossen was elected chairman, by a unanimous vote. Faragoh took over as treasurer. The major, and significant, public event carried out by the HWM was the Writers Conference held at UCLA in October 1943, attended by more than a thousand people. It had broadly based interest and participation, including UCLA faculty, and the support of the University of California president, Robert Gordon Sproul.

Two liberals, playwright Marc Connelly and UCLA theater professor Ralph Freud (Paul Jarrico's wife, Elizabeth, was a student of his), were cochairmen. The general purpose stressed a nonpartisan unity among educators and writers to further the war effort. There was, however, a strong doctrinaire approach and program, particularly stressing the writer's function in the *postwar* world, an emphasis controlled by its Hollywood party organizers. As Lawson insisted at an initial steering committee session, the promotion of the writer's "social function" was "a matter of elementary duty and terrible urgency" in the coming fight between liberalism and reaction. At another planning meeting, Allan Scott called for an emphasis at the Congress on the "unconscious fascism" that threatened the nation in the postwar period. In support of Scott, Rossen stressed the need to foster awareness of the way that the forces of reaction were attacking the Office of War Information because they claimed it was run by radicals, referring particularly to attacks made by Congressman Martin Dies and his committee.[15]

At the Writers Conference there were small-group panels as well as general meetings and addresses. As Rossen later told the HUAC, "We [the Communist participants] met quite regularly in terms of fraction meetings and discussed the whole program of the Writers' Congress, at first in a general sense and later on a kind of detailed sense, in terms of what was to go into the various panels, in terms of the editing of the presentation of the thing." One result of this "editing" was the selection of panel topics and the selection of party members as chairmen of the panels: for example, Minority Groups, Ring Lardner Jr.; American Scene, Robert Rossen; Feature Film, Richard Collins; Nature of the Enemy, John Wexley; Problems of the Press, Melvin Levy; Pan American Affairs, Louis Solomon; Training Films, Bernard Vorhaus, and so on.[16]

Through this period, however, at several meetings with Earl Browder, which Rossen attended, the writers were cautioned not to "heavily weigh pictures" with too much direct propaganda. This position was in line with Browder's Popular Front strategy of accommodations and alliances. Rossen's major speech at a general session of the conference took this approach. He spoke on "An Approach to Characters," the speech then published in the *New Masses* as "New Characters for the Screen" in its January 18, 1944, issue. The speech was a forward-looking call for using the opportunities created by the ideals of the war effort to create "responsible films" (i.e., socially responsible) that would present strong, positive characters who could stand up to corruption and oppression in society and help effect social change. In light of all that happened in the following years, one of his key terms, used in an optimistic passage in his address, has an ironic foreshadowing: "We are still afraid of being betrayed, and that fear goes deep. We've been sick, and this has reflected itself in everything that we've written in the last twenty years. Our stories have been stories of frustration, of defeat. . . . Well, the average man isn't afraid of being betrayed. He doesn't think it can happen anymore."[17]

In his address, Francis Faragoh was more in tune with classic party terminology in stressing the writers' "duty" to their nation "and its allies": "[with] no room for the defeatist, the cynic, the special pleader, the appeaser, the diversionist."[18]

Through this period Rossen and others took part in the Writers Clinic, now organized by the HWM, which conducted a series of workshops, continuing the kind of sessions conducted by the League of American Writers School since 1940. In 1942, Rossen gave several lectures on developing dramatic action in a script. At a Writers Workshop conference in June of that year he was a featured speaker. His address indicated the twofold emphasis of the campaign to raise the consciousness of writers: to further the war effort and to promulgate socially "valuable" ideas. "The screen," he said in his lecture, "can be the great propaganda medium of the war because it brings to audiences a visual sense of human beings, character, actions, but today these techniques must be in terms of *our new* [emphasis added] kinds of social thinking." At the closing session the conference passed resolutions

calling for the immediate opening of a second front in Europe, for the support of longshoremen's leader Harry Bridges, and for the condemnation of
actions of the attorney general.[19]

Organizers of and participants in the two series of workshops included
Rossen, Jarrico, Lawson, Donald Ogden Stewart, George Sklar (a prominent
thirties agitprop playwright, but never a major screenwriter), Lester Cole,
Collins, Carl Foreman, and Barzman, among others. Notes from one workshop suggest the typical approach in discussing scripts: Would it be a violation of the work of Herman Melville if the positive elements were stressed
and the defeatism eliminated? The movie *Humoresque* (which starred John
Garfield) should oppose the "art for art's sake" concept, which "ultimately
led to fascism," with a concept of "people's music." In a discussion of a
proposed script about the Civil War (the American one), "The point was
stressed that history had to be re-examined in terms of historical truths
from a Marxist viewpoint."[20]

The optimism of Rossen's address to the Writer's Conference in 1944
was not mirrored in the developing tensions of his personal relationship
with the apparatus and demands of the party. In 1943, he was present at a
meeting in which Albert Maltz complained that his time and he were being used too much for party purposes and not enough for his development
as a writer and artist. (This was not the Maltz "trial" of 1946.) Maltz was
soundly rebuked by Lawson and others and told that his first function was
to be a Communist. The meeting stirred up Rossen's own worry that he was
being "made into what I consider a cliché word, by this time, a party hack
. . . and now the Party is no longer interested in your creative development.
. . . You begin to suddenly see you were being used."[21]

In 1943 and 1944, however, these feelings were much more tentative,
though they were mixed as well with concern for the plain physical demands on his time, even by valuable party-related activities such as the
HWM. The next turn of events at the HWM added to his growing sense
that he needed to reclaim his time and himself. Early in 1944, when his
term as HWM chairman was about to expire, Rossen was approached by
Lawson, whom he termed "the persuader," with the party's position. Since
Earl Browder's wartime Popular Front strategy was working so well, the
party wanted to capitalize on that momentum and attract "more people
. . . to strengthen the Party." And so it had been "decided at that time it was
important that a man who was not a member of the Communist Party be
chairman of the organization as part of the move to broaden the popular
front." Rossen was, therefore, to bow out gracefully.[22]

It was indicative of Rossen's conflicted relationship to the party at this
time—and of the internal complications involved in breaking free of one's
own mind-set as well as party control—that despite the conflict over his
chairmanship of the HWM and his qualms, as he put it much later, of be-

ing "used," he had still been especially active in party matters in 1943 and on into 1944.

Two such occasions were related to the HWM and involved quite different interactions with John Howard Lawson. In the summer of 1943, Lawson was assigned the task of arranging for the Hollywood segment of a visit to the United States by an official of the Soviet film industry, Michael Kalatozov. Rossen, as HMW chairman, was then given the task of arranging for sponsors and organizing events, including visits to studios and members' homes. Most of the details, of course, were handled by others, including Los Angeles County party officials. Rossen was the official sponsor of a large reception at the Mocambo nightclub (which that year was the scene of a more infamous event in which, half under their table, director Anatole Litvak had fondled the bare breast of actress Paulette Goddard). At the HWM event, Kalatozov had called for greater commercial and artistic ties between Soviet and American filmmakers.[23]

The second event was more adversarial. An Italian film historian, Gaetano Salvameni, was scheduled to address an HWM seminar being held at the Hollywood Women's Club. However, in a prior speech Salvameni had, to the party's surprise, been critical of Stalin, the Italian Communist Party and its leaders, and CPUSA leaders. His address at the HWM seminar was canceled. To stem press criticism, Lawson asked Rossen to use his goodwill with the Hollywood and local press corps, especially an influential radio commentator, to insist that the cancellation had nothing to do with his anti-Communist statements—to show that no freedom of speech was being impaired![24]

In March of 1944 Rossen again worked with Lawson to aid in the suppression of free speech that the party did not agree with. Ulrich Bell, an independent political idealist, had come to Hollywood to promote the program of his organization, the Free World Association. In a full-page ad in the Hollywood *Daily Variety*, he presented his ten-point policy for pursuing world peace at the end of the war. Unfortunately, his program differed from the party's position on postwar peace on at least one major point: To achieve peace, his principles asserted, the world needed to disavow both Communism and Fascism. At meetings held in Hollywood, Lawson and Rossen organized opposition to this point and called for its elimination, but the ten points remained unchanged.[25]

It was also in 1944, however, that Rossen's conflicts with the party and within himself about the party produced a major decision: to move to New York City with his wife, Sue, and their three children. "In other words," he was to tell the congressional committee in 1953, "I was ready at that point to start away, to start to move away, from the party, definitely. I had tried to do it by moving away from Hollywood in 1944. I had done nothing for a year. I was very disturbed by a great many things that were going on in the party, and my own work. I moved away from Hollywood and came here [NYC]."[26]

Nonetheless, despite his being "disturbed," on this rocky path toward leaving the party, he still did not break away completely from party-related activities while he was in New York City. On January 25, 1945, for example, the *New Masses* reported, he was chairman of a *New Masses* Cultural Awards Dinner at the Hotel Commodore. Somewhat ironically, considering later events, he accepted an award that night on behalf of John Howard Lawson. On May 9, 1945, the *Daily Worker* announced that he would be a guest lecturer at the Communist-controlled Jefferson School for Social Science.[27]

After about a year of refueling, he returned to Hollywood. As Ames Billiards was for Fast Eddie Felson, the Hustler, it was the only game in town. *Edge of Darkness* had been Rossen's last script for Warner Bros. He was now free to be an independent screenwriter, and subsequently a director. Working with Lewis Milestone again would be a valuable asset for both prospects—and a fond and fulfilling personal experience.

Although he had begun to turn away from the Communist Party, he did not turn from the humanistic ideals that he had long held, that had led him to join the party in the first place. Rather, these were to receive more direct, more artistic, and less conventional expression in the next two films that he worked on with Milestone. The first of these was *A Walk in the Sun*, released early in 1946, a film about men at war that was not antiwar, but rather pro-humanity in the face of the brutal facts of war. They attempted to record the mood and meaning of a company's six-mile walk after a landing in Italy. The unique structural emphasis on periods of walking and waiting suddenly interrupted by the violence that is always out there somewhere as they walk is a realistic yet lyrical contribution to the depiction of the nature of war. It immerses us in the lives of the men with artful photography; carefully planned, almost choreographic movement; and a kind of folk lyricism in the dialogue, reminiscent of the plays of Clifford Odets. Though carried to an excess of folksy street poetry, the repartee, the repeated favorite sayings are shown as a way of coping with what seems to the men as an endless repetition of foot-slogging and dying, even a way of just filling the time. Wisecracking, philosophizing, they bitch and gripe to keep on going, joke to keep from crying. "Nobody dies," the men ironically mutter, and trudge on to another fight and another death.

At this time events in the world and the party began to propel Rossen further, though still with contradictory and wavering steps, toward a final exit from the party: Soviet aggression in Europe, the onset of the Cold War, the Conference of Studio Unions strikes, the battles and shifts in the party and its policies. Rossen's doubts were exacerbated by these shifts of the party line. He cited being affected by "the bankruptcy of Communist

Party thinking," and "the deep cynicism of the Communist Party" when the Duclos letter produced a complete reversal of the position of the CPUSA and its attendant satellite organizations. The reversal now damned peaceful coexistence and caused the sudden denunciation and removal of formerly venerated leaders such as Earl Browder. And so he began to realize, he said, that "the same reasons why you go into the party are the same reasons which make you go out, which is ultimately the discovery that the idealism that you were looking for, the fighting for the ideas that you want, are just not in the Communist Party."[28]

Sometime in 1946 or early in 1947, Rossen began to demonstrate his reservations by not paying his dues regularly. (This would seem to be the basis for later vituperations on how miserly he was, how deceitful and hypocritical he was in his proclaimed loyalty to the party.) In testimony in 1951, Richard Collins testified that there was even a meeting to discuss whether Rossen should somehow be forced to pay his dues or just be thrown out.[29]

The wartime unity of nations was fading before the increasing tensions and threats of the Cold War. The rosy wartime world of the Left in Hollywood had become a bit of a jungle itself, like the world of Rossen's postwar film *The Strange Loves of Martha Ivers* (1946). These tensions, out in the world around him and within himself, permeate this film, released in 1946 by Paramount. It is Rossen and Milestone's venture into the dark world of film noir. Rossen gives strong and dramatically vibrant social film shadings to the noir motifs—femme fatale, dark past, corrupt and unyielding society, a pervasive sense of fate and doom, striking visual contrasts of light and shadows. The film marks an important stage in his dramatizing how the public violations and betrayals, the corruptions of capitalist power, develop as well *within* a character, corrupt intimate interpersonal relationships, lead to the betrayal of one's self, even of love itself and the ability to love. When young, the wealthy and powerful heiress Martha (Barbara Stanwyck) had been betrayed by those professing to help her. Though immensely wealthy and publicly powerful—her inherited wealth and company control a whole town—Martha cannot control her own inner demons. She lives in a destructive marriage with her weak district attorney husband, Walter (oddly, Kirk Douglas), whom she controls and is destroying. The weakest element in the film is the positive figure, the vital independent loner Sam (Van Heflin) who wanders back into town, is tempted by Martha, but leaves, as she and Walter die while embracing in a kind of last revenge at themselves and life.

After working on a story of gambling house gangsters and warring lovers, *Desert Fury* (1947), which was mangled by production conflicts after he left the project, Rossen rewrote a previous version and was given his first opportunity to direct on *Johnny O'Clock*, also released in 1947 by Harry Cohn's Columbia Pictures. Although *Johnny O'Clock* is limited by the basic murder mystery plot, it does have echoes of Rossen's major character patterns. Its gambling casino tough guy (Dick Powell) is, slowly, given some reason to give up his cynicism and total concern for number one in a dog-eat-dog world. By allowing the feelings engendered by his relationship with a hardheaded but openhearted woman (Evelyn Keyes), he acts against his corrupt gangster partner to right a wrong, not just to make sure he gets his money.

At this point—while his ties to the party were beginning to twist, turn, fray, and erratically unravel—Rossen next worked more closely on a film with members of the Communist Party than in the production of any other film of his career. John Garfield had set up a production company with Bob Roberts, a Communist Party member, and they had a deal with left-oriented Enterprise Pictures for a boxing film, *Body and Soul*, with an initial script by influential party member Abraham Lincoln Polonsky.

The record is not clear, nor are his statements, as to any exact date that Rossen defied the party and finally, clearly, irreparably left it. The stages of his final break with the party surround the first HUAC hearings in 1947, when Rossen was one of the original Nineteen subpoenaed, and their aftermath. Rossen's recollections tend to focus on his taking part from then on only in meetings and activities relating to the HUAC investigation and its legal and professional consequences—both before and after the first hearings. The first of these meetings was held immediately after the issuance of the subpoenas when the group met with the four lawyers who would become the core of the legal team. Most, if not practically all, of the party's activities in Hollywood through this period—and everybody's chief personal concerns—had to do with the hearings. So Rossen's emphasis does not seem to contradict some instances of his continuing participation in actions of the party as he moved toward this complete break.

Following the hearings, the Nineteen were still thought of as a unit and further hearings were thought to be imminent. Rossen attended a number of events and meetings. One was a reception in honor of the Hollywood Nineteen, held on November 2, sponsored by the Civil Rights Congress. At the event Ben Margolis, the lead attorney for the Ten, defined the purposes of the strategy further: "what the Supreme Court does," he said, "depends to a large extent on the political climate of the country."[30] Their job was to expose the HUAC as an "enemy of the people" to produce the proper climate. Rossen was one of the eighteen signers of a petition to the House of Representatives to overrule the committee's citations.

Similarly, after the Ten were convicted, Rossen was later one of the signers of the amicus curiae brief submitted to the Supreme Court on behalf of John Howard Lawson (as the test case) and the others.[31]

Even as late as 1949, the Ten and others did consider Rossen connected enough to confront him about the correctness of the ideological stance and content of *All the King's Men*. It may well be symbolic, even symptomatic, of his attitude at the time that for a while he took part in that thought-control session, and then he got up and walked out. Infuriating and demeaning as that meeting was, it proved easier, and far less painful, to walk out of that room than to walk out of the party and leave behind one's life in the Communist Party in Hollywood.

7

The Consequences of Ideology: The Emblematic Battle of *Body and Soul*

Through the decades, the depiction of the battle of *Body and Soul* (1947) has been a sharply focused, abrasive epitome of the way that the ideological dualism of heroes and villains—of the forces of light and darkness—has not only influenced the judgments of moral character and the history of Hollywood politics but also distorted the facts of the history of films and filmmakers, betrayed the truth. In this battle, the conventional wisdom pits Abraham Polonsky, the quintessential "moral exemplar" and Hollywood Marxist intellectual, against Robert Rossen. The battle becomes a key example in the promotion of Polonsky as a quintessential film artist and theorist—itself a key example of the exaggeration of the art and films of those Communists seen as heroic martyrs. The corollary is the diminution of those who did testify—like Rossen—as both a man and a filmmaker.

Paul Buhle has been highly influential in establishing the conventionally accepted, ennobling view of the stature of Abraham Polonsky. Buhle is not only an indefatigable writer and editor of books about blacklistees and their films; he is a major contributor to such left, and new left, political publications as *The Encyclopedia of the American Left* (1990), of which he has been a coeditor. For Buhle—as is the case for most of these committed writers—there is a strong, determining correlation between his political ideology and his judgments of films, filmmakers, and film history. As historians Harvey Klehr and John Maynard Haynes, among others, have catalogued and analyzed, his facts and his generalizations are as inaccurate, his arguments as fallacious in his political writing as in his writing about film history. One example among a myriad is particularly apt, considering the central place the Soviets' treatment of Jews has in the remarks of both those who cooperated with the House Un-American Activities Committee (HUAC) and those who didn't.

Buhle has regularly argued against the claims, and evidence, of espionage by party members and followers. He has, for example, insisted—against the reality of massive documentation—that "as of the late 1990s, documents examined in the Soviet Union or reprinted for scholars offered little that was new in regard to illegal or secret work by Soviet sympathizers." In an intriguing final twist in one of his articles, Buhle concluded that the bulk of whatever he called mere "intrigues" did exist were done for—Israel. "Little was said within the Left or outside it concerning the *largest* [emphasis added] incident of illegal activity: the shipment of arms and assorted war materials to the new state of Israel." Neither the sources Buhle cites nor a thorough search by Haynes and Klehr revealed a shred of evidence for this claim. Not content, Buhle embellished his fantasy history: "Among those Americans wounded or killed in battles protecting Israeli gains from Arabs, Communists played a prominent role." As Israeli historian Yehuda Bauer said, the claim was "sheer nonsense."[1]

In his role as *film* historian of the Left, Buhle has not only consistently had high praise for and lofty interpretations of films of Abe Polonsky; he has been equally effusive in his definition of Polonsky's role in film history, popular culture, the Marxist intellectual world:

> When Polonsky scored a hit with *Body and Soul* [sic], he reached his moment of mass culture truth.

> But among Hollywoodites themselves, he continued to loom large as the last of the serious 1940s Marxist thinkers and the finest aesthetician among the disappearing circle of Golden Age activists.

> The left-wingers around Polonsky—many of whom admired him as their foremost artistic figure. . . .

> Such key films of the 1940s as Polonsky's *Force of Evil* are acknowledged precursors of the art cinema in Europe and Japan.[2]

A central example of Buhle's approach to Polonsky is his repeated and exaggerated, indeed inaccurate, definition of Polonsky's central role in the development of film noir. As is seen from its beginnings with such films as Billy Wilder's *Double Indemnity* (1944), film noir represented a response (tongue in cheek or serious) by a wide variety of filmmakers to the films of wartime patriotism and postwar optimism that the studios thrived on. Its bitter, ironic attitudes were projected by its style of shadows and striking angles, strong black-and-white chiaroscuro contrasts, images of the night in the big city, darkened rooms, rain-glistening streets, the glow of streetlights and windows masked by shades and venetian blinds. It was an attitude and style, a mood, much influenced by the pessimism and fatalism, the romantic flourishing of sadness, in German and French films (often designated "poetic realism") of the thirties, and by the influx of German and French filmmakers in the Hollywood industry. Its tone and narratives were derived from tough-guy mysteries and pulp fiction—individual stories and novels often used as the basis of the films. It was a world of fatalistic doom of dreams, of inevitable betrayal and corruption, often centered on fascinating variations on the theme of the femme fatale, a theme also derived from German and French culture.

Two of Polonsky's scripts, *Body and Soul* and *Force of Evil* (1948), can conceivably be placed within the circle of attributes of film noir. Of the two films, the stronger, more vibrant visual imagery of *Body and Soul* resonates more with noir tones, but that imagery and tone were, for the most part, the result of the director, Robert Rossen, and his cinematographer, *not* Polonsky's script. But still, the two films are really only on the periphery of the collage of tone, style, and theme that in any meaningful sense is film noir. In one central aspect, for example, in the two films, and most others written by Polonsky, the central character grows in consciousness, in progressive social clarity, and lives to face and/or fight another day; whereas in the basic trajectory of noir narrative, he cannot escape his defeat and doom. The two films are certainly not in the center of the style or movement; they are by no means the most significant, influential examples of it.

On the limited basis of these two films and their passing resemblance to the noir classics (and, of course, the total absence of Robert Rossen from the discussion), Buhle places Polonsky in the forefront, seemingly the leader, of the movement: "Polonsky and the other artists working in this vein, which admiring French critics designated *film noir*." Elsewhere, Buhle rhapsodizes, "The noir master's imprint on the crime film and the noir mood." Or to extend the claim in *Blacklisted*: "One [*Force of Evil*] of the deservedly most famous films of the Hollywood left, and along with Polonsky's two scripted pre-blacklisted films, *Body and Soul* and *I Can Get It for You Wholesale*, part of the classic trilogy of Noir's Marxist master."[3]

Indicative of the way that the orthodox ideological interpretation and judgments of the blacklist period are spread in the mass media through unexamined assumptions and appropriated phraseology is the *New York Times* obituary for Polonsky. It picks up and further promulgates the phrase in the *newspaper of record*: "an early master of Hollywood film noir." The obituary goes on to echo Buhle's statements about *Polonsky's* achievement in *Body and Soul*.[4]

The standard image of Polonsky—as encapsulated in the idolatry of the biography by Buhle and Dave Wagner, *A Very Dangerous Citizen*—has several strands to its narrative. He is seen as a mentor and a master, a unique and major film artist and theorist; as a "moral exemplar," standing up to and victimized by the blacklist; as an erudite, thoughtful Marxist intellectual, distanced and aloof from the structure of the Communist Party, its leaders, and its day-to-day actions and party-line demands. In later years, he did criticize the party and the incompetence, dogmatism, and intellectual limitations of its leaders. His name, it is true, does not appear on all the favored calls, open letters, sponsorships, and so on, that so many others participated in.

In the real world of Communism, however, he did (even as the limited accounts that are available indicate) take on a much more active role in Communist Party operations in Hollywood than the myth of his above-the-fray posture and intellectual purity portrays. He did carry out the party line as a regular functionary in the Hollywood branch of the Communist Party of America. As an unnamed informant told the FBI in 1951, "POLONSKY was one of the real CP leaders in Hollywood. . . . From that time [his arrival in Hollywood], POLONSKY was always a leader in the CP and one of the few men who could successfully challenge the views of JOHN HOWARD LAWSON on any particular issue."[5]

He often served as an organizer and mentor in the recruitment of new members to the party and as a liaison with the Communist Party apparatus in enforcing discipline on those who were members. Two examples: When Sterling Hayden was a new member, he attended discussion meetings that were held at Polonsky's house. Yet, he testified, oddly enough, that at first Polonsky himself was not in attendance. When he did appear, he led the discussions. Abe Burrows, in his testimony, told of Polonsky calling him to arrange a meeting with John Stapp, a full-time Southern California Communist Party organizer, and Polonsky at Polonsky's house. Polonsky, he said, criticized him for not being active enough in party organizations and insisted he take a more conscientious role. Stapp, Burrows said, said nothing. When Burrows continued to be noncommittal, Stapp got up and—"it was like a gangster movie"—left with a scowl and a meaningful nod at Burrows.[6]

Far from remaining aloft and aloof in his ideological tower, Polonsky was an active participant and leader in major party campaigns. During the height of the organizational, ideological, and ultimately physical conflicts of the Conference of Studio Unions strike against the studios in 1946, meetings were held every two weeks, Stanley Roberts testified, at the home of Abe Polonsky. John Stapp was there as the liaison to the county party organization. John Howard Lawson was there, though Roberts felt he was treated "only as an elder statesman." Roberts said it seemed that the real leader of the meetings was Polonsky and that he was "the actual successor to Mr. Lawson in the Hollywood picture." Polonsky not only loyally promoted the strike; he manned the picket line and later liked to brag that he had "personally hurled a couple of writer-scabs onto the street."[7]

In vivid terms, writer Leopold Atlas remembered Polonsky's participation at party meetings where several "clubs" (sections, fractions) would meet and leaders enjoyed "axing away at experts from your clubs. . . . Trumbo, a brilliant speaker, taking Lester Cole apart, piece by piece. Or Herbert Biberman, a sterile, pedantic speaker, hammering at someone else. Or Polonsky, the fiery type, going into old fashioned Union Square soap box oratory."[8]

When, in late 1947, the Screen Writers Guild was debating Hugo Butler's resolution to support the Hollywood Ten, Polonsky was a leader in the fight for the resolution. He provided a strong dose of that oratory, but the proposal was defeated by a large margin. When Polonsky and other Reds continued to protest and vowed to continue the fight, Stanley Roberts began to argue with him, asserting, he testified, that such "tactics could only wreck the Screen Writers Guild." He went on to testify that "it was then that Polonsky came out openly with the statement that if we wrecked the Screen Writers Guild we will build another one. 'If need be, we will wreck twenty to achieve what we want.'"[9]

This aspect of Polonsky's life is not discussed in Buhle's extensive writing about him, or in interviews or other writing. The typical corollary to this selective idolatry in the dualistic history of ultimate heroes and villains is, in this case, to not only diminish the value and meaningfulness of the films of Rossen, but to also besmirch his character. Buhle is, again, a key shaper of what is passed on as conventional opinion, not only with his own remarks but with his extensive quotation of blacklistees in a number of books.

The following is a typical exchange between Buhle and Polonsky in *Tender Comrades*:

> *Buhle*: People say that when Rossen didn't make the cut as one of the Ten he was outraged. He thought that he was the great Hollywood Communist artist.
>
> *Polonsky*: You wouldn't want to be on a desert island with Rossen, because if the two of you didn't have any food, he might want to have you for lunch tomorrow. . . . He was talented like Elia Kazan was talented, but like Kazan he also had a rotten character. In the end they both became stool pigeons. I figured all along that Rossen couldn't be trusted.[10]

The essence of Buhle's distorting pattern of valuation of Rossen as filmmaker is seen in his entry on *Body and Soul* in *Blacklisted*, the encyclopedic listing of left-wing movies. He begins, "One of Polonsky's two master works of this period." In the subsequent paragraphs he does not mention Rossen once.[11]

Polonsky and Buhle often merge in their denigrations of the work and character of Rossen. The following exchange appears in *Tender Comrades*:

> *Polonsky*: He was a good Warner Brothers writer; he made their kind of "social" pictures. He had that idea of himself.

Buhle: His pictures frequently seem a mishmash of blue-collar melodrama and art film, as though he had always wanted to do both types of films and constantly mixed them up.

Polonsky: You have him down cold.[12]

Buhle then repeats this reductive approach and theme in several books. In *Radical Hollywood* he says, "[After testifying] Rossen made several unsuccessful films hitching avant-garde themes to blue-collar backgrounds." And again, "As Abraham Polonsky observed, "The insecure former proletarian artist desperately wanted to create 'real' art, but his art was best suited, after all, to the Warners style."[13]

The treatment of *All the King's Men* (1949) in several of Buhle's books is indicative of the grudging praise, reductive ideological interpretation, and caustic personal barbs in his approach to individual Rossen's films. In *Radical Hollywood*, Buhle states, "The most highly awarded movie by a prospective blacklistee, *King's Men* was Robert Rossen's triumph and very likely his corruption. Succeeding brilliantly on his own terms as writer-director, Rossen delivered the artistic self-congratulations of the parliamentary democratic system that rightward-drifting American liberals longed to hear by this time."[14]

In *Blacklisted* Buhle sees only political compromise as the basis of its success: "Voted best film of the year by the New York critics eager to make a safely liberal political choice." At another point, Buhle compares the film unfavorably with a mediocre Clark Gable western, *Honky Tonk*, which is said to go "deeper, beyond easy individualist moralism." In another book, Buhle comments, "The film compares poorly to a number of earlier Rossen films."[15]

But it is the battle over *Body and Soul* that is the core of this legacy of ideological distortion. *Radical Hollywood* makes the film totally a creation of Abe Polonsky: "Polonsky's two great films bring us back to one of the ironies of the blacklist in Hollywood." Again, and more fully: "Abraham Polonsky's 1940s films *Body and Soul* (1947) and *Force of Evil* (1948) quite simply embody the highest achievement of the American Left in cinema before the onset of repression." Polonsky, of course, sees it that way himself. In *Tender Comrades*, he says, "*Body and Soul* turned out to be a tremendous success. My script is the fundamental reason it turned out the way it did, although it was a wonderful job James Wong Howe did."[16]

But taking all the credit is not enough. For Polonsky also had to overcome Rossen's immorality in almost destroying the film: "No one co-directs with Robert Rossen. You keep trying to prevent him from spoiling the picture, and writers hardly ever win those fights. We [sic] made Rossen promise that he wouldn't change a line on the screenplay, and then we found out he was handing out pages on the set, anyway. That was his character." Buhle typically expands this claim to that of "coworkers": "Rossen struck co-workers as personally competitive almost to the point of mania."[17]

There was, however, an impartial observer of the course of events. Robert Aldrich, who went on to become one of the important directors of the postwar era, was there, on the set during the entire shooting schedule. He has quite a different version of the story—of who actually did the destructive interfering.

At the time, Aldrich was working for Enterprise in several capacities; on *Body and Soul* he was the production manager and assistant director. He had two major impressions of what happened during the production. In later interviews and reminiscences, he iterated and reiterated that he had "reservations concerning *Polonsky's* [emphasis added] interference on the set." Secondly, he remembered that Rossen and James Wong Howe, the cinematographer, hit it off from the start. Rossen, he recalled, had strong ideas about what he wanted. He and Wong Howe worked out each scene meticulously, adjusting dialogue, movements, patterns in relation to camera angles, movements, techniques. He encouraged Howe to try, again and again if necessary, whatever he could to get the visual effects that he (Rossen) wanted. Their concern for every detail and their experiments did push the film over budget, which caused Aldrich some trouble; but he felt that the results of Rossen's experimenting "worked beautifully" and produced the only financial success Enterprise had: "it had one hit and nine disasters. The hit was *Body and Soul*."[18]

Aldrich insisted that it was Polonsky's actions that were extreme and not productive: "Abraham Polonsky, although he'd written a marvelous script, really interfered too much."[19]

In Polonsky's version, Rossen was attempting to destroy his self-proclaimed "masterwork" by wanting to make script changes—almost every day! The producers, Polonsky claimed, even threatened to fire Rossen if he didn't stop meddling with Polonsky's work. Polonsky had never had a film made from his exact script before. Rossen was one of the most knowledgeable script writers of the thirties and forties; had written thirteen screenplays that had been produced and had worked on many more; had worked with and learned from skillful directors like Lewis Milestone; had directed a movie the year before and produced two. As Rossen had experienced, major directors are always changing scripts or insisting on rewrites when they have the power but not the ability to do it themselves. Rossen's mentor as a director was Milestone, for whom he had written three scripts. The excellence of Milestone's films was due in part to his method of working closely, and demandingly, with writers, of making daily changes in response to the palpable realities of day-to-day shooting: He so infuriated Lillian Hellman that she even threatened to quit and give back her considerable salary over their disputes on *The North Star* (1943).

And yet despite this difference in experience and expertise, despite the standard practices on Hollywood movies, Garfield did vacillate. He often deferred to Polonsky and to party loyalist Roberts, who in turn allowed Polonsky to interfere to an extreme degree, to bring to the making of the film the domineering role he was accustomed to within the party. That Rossen's loyalty to the party was already beginning to be questioned added to the unsettling of the usual pattern of power and control on a production.

Ideology and party discipline, and Garfield's insecurity and awe of an erudite major Marxist intellectual and Party leader, triumphed over friendship and over the reality of personal experience. Still, the mythic version of Garfield's extreme opposition to Rossen, of this unified stance against the maniacal director defies logic and the reality of the situation, as recounted, for example, by Aldrich.

In several interviews Rossen commented on his relationship with Garfield during the filming. For example,

> So we all talked shorthand—fighting had to have truth if nothing else. I knew Garfield ten—no more than that—at least fifteen years before. We used to meet at the Intervale Avenue Subway station, and I knew him as an actor. I didn't have to direct him in certain parts of the film. All I had to say was yes or no because he totally understood it. . . .
>
> I think John Garfield was excellent in *Body and Soul*. He is of course an experienced actor, but he was better there than anywhere else. That is because the setting in which he was to play was not unknown to him. It was a part of New York, a life, that he knew and that he understood without ever thinking about it. During the filming I rarely had to advise him. It was no trouble, he found it from within himself without seeking. When a take had to be redone, he knew why quite as well as I.[20]

Rossen had been a longtime mentor for the various career and political problems of Garfield. As Robbie, Garfield's wife, said, Rossen was not only "the favorite screenwriter" during Garfield's Warner Bros. period; he was "one of Julie's most devoted friends."[21] Rossen had tried to get Garfield the central role in *The Roaring Twenties* (1939). On three previous films, he had written the scripts that established and shaped the Garfield persona and image. On *The Sea Wolf* (1941) he had felt that Garfield was not suited for the role he was seeking—the alienated, indecisive writer Von Leyden. Rossen built up the part he thought suited Garfield's temperament, image, and political beliefs—Leech, the tough seaman who leads the rebellion against Wolf Larsen. Garfield took that part and was a great success. For *A Child Is Born* (1939), he had advised Garfield not to take the costarring role because the script he was writing focused strongly on the woman. Garfield took his advice. "Nice-guy" Jeffrey Lynn got the role.

The two had much in common, though in some ways it was their differences that set the nature of their relationship. They both grew up on the East Side in the same Rivington Street neighborhood. They both had done some boxing, but had done more of their fighting in the streets. Both had been drawn to the theater, had similar aggressive personalities—energetic, driving, magnetic. But Garfield didn't have Rossen's education or intellectual bent, or his inner strength and security. He had not developed as much intellectually, politically, even artistically in terms of theory and understanding. Along with Lewis Milestone and Clifford Odets (who was Garfield's oldest friend and original role model), Rossen became one of those who guided him in his early career decisions at Warner Bros. and his entry into the political and social circles of the Hollywood Left. Garfield was an eager, greedy student, but by all accounts he never quite mastered the material.

Garfield loved to hang out in the writers' corner of the Warner's commissary, where Rossen and other contract writers would spend more than just their lunch hours. In those days they were required, as employees, to be on the lot for an eight-hour day, and so they used the commissary as their social club, pursuing everything from talk of Stanislavski or Marxism to pinochle—and especially a lot of kidding and verbal jousting. Garfield relished the intellectual camaraderie, wanted to soak it all up as quickly as possible, even loved being the target of much of the kidding. The Epstein twins, who wrote several of his films, loved stories about him. Garfield: "Okay fellas, let's have ourselves a real intellectual discussion." Phil Epstein: "Sounds fine, but who's going to represent *you?*" They loved to catch him in his literary frauds—claiming to have read all of Stendahl, for one—and in his almost Marx Brothers–like malapropisms (*obsolescence* for *absolution*). Rossen is credited with one of the most memorable exchanges. Garfield was complaining about a studio executive who he claimed was a "congenial idiot." Rossen: "The word's *congenital*, Julie. A congenial idiot is what *you* are."[22]

Rossen often commented on his methods of working. In a late interview, he discussed what he believed was the value of making creative changes on a script during filming, of responding to the moments of production as they occurred: "[Sidney] Lumet will always do a good picture, but never a great one. He lacks the one thing: spontaneity. Everything is too laid out. . . . Anybody who likes to work in studios likes to work in them because you cannot improvise. You go on location in a real setting and everything around you leads you into another idea. You can go down looking for this and you find that. You've got to have the guts to have this spontaneous quality of getting it right away."[23]

Rossen also explained to several interviewers how he worked with James Wong Howe to get the authenticity and yet the heightened emotional ambiance of the drama. He had talked with Roberto Rossellini about his methods and learned from him the use of Eyemos, newsreel cameras, to capture the spontaneity he was after. He had Wong Howe use several such cameras at once in the fight scenes. "I was the first to use Eyemos without concern for sight lines . . . we were the first to shoot Eyemos right into other lenses."[24]

In the orthodox myth about the film, a crucial dispute occurred over the ending, but that it was a dispute is open to dispute. This "dispute" is held up as the prime example of Rossen's attempt to damage the movie. It involved a valid if extreme difference of opinion. Rossen (possibly with his powerful ending for Cagney in *The Roaring Twenties* in mind) had an idea about a tragic ending in which Charley would be killed after refusing to throw the final fight and winning. Polonsky wanted the upbeat ending that was eventually used. According to Aldrich, after Rossen considered both approaches in more detail, he also supported the upbeat ending, while others still wanted to consider the tragic approach. At the time, Aldrich too "thought that [the tragic ending] was the proper ending for the picture." Later, however, he decided that "the current ending was appropriate for the film as it stands today."[25]

However, in shooting the ending used in the film, Rossen insisted on toning down the rhetoric. He eliminated the triumphant proletarian flourishes, condensing the final dialogue to Charley's brash defiance, "What can you do, kill me? Everybody dies!" The last phrase is used as an ironic counterpoint to the gambler Roberts' callous use of the words in responding to the death of Ben. It clearly picks up on the repeated refrain Rossen had used in *A Walk in the Sun* (1946): "Nobody dies."

It works; it might have worked as a tragedy. Some reviewers thought the latter would have been better. Ronald Bergan, for example, complained about the "happy ending that dodged the issues raised."[26]

Rossen gives the easy optimism of the ending some sense of unfinished business, some worrisome foreboding by having Charley and Peg walk back through shadowy dark streets until they see the lights ahead in the windows of Ma's apartment.

It is ironic (about the film, not *in* the film) that whereas Rossen's unused ending had Charley's dead body unceremoniously dumped against a brick wall in an alley, Polonsky's ending for his own *Force of Evil* has Joe Morse's brother's dead body unceremoniously dumped against the stone wall of the steps down to the river.

Polonsky's grandiose party-line rhetoric for his intended meaning of the ending for *Body and Soul*—repeated in several books and interviews—illustrates the context for the adversarial fervor of his remembrance of the conflicts over the film. He saw the film as a fable, but "not a fable about Charley Davis; it is a fable of the working class"; and it would be "crazy" to kill off "the proletariat." For in his grandiose conception of the theme, Charley "discovers a moral and (in the broader sense) political need to rejoin the working class, regardless of the personal price." As Buhle paraphrases Polonsky's concept of the ending, it is "a knockout blow for the working class's enemies, with Garfield the proletariat's symbolic representative, during the last moment when a sweeping labor victory over postwar capitalism could still be imagined."[27] It was the "last moment," apparently, because of the fascistic hardening of the capitalist cold war and the injustice of Walter Reuther starting to ban the Communist-led unions and their leaders from the Congress of Industrial Organizations. And for this apocalyptic proletarian fancy, we have *Charley*, the rich, immoral prizefighter, as a symbol of the workers and the pure labor movement.

Rossen's alleged "interference" did not almost destroy the film. His adaptations of scenes and development of visual sequences made it a better film—more vivid in cinematic terms, fuller, richer in human feeling and drama, beyond the themes that he and Polonsky did generally agree on. His view of the film's materials and Polonsky's script show the definite influence of the social drama of the thirties, especially as structured in Odets' *Golden Boy*. With this shared background, Polonsky's script embodies characters, themes, and narrative structures that Rossen had already begun to use in his own screenplays—the structures and themes that are central in the left-wing canon. The treatment of the gambler-gangster figure as a symbolic, thematic figure is also a central element in the genre films of the thirties, including the films written by Rossen. The central thrust in Polonsky's script is the moral testing of the young man from the slums, with the élan of the protagonists in Rossen's films and a skill, an art, a gift—boxing—that he betrays, as he betrays the better part of himself, and those around him.

Charley buys the values of Roberts, the gambler-gangster, the capitalist corrupter and violator. "I just want to be a success." "You know, every man for himself." But in the business of boxing he encounters the very economic corruption and violation that had originally trapped him. He, too, becomes, in the words of his best friend, Shorty, "a money-machine," lets Roberts own all of him, body and soul. He breaks with his family and with Shorty—whose death he indirectly causes. In the thematic pattern we've seen developing in Rossen's previous films (and which he again probes more deeply in the future), Charley turns against true and fulfilling love, faithful and sharing personal relationships. Peg is the too perfect and patient artist, the woman of both beauty and soul. She understands him, but with firm morality will not go along with him down this false path. He turns instead to the unfaithful lure, the fur-draped body of glamorous Alice, the false prize of economic success, the follower herself of easy money and all it can buy. In his entourage, he does keep one connection to decency, the black sparring partner, Ben, whose title he had taken, whose death he is also indirectly responsible for.

The lure of money and success has been so strong for Charley, it takes the impact of the death of Ben—now his friend and sparring partner—to spur him to reclaim himself and stand up to the gambler-gangster who is now betraying him by forcing him to throw a championship fight. During the fight Charley finally decides to refuse, and wins. Thus, he "betrays" his agreement with Roberts, but this time, for the right cause. Whatever Polonsky theorized about the film's narrative structure, there are intimations here of the ironies and paradoxes of real-life testifying to come. By not being "loyal" to the organization and its dictatorial leader, Charley chooses and asserts his true and better self. The film's pervasive climate of betrayal resonates with the tensions within Rossen and others who were trying to define or end their loyalty to the Communist Party.

What Polonsky defined as damaging "sentimentality" was the full-hearted, full-blooded *sentiments*, the human emotionality that Rossen's direction got into the film: the palpable real feelings between Charley and his family, the undercurrent of his sense of loss and guilt even as he betrays them. Rossen transformed a tightly, rather coolly, patterned script—the speeches pared down by Rossen—into a vibrant, strikingly visual film and experience. This human dimension—beyond the meaningful speeches and the symbolism, the social themes—is captured in the ways in which scenes in the script are developed as images and interactive drama: the patterns of people within shots and their movements and gestures; the shifting patterns of the characters within shots and scenes as emotions and responses develop and shift between and among them; the patterning through revealing, clinching camera angles; the forceful punch of accelerated editing and moving in to closer shots for emotional climaxes. Characters interact emotionally, but they also interact *visually* with each other and with the physical environment that surrounds them. These were the methods and purposes on which Rossen worked with Wong Howe. A shot analysis of one key scene can illustrate this kind of cinematic shaping of a scripted scene.

Charley's return to Ma's apartment—when he attempts to reconnect his life to her and Peg, but still on the terms of the life he has trapped himself in—is played out amid the things of Ma's kitchen. At the center of a series of patterns and shots is the table in Ma's kitchen, the center of that moral universe—of family and love, friendship, loyalty, and trust—that he has betrayed. The kitchen table is the fulcrum of the shots that follow, as the three of them are seen in patterns and relationships around it. Peg is sitting at the table with Ma; Charley, uneasy, is prowling behind them, then around to the front of the table, away from them, isolated, the table now between him and them. He knows he must tell them he's agreed to throw the fight. He needs the money. We cut to a reverse angle, see him from behind them, between them, caught between them, still separated by the kitchen table from them. He can't hold it in anymore. In a series of closer shots of each, he tells them. When they don't accept his justification, he explodes—as he is seen again from behind them, between them, but now, knowing they are judging him, defiant.

In the brilliant final series of shots: We cut to the angle toward Peg and Ma as Peg gets up, then to a medium shot past the back of Charley's head as she comes closer, her face now in close-up, with close-in fury. Her speech is made dramatic, physical, palpable in their shared pain as the words interact with her slapping him and with the dynamics of cuts back and forth to each of them, past the other's head. "I'm like the rest of them. So you want your money back, well, take it back . . ." Slap, forehand, backhand. Cut. Slaps. Cut. Slaps. Cut. Slaps. Cut. Cut. ". . . and everything else you've given me. Here, what everybody gives you. The long years of happiness. The promises broken, the lonely nights." The last cut is to his face, sad and defeated, lost, as she then pulls back and out of the shot and we hear her begin to sob.

The major critics responded to the tangible embodiment of human feeling, the sensory power that this combination of narrative, dramatic energy, and visual imagery had achieved. In the *New York Times*, Bosley Crowther responded, "Robert Rossen has directed with such an honest regard for human feelings and with such a searching and seeing camera." James Agee, the period's foremost critic, perceptively assessed the elements of the film. It had, he wrote, "a general quality of tension and of pleasure in good workmanship." He thought that "the script, discreetly leftish about commercialism in prize fighting, is really nothing much," but that the film "was almost continuously interesting and exhilarating while I watched it, mainly because everyone had decided to do every scene to a finish and because . . . scene after scene came off that way."[28]

In contrast, (briefly) in *Force of Evil*, where Polonsky directs his own script, there is little of the strong and dramatically used visual imagery Rossen created in *Body and Soul*—except for a nice ironic street shot at the very beginning that contrasts the buildings of Wall Street with a small church and its spire, as well as some montages of money and gambling (montages that are a staple of Rossen's films) and the fine ending at the stone steps down to the river. Instead, there are speeches and orations, mainly by Joe Morse (Garfield). As critic Raymond Durgnat commented, "Further, instead of breaking down complexity into images, Joe explains his thoughts (and nearly everyone else's), Doris hers, and Leo and Leo's wife his, and so on, in conversation."[29] The conversations are generally developed in rather dull patterns of shots. The "love" affair has no emotion or passion in it. The innocent, tiny Beatrice is merely there as a foil for Joe's lengthy and showy speeches about the world as a jungle, innocence wanting to be wicked, it being evil not to take for yourself, and so on—speeches delivered to her in a lobby, a taxi, a park, a restaurant, an apartment, and so forth. Unlike the development of the characters in Rossen's films, Joe does not show development or any change in the body of the film, as Durgnat also noted. Joe has not the slightest uncertainty or inner dispute until his sudden growth of consciousness at the very end when, after finding his brother's body, he realizes something has to be done about such things and he decides to help. The physical-visual plot climax is an awkwardly shot cliché, a shootout in a totally dark office, apparently an obligatory gesture, with a forced symbolism of moral darkness, to the tenets of the crime genre that Polonsky believed he was transcending.

The other screenplays of Polonsky that were produced were a limited and erratic body of work. The first, *Golden Earrings* (1947), starring Marlene Dietrich, was extensively rewritten by others. It ended up as a halfheartedly whimsical view of free-spirited Gypsies who, caught in the turmoil of World War II, take some time out from their exotic wanderings and romances to help the allied underground to fight Fascism. Critics found it comical in ways that were not intended.

More determinedly and directly than any of the other Hollywood Communist writers, Polonsky attempted to create films that expressed his political beliefs and his philosophic concepts. He wrote one more screenplay, in 1949, before he was blacklisted—*I Can Get It for You Wholesale*, from the novel by Jerome Weidman. It was released in 1951, with rewrites by Oscar Saul and others. As he often did, Polonsky claimed that they had fatally weakened what he had constructed as an elaborate, major critique of American society: a "sardonic" depiction of the moral conflicts in the New York garment industry as a symbol of the crisis in contemporary capitalism and even as an example of the connection of the business mentality with male attitudes toward women.[30]

While he was blacklisted, Polonsky wrote a number of scripts for television, was a regular writer for the popular show *You Are There*, with Walter Cronkite as narrator. Despite his frequent complaint about the censorship of McCarthyism, he managed regularly to wrench the reality of the historical characters enough to dramatize his opinions about the current state of anti-Communism and America. Three examples:

- Poet Andrew Marvell: "I am not like those in the land, who having shared the life of the republic, would now find safety by being first to cry down their old companions. . . . He who dies after his principles have died, sir, has died too late."
- Nathan Hale: "I know I'm quite young. Nevertheless, I am too old to betray what I believe is just."

- John Milton: "When a king forbids books and free thought, it is his nature; but when a free government does so, that teaches men to hate such governments as if they were hating tyrants."[31]

The most directly propagandistic of Polonsky's distortions of historical reality to promote his criticism of the evils of the American government was a script for a television movie that was never produced: *An Assassination on Embassy Row*, written in 1981. He uses the 1976 assassination in Washington of Orlando Letelier, a respected Chilean economist and former ambassador to the United States, to indict the CIA as the epitome and instrument of American imperialism and aggression.

This is Polonsky's version of the story: "Agent Michael Townley of the Central, Intelligence Agency originally outlined the murder, and right wing Cuban exiles set it in motion." Polonsky depicts Townley as "the CIA's point man in Chile." In the screenplay, the independent FBI agent investigating the case calls him "just an American boy scout type with merit badges in electronics and assassination, the whole thing tied together with a nickel's worth of Anti-Communism." His evil is the American government's evil. As Buhle paraphrases, "Make that the banality of imperial evil, American evil, exactly the evil that Polonsky's adversaries, including cold-war liberals, had repeatedly insisted did not and could not happen at the hands of government agencies in free America."[32]

The actual story is quite different. All objective and authoritative studies of the incident and its context—including Peter Kornbluth's *The Pinochet File: A Declassified Dossier on Atrocity and Accountability*, which collates declassified government documents with a myriad of other sources to appraise, and judge, the government's relations with the Pinochet regime—all agree: Michael Vernon Townley was not an agent of the CIA; he did not work for the CIA in any way. He was a fascinating, erratic American who for years had worked for Chilean security and assassination squads, the clandestine Brigada Exterior and DINA, the official Chilean security agency. He was a favorite of, known as "the leading assassin" of, the notorious security chief, General Manuel Contreras. The CIA did not conspire with these Chilean security agencies to assassinate Letelier. Using extensive sources, Nathaniel Davis, in *The Last Two Years of Salvador Allende*, also concluded that "none of the accounts presents any evidence that the CIA—or the U.S. Embassy—sponsored Townley."[33]

Polonsky never discussed any screenplays he had written, might have written, or worked on while blacklisted, but it is well-known that toward the end of the blacklist period, he wrote *Odds against Tomorrow* (1959) for Harry Belafonte—part botched-heist thriller, part study in racism. The critics' opinions varied widely. *Newsweek*, for example, called it "one part message, three parts mayhem." In 1968 and under his own name, Polonsky was the main screenwriter on the police drama *Madigan*, directed and much revised by Don Siegel. But it was *Tell Them Willie Boy Is Here* that was his major post-blacklist film, released propitiously in the summer of 1969 at the height of the youthful rebellions of the late sixties. It taps into the zeitgeist of the time, yet it is an odd anachronism in its neat characterizations, its solemn narrative patterning, its moral-pinpointing dialogue—unlike the whole new flair, the ironic art of contradictions, of films like *Bonnie and Clyde* (1967), *Little Big Man* (1970), or *McCabe and Mrs. Miller* (1971). An independent young person of color, a native American (Robert Blake), is "forced" into an unintentional murder of his love's father, and must flee with her. (With an odd irony, it is not unlike the situation faced by John Garfield in 1939's *Dust Be My Destiny*, written by Robert Rossen.) He is relentlessly pursued by the forces of the white, "imperialistic" law (Robert Redford). Buhle paraphrases Polonsky's lofty intentions: "to examine the neo-colonial system and transcend his earlier films' questions about the domestic price of capitalism." Or as Polonsky defined what he was depicting: "Civilization is the process of despoiling, of spoliation of people, which in the past we considered a victory, but now we suspect is a moral defeat for all."[34]

Polonsky's final film as director was a strange one, *Romance of a Horsethief* (1971), not written by him. The loosely structured narrative follows the raucous escapades, touched with the fantastic, of two hard-living, loosely rebellious Yiddish-speaking Jews in a wilder version of the type of setting much beloved in *Fiddler on the Roof*. Typical of the Left's inflating the significance of banal films written by blacklistees, Buhle praises its helter-skelter mélange as "Polonsky's contribution to the concept of the collective hero, a shift from the lone protagonist to the revolutionary mass."[35]

Polonsky wrote three more scripts that were filmed, all after the usual extensive rewriting. Not one substantiates the mythic claim of "the finest aesthetician." *Avalanche Express* (1979) was a muddled spy-thriller. *Monsignor* (1982) entangled papal intrigue and economic corruption, wartime intrigue and danger, star-crossed love, Polonskyan "poetic" dialogue, and even a few Sicilian gangsters. Janet Maslin in the *New York Times* called it "the most extravagant piece of Hollywood junk since *Mommie Dearest*."[36]

His final script was, fittingly, one last attack on stool pigeons and praise of moral heroes during the time of the blacklist. It is one among many television programs that show the assimilation of the left-wing stereotypes by the popular media. *Guilty by Suspicion* was shown by HBO in 1991, and one last time, Polonsky's script was changed and revised severely by others. He wanted his hero, played by Robert De Niro, to be a former Communist who would stand up to and expose the immorality of the Inquisition. In the film as produced, and as is typical of the films of this type, he is the usual innocent non–Communist Party member, unfairly pilloried in the tritely didactic blacklist narrative pattern.

More than half a century earlier, in 1947, while *Body and Soul* was being filmed, the threatening steps of the prelude to the first HUAC hearings were being taken. Before it was released in November of 1947, the hearings had been held. The tensions during its production were heightened by the growing tensions within the Hollywood community in facing the onslaught of the hearings and blacklist. The distortions in the historical depiction and interpretation of those tensions in the making of the film are a miniature paradigm of the distortions in the later history and moral judgments of the period.

Part II

THE HEARINGS BEGIN: PARTY DISCIPLINE AND THE REALITIES OF THE SOVIET WORLD

8

The First Hearings, 1947:
The Strategies, the Combat,
and the Consequences

At the time of the first hearings in late October of 1947, Joseph North in his "Crossfire" column in *New Masses* was defining what he saw as the context of the event: "Fear of the Soviet Union as the social revolution in action is increased by the growing insecurity of the capitalist world. Instead of putting on the brakes to check our descent into economic chaos, our leaders are flinging words at the Soviet leaders and now at those who also take a stand in the struggle for freedom."[1]

Interestingly, in the course of the editorial he did not refer to *Communist* leaders nor *Communism*. At the hearings, the ten Hollywood Communists who appeared also shied away from these words or the phrase *Communist Party*—unlike John Howard Lawson in his proclamation in 1934, "I do not hesitate to say that it is my aim to present the Communist position, and to do so in the most specific manner."[2]

Actually, Lawson did use the C word once, and significantly—toward the end of his abbreviated testimony, before his contumacious, disruptive denunciation of the committee caused the questioning of him to be cut short. When he had been asked the famous "Are you now or have you ever been" question, Lawson answered, "The question of Communism is in no way related to this inquiry, which is an attempt to get control of the screen and to invade the basic rights of American citizens in all fields."[3]

In his written statement (which he was not allowed to read, but which was distributed), he took the theme further into flamboyance: "They [the Committee] want to muzzle the great Voice of Democracy. Because they're conspiring against the American way of life. They want to cut living standards, introduce an economy of poverty, wipe out labor's rights, attack Negroes, Jews, and other minorities, drive us into an unnecessary war."[4] The following nine witnesses followed this same direction of discourse—not only in avoiding the word or any of its variations (except for an impersonal, insignificant instance or two), but in defining the issue as he did, and at the same level of demagogic hyperbole. The hearings were an invasion of their rights of normal political activity and association. That is, the unstated Party in question was a normal American political party.

The tactics and themes that Lawson and then the others followed in these hearings had been defined and organized in a series of strategy meetings. In a striking pattern of script-like conformity, the testimony and written statements of all of the Ten followed Lawson's lead in carrying out this predetermined set of motifs: In their confrontational, combative performances (Lawson: "I am not on trial here, Mr. Chairman. This Committee is on trial here."). In their reiterated insistence that they *were* answering the questions in their own way (Lawson: "I wish to frame my own answers to your questions, Mr. Chairman").[5] In their insisting on their right of normal and patriotic political activity and association. In their emphasis on the committee's seeking to destroy the Screen Writers Guild. In their associating their situations with that of oppressed minorities such as Jews and Negroes. In their asserting again and again that their freedom of speech was being attacked.

This consistent pattern of responses was not mere coincidence. It was the result of strategies and tactics first discussed at a meeting in Hollywood in May—months before the subpoenas were issued on September 21—and then implemented in detail through later meetings and then in sessions on the train to Washington and in Washington hotel rooms, mainly in a large suite at the Shoreham Hotel.[6]

The warning had been sounded early in 1947—after the crucial and inflaming conflicts of the Conference of Studio Unions strikes. Appearing in Washington in March, the producers' spokesman Eric Johnston had proclaimed that "Communist infiltration" of the industry had been defeated. In the April 11 issue of the *Hollywood Reporter*, Jack Warner had called for "an all-out fight on Communism." On May 9, the inflammatory (and eventually indicted and convicted) J. Parnell Thomas came to town for a brief series of closed hearings. As reported in *Daily Variety*, Johnston met with Thomas and pledged the "full cooperation" of the producers and stated that we "are just as anxious as any member of the Committee to expose any threat to the screen and to the American design of living." But, he insisted, it should be done in a "fair, dignified and objective" manner. Among the "fair, dignified and objective" statements at the closed hearings that were leaked to *Variety* was Rupert Hughes' proclamation that "the Screen Writers Guild was lousy with Communists." At the close of these closed hearings, Representative Thomas proudly announced that "hundreds of very prominent film capital people have been named as Communists to us." After a meeting on June 2, the Producers Association announced a three-point program. They insisted on a fair and open investigation. They would not employ "proven Communists if they can influence film content" (whatever that could mean!). They would hire James Byrnes, former secretary of state, to represent them before the House Un-American Activities Committee (HUAC) and the public. None of this program was implemented.[7]

On July 23, H. A. Smith announced for the HUAC, "I plan to hold a number of meetings with industry heads, and the full resources of the House Committee and our investigative staff are at the disposal of those who want to put their house in order before Congress does it for them."[8]

It was clearly time to organize some conferences and deliver some speeches. At a July 11 conference on "Thought Control in the U.S.," held at the Beverly Hills Hotel, Henry Wallace, about to become the leading figurehead for Communist Party positions, was one of the speakers. In an address by Albert Maltz, later published as "The Writer as the Conscience of the People," Maltz spoke with the hyperbolic rhetoric that he, and others, would use at the hearings and about the hearings. "What a loathsome spectacle in our national life, when individuals who are the political scum of our nation are seated in Congress, and are given the power to intimidate citizens. . . . But these eleven [a reference to others, not the Hollywood witnesses] have refused to be intimidated. These eleven refuse to turn the names of anti-fascists over to the mercies of those who would reduce America to one vast concentration camp."[9]

It was also clearly the time to devise a strategy, and the meetings began that resulted in the strategy employed by the Ten to face these "fascistic" threats. On September 11, 1947, forty-three subpoenas had been issued, but subsequently only nineteen people had been summoned to the October hearings in Washington.

There has been some debate and disagreement over the conduct of these meetings. Robert Kenny, a most idealistic liberal and former California attorney general, was one of the legal consultants, but attended only some of the meetings. In his typically naïve idealistic view, "We were always determined that they would arrive at their own decision of conduct before the committee. That's what really happened, for the decisions were their own. And it was not a collective decision." Bartley Crum served as legal consultant for some of the Nineteen, but he was present at only a few meetings—mainly toward the end of the process. He stated that he had wanted Edward Dmytryk and Adrian Scott to testify, but that any such attempt was blocked by the unanimity rule that had been established. Dmytryk later testified that "people like Herbert Biberman" advocated prepared positions from the start, such as this so-called "unanimity rule" that was euphemistically proclaimed as showing how everyone agreed, but that, Dmytryk pointed out, actually was a means of control: Any individual's action must have the unanimous consent of the group.[10]

While individuals were "advised" to talk to attorneys separately, Dmytryk recalled, that was to avoid the danger of "conspiracy." The main "attorneys gave the same advice to everybody." He had agreed that they would "pool our attorneys but we [he and Adrian Scott] went into it without realizing that the thing was carefully planned by a certain number."[11]

One of the meetings of the Nineteen was held at the home of Robert Rossen. At one point of this evening, Rossen, once again upset at the insistence on discipline, came out of the room in which they were meeting and told his wife, Sue, "We apparently just can't tell the truth." The strategy of the lawyers, he told her, was "to protect the Communist Party."[12]

The "unanimity rule" was a way of establishing party discipline, even on those not in the party. When screenwriter Howard Koch told the group that since he wasn't a Communist, he wanted to state he was not a Communist, he was vehemently opposed and subsequently put under pressure to relent. (He was not called to testify.) After the hearings, however, Koch placed an ad in the *Hollywood Reporter*, stating that he "had never been a member of the Communist Party," but reserved the right to refuse to say so before the HUAC. In the ad he asked people in the industry to "defend ourselves by defending each other." In his memoir, *As Time Goes By*, Koch recounted that at the meetings of the Nineteen, "My proposal was for all us to speak out and defend affirmatively our own and each other's political beliefs and associations."[13] His version of what that meant was not the same as that of the party leaders.

Whatever the variation in the later reports from different factions, the result clearly shows that the insistence was on the party's version of unanimity, a new variation on the strategy of a showcase united front.

The chief architect of the plan was Ben Margolis. Dmytryk recalled knowing him from earlier "fraction meetings" of party members, one of which was held at Margolis' home. Margolis and his colleague Charles Katz were the only lawyers who were at all the meetings and at the many individual coaching sessions. Both had previously (and subsequently) participated in many cases and campaigns for the party and party members. At that time they were both opposed to having anyone take the Fifth Amendment. That, they believed, would play into the hands of the committee because "to intimate that their political beliefs could conceivably be seen as criminal under our country's institutions would in fact be tacitly to concede in the public eye what Dies and Rankin had long been trying to prove." However, in later cases and hearings, when saving the defendants (and not propaganda) was the objective, Margolis and Katz *would* advise later "testifyees" and California party leaders to take the Fifth.[14]

Katz commented after the hearings that they were agreed from the start that "we wanted to destroy the committee, and it was an objective that seemed realistic at the time." Margolis discussed this real goal, the party's

goal, and the basis of his strategy in a letter to Kenny: "We shall undoubtedly receive many setbacks. Only by proper utilization of each stage of the
proceedings, and of setbacks themselves, can a case like ours achieve the necessary public support. . . . Then the public can understand what the fight is
about. . . . The presentation of these issues will advance our objectives even
though the court rules against us." These "objectives" were the point, not the
best defense for the witnesses. For the "stages" of *their* losses, the witnesses'
losses, can be used to advance the party's objectives, its positions, and its
policies in the eyes of the public. In his speech at the Civil Rights Congress
celebration of the Nineteen, Margolis focused on the need to change the
"political climate of the country," to work to see the people "united, and
the committee exposed as an enemy of the people." He worked hard at
that strategy, coaching his players through the five long days on the train
to Washington, improvising mock hostile question and answer sessions,
rehearsing the agitprop drama that they were to perform. As Ted Morgan
cogently commented on the result in *Reds*, "Margolis turned the hearings
into a show trial abounding in disruption and confrontation."[15]

Margolis already had had a lot of practice. He and Katz had represented
Harry Bridges and Jeff Kimbre in tumultuous labor disputes. In the early
forties they had toured the state, following the speaking trail of loud but
inept anti-Communist State Senator Jack Tenney. After each Tenney appearance, they would conduct loud rallies and create demonstrations
and protests.[16] Margolis had played a major, and complicated, role in the
defense of the accused in the Sleepy Lagoon murder case in 1942–1944,
in which seventeen young Mexicans were on trial for a murder that had
occurred near a reservoir in East Los Angeles known as the Sleepy Lagoon.
Their original lawyer consistently created a pattern of chaos and disruption
in the courtroom, produced angry and hostile, confused and contradictory
rulings by the judge, and interfered with a clear and effective presentation
of the prosecution's case. *After* the conviction, however, Margolis stepped
in to conduct the appeal. The party stepped in as well. The Sleepy Lagoon
Defense Committee was created *after* the conviction. Fund-raising rallies
were held *after* the conviction; dinner parties in Hollywood, public and
radio appearances—all held *after* the conviction. Blacklisted screenwriter
Guy Endore, pamphlet writer extraordinaire, wrote one in which he said
that one could not help thinking that it was pro-Fascist subversive elements
who were behind the trial and conviction. Dalton Trumbo was not to be
outdone. He too wrote a pamphlet.

On appeal in that case, Margolis skillfully used all that the constant
uproar and confusion had created at the trial. In 1944 the appellate court
agreed that there was extreme judicial bias and a lack of sufficient evidence
to convict either of conspiracy or of murder. The convictions were overturned, and the party basked in the light of the positive publicity. It was

the appeal—the "utilization of the setbacks"—that would "advance our objectives" most effectively.[17]

In a case in the fifties, Margolis employed the strategy in defending Communist union leader Claude Jencks. He thought so well of the tactic of confrontational denunciation that he used it during his own time of testifying in 1952. At that time, Margolis began his attack from the very beginning of his testimony: "almost from the first day that I can remember I have hated tyranny and that is why I feel the way I do about this committee. . . . I have nothing but contempt for this committee, and I will show it as long as I am here." And he did.[18]

In the case of the Hollywood Ten, the strategy was seen by many as ill-advised and self-defeating for those about to be called—and subsequently as destructive for many others in Hollywood. As it was carried out, at the hearings and after, it resulted in an immediate collapse of any unity that had been reestablished among the Hollywood radicals and liberals in organizing to combat the HUAC and defend the Nineteen. Director John Huston had been one of the organizers—according to the legend, over martinis at Lucey's restaurant across from Paramount—of the committee for the First Amendment, the name given the initial broad coalition in support of the Nineteen. He and Philip Dunne met with the unfriendly witnesses before the hearings. Dunne, one of the most prominent screenwriters in Hollywood, was an outspoken and busy fighter for liberal causes. He recalled that early on he and others had advised the Nineteen and especially those who were most likely to be called first to quietly claim violation of their rights and then outside the committee "declare their political affiliation." When he and Huston met with the group, they proposed a novel approach to them. They should "respectfully" refuse to answer under their privilege of the First Amendment, hold a news conference, have Supreme Court Justice Felix Frankfurter put them under oath, and then answer all questions. Huston and Dunne were "greeted by stony silence." In contrast, in his memoir *Hollywood Red*, Lester Cole indicated how that kind of action would undermine the purposes of the strategy taken. He pointed out, "It was argued that acknowledged membership would harm my effectiveness."[19] That is, effectiveness in acting as a Communist.

After the Ten's performance at the hearings, Dunne was appalled. He commented, "They'd come up with this cockamamie idea of saying I'm trying to answer the question in my own words, and then delivering a diatribe against the committee." Huston decried the loss of public sympathy for the witnesses and for the principle behind their defense. "You felt your skin crawl and your stomach turn. I disapproved of what was being done to the Ten, but I also disapproved of their response. They had lost a chance to defend a most important principle. . . . Before the spectacle, the attitude of the press had been extremely sympathetic. Now it changed."[20]

After only a few of the displays, producer Dore Schary, who was to take over as head of MGM in 1951, agreed: "I suggested to Scott, Dmytryk, and Katz that I believed that they could keep the majority of public opinion on their side by avoiding the histrionics of those members of the Ten who had preceded them to the stand." Later, liberal journalist Richard Rovere acidly remarked, "The investigators and the investigated have seemed richly to deserve each other." Dorothy Healey saw it more philosophically, and in a sense morally: "I don't know, though, I do think in retrospect that it would have been better for—what? Morale or solidarity, I guess—if individuals who had been put on the spot had identified themselves politically."[21]

Ted Morgan believes "the Ten didn't realize that they were thrown to the wolves to improve the Party's image." The most striking, ironic point, however, is that, in the long historical run of things and of the influential shaping of that history, their image, collective and individual, was actually improved—despite their loud behavior and the moral silence it embodied. As Ronald Brownstein captured the irony, "The inquisition would be a victory from which Hollywood conservatives never quite recovered."[22]

Victor Navasky established the litany early in the decades of deification. They were "moral examples. . . . They taught us how to act." He hoped, in the phrase that would become an oft-repeated paradigm, that he too would have been able to "behave decently," as they had. Ring Lardner reminisced many years later that "we did the only thing we could do under the circumstances, short of behaving like complete shits."[23]

Historian Tony Judt, on the other hand, has been firm and consistent in his opposition to the decades of this mythmaking: "But we need to learn the truth about Communism: that it was a singularly dishonest confidence-trick whose consenting victims include its distant apologists in England and America, who enthusiastically sent others on the road to hell with the very best of intentions."[24]

In the immediate aftermath in the late forties, the behavior of the Ten and the Communist Party had more direct consequences. Dore Schary was "convinced," even later, "that if the Ten had taken the course I suggested, the disaster that followed the hearings would not have taken place, despite Hedda Hopper, Westbrook Pegler, and the Motion Picture Alliance for the Preservation of American Ideals, which was the wordy title dreamed up by strong right-wing opposition in Hollywood."[25] Schary may well have been too naïve. However, even though testifying would not have saved the jobs of the Ten and others, a different, more honest (and more moral) strategy might well have changed the climate of public and media opinion about Hollywood to the point of inhibiting the actions of the producers, giving them some basis and even courage on which to stand up to the pressures of the Right, allowing a freer range of options and consequences for others caught up in whatever process would have then developed.

At any rate, the producers had certainly been handed their rationale, and their excuse, by the performance of the Ten. They were given the basis for a public relations justification to once and for all—or so it must have seemed—put an end to the decades of battles with the disruptive Communists and their defenders. On November 25, after a conference at the Waldorf Astoria Hotel in New York City, the members of the Association of Motion Picture Producers issued "The Waldorf Statement." A group headed by lawyer Mendel Silberberg wrote the statement. Silberberg was a prominent stalwart of the Jewish community in Los Angeles, and a confidante and adviser of many of the Jewish movie producers and magnates. After the HUAC hearings, Dunne had met with Silberberg to enlist his aid in heading off a looming blacklist. Still trying to work out his own strategy, at that point Silberberg did concur, fearing, it was said, that once it was started, the Jews would suffer. Dunne and Silberberg then met with a number of studio heads, with no conclusive results. Silberberg, however, was still worried about the negative impact of the performance of the Ten at the hearings and of what continuing performances would unfold. And so at the Waldorf conference, he had decided on what he deemed the best way to mitigate the damage to the industry—and the Jews. He drafted the statement for the association. As Neal Gabler wrote, "No one in Hollywood was more conscious of the image of Jews in the public mind. No one was more keenly aware of the practical consequences of the Hollywood Jews' seeming to harbor Communists. No one more accurately represented the Hollywood Jews' fears and hopes."[26]

In its four paragraphs of explanation and definition, Silberberg's version of these hopes and fears announced that because "their *actions* [emphasis added] have been a disservice to their employers and have impaired their usefulness to the industry," the producers "will forthwith discharge or suspend without compensation" the Ten until they are acquitted of contempt or testify under oath that they are not members of the Communist Party. And more importantly, the producers felt it possible to go further without any danger of public disapproval and with the further justification of Federal policies and definitions: "We will not knowingly employ a Communist or a member of any party or group which advocates the overthrow of the Government of the United States by force or by illegal or unconstitutional methods. . . ." The statement did concede, "There is the danger of hurting innocent people . . . we will invite the Hollywood talent guilds to work with us to eliminate any subversives, to protect the innocent, and to safeguard free speech and a free screen whenever threatened."[27]

Schary later commented how he was dismayed by the producer group's action and statement. While they proclaimed their protection of the innocent and free speech, they were really signaling and implementing the opposite.[28] Whether in principle, in anger or selfishness, or in fear, they had succumbed to the pressures of right-wing zealots. For all their own motives—individual and collective, principled and invidious—the producers to all intents and purposes created the blacklist. It was a term, and an implication of fearful and greedy betrayal that they never accepted—or at least publicly testified to.

Some years later, in 1961, Lardner wrote an article for the *Saturday Evening Post* of October 14. In part it was a reprise of an earlier reminiscence, "My Life on the Blacklist," but it was in great part an indictment of the attack on civic liberties. Roy Brewer wrote a rebuttal. When the *Saturday Review* refused to publish it, it was published in the *American Legion Magazine* in March of 1962. Still using the evangelical rhetoric of his passionate anti-Communism, Brewer did attempt to review the basis of his own role in that period's events, providing a rationale for what he saw as his necessary but sympathetic firmness in fighting Communism. In one passage, Brewer states, "What he [a banker friend of his] had failed to recognize is that communism is not a political belief, but is, in fact, a world-wide organization of gangsters which is irrevocably dedicated to destroy every government in the world that it does not control. Many of the persons in it are deceived as to its real nature but as long as they are subject to its discipline they can never be trusted and their very presence in the industry destroys public confidence in it."[29]

As Huston, Dunne, and Schary, among others, realized from the start, the behavior of the Ten at the first hearings in October 1947 contributed to the momentum of the crusade of the Right in Hollywood. The Ten thus played their own paradoxical role in the development of the blacklist and in the collapse of any effective coalition that might have combated it. Here are a few typical samples of three of the tactics that carried out the strategies and themes developed in the many sessions of preparation: (1) refusing to testify by saying you are testifying, (2) being confrontational and combative, but at the same time, (3) defending the right of normal political association.[30]

The climactic Lawson variant on the I-am-answering tactic:

The Chairman: Now, do you care to answer the question?

Lawson: You are using the old technique, which was used in Hitler's Germany in order to create a scare here—

A shouting match ensued, with seven fragmentary exchanges. Finally:

The Chairman: That is not the question. That is not the question. The question is, Have you ever been a member of the Communist Party?

Lawson: I am framing my answer in the only way in which any American citizen can frame his answer to a question which absolutely invades his rights.[31]

Lardner, son of the novelist and short story writer, probably had the sharpest wit, the most comfortably debonaire sophistication of the group. In his brief testimony, he played constant variations on the almost comic routine-like sequence: Yes, I am going to answer, but first I have to . . . , first I need to . . . , all building to his well-honed punch line.

After a number of such parries, the following exchange took place:

The Chairman: Are you a member of the Screen Writers Guild? Now you answer it yes or no.

Lardner: Well, I am saying that in order to answer that—

Stripling: Mr. Lardner, are you now or have you ever been a member of the Communist Party?

Lardner: Well, I would like to answer that question, too.

A bit further on, Lardner said, "I am trying to answer the question by stating, first, what I feel about the purpose of the question."

After several more attempts by the chairman and Stripling, the chairman's fervent flag-waving buildup to his repetition of the big question presented the perfect opportunity for Lardner's "topper": "It depends on the circumstances. I could answer it, but if I did, I would hate myself in the morning."[32]

Trumbo, who never liked to be topped by anyone when it came to being a phrase crafter, contributed his own, typically more verbose, variation on the theme. He was, as Paul Jarrico remembered, "the most original, the most flamboyant, the most unique of all the characters I knew on the left. . . . He was a fabulous bullshitter." And he loved to act out that role, jaunty and acerbic, yet with a good full heart beneath the prideful breast.

At one point, Trumbo said, "I understand, Mr. Stripling. However, your job is to ask questions and mine is to answer them. I shall answer 'Yes' or 'No' if I please to answer. I shall answer in my own words. Very many questions can be answered 'Yes' or 'No' only by a moron or a slave."

After several attempts to get an answer, the chairman asked, "Are you answering the question or are you making a speech?"

After several more attempts have led to more interrupted speechifying:

The Chairman [sounding more and more and more like an exasperated Groucho trying to get a straight answer out of Chico]: Now, you are making another speech, or is that the answer? Well, can't you answer by saying "Yes" or "No" or "I think so" or "Maybe" or something like that?

Trumbo: Mr. Chairman, I should like to accommodate you. May I try to answer the question again?

For *his* topper, Trumbo created a sly reversal of roles. When asked the "sixty-four-dollar" question, he in return asked several questions about a party card that he claimed was illegally shown to the press—"Is that true?" he asked.

Stripling: That is not true.

The Chairman: You are not asking the questions. . . .

Trumbo: I was.

The Chairman: The chief investigator is asking the questions.[33]

Alvah Bessie, who had gone to Spain in the Abraham Lincoln Battalion, was always more sober and intense about his beliefs. He was nowhere near the success as a screenwriter that Lardner and Trumbo and some of the others were, and never fancied himself a wit. His answers that were not answers were serious ideological speeches.

Stripling: Do you refuse to answer the question?

Bessie: I have not refused, but I must answer the question in the only way I know how, and that is, that I believe that such a question violates my right of association.[34]

His "answer" to the sixty-four-dollar question was one of the longest speeches allowed any of the witnesses. It even attempted to use General Eisenhower as one, like himself, who refused to reveal his political affiliations. When asked the question again, he insisted he had already answered it. When it came down to the "Yes" or "No" level again, he insisted he had already answered it several times.

Lester Cole was the last to testify. His answers were less heated, his demeanor more controlled, even smug in his unwavering sense of his righteous cause, which, thus, needed no spinwheel fireworks.

When asked if he was a member of the Screen Writers Guild, Cole said he wished to answer in his own way. When, after several exchanges, he was asked the big question, he returned to the subject of the Screen Writers Guild, starting to get in the claim that he had not been allowed to make earlier: "I believe the reason that question is being asked is that there is an election in the Screen Writers Guild in Hollywood that for 15 years Mr. McGuiness and others."

After being interrupted and after several more exchanges, the question was put again, and Cole gave his defining answer, more straightforward than most: "I want to reply in my own way and at times when I feel it is proper."[35]

This provocative pattern of counterattack regularly implied and advanced the theme that was the real core, the crux not only of their strategy, but of their system of belief and its consequences. That crux was touched on in Bessie's response: His right of association, of political association, was being violated. For the core of this morally ambiguous aspect of their ideology, and the influential deceit that was carried forward through the years, was this: The Communist Party of the United States was merely a normal political party and membership in it was no different in its basis and consequences than membership in the Democratic Party or the Animal Rights Party. And so a citizen's rights to membership in it, support of it, could not be treated by the government any differently than a citizen's rights to membership in any other organization, political or not.

From this perspective, anything the HUAC, or any other arm of the government, did was an attack on democratic principles. As Cole phrased it with more of an attempt at rhetorical wit than usual, "This committee is waging a cold war on Democracy."[36]

Bessie elaborated on this position in his written statement to the HUAC: "that this body is totally unconstitutional and without power to inquire into anything I think, believe, uphold, and cherish, or anything I have ever written or said, or any organization I have ever joined or failed to join."[37]

In his variant on developing this theme, Herbert Biberman gave a brief testimony that was marked by the interrupting, fragmented give-and-take of a musical comedy duet or the telegraphic dialogue pattern of a twenties expressionist drama:

Biberman: It has become very clear to me that the real purpose of this investigation—

The Chairman: (pounding gavel) That is not an answer to the question—

Biberman: —is to drive a wedge—

The Chairman: (pounding gavel) That is not the question—

Biberman: —into the component parts—

The Chairman: (pounding gavel) Not the question—

Biberman: —of the Motion Picture Industry.

Mr. Chairman: (pounding gavel) Ask him the next question.

Biberman: And by defending my constitutional rights here, I am defending—

Mr. Chairman: (pounding gavel) Go ahead and ask him the next question.

Biberman: —the right not only of ourselves—

Stripling: Are you a member—

Biberman: —but of the producers and of the American people.

Stripling: —of the Communist Party?

Biberman's written statement focused more clearly on all the slogans involving the rights of citizenship, of political activism—and without interruption: "It is not force or violence this committee is investigating, but earnest, unceasing citizenship. . . . It is because I am an active citizen that I am here . . . because I committed the sin of devoting ten years to energetic advocacy of my faith in the American people under our Bill of Rights. I believe the American people will not give up the holy struggle for a peaceful world, will not be bullied into an hysterical war."[38]

Albert Maltz was himself amazed when he was allowed to read his statement aloud. Paul Jarrico saw Maltz as "a rather humorless man who took causes in which he was involved very personally."[39] In his statement to the HUAC, Maltz emphasized that his situation was like that of all Americans who take part in political activities and groups for what is good and just:

> I maintain that this is an evil and vicious procedure; that it is legally unjust and morally indecent—and that it places in danger every other American. . . .
>
> Very well, then, here is the other reason why I and others have been commanded to appear before this Committee—our ideas. In common with many Americans, I supported the New Deal. In common with many Americans, against Mr. Thomas and Mr. Rankin, the anti-lynching bill. . . .
>
> I claim and I insist on my right to think freely and to speak freely; to join the Republican Party or the Communist Party [one of the rare and rather facetious exceptions], the Democratic Party or the Prohibition Party.

After his reading, he was asked if he was a member of the Screen Writers Guild. "Next you are going to ask me what religious group I belong to. Any such question as that is an obvious attempt to invade my rights as a citizen under the Constitution."[40]

Lawson played many variations on this theme, such as, "It is absolutely beyond the power of this Committee to inquire into my association in any organization."

And in his written statement he elaborated and elaborated, reaching the level of exaggerated, vituperative rhetoric that disturbed many who had hoped to defend him and the others:

> For a week, this Committee has conducted an illegal and indecent trial of American citizens, whom the Committee has selected to be publicly pilloried and smeared. . . .
>
> I am forced to appear here as a representative of one hundred and thirty million Americans because the illegal conduct of the Committee has linked me with every citizen. . . . No American will be safe if the Committee is not stopped in its illegal enterprise. . . .
>
> [This Committee] is serving more powerful forces. Those forces are trying to introduce fascism in this country. They know that the only way to trick the American people into abandoning their rights and liberties is to manufacture an imaginary danger.[41]

In 1948 Gordon Kahn, who was subsequently blacklisted, wrote *Hollywood on Trial*, the first paean to the Ten. He summarized in print this central claim of the witnesses. "Almost at once it became clear that deeply underlying this attack on screen freedom, and implicit in it, was an attack on the essential idea of American liberty . . . the onslaught against civil liberties. Here, all wrapped up together, were the truculent attempt to establish censorship over the screen; the invasion of the privacy of individual belief by the drumhead trial."[42]

Elia Kazan saw it differently: "I believed it was the duty of the government to investigate the Communist movement in our country. I couldn't behave as if my old comrades didn't exist and didn't have an active political program. There was no way I could go along with their crap that the CP was nothing but another political party, like the Republicans and the Democrats. I knew very well what it was, a thoroughly organized, worldwide conspiracy."[43]

The evidence bears out Kazan's contention. The party that, like the elephant in the room, was hardly ever mentioned by the witnesses, was *not* a normal independent American political organization. It was controlled by and carried out the directives of the Soviet Union and the Comintern. It was supported financially by the Soviet Union and the Comintern. It actively engaged in espionage against the United States. It was constant in its obedience to the ever-changing international Communist party line.

9

Testimony and Silence: Just a Democratic Political Association and the Secret World of Communism

At the first hearings, the central motif of the claims by the Ten—and afterward by them and by others—was that their constitutional right to normal political association and activity was being unconstitutionally, even fascistically, violated. The flaw in this reiterated chorus, which blurred and damaged other possible constitutional protests, was the reality of the Communist Party that they were part of. The facts of the control and support of the Communist Party of America (CPUSA) by the Soviet Union and the Comintern not only place these claims in a different legal context; they place the silence about these facts during the hearings and in the years following in a different moral context. As Yevtushenko perceived, this kind of silence is a lie. It is a lie that aids and abets—at whatever distance—the actions that are evaded and ignored. And so, however minor the degree, it makes morally complicit in those actions the silent ones.

We can begin a review of these accusing facts of the real secret world of the CPUSA with a focus on money, Comintern rules and regulations, and espionage.

For decades—even into the eighties—the CPUSA annually received clandestine funds from the Soviet Union in the millions, the largest funding per capita of membership of any of the worldwide Communist parties. This financial support by a foreign government and its international organization, the Comintern, was never revealed or admitted. Indeed all evidence was carefully hidden and suppressed in a deceitful response to claims that such subsidies existed. Unfortunately, the cover story was generally accepted by historians for many decades, and it is still promulgated by some. Some of this funding was a kind of general periodic stipend, but much of it was designated for particular needs and projects, including espionage. All of it has been documented in specific exchanges of requests and responses and financial records down to the penny.[1]

Even as early as 1919 and 1920 the Comintern (as shown in a Comintern account fact sheet) sent Russian gold and jewels valued at several million dollars to help found the Communist movement in America. John Reed, author of *Ten Days That Shook the World,* was one of the four couriers who were to distribute the "goods" as directed. By the early twenties, stipends were sent on a regular basis. On March 6, 1923, for example, a document from the CPUSA to the Comintern reports with specific details how it spent a subsidy of $30,950 received in December 1921 and subsidies totaling $49,429 received in June and July 1922. That was a lot of money at the time; not all amounts were that high—a document for nine full months of 1926 showed a total of $44,864. The Soviets were quite considerate. A 1923 document concerning an allocation of $37,500 to the American party states that the Americans should appeal for more aid "if this is not sufficient." Party leader Charles Ruthenberg was not at all shy in responding, "The sum for 1923 is far from being sufficient." Others were equally outspoken. On September 26, 1928, Jay Lovestone, later a strong anti-Communist and labor leader, wired Bukharin and Molotov directly: "Bukharin Molotov insists you execute your promise rendering immediate substantial financial assistance cable money immediately."[2]

A conservative estimate based on all known documents is that through the twenties, Moscow accounted for anywhere from one-third to two-thirds of the budget of the American Communist Party in any given year.[3]

During the thirties, the CPUSA averaged only between ten thousand dollars and fifteen thousand dollars a year in direct Comintern subsidies, but interestingly despite the depression, the American party was deriving more income from property it had acquired and from wealthy supporters. However, a more significant reason for the reduction was that in this period while Stalin had reduced the Comintern's budget, he had increased the amount that the NKVD and other Soviet intelligence agencies would directly receive to subsidize their espionage activities. Thus, money for espionage activities in the United States was allotted in different ways, and not shown in Comintern records.[4]

During the forties, the "secret apparatus," the covert arm of the CPUSA that was directed by Rudy Baker, continued to receive operating funds from both the NKVD and the Comintern. The methods could have been part of a spy movie. A cable of February 13, 1940, from Baker and Earl Browder to Georgi Dimitrov states, "We propose you send several 1000 bill [sic] every two or three weeks, scilfully [sic] concealed inside cover English edition book published cooperative publishing society and addressed Mr. A Spritzman 1709 Boston road Bronx New York." Totals for these years exceeded those in the thirties; a year-end report for 1943 showed a total of $30,145.[5]

Large yearly payments continued into the eighties. As the party was struggling to even stay in existence, the Soviets increased their subsidies in hopes of producing a resurgence—as they were doing for Communist parties all over the world. In 1963, for example, they supplied a total of $15,750,000 to eight-three national parties. From 1953 to 1984 the CPUSA received a total of $42,102,000 (somewhat less than was given both the French and Italian parties). As late as 1976, the U.S. party received $1,997,651, and in 1987 an even $2 million; still, Gus Hall, party head from 1959 on, complained to the Central Committee that it was not enough. Inexplicably, in view of the state of the CPUSA and the Soviet Union at that time, the stipend was raised to $3 million in 1988.[6]

Even major CPUSA officials were sometimes used as couriers. Max Bedacht, head of the party-controlled International Workers Order, in the thirties was used to bring money directly to Browder. The oddest case is that of the Childs brothers, Morris and Jack. They were senior party members. For more than twenty years, 1958 to 1980, they carried Soviet funds to the CPUSA, totaling millions of dollars. What the party didn't know, however, was that the FBI had recruited them in 1958. They were reporting it all.[7]

The only form of repayment ever required was total obedience to the Soviets' policies and requests, but that obedience would have been given anyway. It was embedded deep within the nature, the very basic form of existence of Communist parties throughout the world. An independent local party was a contradiction in terms.

And yet in the fifties and ever since, claims such as these have been made and supported as gospel: "We had no connection with the Russians; we asked nothing from them and received nothing in return." And, "There was no truth to the government's charge that we were subject to the Soviet Union."

The strict and detailed pattern for the relationship of local parties to the Soviet Union and the Comintern, the definition of the rules and regulations for total control and obedience, was established at the Second Congress of the Comintern in the summer of 1920. Its significant "Twenty-One Conditions" became the veritable constitution for Communist orthodoxy throughout the world. They were the machinery for the long-term program for an "international workers' revolution" as laid out by Lenin at the Eighth Party Congress in March 1919: Since the Soviet Republic was "living not merely in a state, but in a system of hostile states," it was "inconceivable that the Soviet Republic should continue to exist for a long period side by side with imperialistic states. Ultimately one or the other must conquer." And so the Comintern conditions stated, "Workers' parties all over the world" would have a vital role in that conquest, for "the international proletariat will not sheathe its sword until Soviet Russia is incorporated as a link in the World Federation of Soviet Republics."[8] (Looking ahead, we might note that the unchanging goals of such proclamations and policies as these, repeated through the years in varied ways, give the lie to the claims of "revisionist" historians that Soviet aggressions during the Cold War were the necessary defensive response to U.S. imperialist threats and aggressions.)

These "conditions" set up requirements for all phases of the organization and actions of member parties. The key to them all, the very basis of the relationship, was that "all decisions by congresses of the Communist International as well as by its Executive Committee are binding on all parties." After several years of uneven implementation of some elements of the conditions, the Fifth Comintern Congress was even more forceful in its demands for what it called the full "Bolshevization" of all member parties. This time it added a crucial new element to its demands—a direct demand not only on parties, but on party *leaders*, calling for their absolute orthodoxy and loyalty; implied was—"or else." The journal of the United Communist Party, *The Communist*, proclaimed in April of 1921, "The Communist International has acted! . . . It is binding on the convention and on the representatives themselves. There will be no modification. . . . The highest authority . . . has spoken."[9]

The most extreme of the demands of loyalty—and the most morally crucial—was participation in espionage. In the legal debates and conflicts in the forties and fifties over investigations and government regulations, the central issue was twofold: Was there a major threat of espionage and subversion, and was the CPUSA not only controlled in general by the Soviets, but actively involved in Soviet espionage—and thus other than a normal political party?

THE REALITY AND THE EXTENT OF ESPIONAGE

A number of current commentators, using collations of the various sources now available, have used the figure of two hundred as a round number for the total of known Americans in various parts of the U.S. government who were espionage agents or "agents of influence" (i.e., used to report on policy and most importantly to influence policy). However, the most definitive statistic so far for any aspect of subversion, not only within the government, is supplied by Harvey Klehr and John Earl Haynes. They analyzed the Soviet cables that were translated before the program called Venona was stopped. Venona translated a small percentage of the three thousand secret Soviet telegraphic cables intercepted and collected from 1939 to 1947. Klehr and Haynes find they can "identify 349 citizens, immigrants, and permanent residents of the United States who had a covert relationship with the Soviet Union." They can identify the true names of 171, with 178 still known only by code names. In addition, they have identified 139 others from collating other sources—making a total of 488 (although a small number of those in the second group may be among those known only by code names in Venona).[10]

Following is a brief checklist of major categories and names—with some typical statements by Soviets as found in documents in a variety of sources:

Government

Through the thirties and forties, three of the most active groups conducting espionage were led by Gregory Nathan Silvermaster, Victor Perlo, and Harold Ware. These organized groups involved some three dozen people who worked for various departments and aspects of the government. Participants were often shifted from one to another or to independent connections to a Soviet controller. Alger Hiss, for example, was subsequently controlled by Military Intelligence, and was not in the KGB archives. His absence from the latter, as we will examine later, was used in recent years in a fallacious public relations campaign to still "prove" his innocence.[11] (See chapter 13.)

Indicative of the heavy espionage traffic, Soviet documents show that in eight months of 1944, the Silvermaster network alone passed 386 significant government documents to the NKVD. KGB records show that in 1943, the network controlled by Itzhak Akhmerov delivered 211 reels of microfilm of government documents to Moscow; in 1944, 600; in 1945, 1,896. Haynes and Klehr estimate a total of 68,256 pages of documents were passed along in 1945. Akhmerov wired to Moscow that after some problems, "Now Silvermaster is carrying out enormous work and giving our government a complete picture of American politics on all questions."[12]

Harold Glasser was one of the most prolific of the Communist spies—although not discussed as much as some of the more famous. A 1945 NKGB report, for example, shows that in five months, 74 documents supplied by him had been passed on to Stalin and other Soviet leaders. The contents, according to Allen Weinstein and Alexander Vassiliev, were "all of critical interest to the leadership of the USSR." In *The Haunted Wood*, their partial list of 1945 materials forwarded by Glasser covers almost three pages of text (in small typeface).[13]

A significant special group, involving eight known participants, and possibly more, was organized to infiltrate the OSS (Office of Strategic Services; forerunner to the CIA) in its earliest years. Earl Browder and Eugene Dennis personally took part in creating this strategy. Placed in a related army security unit was William Weisband, who in 1947 informed the Soviets of the Venona project—a devastating revelation that cut short a major source of counterintelligence information. A 1948 memorandum indicates the importance of his contribution: "For one year, a large amount of very valuable documentary material concerning the work of Americans on deciphering Soviet ciphers and analyzing open radio-correspondence of Soviet institutions [Venona] was received from ZHORA [Weisband]." Even during this period of intense investigations, Weisband continued to supply information to his handlers until 1950, when they deemed his participation too dangerous to their operations.[14]

As to those who were "agents of influence": The most significant were Alger Hiss and Harry Dexter White, assistant secretary of the treasury, although both also participated in actively passing along valuable documents, among other postwar economic policies that were beneficial to Soviet interests. White created a program that allowed plates for printing new German marks to be placed in Soviet hands. As a result, for example, in the U.S. zone of Germany there was initially 78 billion in new marks; in the Soviet Zone, 105 million. Under Soviet control, White developed and encouraged Treasury Secretary Henry J. Morgenthau to attempt to enact a program that would have reduced postwar Germany to a weak agricultural state—and probably allowed the Soviets/East Germans to take over all of the divided country. In the early stages of the United Nations, White, along with Hiss, developed financial proposals that also were to be to the Soviets' benefit. At the Tehran and Yalta conferences—which Hiss helped plan and then attended—Stalin knew of the contents of highly classified British and American documents concerning policy and negotiating positions.[15]

Back in 1941, recently unearthed documents show, White was instrumental in creating an intransigent, demanding policy and negotiating positions that were intended to heighten tensions between the United States and Japan and thus deflect any Japanese interest in Soviet territory in the Far East. In attempting to implement this strategy, White was assisted along the way by Lauchlin Currie, an administrative assistance to Roosevelt, who was active among the Soviets' networks, and by Owen Lattimore, especially in an influential cable report of November 26, 1941, while Lattimore was the American adviser to Chiang Kai-shek.[16]

On July 3, 1941, the Soviet *rezident* in New York, Pavel Pastelniak, reported to Moscow that intelligence data shows "Japan intends to . . . undertake an attack on the Soviet Union. Sources 29 and RICHARD [White] are confident in the reliability of this information." As a result, orders from Moscow called for pressure on their American contacts to threaten Japan with harsh sanctions to distract their attention from the Soviets. In November Pastelniak reported that Robert (Silvermaster) and Richard (White) were "actively participating" in recommendations to Roosevelt "to prevent and impede Japan acting against the Soviet Union."[17]

Their efforts were controlled by agent Vitali Pavlov, sent to Washington to manage what he named "Operation Snow." Years later Vladimir Karpov, editor of *Novy Mir*, a leading Soviet journal, described the operation: "Harry Dexter White was acting in accordance with a design initiated by Akhmerov and Pavlov. . . . The essence of 'Operation Snow' was to provoke the war between the Empire of the Rising Sun and the USA and to insure the security of the interests of the Soviet Union in the Far East."[18]

Nevertheless, despite all, years later novelist Howard Fast said, "I believe that in those years there was little I did not know about the Communist Party, and I am ready to swear under oath . . . that there was no member of the Communist Party in the State Department . . . The very thought, for anyone who knew the Party, was idiotic."[19]

And as for spies? Ring Lardner Jr., too, could see it only as idiotic: "But about the dumbest thing a Soviet spy could have been . . . would have been to join the Communist Party of the United States."[20]

Technology and Science

Soviet archives reveal that at one point the Soviet controllers had worked with a total of forty-nine American "engineers" (although the term probably included scientists).[21]

A central ring in collecting and passing to the Soviets a vast amount of technological materials was a ring organized and led by Julius Rosenberg. These materials ranged from new inventions, to processes, to adaptations of known equipment and systems and important military advances such as the proximity fuse for artillery, and eventually to the atomic bomb. In this group were Joel Barr, Alfred Sarant, Morton Sobell, and William Perl, among others who passed in and out. They were controlled at one point by Alexander Feklissov. Years later Feklissov revealed that by 1946 the group had delivered more than twenty thousand pages of military technology to the Soviet Union, including the design plans and technical drawings for America's first jet fighter, the F-80, and advanced military radar.[22]

Using Soviet network documents, a U.S. government report summarized, "The Soviets estimate that by using documentation on the US F-80 fighter their aviation and radar industries saved some five years of development time . . . one of the most successful individual exploitations ever of Western technology."[23]

Among the small percentage of Soviet cables deciphered, in 1944 and 1945 alone, twenty-one deciphered cables deal with Rosenberg. In 1944, New York informed Moscow Center that Rosenberg was receiving so much intelligence from his agents that he was finding it difficult to cope, and even to find enough film. "We are," the report said, "afraid of putting LIBERAL [one of Rosenberg's several code names through the years] out of action with overwork." In November of that year his controller, Semyonov, reported, "His group ran on the principles of a Communist Party group, and he [Rosenberg] ran it as a Party organizer."[24]

At one point the Rosenberg group was connected to two of the most important American couriers, Lorna and Morris Cohen, who had their own satellite network. When the Rosenbergs were arrested, the Cohens escaped to Mexico and then Moscow. Some years later they turned up doing espionage work in England, as Helen and Peter Kroger, until arrested by British Intelligence.

Interconnecting as well with Rosenberg and his group was Harry Gold, another active courier and one of the few participants in this work who was not a Party member. Gold served as courier for the most important Atomic spy, Klaus Fuchs, as well as for the most valuable American Atomic source, Theodore (Ted) Hall, and for other scientists and engineers, such as Abraham Brothman and Alfred Slack.

In 1943, the NKVD's 10th Section, in charge of this "Scientific Line"—part of a precise demarking system organized by Moscow Center—reported twenty-nine active agents in the Manhattan [Atomic] Project. Numerous scientists referred to by code names in Venona and other reports have still to be identified. In 1946, 659 scientific reports were delivered to Lavrenti Beria himself, in charge of Soviet atomic development, 33 in one delivery on August 28, 1946.[25]

But John Wexley, among others, still would not believe a word of it: "The climate of fear was tremendous . . . You know, the Communists had stolen the atomic bomb in some way or other. They were *muzhiks*; they weren't capable of making their own bomb, so they had to steal it from us!"[26]

Gold, of course, became the courier for David Greenglass, recruited by Julius Rosenberg and eventually a main government witness against him. The government case against the Rosenbergs was hampered by its inability, or refusal, to use the many Venona documents that clearly proved Rosenberg's atomic and other espionage because they did not want the Russians to know they had all of that data and the means of translating the documents. They did not know at the time that Weisbard had already informed the Soviets about the Venona decryptions.

Ted Morgan commented on the broader damage and confusion caused by the government's refusal to release the Venona data in any form: "The release of Venona would have nipped McCarthyism in the bud, for the true facts about real spies would have made wild accusations about imaginary spies irrelevant. . . . Venona would have revealed unstinted spying, abetted by the American Party. It would have led to the prosecution of disloyal public servants. It would have stifled the outcry that Communists were innocent victims of Red-baiting and witch-hunts, and shown that McCarthy was inconsequential to the issue he rode to fame."[27]

The Role of the CPUSA

The great majority of people involved in espionage in the CPUSA *were* members of the Communist Party, which correlation is more than a mere coincidence. The CPUSA was active in collaborating with the Soviets in recruiting, organizing, and helping to manage agents such as those just mentioned. Cables and other documents show consistent interactions with Moscow in recommending potential candidates, arranging connections, settling disputes and problems, changing procedures, and so on.

Vasili Mitrokhin, former head of the Soviet Intelligence Archives, summarized the evidence: "During the second World War the CPUSA had played an important part in assisting Soviet penetration of the Roosevelt Administration, the intelligence community, and the Manhattan Project." The assistance had continued after the War, but Mitrokhin explained that trials of leaders, investigations, and loyalty programs "forced it into a largely underground existence" producing "a dramatic decline" in the assistance offered by the CPUSA. Mitrokhin complained that even such an effective agent as Rudolph Abel (Vilyam Fisher) was now able to recruit less American "Volunteers" because "he did not have the active and enthusiastic assistance of a well-organized American Communist Party to act as talent spotter and assister."[28]

Mitrokhin confirmed Elizabeth Bentley's statement that in March 1944, party chief Earl Browder passed on to her a group of Washington bureaucrats who had been sending him intelligence which he had passed on to Jacob Golos [Bentley's controller]. When the Soviet controller decided to change Bentley's function, she appealed to Browder for help in remaining the courier for the Washington networks. He told her, "Don't be naïve. You know that when the cards are down, I have to take my orders from them." Also in 1944 a Soviet memo, for example, praises CPUSA "cooperation in access to research . . . since 1942."[29]

An interesting example is the case of Steve Nelson, a highly visible party official on the West Coast, often referred to as a victim of the Smith Act prosecutions. He was also part of a secret underground commission. Documents show him meeting with Vasily Zubilin (real name Vasily Zarubin), a major controller, to receive money for recruitment and courier work. Early in 1943 a cable from "Son" (Rudy Baker) to Dimitrov states, "We have assigned one responsible person in California (Mack) [Nelson] to be responsible for all our work there." About the same time the FBI bugged a phone call between Baker and Zubilin that made the same point: Their project was to receive technical information from Joseph W. Weinberg and others at the U.C. Berkeley Radiation Lab, run by Robert Oppenheimer in 1943. This plan was one stage in the major espionage project at the atomic research facility at Los Alamos. In response to instructions from General Pavel Fitin, head of the Foreign Intelligence Directorate, in June of 1942

Zubilin assured him, "We are taking further measures to plant our reliable sources in Los Alamos."[30]

At one point Moscow Center even warns Zubilin about being too over-eager in recruiting through the party: "We permit the use of the Communist Party members illegal intelligence capability . . . as a supplement to the residency's operations, but it would be a mistake to turn those capabilities into the main basis of operations." This was after Zubilin had ordered leaders of the CPUSA to identify and analyze more supporters in government establishments suitable for work as agents.[31]

Senior members of the party were regularly involved in a number of espionage functions, from Browder and Dennis on down. Browder, by all accounts eager and excited about the clandestine work, often acted independently, in great part acting as recruiter for party members to join the espionage networks.

After Browder had been deposed in 1945, the NKGB in America wrote memorandums supporting him and praising him for his assistance in their work. Both a 1945 and a 1946 memo place his first espionage activity in 1933: "Starting in 1933 and into 1945," said the April 1946 memo, intended for Stalin himself, "Browder rendered the NKGB . . . and the GRU . . . help, recommending to our representatives in the U.S. a number of illegal members of the U.S. Communist Party for agent work." The message goes on to specify numbers of people at different times: eighteen, twenty-five, and several instances where the number is missing in the transcribed message. The 1945 memo had listed specific instances in which Browder worked with three major Soviet agents: Peter, who was also known as J. Peters; Bill, who was never identified; and Jacob Golos. The memo commented, "[Golos], being our important group handler for a large number of agents made up of local citizens [a term often used for Party members], was the main person entrusted for a connection with [Browder] from 1937 to 1940." It also praised Browder for recruiting "verified persons from the local compatriots for use as agents, illegal couriers, and illegal group handlers."[32]

While Browder was in prison from late 1940 until early 1942, Eugene Dennis (code name Ryan) filled in as the coordinator between the Soviet apparatus and the CPUSA members. One set of correspondence between Dennis and Dimitrov involves the Communist penetration of the OSS. While Dimitrov had applauded the operation, he felt that it was becoming dangerous—in one of his favorite, and important, terms, *counterproductive*. Milton Wolff, the former commander of the Abraham Lincoln Battalion (always promoted as a *Brigade*, which it wasn't), was continuing zealously to recruit people for espionage work, and Dimitrov wanted him stopped. Just before Browder's sentence was commuted and he was released, in June of 1942, Dennis complied, and thus acted to actually *stop* an espionage activity: "We fully agree [of course] with your proposals regarding the activities of Wolff and we have taken all necessary measures for their discontinuation."[33]

Father and Son

But the most organized phase of Browder's espionage was done in conjunction with Rudy Baker. His most extensive role in the party's "secret work" (as it was named in clandestine party documents) was that of "Father" in the CPUSA's most organized espionage program, now referred to as the Brother-Son Network. The familial terms were the code names of the leaders of the operation, though, oddly, in a number of documents the code was broken and actual names were used for one or the others. "Son" was Rudy Baker, the actual operating head of the network. "Brother" was the ubiquitous Georgi Dimitrov, head of the Comintern. Most of the known correspondence was between Brother and Son, but a good deal was to or from both Son and Father, who was often supervisor, consultant, participant. In a 1943 report to Dimitrov, Baker explained that although for security reasons "our apparatus is kept strictly isolated from the party . . . periodically all questions are discussed and considered by son and father." He went on to describe several instances for which he turned to Browder for his final decision.[34]

Baker was an intentionally mysterious and anonymous character. He was born in Croatia, probably as Rudolph Blum. Even before he joined the American party at its formation in 1919, he had been an active revolutionary and served two short prison terms. Early in his Communist Party career he was schooled at the International Lenin School in Moscow from 1927 to 1930. The earliest indications of Baker's espionage work are from the early thirties. At that time he was referred to as both Bradford and Betford, later sometimes as Al. A 1935 letter from Browder to Dimitrov refers to Baker as "Comrade Bradford"; it informed Dimitrov that Bradford was the choice to head the Pan-Pacific Trade Union Secretariat, one of the Comintern's espionage networks for the Pacific basin.

In 1938, Baker took over as head of all the CPUSA secret work. In a January 28, 1939, report, labeled "Top Secret," that Baker wrote for Dimitrov—"On the Work of the CPUSA Secret Apparatus"—he explained that the previous control of that work had been too dangerously in the hands of the known Communist J. Peters. Comrade Browder, he diplomatically said, "was above all concerned that this work be passed on to me in such a way that my participation in the work of the special apparatus not become generally known, as had been the case with Comrade Peter." While Browder and four other party leaders knew of his appointment, he explained that he would keep his post on the CPUSA Central Control Commission, so "there is no reason for anyone to reflect or puzzle over what sort of work Baker is doing. . . . Baker's special work goes unnoticed and unknown." In the report he dealt at length with more than espionage itself. He stressed that measures were needed to safeguard the security of their own systems of collecting information. These measures included "the exposure and weeding out of enemies," improving methods of investigation and communication of data because "spies and traitors" and "espionage agencies, chiefly their Trotskyist and Lovestoneist sections, have become more sophisticated and wily." One of the measures that needed to be taken was stealing documents from Lovestone Socialist files.[35]

In this Party document, Baker went on at great length to demand the improvement of security measures against Trotskyite and Lovestoneite spies. In the course of the discussion he refers to work being done by "Communists [who have] found their way into that Commission [The La Follete Commission] through the Communist faction of Washington officials." Their work, however. was being undermined by such Trotskyite traitors as "Leech and Wicks."[36]

As Son, Baker sent yearly reports to Dimitrov, as well as communicating regularly on specific matters. In the year-end report for 1942 he talked about his coordinating activities with Cooper (Zubilin). Because of the war, international mail was too insecure, so he had begun sending material through Zubilin. "We are cooperating very closely with Cooper" and have "loaned George . . . to Cooper for auto-building work." George, he said, was an excellent auto-builder—that is, short-wave radio operator, also called a "driver." In this passage, Baker also refers to an agent code-named Merton, who has not been identified. Back in 1939, after the Nazi-Soviet Pact, Dimitrov had begun to insist on using an "automobile man." In several memos he began to demand, "It is of great importance to organize with the necessary reserves the automobile connections." Son dutifully organized what older Brother wanted, so that by 1942, he was able to report successful short-wave radio links to Party sources in South America and Canada.[37]

After the war and after this extensive activity for the CPUSA, Baker decided to return to Yugoslavia and serve international Communism through the establishment of the Communist state there. However, as the conflict developed between the Yugoslavian leader Marshall Tito and Stalin, he chose—in his own paradoxical mixture of motives and after his years of battles against deviationists—to side with Tito.

In the postwar period, even while security investigations were intensifying, the Soviets still were attempting to increase the effectiveness of their espionage operations in America. A key figure in these final, and valuable, attempts was Rudolph Abel (Vilyam Fisher). While he had been active in New York City since 1946, he was given more authority and a wider circle of agents beginning in 1948 and again in 1949. He was instrumental in bringing the Cohens back into active work until their flight to Mexico. His most important work involved nuclear physicists, including Hall and the still unidentified Aden, Serb, and Silver. As the post-Soviet Russian intelligence service concluded, "the VOLUNTEER group [Abel's group] . . . were able to guarantee the transmittal to the [Moscow] Centre of supersecret information concerning the development of the American atomic bomb." Abel continued his espionage work until he was arrested and convicted in 1957; in 1962 he was exchanged for U2 pilot Gary Powers.[38]

In response to the extent of this secret work, Klehr, Haynes, and Firsov, in their definitive *The Secret World of American Communism*, concluded, "But the Communist Party of the United States of America was also a conspiracy financed by a hostile foreign power that recruited members for clandestine work, developed an elaborate underground apparatus to collaborate with espionage services of that power."[39]

Nonetheless, much-quoted and influential Cold War historian David Caute wrote in 1977, "There is no documentation of a direct connection between the American Communist Party and espionage during the entire postwar period."[40]

And taking a different, rationalizing approach, Ellen Schrecker, with a typical New Left romanticism about a heroic progressive past: "The men and women who gave information to Moscow in the 1930s and 1940s did so for political, not pecuniary reasons. . . . It is important to realize that as Communists these people did not subscribe to traditional forms of patriotism; they were internationalists whose political allegiances transcended national boundaries. They thought they were 'building . . . a better world for the masses,' not betraying their country."[41]

But as William Phillips in *Partisan Review* saw it, "Some were Communists . . . [and spies] . . . and what one was asked to do was defend their right to lie about it."[42]

10

The Lie Deep within the Silence: The CPUSA and Obedience to the Destructive Policies of the Soviet Union

Espionage—eminently important as it was—was not the only form of the Communist Party of America's (CPUSA's) obedience. More widespread throughout the organization and its individual members and followers was obedience to the policies of the Soviet Union. An organization whose policies, strategies, and activities are strictly obedient to the policies, strategies, and goals of a foreign nation is not a normal political party. The obedience of the CPUSA and of its members to Soviet-Comintern policies and shifts of policies resulted in decades of evading, denying, and obfuscating the monstrous horrors produced by these policies, maintaining the disguise of the righteous mask. This obedience was the most morally stained illustration of the falsity of the claim implied at the hearings and loudly proclaimed subsequently that the CPUSA was merely a normal political party, that participation in it was merely normal political association.

The sharp-tongued and free-wheeling libertarian pundit Dwight McDonald captured it well in pungent form for all to see in February of 1944: "For a long time the CP has been a branch office of the parent firm in Moscow rather than an American Political Party."[1]

In relation to the Hollywood Party and its adherents, in chapter 4 we've touched briefly on the whirling merry-go-round of their overnight turnaround over the signing of the Nazi-Soviet Pact of August 23, 1939—and then the subsequent reversed turn after the German invasion of Russia. As was his wont, McDonald cut to the intellectual bone of this kind of political gymnastics: "The effect of this sort of thing on the human mind and spirit after a few years must be appalling."[2]

The shifts in this Soviet policy that the Hollywood adherents were following and rhetorically supporting were part of an organized strategy that the Soviets and Comintern had devised and passed down to all the national parties for unswerving compliance at every level of their organizations. After the signing of the pact, in September 1939, Dimitrov sent Earl Browder (along with other party leaders around the world) detailed instructions on the new policies. Dimitrov had met with Stalin on September 7 to set the exact terms of the Soviet position and resulting directives. In summation, he stated to Browder and the others, "This is a war for imperialist supremacy. [It] is a continuation of the struggle between the rich powers (England, France, the USA), which are the backbone of the entire capitalist system, and the cheated states (Germany, Italy, Japan). . . . At the present stage of the war the Communist's task is to boldly, as befits Bolsheviks, fight against the war, . . . concentrate their fire against the bourgeois dictatorship in their own countries, . . . [and] in the neutral countries (above all the United States) to expose the bourgeoisie as profiteers and marauders of war."[3]

After Nat Ross, the American party's representative at the Comintern, was given detailed instructions, he even requested further information, such as asking specifically in one document what "type of brochures the ECCI considers necessary." Given that information, he went on, "the CC would be able to decide which prominent non-communists among the intelligentsia and the trade union movement could best write such brochures for wide mass consumption and mass influence." The content of such brochures, and any other statements, was summed up in a speech by Robert Minor, Browder's chief aide, at a special antiwar conference attended by two thousand party officials, in which he quoted and paraphrased Dimitrov's instructions. Poland, he said, was a "reactionary multinational state built on the oppression of Ukranians, Belorussians, and Jews. The international proletariat has no interest in the existence of such a parasitical state." As for the Nazis, "Fascism is not the issue," for the main current evil was "British and French Imperialism." The pact was a "landmark in the struggle against war."[4]

Through the period of the pact, the *Daily Worker* regularly reiterated the terms of this policy. For example, since it was "a war between rival imperialisms for world domination, the workers must be against the war." Nonetheless, at one point the Comintern harshly criticized the paper and the party's opposition to FDR's aid to Britain for not being strong enough.[5]

During this "struggle against war," during the duration of the pact, Hitler invaded Poland on September 1 and went on to conquer Denmark, Norway, the Netherlands, Belgium, and France. Russia invaded and appropriated half of Poland, appropriated the three Baltic States—Latvia, Estonia, and Lithuania—invaded Finland, and took over ("liberated") Bessarabia and part of Romania. The Soviets even returned to Germany (for execution) German Communist refugees who had previously fled to Russia. In Poland the Soviets within one year had imprisoned more than 100,000 people and had executed at least 50,000 people. They had deported 108,000 people to the Gulag and 320,00 to exile villages in the far north and Kazakhstan, of whom a large percentage were dead by 1941. In the Baltic states, 75,000 Lithuanians; 60,000 Estonians; and 34,250 Latvians were murdered or deported. Many of those deported died, more than those who were actually executed. As the years went by, the deportations continued. By the time of Stalin's death, more than half a million people had been deported from the three Baltic states, the population of Estonia reduced by 25 percent.[6]

Thus, there were two levels of significance to the pact: (1) the agreement with Germany and (2) the Soviet invasions and subsequent purges, executions, deportations. The pact and its reasons were defended. The subsequent human violations produced by the pact were never mentioned by the American Communists, at the time or even decades later, even when some did allow some doubts about the pact itself.

Typical of this total focus on the logic of the strategic necessity—and ideological blindness to the human cost—are statements, some years later, by Hollwood party stalwarts Paul Jarrico, Lionel Stander, Allen Boretz, and Ring Lardner Jr.:

> Jarrico: "I think the Pact *made sense* [emphasis added] for the Soviet Union. The Pact was the Soviet Union double-crossing the double-crossers [i.e., England and France]. It was a brilliant coup."[7]
>
> Stander: "I was cool. I figured it was a temporary thing, which it was, and that the reason for the Pact was the inability of the democracies to line up with the Soviet Union against Hitler."[8]
>
> Boretz: "When Stalin and Hitler signed the pact, I understood. I understood it was a maneuver."[9]
>
> Lardner: "That their *occupation* [emphasis added] of Eastern Poland and Southeastern Finland were not *aggrandizing* [emphasis added] acts but necessary defensive moves."[10]

Howard Fast *did* note what he called the "movement" of people, but he saw only the usual good intentions of the Soviets as the motive. In his memoir of 1990, he proclaimed, "Russia had . . . moved three million [*sic*] Polish Jews and Ukra[i]nian Jews eastward to get them beyond the reach of the Nazis and their death camps."[11]

In 1947, Jacques Pat conducted a thorough survey of sources, records, interviews; in two articles in the Jewish *Daily Forward* he documented how four hundred thousand of the Jews who fled to the Soviet Union to escape the Germans died during deportation to or incarceration in concentration and forced labor camps.[12]

The official CPUSA position on Poland is seen in this standard *Daily Worker* editorial defense of the Soviets' actions: The "movement" of troops into "Fascist Poland" (not an invasion) was a contribution to "the cause for World Peace."[13]

The official Lillian Hellman position at the time was, as usual, similar. Maurice Zolotow recalled that she, too, argued that the move into Poland was a move for peace and particularly as a move in which "at least half the country would be saved."[14]

And then on June 22, 1941, it all whirled back. Germany invaded Russia. On April 5 the American Peace Mobilization had held an antiwar rally at Randall's Island in New York City. On June 21, it had held a "peace vigil" at the White House as the first event of a National Peace Week. Two days later, however, on June 23, it changed its name to the American People's Mobilization—"For Victory over Fascism"—and canceled National Peace Week. For Dimitrov had already informed the CPUSA that the anti-capitalist and anti-imperialist rhetoric no longer applied; further, the war was now to be seen as "neither a class war nor a war for socialist revolution." It was a "just war of defense. . . . The main task now is to exert every effort in order to secure the victory of the Soviet people and to smash the fascist barbarians." Obeying this demand, on June 28 the CPUSA published its new definitive program, "The People's Program of Struggle for the Defeat of Hitler and Hitlerism."[15]

The League of American Writers followed a similar pattern of obedience. At a congress before the pact, Hellman, Dashiell Hammett, and others of the Hollywood contingent had joined in a call for "the cooperation of this country with other nations and people opposed to Fascism, including the Soviet Union, which has been the most constant defender of the people." Then, in August of 1939, after the signing of the pact, the league had formed the "Keep America Out of War" committee—again with many of the usual Hollywood cast as members. But after the invasion of Russia, in the *Daily Worker* in July 1941, a new call by the League of American Writers was published, its signatures headed once again by Hellman and Dashiell Hammett and featuring many of the Hollywood adherents. Now it was, "A Call to all Creative Workers . . . to demand full support to Great Britain and the Soviet Union in their struggle for the demolition of Fascism."[16]

Hollywood and the CPUSA justified more than the pact with the Nazis and its bloody consequences. More appalling (to use McDonald's apt epithet)—and morally flawed—was their support of the even bloodier events of the Terror within Russia itself. The CPUSA and its organs and followers did not merely follow the Soviet line on these murderous events, did not merely evade and justify. They often cheered and called for more. Nothing is more revealing of this kind of callous indoctrination than its effect on Communist youth. In 1930, while terrible famines were being created by Soviet practices, while millions were already being arrested, executed, and deported

and the first deadly purges were underway against so-called Trotskyite traitors—while all this was erupting, the *Young Worker*, journal of the CPUSA's
Communist Youth League, was demanding, "As for those who plotted and
planned the crippling of Soviet industry and Soviet farming and planned to
have the only workers' country ruled by the lords of money again—to them
DEATH! THIS SHOULD BE THE MESSAGE OF EVERY YOUNG WORKER
TO OUR ENEMY CLASS, THE BOSSES OF THE WORLD."[17]

As the purges of deviationists, capitalist lackeys, Trotskyists, ad infinitum,
exploded exponentially through the thirties, the CPUSA not only continued to support every charge and action; it developed its own program, as
we've noted in the previous chapter, to eliminate deviationists, saboteurs,
and traitors within its own ranks and in renegade groups in the United
States. Until the Popular Front policy turned everything upside down,
Browder and the CPUSA found social Fascists everywhere on the Left and
acted against them. They even went as far as betraying them to the Soviets.
Records that they stole from Jay Lovestone's office were shipped to Moscow, with a note calling attention to the names of "certain persons in the
USSR who are mentioned in traitorous letters which discuss the trials of
the Trotskyist-Bukharin spies." One can imagine what happened to those
"certain persons."[18]

At the peak of the purges, the Moscow trials, and the Great Terror, the
American party continued its blind obedience to the Soviet version of
"truth"—as did its obedient intellectuals, artists, and writers. Browder responded to a series of Comintern directives in a 1935 speech to the leadership of the CPUSA. He stressed "the lessons that we must bring down to
the Party, to every member of the Party, to every worker, to all honest elements, to make them acutely and keenly conscious of it and transmit this
consciousness to the broad working masses in the United States." The *it* was
every single detail of the claims the Soviets were beginning to make about
the network of traitors within Russia. For example, Browder parroted, there
were already "thirty or forty assassin groups" seeking to kill Stalin. "We
cannot," he exhorted, "carry on our defense of the Soviet Union; we cannot
carry forward the struggle for the conquest of power unless we strengthen
this offensive against the Trotzkyite counter-revolutionary ideology, which
is the spear-head of counter-revolution."[19]

As the trials began in earnest in 1936, the Comintern sent a coded cable
detailing exactly the line and details the CPUSA was to promulgate about
the traitors being tried: "picture huge crime of these mean degenerates" who
"made terror . . . the chief method of their counter-revolutionary activity."
The cable listed alleged instructions that had been discovered that called
for "a series of other terroristic actions against leaders of CPSU and Soviet
State, in first place against comrade Stalin . . . established direct connections with the fascist Gestapo. . . . Necessary now to secure full liquidation

of Trotzkyism." Further cables provided more materials for propaganda outlets, stressing in one that "Writing articles on Trotskyism should be entrusted only to most verified and politically qualified authors." A later cable ordered Browder to make sure that the *Daily Worker* made space available for broad coverage of the trial of Karl Radek and his "bloc" in 1937, with specific instructions of what to stress in articles and editorials, with such choice phrases as "a band of wreckers, revisionists, spies, allies of German Gestapo." One set of materials provided actual manuscripts for pamphlets defending the trials.[20]

Browder and the CPUSA worked hard at carrying out the orders, yet they were criticized by the Comintern for not being effective enough. In response Sam Darcy, the CPUSA representative to the Comintern, wrote a defense of the efforts of the *Daily Worker*. He cited publication of such notable articles as "Kamenev Admits Group Had No Mass Base; Terror Only Hope"; "Trotsky Spurned by Masses, Uses Nazi Aid Against USSR"; "Trotsky Gave Orders to Kill Stalin, Kirov, Say Plotters"; "Terrorist Plot by Trotskyists Bared in the USSR; Directed from Abroad by Trotsky to Kill Soviet Leaders"; "People Hail Sentence of Plotters." Facing continuing complaints, Browder in 1937 provided forty-two pages of testimony to the Comintern central secretariat detailing the difficulties they had to face and the extensive measures constantly being taken to carry out their struggle to support and defend the trials and purges. He cites the success of creating a group of eighty-eight "outstanding public figures" (including some of the usual writers) who issued an "Open Letter to American Liberals" in which "they reaffirmed their faith in the Soviet Union" and "condemned this Committee for the Defense of Trotsky." Still, the criticism continued. Often American Communists joined in, complaining to their Comintern representative about the slightest deviations in doctrine in various Party organs, including the *Morning Freiheit*, the party's Yiddish-language newspaper.[21]

The party and its press struggled on to be worthy promoters of the Soviets' horrifying fantasy of necessary terror and liquidation of enemies of the people, whether in small groups of leaders or masses of workers, farmers, and their families. Its "loyal intellectuals" followed their lead. The "open letter" that Browder referred to was published in *New Masses*, February 1, 1937, and *Soviet Russia Today*, March 1937. The letter affirmed the validity of the verdicts and sentences imposed on the "defendants in the trials under attack [who] all confessed fully the crimes of high treason of which they were convicted." The trials "were properly conducted and the accused fairly and judicially treated." After several years of such articles and petitions, an April 28, 1938, article in the *Daily Worker* reported on a petition by the usual artists, writers, and intellectuals (many in Hollywood), with the headline "Leading Artists, Educators Support Soviet Trial Verdict." The petition appeared as an article in *Soviet Russia Today*, May 1938. The writers called on "American Progressives" to support Russian efforts to "eliminate insidious internal dangers." In attacking "The Trotskyite-Bukharinite Traitors," the petition creators supported the CPUSA position that the trials and executions prevented "the fascists from strangling the rights of the people." Among the signers were Lillian Hellman, Lionel Stander, Dashiell Hammett, John Howard Lawson, Dorothy Parker, Lester Cole, Guy Endore, Albert Maltz, Samuel Ornitz, Marc Blitzstein, Irwin Shaw, Langston Hughes, Richard Wright, Morris Carnovsky, and John Garfield. Most of the same had signed the previous letter, as had such regulars as Ring Lardner Jr., Lewis Milestone, Dudley Nichols, Donald Ogden Stewart, Nathanael West, and Theodore Dreiser.[22]

The "necessary steps" to eliminate enemies of the people included such enormities as these examples of terror and liquidation:

In one study of documents concerning the direct actions of the NKVD alone, it has been determined that "during 1937 and 1938 1,575,000 were arrested by the NKVD. Of these, 1,345,000 (85.4%) received some sort of sentence and 681,692 (51% of those who were sentenced) were executed." This study did not include actions of other services or of the results of deportations.

As Stalin told the leaders of the NKVD, "Mount your prisoners and do not dismount until they have confessed."[23]

A former Soviet chief historian, Dimitri Volkogonov, has used other archives as well as those of the NKVD to arrive at the broader picture of the results of all phases of the massive oppression. He has determined that "between 1937 and 1939 from five to five and a half million people had been arrested. Not less than a third of them had been shot, and many of the rest died in the camps." For a close-up, Volkogonov cites as an example: on one day, December 12, 1938, Stalin and Vladimir Molotov personally sanctioned the shooting of 3,167 people.[24]

For a direct parallel to the lives of the Hollywood and American intellectuals (and especially members of the Screen Writers Guild) who defended the Terror: In addition to all kinds of other artists and intellectuals, more than two thousand members of the Soviet writers' Union were arrested, then deported to camps or executed. They actually fared better than clergy, who were by official directive fated for "complete liquidation."[25]

In the period before World War II, forced collectivization and institutionalized forced famine (and related deportations and executions) produced the largest number of deaths—6 to 7 million. Some 5 million of those were in the Ukraine, 2 million of those accused as kulaks, supposed counterrevolutionary bourgeois farm owners and exploiters. There were, in addition, mass deportations from all farm areas: by 1937, 5.7 million households, about 15 million people.[26]

Vladimir Molotov created the detailed plan for the destruction of the kulaks. He outlined three categories: "First category . . . to be immediately eliminated." The second, to be imprisoned in camps; the third, 150,000 households, to be deported. Molotov organized the death squads, railway transport, concentration camps for this destruction.[27]

Forced labor included many more people than kulaks. Through the Soviet period, there were an estimated 28,700,000 "forced laborers." Some key examples follow:

- In the Gulag network of camps: 7 to 8 million passed through by 1940, 18 million by 1953
- In camps of "forced labor without incarceration": 700,000
- At camps in Siberia for "special exiles": 6,015,000
- Total deaths in the Gulag and exile villages: 2,749,163 (This estimate is considered low. It uses various official camp statistics, but cannot account for mass executions, deaths during transport or interrogations, etc.)[28]

The Terror continued throughout World War II; liquidation of class enemies and mass deportations continued in the Soviet Union: in the Gulag camps, 620,386 died between 1941 and 1943. Mass executions and deportations of "dangerous" civilians accelerated as areas were conquered or reconquered during the war: For example, in 1943 alone, Lavrenti Beria supervised the arrest of 931,544 people in liberated territories. In 1944, 500,000 were deported from Chechen and Ingush. Another 300,000 were removed from areas near the Volga, 160,000 from the Crimea. Beria at one point reported to Stalin that 1.5 million had been removed. More than 500,000 died en route or on arrival at camps. Another set of NKVD records reported 145,000 imprisoned after deportations, tens of thousands executed, 340,000 deported to exile villages, 108,000 sent to the Gulag. There were also mass executions of German prisoners of war, estimated at 1 million deaths. As late as March 1947, 892,532 Germans were still in camps.[29]

In response to this monumental destruction, writers at the time and later followed the party line in various ways.

Denial, often accompanied by extreme factual distortions, was maintained, no matter what information was available, as exemplified by the following:

- John Howard Lawson: "The only truly conscious anti-fascist force during the war years was the Communist Party."
- An open letter: Issued by the "Committee of 400" and created by the American Soviet Friendship Committee, this letter was printed in the *Daily Worker* and other leftist publications. Among the 165 names actually affixed were those of Donald Ogden Stewart, I. F. Stone, Max Lerner, Wright, Hammett, Hellman, Vincent Sheean, Clifford Odets, and others. A key claim was that "the Soviet Union considers political

dictatorship a transitional form and has shown a steadily expanding democracy in every sphere."

- Ring Lardner Jr.: "The best hope for mankind lay in the Soviets. Only in Russia were massive construction and planning for the future going on."
- Abraham Polonsky: "The best vehicle for bringing about the socialist transformation of society."
- Maurice Rapf, while director of Film Studies at Dartmouth: "As far as all the revelations about the atrocities that took place in the Soviet Union—the so-called expose of Stalin—by the time it began I was no longer a member of the Party anyway, and I don't believe half of it, either."
- Paul Robeson: "As far as I know, about the slave camps, they were fascist prisoners who had murdered millions of the Jewish people and who would have wiped out millions of the Negro people, could they have gotten a hold of them."[30]

Euphemism and obfuscation served many well for many years as they evaded the horrors of the human reality while, at least to themselves, seeming to face some facts—as in Ring Lardner's comment about the "moral and social *rigidity*" (emphasis added) under Stalin's rule. Other examples:

- Pete Seeger: "Stalin [was a] hard driver. . . . There was an awful lot of rough stuff."
- Lillian Hellman: "I thought that in the end Russia, having achieved a state socialism, would stop its *infringements* [emphasis added] on personal liberty."
- Allen Boretz, on the trials: "I would rather they had not taken place."
- A Left historian, James Weinstein, may have topped them all: "The Soviet and Maoist regimes did *discard* [emphasis added] their native capitalists."[31]

Or there was just the plain *self-blinding illusion* of untarnished righteousness:

- Jules Dassin: "I don't see that the ideas we tried to present were wrong. And the intentions were, as far as I'm concerned, always pure."
- Ring Lardner Jr.: When looking back, he admitted, "I was deluding myself on a number of *points* [emphasis added]," but he still insisted "nor am I admitting my mistakes with any sense of guilt or remorse"—since those "mistakes" were the result of mere "theoretical delusions."
- Dalton Trumbo: "They [American Communists] openly express keen interest in and sympathy with the aspirations of the Soviet Union,

which was the first country to embrace socialism. In this feeling they differ very little from republicans throughout the world who hailed the American Revolution of 1776 as the beginning of a new era in human affairs."[32]

In his major revision of his seminal study *The Great Terror,* Robert Conquest comments on such statements as this: "In fact, those who 'swallowed' the trials can hardly be acquitted of a certain degree of complicity in the continuation and exacerbation of the torture and execution of innocent men." He goes on to point out that in the broad context, what was concealed was "the existence and extent of the mass slaughter and imprisonment."[33]

In the postwar period before the hearings, the "Duclos letter" produced one of the most direct and important instances of instant obedience by the party and its individual members to a Moscow directive. The Duclos letter of April 1945, the most significant of all open letters, as is now known, was written in Moscow in Russian, sent to Paris, and translated and published with the name of the French Communist Maurice Duclos. It called on Communist parties everywhere to assist in the defense of the Soviet Union by taking more adversarial stances toward imperialist governments after the necessary maneuvers of a Popular Front against the Nazis and the partnerships called for by the circumstances of World War II. It can be seen now as a harbinger of the Soviet shift to increased aggressiveness, as was delineated by Zhdanov at the meeting that created the Cominform in 1947. As Earl Browder himself said years later, the Duclos letter was "the first public declaration of the Cold War."[34]

Browder and his programs were the chief victims in the United States of the letter's demands. Duclos denounced Browder's "erroneous conclusions" of accommodation and moderation. In short, "his notorious revision of Marxism" had led to "liquidation of the independent political party of the working class." He, it was clearly implied, and his mistakes must go. By June he was ousted and denounced, even by his protégé, Eugene Dennis, the new leader of the CPUSA. As the *Nation* now said, in affirming the shift—and betraying Browder, "The attitude of the American Communist Party has been such a travesty on a working-class program that to maintain it after the fighting ended would have meant certain political suicide."[35]

Hollywood Reds joined the attack and in the shift to a hard line:

- John Bright: "From a theoretical standpoint, I looked upon it [the Browder period] as backsliding, as a betrayal, really, of revolutionary purposes."
- Michael Wilson, supporting the new line and its attacks on the Marshall Plan: "I came back from the war tough and angry. I was always intolerant of the Browder period."

- Ring Lardner Jr.: He reported how he was "flattered" and convinced when William Z. Foster came to Hollywood to explain the necessity of the shift from Browderism in a series of meetings.[36]

In his testimony of 1953, Robert Rossen saw it quite differently:

Well, now if anybody wanted any manifestation of the bankruptcy, of the Communist Party thinking . . . you had the Duclos letter. . . .

Now, suddenly a letter appeared in France by Duclos. The very people that we had been led to believe for years were the paragons of wisdom, the people in whom all Marxism reposed and could answer all the questions now had been wrong for their whole existence in the party.[37]

Another important illustration of Soviet domination of the positions and actions of the CPUSA—and in turn the members and followers of it—is seen in the creation and support of activity in related organizations, committees, and conferences. In this postwar period, the aggressiveness of the new Soviet policy, the acts of aggression in countries of Eastern Europe, the intensification of purges and terror in satellite nations and again within the Soviet Union—all of this needed, and received, the typical mask of "progressive" campaigns. Chief among these was the worldwide "peace" campaign. It was so extensive, and so successful not only among the usual "intellectuals" but within the general public that even Willi Munzenberg would be ashamed of the pettiness of his own "peace" campaign in the thirties—if he hadn't been assassinated.

The campaign was carried out in great part by the Munzenberg technique of creating broad-based (and Communist-dominated) organizations, committees, conferences, rallies, petitions, and so on. In America these were often called Communist fronts, which has become a term that supposedly exposes the falseness and injustices of anti-Communist investigations into innocent, idealistic organizations and their members. In most instances, such as the peace crusade, the term was far from inaccurate.

The exact thrust of this campaign coupled the traditionally revered ideal of peace with the new danger and fear of atomic warfare. It consistently associated, and directly correlated, *peace* with two complementary messages: defense of the "peaceful" policies and actions of the Soviet Union and attack on the "aggressive" intentions and policies of the United States, including such imperialist aggressions as the Marshall Plan, the Truman Doctrine, NATO, the Berlin Airlift, and so on.

In America the crowning event was the Waldorf Conference for World Peace—in official Comintern terminology, the Cultural and Scientific Conference for Peace. It was held in March 1949—for Hollywood Reds almost exactly halfway between the first congressional hearings of 1947 and the second round in 1951. Though it was a time of pending legal appeals, a slowly developing blacklist, debate and turmoil over careers and loyalties and moralities, many in Hollywood found the time (and were indeed exhilarated by the call to a new major crusade) to join other CPUSA comrades in support of the event and promotion of its cause. The first call was issued in the *Daily Worker* of January 10, 1949, followed on March 8 by an article with full details on the upcoming conference. Joseph Losey (who during the war had staged mass rallies for Russian War Relief), Hellman, and Lawson were on its organizing committee. Hellman and Lawson, along with Clifford Odets and composer Aaron Copland, were among the featured speakers. Copland had recently completed his beautiful score for the film *The Heiress* (1949) and his oft-heard *Fanfare for the Common Man*. Among the organizers, sponsors, signers of invitations, open letters, and calls were what was probably the largest number of Hollywood leftists ever assembled for a single event, including Albert Maltz, Budd Schulberg, Arthur Miller, E. Y. Harburg, Donald Ogden Stewart, Ring Lardner Jr., Dalton Trumbo, Clifford Odets, Paul Robeson, Howard Fast, Charles Chaplin, Jules Dassin, Edward Dmytryk, Dorothy Parker, Lester Cole, Martin Ritt, Gale Sondergaard, and others.[38]

Enthusiastically and widely praised as the supposed result of a spontaneous groundswell of the desire for peace, the Waldorf Conference was in reality one stage of an organized and elaborately orchestrated Soviet campaign.

The concept was first developed at a conference of the Cominform (the successor to the Comintern) in September 1947. The Cominform called for a program to "appeal to men of letters, men of art, culture and science" to promote the Soviet foreign policy for "peace" and "to awaken the people of Europe and the world to the growing danger of a new world war, as a consequence of the ruthless expansionist drive of American big business." The phrasing was a perfect example of the propagandic mask: Attack ruthless expansion to draw attention away from ruthless expansion.[39]

The first implementation of the concept, within several months, was an open letter by twelve Soviet writers, with variations directed at the "intellectuals" of particular nations. In the American version: "We call upon you [writers and artists], masters of American culture, to raise your voice against the threat of fascism, against the instigators of war." The open letter was widely promoted by the CPUSA. In May 1948 *Masses and Mainstream* (successor to *New Masses*) used it as the basis for a call for the development of a new united front against war and Fascism and for the first direct promotion of the American event.[40]

The next major international step was a pair of conferences, the Wroclaw (also known as Breslau) Congress of Cultural Workers in Defense of Peace in August 1948 and the World Conference of the Democratic Women's

Federation in Budapest in September. The Wroclaw, Poland, Conference, also known as the World Congress of Intellectuals for Peace, was the crucial meeting during which future conferences were planned and integrated. Some thirty Americans attended this Congress, including Donald Ogden Stewart, Howard Fast, Albert E. Kahn, and physicist Harlow Shapley, a typical "inveterate" participant in Communist campaigns who was a central organizer and manager of the Waldorf Conference. Ella Winter, still active, mainly in Europe, was an officer at these two conferences. In his memoir, Fast insisted, "The Russians had no part in it."[41]

The Waldorf Conference was the prime-time "opening night" of a whole series of publicized, allegedly public-instigated conferences. A thorough HUAC report of April 19, 1949, despite the bias of its rhetoric, was accurate in defining the purpose of the conference and describing the event as a "supermobilization of the inveterate wheel horses and supporters of the Communist Party and its auxiliary organizations." As Philip Rahv wrote in *Partisan Review* (a Socialist-oriented journal at the time), at the conference the CPUSA would not "tolerate the active participation of anyone who is not ready to defend every policy of Stalin." His criticism was echoed by Sidney Hook and others, especially those affiliated with the liberal anti-Communist organization, the Committee for Cultural Freedom. The committee set up a counter-conference and issued a counterstatement, written principally by Hook and James T. Farrell, that the meetings "revealed the directing hand of the Cominform" and emphasized as "especially disgraceful" the attempt "to convince European public opinion that a Hitlerian regime exists in our country." In his review of the events in his memoir, Hook pointed out that "not a single person openly critical of Soviet foreign policy or of the Communist Party line in any field of the art[s] and sciences had been invited."[42]

When *Saturday Review of Literature* editor Norman Cousins attempted to criticize the totally slanted program at a session of the conference, he was booed and then chastened, to great applause, by vice chairman Hellman, "I would recommend, Mr. Cousins, that when you are invited out to dinner you wait until you get home before you talk about your hosts." (It is a quote repeated with admiration for its wit in many books and articles since.)[43]

Harvard historian Nathan Glazer, in an essay on Hellman's memoir *Scoundrel Time*, had this to say about the conference and Hellman's participation: "I thought then—and I think now—that the defense of freedom required one to expose the Communist organizers of this meeting, required one to demonstrate the obscenity of speaking of world peace under the auspices of a movement whose leaders ran a huge system of slave camps for dissenters, who extirpated even the most modest efforts at independence of mind, who just about then were executing the leading Jewish poets and writers of Russia (even though these poets and writers had served them well). What was Lillian Hellman doing in that company?"[44]

The speech of Aaron Copland, entitled "Effect of the Cold War on the Artist in the U.S.," was the perfect, and sad, symptom of what Cousins, Glazer, and the others were protesting about. A supporter of Communist causes since his youth, Copland said, "I came here this morning because I am convinced that the present policies of our government, relentlessly pursued, will lead us inevitably into a third world war." When he went on to ask the Soviet Union to allow more musical exchange with the United States, he nonetheless blamed the United States because of "the determinedly unfriendly attitude of the Western powers to the Soviet Union. . . . To cut ourselves off from each other is exactly what the proponents [i.e., American proponents] of the cold war would like."[45]

The controversial Soviet composer Dimitri Shostakovich, revered by the American Left for his patriotic wartime symphonies, also spoke at the conference. At the time, during the Zhdanov crackdown on artistic "formalism," Shostakovich's work had suddenly disappeared from the Soviet music scene. Knowing the anti-American basis of the conference, Stalin himself instructed Shostakovich to attend the Waldorf event and agreed to end the ban on his music, which he also told Shostakovich didn't really exist anyway. At the conference, Shostakovich began the speech that had been written for him, calling on "progressive Americans" to oppose the anti-Communist "warmongers." But after stammering out a few sentences, he had to give the speech to the interpreter to finish reading it aloud. Novelist Vladimir Nabokov, who had managed to procure an invitation to the event, wrote, "I sat in my seat petrified by this spectacle of human misery and degradation. . . . This speech of his, this whole 'peacemaking' mission, was part of a punishment, part of a ritual redemption he had to go through before he could be pardoned. He was forced to tell, in person, to all the dupes at the Waldorf conference and to the whole decadent bourgeois world that loved him so much that he, Shostakovich, the famous Russian composer, is not a free man, but an obedient tool of his government." Years later, Shostakovich admitted to a friend and potential biographer that he would have done, said, or signed anything to be able to continue composing, and having his works performed. "I've been a whore, I am and will always be a whore."[46]

The Waldorf Conference was followed in April by the World Conference of Partisans for Peace in Paris (with many of the same Hollywood players listed as sponsors) and a parallel World Peace Congress in Prague. Through the rest of 1949 there were the Congress of the Peoples for Peace in Vienna and one in Rome; the Soviet Peace Congress in Moscow; the American Continental Congress for Peace in Mexico City (with the usual

Hollywood sponsors); and Peace on Earth, a satellite rally in Central Park held in conjunction with the Vienna Congress. At the 1949 Cominform Congress, Soviet delegate Suslov praised these developments, but called for particular attention to be paid "to drawing into the peace movement trade-unions, women's, youth, cooperative, sports, cultural, education, religious and other organizations."[47]

The "suggestion" was brilliantly achieved with the World Peace Conference in Stockholm in March 1950, sponsored, it was claimed, by the Democratic Committee of the World Congress of Partisans for Peace. Its subsequent Stockholm Peace Initiative, Stockholm Peace Appeal, and Stockholm Peace Petition garnered millions of signers. In the United States the CPUSA organized the Sponsoring Committee for the World Peace Appeal. Their chief implementation was the American Peace Crusade (APC), whose office was listed at 1186 Broadway, New York City, the headquarters of the CPUSA. Among their exhortations to the faithful was this official proclamation: "The Communist Party therefore calls on every single one of its members to turn his and her entire activity to this single, gigantic peace effort." The APC spawned hundreds of groups; it obtained more than 2 million signatures in the United States alone for the so-called Stockholm Peace Petition. To promote the petition, at rallies Pete Seeger performed a reworking of a thirties labor organizing song that he composed:

> Put my name down, brother, where do I sign,
> I'm going to join the fight for peace, right down the line.[48]

With Picasso's Dove of Peace as its symbol, this was arguably the most successful mass public relations campaign ever. Still, while it was broadly noted that there had been 273,470,566 signers of the petition, little note was made of the fact that 80 percent of the signers—235,000,000—were from Communist-dominated countries. Picasso's contribution was not his only work dedicated to the anti-American peace crusade. He created a number of paintings and posters, including a devastatingly brutal depiction in 1951 of a phalanx of surrealistic robot-like American soldiers attacking nude innocent women and children in "Man Slaughter in Korea."[49]

The Stockholm campaign stressed the danger of atomic warfare and called for the outlawing of all atomic weapons. This strategy was conceived and implemented because at that time the Soviets feared their nuclear inferiority. In 1953, when the Soviets had been able to detonate their own thermonuclear device, they abruptly suspended the Stockholm Peace Appeal.

Spin-off organizations had continued their activities on into the fifties. There were, among others, a Second World Peace Conference in Warsaw, the Soviet Peace Society in Moscow, the Peiping Peace Conference, the American Peace Crusade, Mid-Century Conference for Peace in Chicago, and Minute Women for Peace. During the Korean War, in a speech and then a public letter to and on behalf of the American Peace Crusade, reprinted in the *Daily Worker*, its codirector Willard Uphaus called for the United States to cease its "aggression" against the Korean people. "Why should we, with our tradition of 1776, frustrate normal revolution in the world with our money?"[50]

Czeslaw Milosz eloquently summed up the kind of betrayal—not only of truth but of countless human beings—that these intellectuals and artists committed in "A Letter to Picasso": "I need hardly tell you what your name, quite appropriately annexed by the Stalinists, has been used to cover up. . . . In fact your weight added to the balance and deprived of all hope those in the East who did not want to submit to the absurd. . . . What would have been the consequence of a categorical protest voiced by all of you."[51]

In this postwar period, celebrities like Picasso and campaigns like the peace crusade served to mask the continuation of Communist terror, this time in East European satellites as well as within Russia itself:

- In 1953 there were more prisoners in the Gulag network of concentration camps than ever before: 2,561,351. (It should be noted that Gulag totals at any given time are based on those still recorded as living *after* hundreds of thousands have died.)
- There were nearly as many people in "special exile" villages.
- In the harshest regions of the country there were 210,000 in new "special" camps for political suspects.
- Of the Germans living in the Soviet Union, 1.2 million were deported to camps.
- Throughout Eastern Europe, and under Soviet control, an estimated 1 million Titoists, Trotskyists, and other enemies of the people were killed in purges, deportations, executions, and imprisonments. A sampling in individual countries:

  - In Bulgaria, "people's tribunals" had sentenced 10,897 people in 1945, 2,138 of them to death. In the next two years a general purge had led to close to 40,000 arrests. New purge trials were initiated in 1949.
  - In Hungary, under the control of the Red Army, by 1947 the former leaders of the country were arrested, imprisoned, and some executed. The chief democratic spokesman, Bela Kovacs, was arrested and incarcerated in a prison in Russia for ten years. In purges in 1948, former Communist hero Lazlo Rajk and several colleagues were tortured and executed. In 1949 there were further extensive purges within the party, leading to months of torture, confessions, and executions. After trials from 1949 to 1953, several hundred thousand were imprisoned and executed.

○ In Poland, before the controlled elections of 1947, 37,000 "dissidents" were arrested. Purge trials began in 1949. In 1952 alone, 21,000 were tried, including 2,500 juveniles. By 1952 there were security files on 5.2 million people, half of the population.[52]

Among the faithful, none of this seemed to matter.

In his brief appearance before the HUAC in September of 1951, Michael Wilson played the peace chord again and again—insisting it was the committee and America that were endangering the peace of the world.

Peace is a word of purity that I have seen this committee try to defile. . . .

Because it is my opinion, sir, that the committee is beating the drums of War. . . . If the profits were taken out of war.[53]

From the late fifties on, Dalton Trumbo had misgivings about the Soviet Union and the CPUSA and engaged in several disputes over what he considered censorship within the party. But in public he did not pronounce these misgivings with his usual flair and verbal fireworks. These thoughts were intra-party, among friends and tender comrades (to use the title of his script about wartime romance in Washington, adopted for other meanings by Patrick McGilligan and Paul Buhle). Nevertheless, in a letter to Albert Maltz in 1972, he defined what he did righteously still see as the "cost" of being a Communist, the real problem of the organization they supported: "Whatever may be said of Communists and the goals they pursued, [all] were animated by a sincere desire to change the world and make it better, even at the cost of affiliating with an organization that had, from its beginnings, been subject to constant government harassment, popular hatred, and sometimes physical violence."[54]

And what did Wilson believe the period taught the blacklisted Communists? "Many of us grew during this period. . . . We attained a more abiding and profound humanism, a greater compassion."[55]

Paul Robeson, on Moscow: "Yes, the Communists march at the front of the struggle for stable peace and popular democracy." Whereas, on the other hand, he told the members of the HUAC, "You are responsible, and your for[e]bears, for sixty million to one hundred million black people dying in the slave ships and on the plantations."[56]

On *60 Minutes*, Lillian Hellman was asked why she was so critical of the United States and yet had never criticized Russia. In her response she said, "I don't really see what one thing has to do with another. I was not a Russian, I was an American."[57]

11

Testimony and Silence: Jews, Free Speech, and the Degrees of Betrayal

In the testimony at the first hearings, two of the major motifs orchestrated within the overall strategy of the party are particularly revealing in juxtaposing the claims of the Ten with the realities of the world of Communism, in exposing the lies within the silence.

These motifs focused on Jews and other minorities, but especially Jews; and, most importantly, freedom of speech and censorship. These were the most impassioned, emotionally vehement, and likely most personally felt of their themes, within the ideological armor that insulated them from the painful contrasts between what they were saying and the real-life contemporary violations on a devastating scale of both Jews and free speech in the Soviet world.

The position taken by a number of the Ten was that the hearings were a part of a pogrom—an attack on Jews and other minorities in the United States. Among these was Adrian Scott, who was probably the least hostile and dogmatic of the witnesses. He believed he had been called among the first Ten for one reason, that his recent film *Crossfire* (1947) had been, at least in part, an attack on anti-Semitism and that the ranking members of the HUAC (House Un-American Activities Committee) were anti-Semitic. Scott's written statement, which he was not allowed to read, was entirely devoted to his and the Nineteen's fight against persecution and the committee's complicity in maintaining and promoting it.

> I wish to speak now about another war. I would like to speak about the "cold war" being waged by the Committee of [*sic*] Un-American Activities against the Jewish and Negro people. . . .

The next phase—total war against minorities—needs no elaboration. History has recorded what has happened in Nazi Germany.[1]

Edward Dmytryk, the director of *Crossfire* (Scott was the producer), touched on more of the usual topics in his prepared statement, but he began by tying suppression of minorities with suppression of freedoms and returned to that correlation several times.

> The dark periods in our history have been those in which our freedoms have been suppressed, to however small a degree . . . that darkness exists into the present day in the continued suppression of minorities. . . .
>
> Is a Committee member anti-Semitic? He will force the producers to blacklist men who deplore anti-Semitism.[2]

It was no surprise that Samuel Ornitz, always so intensely concerned about matters that he felt affected the Jews, was the most emotional and accusatory in his written statement.

> I wish to address this Committee as a Jew, because one of its leading members is the outstanding anti-Semite in the Congress and revels in this fact. . . . I refer to this evil because it has been responsible for the systematic and ruthless slaughter of six million of my people. . . . It may be redundant to repeat that anti-Semitism and anti-Communism were the number one poison weapon used by Hitler. . . .
>
> For when Constitutional guarantees are over-ridden, the Jew is the first one to suffer . . . but only the first one. As soon as the Jew is crushed, the others get it. . . .
>
> Nor did this evil die with Hitler. . . .
>
> I must not fail—nor for one moment falter before the threat of contempt, which word sounds like the short way of saying concentration camp.[3]

However deep and sincere the feelings about the "plight" of Jews in America that underlay Ornitz's ideological hyperbole, there is something bitterly ironic and painfully sad in this blinded, blinkered passion. Until his death in 1957, this man who was so deeply and actively concerned with the plight of the Jews denied and continued to deny the real and actually destructive attacks on Jews in Soviet Russia.

The official Soviet campaign of suppression of the Jews in 1947—the year of these tirades about American pogroms—was not the first instance of anti-Semitism in Russia. Despite the large number of Jews in the movement, actions against Jews were entwined with the terror against the kulaks in the late twenties and early thirties, and with the terror and purges of Trotskyists and others in the thirties. The oppression and killing continued with Molotov's further attack on Jews in the party apparatus in 1939, the execution and deportation of Poles after the invasion of Poland, and the wholesale deportations during World War II. In one ironic instance, in 1944, Nikita Khrushchev, then czar of the Ukraine, had refused to allow Jews who had been imprisoned by the Nazis to regain their homes, farms, and businesses. He complained that these "Abramoviches" were preying on his land "like crows." It was Lavrenti Beria who intervened with Stalin, for whatever unfathomable reason besides competition with Khrushchev, and Stalin ordered Khrushchev to desist.[4]

After the war, the new major campaign started with the purging of the alleged excess of Jews in the *apparat*. Andrei Zhdanov complained it was getting to be "some kind of synagogue," and his chief aide in ideological purification, Mikhail Suslov, an ardent anti-Semite, was quick to start to remedy the situation.[5]

The two major thrusts, however, were against Jewish cultural leaders and Zionists—who were seen as well as agents of the United States. Although for a combination of strategic motives, Stalin had recognized the new state of Israel, his long-nurtured anti-Semitism became obsessive in the late forties, early fifties. During a crisis at the Stalin Automobile Plant, Stalin told Khrushchev, "The good workers at the factory should be given clubs so they can beat the hell out of those Jews at the end of a working day." Two Jewish journalists who had written about the factory were executed, as being complicit in an "anti-Soviet Jewish nationalistic sabotage group." Khrushchev, duplicitous as usual, later commented that anti-Semitism now "grew like a tumor in Stalin's mind," yet he supported the new campaign and explained the necessity of it in *Pravda*. Zhdanov's new cultural terror (known as Zhdanovschina) was particularly harsh on Jewish writers, actors, artists because they were also suspected Zionists. In the fall of 1947, at the very time of the hearings, Stalin ordered Victor Abakunov, the new chief of security, to join the hunt for "every Jew [who] is a nationalist and agent of American intelligence." Abakunov's department widened the spread of arrests and torture of Jews.[6]

On November 21, 1947, less than a month after Ornitz's impassioned attack before the HUAC on the dangers of vicious *American* anti-Semitism, Stalin personally ordered Abakunov to murder the leading Jewish intellectual in Russia, Solomon Mikhoels, who had long acted as chief liaison between the Jewish community and the government. Mikhoels was injected with a poison, battered on the head, and shot. His body and that of his companion were then run over with a truck and left in the snow.[7]

The pogrom continued with more purges, arrests, torture, executions, and a formal Jewish case prepared for a public show trial. One program was a series of attacks on Jewish intellectuals for being "cosmopolitan." In February 1949, *Pravda* asked, "What vision can a Gurvich or a Yusovsky possibly have of the national character of Russian Soviet man?" At one point Soviet records show 110 Jewish prisoners undergoing interrogation in the Lubianka. The torturer, V. I. Komarov, later boasted, "I was merciless with them. I tore their souls apart. . . . I was especially pitiless with (and I hated the most) the Jewish nationalists."[8]

By 1950 the original Jewish Case was closed without a trial, but with no prisoners released and no tortures banned. Instead proceedings were instituted against the Jewish Anti-Fascist Committee and its leaders, while thousands of Jews were purged from the government and government industries. Leaders of the committee were imprisoned in 1950, but not brought to trial until 1952. There were 125 sentences—25 to death "immediately," and 100 to the camps.[9]

In 1950 the first Jewish doctor was arrested, and the final spasm began—the so-called Doctors' Plot to assassinate Stalin and other leaders. The doctor, Professor Yakov Etinger, was tortured so intensely that he died. The arrests of doctors continued into 1952, to be joined by new arrests of Jewish poets and former government officials. In one group, thirteen were executed. On September 8 Stalin gave explicit orders to the chief torturer, "Midget" Riumin, to torture the doctors until they had confessed to killing several Soviet officials, including Zhdanov, who had died of natural causes due to extreme alcoholism.[10]

After several years of unreported terror, the Doctors' Plot was finally made public and official with an article in *Pravda* on January 13, 1953, headlined, "Ignoble Spies and Killers under the Mask of Professor-Doctors." This set off another wave of anti-Semitism throughout Russia. The final stage—never consummated—was to be a program of "voluntary-compulsory eviction of Jews." New concentration camps were being built for the "evicted" Jews.[11]

By 1951—the year of the second extensive set of hearings in Hollywood—the purge of Jews had spread into the Soviet-controlled states of Eastern Europe. That summer, for example, fourteen thousand Jews were deported from Budapest, Hungary, to "labor camps" in the provinces. In the purges within the Communist parties of the Soviet bloc countries, many of those purged were Jews in the oft-repeated "struggle against Zionism and Zionists." The most important of these trials was the Slansky trial in Czechoslovakia in 1952 of Rudolf Slansky and his "Trotskyite, Titoist, Zionist terrorist group."[12]

After Stalin's death, Khrushchev explained to a group of Polish Communists why the purging of the Jews was necessary. "We all know Jews; they all have some connection to the capitalist world because they all have relatives living abroad. . . . Through their connections, the Jews had created a network to carry out American plans."[13]

The wild savagery may have lessened, but the persecution continued. At the time of Stalin's death, there were still 450 synagogues in Soviet Russia;

by 1963 there were only 96. KGB spies were planted in congregations, and religious schools and seminaries were closed, as were Hebrew-speaking theaters. Jews were still being accused of sabotaging the economy, some executed after public "economic trials."

Trumbo, as on all subjects, had his say on the status of Jews in the ideal Soviet state. In criticizing the arguments of anti-Communist New Liberals during the Cold War, he announced, "They must equate 6,000,000 Jews burned and gassed and tortured to death in the territories of Nazi Germany with 3,500,000 Jews living in the Soviet Union under the protection of laws which ban discrimination of any kind."[14]

In contrast, in the spring of 1964, Joseph Birnbaum, after a longtime commitment to Soviet Jewry, founded the Student Struggle for Soviet Jewry. In his speech at the founding meeting, distributed afterward as a pamphlet, Birnbaum said, "So must we come to feel in ourselves the silent, strangulated pain of so many of our Russian brethren. . . . We who condemn silence and inaction during the Nazi Holocaust, dare we keep silent now?"[15]

At the first hearings in 1947, the claim of the beginning of the alleged assault on the Jews of America was frequently interlaced with the theme of the HUAC's attack on freedom of speech and the Ten's defense of it. This theme, in turn, was related to the theme of an attack on the right of political association.

In his prepared statement, Trumbo used four variations on freedom of expression within his first paragraph. Then in his peroration he wrote, "The Committee throughout its hearing has approved even the grossest attacks upon the right of the artist to express his ideas freely and honestly in his work." And in this paragraph he spun several more variations on the theme. And turned, inevitably, to the Nazi analogy: "You have produced a capital city on the eve of the Reichstag fire. For those who remember German history in the autumn of 1932 there is the smell of smoke in the very room."[16]

In the numerous spoken and written statements regarding free speech, one somewhat minor variant was to tie this kind of attack to an attack on the Screen Writers Guild as the bulwark of freedom of expression for writers. Ring Lardner Jr., for example, claimed that any attack on him is an attack on the Screen Writers Guild, which is thus an attack on the motion picture industry and thus an attack on "our whole practice of freedom of expression."[17]

Herbert Biberman stressed the HUAC's attack on the "progressive" Bill of Rights: "this Committee seeks to undo it, by bullying the American people into surrendering their respect for, and their faith in, this charter of individual freedom."[18]

Dmytryk's first line sets the theme of his prepared statement: "It is my firm belief that democracy lives and thrives only on freedom."[19]

Lawson stated, "I will never permit what I write and think to be subject to the orders of self-appointed dictators, ambitious politicians, thought-control gestapos, or any other form of censorship."[20]

Maltz stated, "Right or wrong, I claim and I insist upon my right to think freely and to speak freely . . . and I assert that not only the conduct of this Committee, but its very existence are a subversion of the Bill of Rights."[21]

It had been, of course, in the previous year that Maltz's insisted-on right to think and speak freely was harshly censored—not by the government, but by the Communist Party.

Robert Rossen was present at a meeting of the Nineteen in 1947 when Maltz was one of those who demanded that actor Larry Parks, who had wanted to express a different position, must comply with the strategy of "unity" at the hearings. Parks was among several who had voiced an interest in either testifying to some degree or relying on the Fifth Amendment. Parks relented, but he wasn't called to testify in 1947.[22]

The censorship of Maltz in 1946 was not the first or the last of the enforcement of party discipline on errant writers and the content of their work. Many lesser-known writers were regularly "instructed" in workshops, meetings, and personal consultations. Among the major figures, Rossen, as we saw in chapter 1, was brought up on "charges" over *All the King's Men* in 1949, but unlike Maltz, Rossen did not accept the party's distortion of what free expression was. He walked out.

In the mid-thirties, so did Elia Kazan. Kazan was part of a Communist "cell" in the Group Theater that met to prepare a unified strategy before meetings of the group. After the successful opening of Clifford Odets' *Awake and Sing*, the party had become interested in the group. Kazan was called to a private meeting with culture commissar V. J. Jerome, who instructed him to organize a campaign for the cell to gain control of the Group Theater by establishing a collective, run "democratically" by the actors: that is, through "behind-the-scenes caucuses, block voting, confusion of issues, and other techniques." Despite his misgivings, he brought the message to the people in the cell. In a meeting in J. Edward Bromberg's dressing room, they voted for the plan, despite Kazan's criticisms of it. A special party meeting was then called, headed by a "leading comrade," who attacked Kazan as an opportunist, giving in to right-wing pressures, siding with the "bosses and exploiters" against the "people." Others in the room, in an apartment above a sweet-smelling bakery, joined in. He was being given the chance to, was expected to recant and confess his error. Instead, he walked out and left the party.

Years later, Kazan said, "I couldn't clear out of my mind the voice of V. J. Jerome and its tone of absolute authority as he passed on the party's instructions for our Group Theater cell and his expectation of unquestioning docility from me and the others."[23]

At about the same time, Odets was experiencing a more direct attempt by the party to curtail his right to think and write freely. The plays of Odets in the thirties and later were the most successful—probably the only successful—plays the theater of the Left produced, and the only plays of that milieu to be performed in revivals again and again through the years. After the one-act agitprop *Waiting for Lefty* (1935), the key protest play of the decade, he wrote *Awake and Sing* (1935), *Paradise Lost* (1935), *Rocket to the Moon* (1938), *Golden Boy* (1939), *The Big Knife* (1949), *Clash by Night* (1941), *The Country Girl* (1951), and *The Flowering Peach* (1954). His screenplays (in addition to plays done as movies) included *The General Died at Dawn* (1936), *None but the Lonely Heart* (1944), *Humoresque* (1946), and *Sweet Smell of Success* (1957).

In the mid-thirties Odets faced personal confrontations at cell meetings, or even cause parties, over why he wasn't writing another "strike play" (after *Waiting for Lefty*) instead of the plays about middle-class life that he had turned to. But in his case the main attempt to shape and direct his work was made through continuing criticism of his plays in the party press. The shifting opinions in the articles show the obedience of the critics in following the party's shifting positions on Odets' writing, as they attempt to influence the direction his work would take.

As Odets summed up his situation when testifying in 1952, "And so I persisted in going along on my own line and writing what did come out of my true center. And whenever this happened, I got this violent opposition in the press, and I became further disgusted and estranged."[24]

Even *Waiting for Lefty* had received contradictory reviews by the same critic, Nathaniel Buchwald. In January 1935, Buchwald found that "propelled by his burning revolutionary fervor, and by an essentially clear guiding idea, this young playwright swept the audience off its feet by the sheer power and sincerity of dramatic utterance." Yet in February Buchwald found that "the very gush of his dramatic style has resulted in a woeful looseness of play structure and its strident overtones all but vitiate his message . . . though each episode is eloquent in itself, all of them put together fail to make a play."[25]

What had happened? Soon after *his* "conversion," John Howard Lawson, in the first zealous stage of applying Marxist ideology to a theory of playwriting, had criticized the play as "a dis-jointed, structurally arbitrary piece of writing" because of its author's lack of true Marxist perspective on and understanding of its subject.[26] That immediately became the standard position on Odets, and Buchwald quickly adhered to it.

That position was revealed again in the course of the shifting opinions in reviews of *Paradise Lost*. In December of 1935 it was praised in two reviews. But in the February 7, 1936, *Daily Worker* it was criticized harshly by Jay Gerlando as unreal, theatrical because of its "lack of Marxist perspective. And the Marxists have an advantage in making real characters because they understand the forces that shape human beings." Again, the shift was the result of discipline, the need to follow the approved position enunciated this time by Stanley Burnshaw (though clearly echoing Lawson) in *New Masses*: "It is the lack of Marxism which has deprived the play of its fundamental social truth. It is regrettable to see a left writer proceeding on an utterly false premise, portray as doomed objects of decay that very middle class which will be enlisted as a vigorous ally in the growing people's front against Fascism and war." One could not find a more thorough encapsulation of the threat dogmatic ideology poses for free creativity—or even logical thinking.[27]

Michael Blankfort was a reviewer for the Communist press in the thirties. A novelist and playwright, he wrote a number of successful movies, including *Broken Arrow* (1950), a liberal breakthrough in Western themes; *Halls of Montezuma* (1950); *My Six Convicts* (1952); *Lydia Bailey* (1952); *Untamed* (1955); and *The Juggler* (1953; from his own novel). In later testimony, Blankfort recalled, "I was dropped as a writer by both the *New Masses* and the *Daily Worker*. I was dropped as a writer because I refused to fit my reviews into the political theory of the moment . . . the current Party line at the moment of the plays." He cited two examples, both involving plays by Odets. In January 1935, when the party was praising Odets for *Waiting for Lefty*, he wrote a negative review of *Awake and Sing*. Joe North, editor of *New Masses*, refused to print it. In December 1935, however, he wrote a positive review of *Paradise Lost* for the *Daily Worker*. When he was asked to reconsider, he refused. The contrary review, attacking the play, was the one written by Gerlando.[28]

In Hollywood in the late thirties Budd Schulberg, the son of Paramount executive B. P. Schulberg, was a young screenwriter. In a later novel, *The Disenchanted* (1975), he presented a fictionalized account of his ill-fated collaboration with F. Scott Fitzgerald for a film, eventually written with others, called *Winter Carnival* (1939). His later major screenplays were *On the Waterfront* (1954), *The Harder They Fall* (1956), *A Face in the Crowd* (1957), and *Wind across the Everglades* (1958). In 1937 Schulberg published a story in *Liberty* magazine that was a sketch for his novel *What Makes Sammy Run?* When he went on to write several more related stories and said he wanted to write the novel, he was called to a meeting of young Communist writers. At the meeting he was told it was "a destructive idea"; that "it was much too individualistic; that it didn't show what were called the progressive forces in Hollywood." He was asked to talk to Lawson. Lawson told him to write an outline for further discussion, along the lines of a proletarian novel about the worker in Hollywood.

Instead, Schulberg went off to Vermont with his wife, Jigee, to write the novel, which was a sardonic depiction of the power structure of Hollywood. Sammy is a young man on the make, who happens to be Jewish, who is willing to step on anyone, including those who are trying to step on him, to get to the top of the heap.

When Schulberg returned with the novel, more meetings were called, including another meeting with Lawson and a meeting with V. J. Jerome, who was in Hollywood at the time. All wanted him to defer publishing the novel. Jerome, he recalled, went further, telling him his whole attitude about the role and duty of a writer was wrong, even his attitude about the peace movement during this period of the pact. He published the novel anyway, early in 1941.[29]

The book was reviewed by Charles Glenn in both the *Daily Worker* and the *People's World*. Glenn's initial review was published on April 2, just days after the book was published. Eager for his scoop, the young reviewer rushed into print with a generally favorable review. The power structure rushed into action, meetings spread as quickly as angry shouts. Schulberg was attacked for publishing the novel, for being anti-Semitic.

Glenn was hit by a barrage of "discussions." Madeline Ruthven and Lawson were among those demanding a retraction. Glenn later claimed that at first he had refused, but had eventually capitulated. "I was young enough in the Party then that it was still like a church. I have never ceased regretting the retraction." However, despite any such regret, his obedience and loyalty to the party still controlled his emotions and his behavior: "Ten years later I still wanted to apologize to Budd, but I didn't have the guts, and by then Budd had used me as his cop-out. As bad as I felt, I knew I'd feel worse if I had to consort with a stool pigeon."[30]

However, in his retraction, in the *Daily Worker* and *People's World* of April 24, 1941, Glenn did not mind consorting with disciplined deceit. "On the basis of quite lengthy discussion on the book, I've done a little re-evaluating. . . . It's rather important that this re-evaluation be done, not in the light of breast-beating, but in the light of constructive self-criticism. . . . It's necessary criticism because until the attitude reflected ["my superficial subjective attitude"] is cleaned up, Hollywood will not and cannot be considered the force for peace [*sic!*] and progress it is and can be."[31]

Among the fascinating reversals within his two articles are the following:

1. All critics, no matter their carping standards, will have to admit they've found the Hollywood novel. . . .
2. The first error I made was in calling the book the Hollywood novel.

1. Former works on the film city have been filthy with four-letter words, spoken and implied. . . . None of these things hold true for Schulberg's novel. There is nothing vulgar in what he says. . . .

2. We do not intend to go into all the aspects of the conscience of a writer, a conscience that allows him (with full knowledge of the facts) to show only the dirt and the filth.

1. Characters [in former books] have been drawn black and white. . . . None of these things hold true for Schulberg's novel. . . .
2. Some day the story of the Guild will be thoroughly told, and done in all the shades of gray . . . not on the plain blacks and whites drawn in Schulberg's book.

1. Writing in the first person, Schulberg tells of the good and the bad. . . .
2. In a full-drawn portraiture of either Sammy Glick or Hollywood, the people must be seen in action, living the lives they lead. Even more effective would be the filth of Sammy Glick counterposed to the cleanliness of the people.[32]

Lilllan Hellman's play *Watch on the Rhine* was given this critical turn-around treatment, with an extra Albert Maltz reversal. Since the play had opened during the period of the Nazi-Soviet Pact, its call for a resolute stand against Fascism was sharply attacked in the party press. The *Daily Worker* found it unacceptable on many levels, even going off on a tangent to attack its failure to mention that the working class was leading the struggle for a better world and of course to point out "that a land of socialism has already established the permanent new life of peace and freedom." Alvah Bessie's article in *New Masses* called it "a network of fallacies, both dramatic and political . . . [which could be] misused by those who would like to whip us or cajole us into imperialistic war under the banner of fighting fascism in Germany." In 1943, however, when the rather inferior film version of the play opened, the *New Masses* found it an "artistic expression of the ideals and aspirations of the best people of our time—the fighters in the ranks of anti-fascism." In his February 1946 article "What Shall We Ask of Our Writers?" Maltz criticized this reversal as an example of the destructive kind of application of rigid doctrine in judging the value of a writer's work. After the subsequent attack on him by his party colleagues, he "recognized" that his judgment on this matter, and others, was shortsighted and faulty.[33]

One more sample of the invasion of an artist's free thinking: In 1945 Dmytryk and Scott were called in for *their* series of "discussions" over *Cornered* (1945), a variation on the film noir genre in which former pilot Dick Powell, like a private eye, seeks to avenge the death of his brother in a quest that takes him to Argentina. Its elaborate plot twists involve Fascist and anti-Fascist expatriates living in Buenos Aires. The three, along with the same writer, John Paxton had had a great success the year before with *Mur-*

der My Sweet (1944), an iconic noir based on Raymond Chandler's *Farewell My Lovely* (1940).

The meetings began over a dispute with John Wexley, who had written an earlier draft of the movie. Dmytryk "just didn't like it. While his script was highly anti-fascist, I didn't so much object to its sentiments as to its wordiness and generally uncinematic treatment. . . . The picture was undramatic, too many speeches . . . long speeches, propaganda—they went to extremes in following the party line on the nose." Paxton was called in to do a new version. Wexley protested and demanded a party meeting, once again led by Lawson. The attack claimed that by removing Wexley's lines they "were making a pro-Nazi picture instead of an anti-Nazi picture." When Dmytryk and Scott refused to back down, a second and then a third meeting were held. Maltz was present at the meetings and, to Dmytryk, seemed to be upset at Wexley's complaints and more sympathetic about his position, although he ended up supporting the others. It was shortly after these meetings that Maltz, possibly still troubled by what had happened, wrote his renegade *New Masses* article. In the Dmytryk-Scott sequence, Lawson then wanted to talk to Dmytryk and Scott alone. At lunch at the Gotham Café on Hollywood Boulevard he berated them for not accepting party discipline. "If we felt that way, it would probably be better that we get out of the party. He said, 'When you decide that you can accept Party discipline, we'll explore the situation again.'"[34]

In 1951 Dmytryk looked back on the relationship between the party and freedom of thought and expression, the party and truth. "The average person who goes in finds there is no freedom of thought; that the discipline is a very harsh one. . . . The Party has a very good explanation for everything that troubles a man. If he says he doesn't have freedom, the great explainer, whoever he is in that locality, will point out that he has freedom to tell the truth; that the Communist Party has discovered the ultimate truth; and within that limit he can speak. Anything outside of the Party line is a lie."[35]

A broader significant example of the party's stifling of free expression, especially of those who dissent from the party's line and policy, affected a larger group of people than the Hollywood Reds and was demanded by basic Comintern strategy and ideology. If the thought and speech differed from the current "truth" of the party, the freedom to express that thought did not deserve to be defended, or even allowed. This illustrative incident occurred shortly after the Schulberg episode. After Hitler had invaded Russia, the party had not only turned from peace to necessary war, but from support of labor strikes to a no-strike policy. At that time, the Socialist Workers Party (SWP), which the Communist Party deemed Trotskyist, still opposed the war and defended labor's right to strike. Union leaders who spoke out against the no-strike policy were called "agents of Hitler" by party spokesmen and the party press. When twenty-nine SWP labor leaders were indicted under the Smith Act in 1941, the Communist Party defended the government's action and applauded their conviction. A *Daily Worker* editorial compared the policy of these men to the Nazis: "The leaders of the Trotskyist organization which operates under the false name of Socialist Workers Party deserve no more support from labor . . . than do the Nazis who camouflage their Party under the false name of National Socialist Workers Party."[36]

When the defendants appealed, the Communist Party actually submitted a brief in defense of their *conviction*, with a collection of documents arguing that their statements revealed them to be subversive and dangerous. One, entitled "The Fifth Column Role of the Trotskyites in the United States," claimed that "being a sabotage organization . . . the Trotskyites do not require a large organization. . . . This core of saboteurs is small, but its underground influence is large. Remove the core and you wreck a strong fascist weapon in America."[37]

A similar decision was made in 1949, to exclude the defense of Trotskyites from any campaign to support defendants in the current postwar Smith Act trials. The call for this exclusion and an inflammatory anti-Trotskyite speech by Paul Robeson were roundly cheered by the delegates. "Would you give civil rights to the Klu [sic] Klux Klan?" Robeson asked. "These men [Trotskyites] are the allies of fascism."[38]

Attacks on the Right to speak freely of all those who differed, especially those who could be labeled Trotskyite, were long a central aspect of the "line" and activities of the Communist Party of America (CPUSA)—and its Hollywood adherents. When Leon Trotsky himself was scheduled to speak in New York City in 1937, the party press, rallies, pamphlets, and so on raised protests, calling for the banning of the speech of this Fascist sympathizer. The chief topic of his speech was the monstrous lies of the Moscow trials and purges. When a commission, headed by the American philosopher John Dewey, was being formed to investigate the Soviet charges against Trotsky, a protest campaign was mounted—calling for the banning of this un-American defense of a Fascist sympathizer. There was the typical "An Open Letter to American Liberals," signed by the usual "intellectuals," including Hellman, Hammett, Lardner, Lawson, Dorothy Parker, Nathanael West, and others.[39]

A few years later, in August of 1940, Trotsky's right to speak freely was more effectively annihilated with an ice pick to the back of the head. No protests were raised in Hollywood. By a series of connections, the CPUSA was complicit in his execution—as ordered from the very top, Stalin. Through the Comintern, it was arranged with the CPUSA that two American Communists would be part of the apparatus that tracked Trotsky for years and finally killed him. Sylvia Franklin insinuated herself into the headquarters of the American Trotskyite party, indeed, as secretary to its leader, James Cannon; and so she was privy to much crucial information about Trotsky's plans. The second American, Ruby Weil, also masquerading as a Trotskyite, befriended an idealistic young woman named Sylvia Agelof, who was dedicated to working in the Trotsky movement and ended up unwittingly assisting in his murder. Through Weil and Lev Zborowski (a Soviet agent who had managed to become Trotsky's key representative in Europe), Agelof was introduced to Ramon Mercador (as Jacques Mornard). After a whirlwind romance, she became his lover. With great excitement, she became Trotsky's secretary in Mexico and innocently introduced Mercador to Trotsky, vouched for him so that he could enter the guarded compound easily. Now known as Frank Jacson (he told Sylvia he had to use that name to evade military service), Mercador developed his plan of attack, penetrated Trotsky's physical and emotional security, and, finally, his skull.[40]

At the HUAC hearings in 1947, the climax of the litany of righteous protests in defense of freedom of expression erupted, with the beautifully placed "beat" of a well-wrought screenplay, at the close of the testimony of Dalton Trumbo. As recounted in chapter 8, his whole testimony was a series of witty exchanges over whether he was answering the question or not, including the unique "Mr. Chairman, first I would like to know whether the quality of my last answer was acceptable?" At the climax, after the reversals of who is asking the questions that were triggered by Trumbo's question about an alleged party membership card, the chairman gave up.

The Chairman: Excuse the witness (pounding the gavel). Impossible.

Trumbo (shouting as he is led from the witness chair): This is the beginning—

The Chairman (pounding the gavel): Just a minute—

Trumbo: Of the American concentration camp![41]

That for many, and that for many years afterward, this was not mere hyperbolic rhetoric is indicated in a statement by actress Karen Morley decades later: "There were strong fascist elements on the march, and there was great fear as to what could happen. By the provisions of the McCarren Act, six concentration camps were set up. And it was quite clear who would have been sent to them. It was in this atmosphere that people informed, and I believe they didn't know whether they were only taking our jobs away or sending us off to something much, much worse. I think the informer realized the full extent of this, and that's why I personally don't forgive them."[42]

While the specter of concentration camps in America was being raised at the hearings, millions were being sent to the real concentration, and death, camps in Russia and its satellites.

During World War II, even so basic a "right" as a soldier's surrender when facing annihilation had been denied. Orders 246 and 270 declared such attempts at survival as treason, punishable by death. Further, Order 270 declared that the "family is to be arrested as a family of a breaker of the oath and betrayer of the Motherland." During the war, more than 421,000 were sent to the Gulag for these "crimes" against the state.[43]

At war's end, as the Soviets reconquered territory and "liberated" prisoner of war camps, hundreds of thousands of Russian soldiers were arrested en masse and sent to *concentration camps* in Russia because their wartime existence in foreign lands made them potentially dangerous dissenters and deviationists. Many were killed—as were many other deportees from newly liberated territories. At the Yalta Conference the three Western allies assisted in this oppression. They accepted Russia's demands for the repatriation of prisoners of war and civilians in the occupied zones, areas recaptured in Russia and in other Eastern European nations. The Soviets turned this into "enforced" repatriation. From the last months of 1944 through January 1945, at least 320,000 Russians who had been prisoners of war were deported to "filtration camps," to be studied as to their appropriateness for being sent on to the Gulag. By August of 1945, 1,545,000 former prisoners of war and 2.5 million alleged "Russians" were taken from the occupied zones and sent to various levels of concentration camps in Russia. These postwar repatriates were added to the 1.5 million deportations that Beria enthusiastically supervised during the war. Of these, the NKVD reported 375,000 had died; others estimate more than 500,000 died through executions or transport to or detention in the camps.[44]

In addition, at the close of the war another 2 million people were deported from their home areas *within* Russia on the basis of ethnic and political classifications that allegedly threatened the security of the nation. All in all, close to 6 million people passed through the various prisons and types of camps within two years of the end of the war—within the two years that led up to such statements as Trumbo's about concentration camps.[45]

From the war's end through the very time of the HUAC hearings and into early 1948, Khrushchev himself supervised the expulsion of "harmful elements" from towns and villages in the Ukraine; almost a million were arrested, the great majority sent to concentration camps. In 1946, 53,000 collective farm workers were sent to the camps for theft of grain or bread, in 1948 more than 38,000 for being "parasites"—not filling quotes or allegedly not working hard enough. When a renewed emphasis on collective farms produced another famine in the south, the government instituted harsh new collective farm laws, particularly two decrees of June 1947 that were aimed at people who protested against or allegedly interfered with the new farming laws. In the year of the hearings alone, 1947, 380,000 people were sentenced to camps. By 1953, 1.3 million had been sentenced, 75 percent for more than five years.[46]

At the same time as the hearings in 1947, a new sequence of trials began in Russia and continued for several years, purging party leaders and members who were potential dissenters and "wreckers." Hundreds of thousands were arrested and sent to various kinds of camps. New "special" camps were set up particularly for those accused of active *dissent*: in official Soviet terminology, "spies, diversionists, terrorists, Trotskyites, right-wingers, Mensheviks, Social Revolutionaries, nationalists, white emigrants, and participants in other anti-Soviet organizations."[47]

After the war the Soviet-controlled states of Eastern Europe added to the resurgence of terror. A brief sampling:

- In Hungary, during the war and after, 75,000 civilians and more than 100,000 prisoners of war were sent to the Gulag.
- After the war, supported by Soviet troops, 600,000 out of a population of 9 million were moved from their homes, some deported to other countries, some sent to newly constructed "labor camps." Similar camps were created in Poland, Czechoslovakia, Bulgaria, and Poland.
- In East Germany, 240,000 were imprisoned in special camps in the first five years of Communist rule; 95,000 were still in camps in 1950.
- In Lithuania in 1947 and 1948, 50,000 "bandits, nationalists and family members of the two categories" were sent to camps for the "specially displaced" and 30,000 to the Gulag. In a two-day period in 1948, during the "Operation Spring" collectivization campaign, the NKVD arrested 36,932 men, women, and children and sent them to labor camps. In that campaign, besides those sent to camps, 21,258 were executed. Throughout the three Baltic states, by 1953, 200,000 people had been convicted at hasty, rigged trials as "elements who are hostile and dangerous to the Soviet regime."[48]

One of the most striking and bitterly ironic examples of the realities of Soviet control was their use of the notorious Nazi concentration camp Buchenwald during this period. It (and several other lesser known Nazi camps) were among the eleven special camps set up under the direct control of the NKVD as both internment camps and transit points for people suspected of having collaborated with the Nazis during the war. Those imprisoned, and killed, were not leading Nazis, but writers, intellectuals, judges, lawyers, businessmen, even those who were known to have opposed and fought against the Nazis. Over a five-year period, some 250,000 entered these camps; 95,000 died.[49]

After Trumbo had left the party, he and liberal columnist Murray Kempton engaged in an exchange of a series of letters in 1957. In one letter, Trumbo allows that "we seek so passionately that we strike down all who seem to stand between us and the answer, or even those who assert a different answer. We have [all] been touched with the madness of moral infallibility." And yet, in another exchange, when Kempton asked him about the Soviets' record of such betrayals and violations as those sampled here, Trumbo evaded any direct response or allowance of any kind of personal complicity: "I never believed in the *perfection* [emphasis added] of the Soviet Union. . . . So I don't feel impelled to penitential cries."[50]

Part III

THE TIME OF THE BLACKLIST—
AND THE TIMES SINCE

12

The Time of Turmoil, 1947 to 1951: Hollywood Besieged, Crusades Continue— Wallace, Peace, and Korea

On Thanksgiving Day of 1947, most of the Nineteen were among the large crowd having their turkey and trimmings in the pleasant courtyard of the El Patio Theater in Hollywood—before they all went into the auditorium for speeches, auctions, and a round of fund-raising. Enthusiasm was still high in this fall of 1947, optimism jostling with anxiety and anger, fears kept at the gates by the spirit of a righteous crusade. They were attending "A Thanksgiving Meeting with the Ten," one of a number of fund-raising functions attended by a broad political spectrum of supporters of the Ten's proclaimed defense of freedom of speech and the Constitution at the first House Un-American Activities Committee (HUAC) hearings. There was, for example, "Election Night with the Ten," at Hugo Butler's home; but for those in the inner circles there was the very expensive fund- and spirits-raising party "New Year's Eve with the Hollywood Ten" at Lucey's Restaurant.[1]

The new year, 1948, and the years that followed were not the years of the concentration camp, as had been predicted by Dalton Trumbo and others. As optimism and unity waned, they were indeed the years of turmoil—a time of turmoil in the movie and entertainment industry, in the Communist Party and its satellites, and within individuals. Through the eleven days of the 1947 hearings, eight of the Nineteen had waited in the wings, never called to the stage. In the years that followed they and many others were left still waiting, their lives and careers precariously suspended—some literally suspended—as they tried to choose among the options seemingly available, tried somehow to manage their lives.

For the Ten the blacklist had begun; for others, it began to spread, but slowly. Not until the next round of hearings in 1951 did the blacklist develop the full procedures and momentum that would overtake the lives of hundreds. Still, in these first limbo years—from 1947 to 1951—threatening pressures were mounting. This was especially true for those known to be in the party or very close to it, and not only the Ten. Even before the 1951 escalation or any further subpoenas, some who had contracts found they were terminated or not renewed, some freelancers got no offers, some feared subpoenas and began to emigrate, though the number of those who emigrated before actually being subpoenaed increased after new hearings were initiated from 1951 on.

In the days following the hearings, there was for the Left the energy and adrenalin rush of idealistic combat, fueled by anger, personal and ideological. Immediately after the close of the HUAC session, the Civil Rights Congress organized a rally in New York City, at which hundreds cheered the Nineteen and their vows to fight on. Their arrival in Los Angeles drew hundreds again; Ring Lardner addressed the crowd, telling them that the HUAC had been dealt a blow (referring to their "success" in causing, or so they assumed, a curtailment of the hearings), but that the fight was not over. On October 15, 1947, the Progressive Citizens of America (PCA) held a fund-raising rally at the Shrine Auditorium, staged dramatically by director Joseph Losey (soon to depart for England, never to return). On November 16, the PCA organized a larger rally at Gilmore Stadium. HICCASP (Hollywood Independent Citizens Committee of Arts, Sciences, and Professions) continued the money-raising meetings and rallies it had started after the subpoenas were delivered.

Early on, liberals in the original support group, the Committee for the First Amendment, stayed in the campaign. They held meetings with studio officials, seeking compromises, even promises. They announced a project of ten radio broadcasts and a speakers bureau. But it was indicative of the short-lived nature of this unity that the discussions got nowhere; after a program entitled "Hollywood Fights Back" on October 26, the radio broadcasts and the speakers bureau disappeared. The Committee for the First Amendment drained away. Some of its leaders (William Wyler, John Huston, Philip Dunne) continued the fight individually, but with increasing disapproval of the statements and actions of those whom they were defending.[2]

Soon it was the Ten themselves, and their party comrades, who had to be the most active in developing the activities, promoting the enthusiasm, raising the money for their own defense. Throughout 1948 the Hollywood party conducted frequent strategy meetings, some for the Ten, some still for the Nineteen, and for others already threatened or about to be threatened by subpoenas and loss of work. Of the Ten, Herbert Biberman was (in the praise of Albert Maltz) "the super dynamo behind all our activities." He and party activist Pauline Finn were the mainstays of the Freedom from Fear Committee, and its satellite, the Committee to Free the Hollywood Ten. They organized publicity, speeches and pamphlets, money-raising, legal briefs, and speaking tours for the Ten, which continued on into 1949 even as energy and funds were depleted.[3]

In the first burst of activity in 1947–1948, it was estimated that more than $150,000 was raised, but as the enthusiasm waned, so did the donations. By October of 1948, Maltz was writing to his colleagues, "We are financially and physically depleted."[4]

In a letter to Maltz in August of 1949, Dalton Trumbo tells him that he can't help at that time because his own funds are depleted and he has a family to support. Along with Lester Cole, however, Trumbo was one of the most well-traveled of the group. He and Cole and others were sent around the country in a tour organized by the CPUSA (Communist Party of America) to raise both money and consciousness, speaking to affiliated front groups, but also at nonaffiliated events arranged by the front groups. In his speech at a fund-raising luncheon of the City Club in Cleveland, Cole used his usual peroration:

> The man who admits he is a Communist or is interested in Marxism under such conditions of whipped-up hatred is free only to reap the whirlwind of a savage, hysteria-driven mob. Such a man is either a fool or a martyr.
>
> And the man, who in such an atmosphere of diseased morality, under pressure of inquisition, seeks to save himself by admitting he was a Communist and accommodate his inquisitors with the names of others, vainly hoping to divert the violence from himself, is both a fool and a coward. I trust I am not a fool. I have no intention of being a martyr. And I pray I'll never be a coward.[5]

Once again, the extreme nature of the Hollywood Reds rhetoric—and particularly their attaching their cause to support of the current crusades of the international Communist movement—were alienating the liberals, destroying the possibility of a viable unified front to combat the unleashed power of the Right.

Looking back a decade later, even Trumbo complained about the party's use of the Ten and others for its own strategies: "From 1948 to the present time, the most prominent of the blacklistees have been exploited for every left-wing cause that came down the pike, regardless of the effect such exploitation might have upon their own blacklist fight." The effect, he concluded, "increased rather than diminished their public disrepute, and rendered immeasurably more difficult the winning of their fight."[6]

Several attempts were made to have individuals influence their guilds to defend the Ten. But the political climate had shifted. There were certainly other factors: the pervasive climate of anti-Communism in the country, rational and irrational, and, as well, a more localized economic concern—a fear that the momentum of the crusade of anti-Communism and the combative extremism of the Communists were endangering the well-being, work, and profits of the industry in the eyes of the public. Whatever of the welter and ambiguities of these beliefs and fears, it still was indicative of the disaffection with the Ten and desertion from their cause that all attempts to gain support of the Ten in the guilds were soundly rejected. At the Screen Directors Guild meeting of December 1, 1947, Robert Rossen rose to speak. He proposed a guild protest against the "firing" of Edward Dmytryk; it is not clear if he was acting out of personal concern for, and affinity with, Dmytryk, or as a spokesman for the Nineteen and the party. According to the *Hollywood Reporter*, he was actually booed. The members then passed a resolution requiring all Guild officers to sign the Taft-Hartley "non-Communist" affidavit.

In early January 1948, Hugo Butler—not among the Nineteen but soon to be blacklisted—proposed to the Screen Writers Guild (SWG) membership that the guild call for the reinstatement of the writers already fired and provide them with legal counsel for civil suits. Reflecting the shift in the SWG that had produced the all-guild (anti-Communist) victory in the executive board elections, Butler's proposal was voted down.[7]

A few similar proposals were raised at various meetings of the guilds over the next two years. One of the last was also futile; it produced a major anti-Communist statement in response. Character actress Gale Sondegaard, the wife of Biberman, was one of the first eight radicals subpoenaed for the 1951 set of hearings. She petitioned the Screen Actors Guild (SAG) to support her and any other actors called to testify. The SAG executive board's response, published in *Variety*, was strong and harsh. It criticized Sondegaard's statements as an attack on the HUAC in the language of the Communist Party press. "The Guild Board," it stated, "totally rejects this quoted typical Communist Party line. . . . The Guild Board believes that all participants in the international Communist Party conspiracy against our nation should be exposed for what they are—enemies of our country and of our form of freedom." In conclusion, the letter defined the Screen Actors Guild's current policy: "If any actor by his own actions outside of union activities has so offended American public opinion that he has made himself unsaleable at the box office, the Guild cannot and would not want to force any employer to hire him. That is the individual actor's personal responsibility and it cannot be shifted to the union."[8]

The SAG's 1951 policy was no surprise, since in 1947 the membership had already voted in Ronald Reagan for his first term as president of the guild, and Reagan's anti-Communist stand had grown even stronger and more outspoken. Policies in SAG, and the other guilds and unions, shifted from any focus on the Ten to a concern for loyalty oaths. In January 1948, SAG, after a resounding 1,307 to 157 vote, had required its officers to sign non-Communist affidavits, in compliance with the Taft-Hartley law. In October 1950 SAG officers had proposed an industry-wide loyalty oath, as was in effect in the Truman federal government loyalty program. The proposal was not acted upon, but in June of 1951 SAG leaders, in response to Sondegaard, again took the lead in opposing Communism in Hollywood. In July 1953 SAG members voted to require all new professional actors to sign a loyalty affidavit.[9]

By 1951 the SWG's policy had developed along similar lines. The contrast was striking. In 1947, after the hearings and the Waldorf Declaration by the producers, the SWG had filed a suit for breach of contract, demanding an injunction to void the declaration. Later, it dropped the suit. As the second round of hearings began in 1951, its new president, Karl Tunberg, spoke to the HUAC in a public meeting to explain how the SWG had cleaned its own house, was capable of policing itself.[10]

In the Screen Directors Guild there were several twists and turns while traveling in the same direction. In one sequence of events in October of 1950, a conservative faction on the board, led by Cecil B. DeMille, had manipulated guild rules to push through a new bylaw to require a loyalty oath of all members. Eventually, on October 22 a full membership meeting was finally held at the Beverly Hills Hotel. Though they seemed to have a majority of the guild in favor of their position at the beginning, the DeMille faction was so outrageously extreme in its comments that after many over-heated hours, the tide began to turn. John Huston delivered a strong speech against the proposal, and finally even John Ford rose to deliver his famous denunciation of DeMille: "My name is John Ford. I am a director of Westerns. [I am] ashamed at what looks to me like a blacklist. I don't think we should . . . put ourselves in a position of putting out derogatory information about a director, whether he is a Communist, beats his mother-in-law, or beats dogs. . . . I don't agree with C.B. DeMille. I admire him. I don't like him, but I admire him." The members then voted against the new bylaw. After this victory, however, guild president Joseph L. Mankiewicz, in a letter to the membership, called on the members to show their loyalty in the fight against Communism by *voluntarily* signing an affidavit.[11]

These developing policies in the guilds, and in the trade unions as well, were given a practical, working focus and definition as specific policies and procedures by the Motion Picture Industry Council (MPIC). The MPIC was organized and its policies shaped by Roy Brewer, who was already the most active leader of the Motion Picture Alliance and, as the executive of the Hollywood IATSE (International Alliance of Theatrical Stage Employees), the controller of labor activities in the industry. He also organized the Labor League of Hollywood, whose main function was to oppose any Communist presence in any unions or guilds and endorse anti-Communists for executive board positions.

In the new MPIC, Brewer, and fellow founders including Reagan, brought together groups and individuals from unions, guilds, and producers organizations to coordinate anti-Communist activities in Hollywood, to facilitate rehabilitation procedures, and to conduct public relations campaigns to stress the motion picture industry's success in fighting Communism. In March 1951, the MPIC announced that its position was to support "any legally constituted body that had as its objective exposure and destruction of the international Communist conspiracy." Still, in defending the actions taken within the industry, there were occasions on which Brewer and his organizations differed with and even criticized what they considered counterproductive extreme organizations like Red Channels and even criticized the HUAC for being too negative about the current state of loyalty in the industry. Reagan worked closely with Brewer in this organization, as well as in a related organization of producers and distributors, the Council of Motion Picture Organizations, whose main function was to conduct public relations operations to convince the public that Hollywood was getting rid of its Reds. In a guest column in the *Hollywood Citizen News* of July 30, 1951, Reagan averred the Communists in Hollywood had "failed completely . . . [but] not before the communists had fooled some otherwise loyal Americans into believing that the Communist Party sought to make a better world. Those dupes know today that the real aim of the Communist Party is to try to prepare the way for Russian conquest of the world."[12]

Starting in 1948, the Ten also met with no greater success in their criminal cases. All had already been blocked from employment. John Howard Lawson was the first to be tried for contempt and convicted in April 1948. Dalton Trumbo was convicted on May 5. By agreement, trials for the other eight were held in abeyance until the result of appeals had been determined. The appeals court upheld the convictions in June of 1949, and the Supreme Court refused to accept the case in April of 1950. The other trials were then briefly conducted and convictions obtained. Lawson and Trumbo began to serve their sentences on June 11, 1950, and all were subsequently sentenced. All were out of prison by May of 1951, just as the second round of hearings was underway.

The civil suits filed for breach of contract and conspiracy to deny employment did achieve some success. After several years of complications and reversals, in both directions, six of eight suits were lost and two settled for a total payment of $259,000, about half of which (after legal fees and expenses) was split among the group.[13]

Even in the first months after the hearings and into 1948 and 1949, those of the Hollywood Left soldiered on in support of the other political causes promoted by the Comintern and the CPUSA. Primary among these party-organized and controlled causes were the interlaced campaigns of Henry Wallace for president and the latest version of the international crusade for peace and its corollary, the attack on the threatening aggressive policies of the United States.

The first new point of focus was the presidential campaign of Henry Wallace. In 1947 and 1948 it became for the party and the Soviets a new attempt at rebuilding the kind of Soviet-defending Popular Front that had been created in the thirties. As had been the case in the earlier decade, the crusade for peace, as the proclaimed and popularly acclaimed principles of the Soviet Union, masked the aggressive strategy and actions of the Soviet Union in the deepening Cold War. One key center of early activity in the development of these foreign policy positions was the PCA. It had been formed in 1946 after the collapse of any harmony among leftists and liberals in previous political action groups such as ICCASP (Independent Citizens Committee of the Arts, Sciences, and Professions) and HICCASP. While it was a new means of seeking throughout the country to enroll liberals as well, the PCA was controlled by Communists, who also dominated its Hollywood branch. Lillian Hellman and Gene Kelly were among many of the Hollywood Left whose names graced the organization's letterheads and calls, open letters, and so on for the "cause," which continued the pro-Soviet policies initiated by the radical wings of the previous organizations. A constant champion of these policies and regular presence at rallies and conferences was Henry Wallace. During the war, Wallace had been almost rapturously embraced by the Hollywood Left when he was the featured guest at a series of events in February 1944. At a series of small gatherings and a giant rally at the Shrine Auditorium—sponsored by the Free World Association—Wallace stressed the value and necessity of cooperation with the Soviet Union not only during the war, but during the peace that followed.[14] No speaker, no words, could have been more welcomed.

After Wallace had been superseded by Harry Truman as vice president, Truman had become president after Roosevelt's death. Wallace had become more and more outspoken, and frequent, in his criticism of American foreign policy. At an ICCASP rally in New York City in September 1946, he directly attacked Truman's policy toward the Soviet Union; it was, he believed, the United States that was the danger. "I realize," he said, "that the danger of war is much less from Communism than it is from imperialism." The path became clear: He would be a third-party presidential candidate and the new party would be called the Progressive Party. And it was not accidental or independent.[15]

As two Soviet memos of April 10, 1947, show, at meetings in Moscow Morris Childs, CPUSA representative to the politburo, had requested direct advice as to whether Wallace should seek to battle Truman within the Democratic Party or run a third-party campaign. In response, Foreign Policy Deputy Director A. Panyushkin was cautious. He advised that unity of action in the workers movement was vital to such a third-party attempt, and that unity was not yet present in the United States. No further memos are available, but the CPUSA was encouraged enough to move ahead with the third-party plan. They began to create a broad coalition of progressive supporters, including of course Wallace himself, but could only gain limited support within the labor movement.[16]

In the same month in 1947 that the HUAC hearings began in Washington, the Soviets' Cominform (successor to the Comintern) met for its inaugural meeting in Poland. While it did not issue a specific directive on a plan for a third party, its general strategic statements implied this and encouraged the U.S. party to go ahead with its plans for a third-party campaign. The CPUSA and the PCA began to implement that plan. In December of 1947 a party leader, Robert Thompson, led a meeting with labor leaders to try to forge the kind of unity Moscow had prescribed, as he let them know the decision to go ahead had been made. In December Wallace declared he was a candidate, and the Progressive Party was announced. Dwight MacDonald pointed out that Wallace "devotes one-fifth of his current campaign book *Toward World Peace* to a detailed defense of Russian foreign policy and a mendacious whitewash of such internal Soviet scandals as the suppression of the Trotsky opposition, the forced-collectivization famines, the Moscow Trials, and the forced-labor camps. Can you imagine the American Firsters issuing a similar campaign document defending the concentration camps and the Reichstag fire trial?"[17]

The scorn of anti-Communist liberals had no effect on the converted and the hopefully converted. In Hollywood, in March of 1948 most of the Ten and the Nineteen and other party members took time, energy, and money away from legal defense activities to form the Hollywood Wallace for President Committee. For a time liberals like John Huston joined in, but first drifted, then scurried away. Others, like Philip Dunne, opposed the move from the onset. When Huston had solicited his aid, Dunne later said, "I listed my objections to the Wallace candidacy. But he did take it on and the most prominent members of it were the Hollywood Ten." The Hollywood Wallace for President Committee joined the party's campaign to obtain signatures to place Wallace on the ballot. The party hoped to reach a safe 450,000 by the end of February. Using an organization called Field Theater, Hollywood Reds, followers, and unknowing supporters created a series of traveling shows to promote this campaign. Officials from the central party headquarters in New York spent weeks with the Californians to ensure the success of the campaign that they considered vital. Documents show one reason for their extreme interest: They wanted to use Wallace and his campaign as a hunting ground for new party members in the face of government pressure, impending trials, legal and underground expenses.[18]

A cadre of Communist Party activists formed around Wallace. On the basis of FBI reports, Venona transcriptions, and other documentation, Ted Morgan in *Reds* concludes, "It is indisputable . . . that the Progressive Party was the brainchild of the Communist Party, which launched it, staffed it, micromanaged it, and found a willing spoiler in Henry Wallace, who mistook Communist backing for mass appeal." Back in April of 1948, Congress of Industrial Organizations president Phillip Murray had already announced, "The Communist Party is directly responsible for the organization of a third party in the United States. There is no question about that." But as the campaign developed, Wallace and his supporters denied this control. When questioned, Wallace responded that it was inevitable that "all Peace-loving people in times like these should be attacked as Communist dupes"; that "anyone who will work for Peace is okay with me"; that "neither the Communists nor the Fascists [sic] will control my policies."[19]

During the campaign, Lillian Hellman was among the most active and vocal of Hollywood Reds in support of Wallace and his call for peace with the Soviet Union. Earlier, in October 1947, she too had raised the issue of the HUAC hearings to the hyperbolic level of Nazi-like conspiratorial warmongering. She too had published a protest, an editorial titled "The Judas Goats," printed in the SWG magazine:

> A sickening, sickening, immoral and degraded week. And why did it take place? It took place because those who wish war have not the common touch. Highly placed gentlemen are often really gentlemen, and don't know how to go about these things. Remember that when it was needed, in Europe, they had to find the house painter and gangster to make fear work and terror acceptable to the ignorant. Circuses will do it, and this was just such a circus. . . Has it anything to do with Communism? Of course not . . . those are frightened men [i.e., the producers] and you pick frightened men to frighten first. Judas goats; they'll lead the others, maybe, to the slaughter for you.[20]

Hellman became chairperson of Women for Wallace, regularly defending his campaign against the charges that it was dominated by Communists. One of her favorite lines at luncheons and meetings around the country was, "These days a Communist is anybody who thinks maybe a dividend check should be higher." She told others working in the campaign that if she found that the claims that the Communists were in control were true, she would resign. In her 1977 memoir *Scoundrel Time*, however, Hellman, admitted that she had known of the Communist infiltration of the Wallace campaign, but insisted that they had not *controlled* it. She claimed that she had told Wallace that indeed there were Communists in his party, but that it was so obvious, they were harmless and not acting under any centralized control. After the election, she broke with Wallace for his still denying he had any knowledge of Communist participation.[21]

In *Scoundrel Time*, Hellman did more than admit there were Communists in the Wallace campaign. In a typically euphemistic and evasive way, she allowed that she and others had mistakenly not seen some of the "sins of

Stalin Communism" [emphasis added], but she still claimed, "But whatever our mistakes, I do not believe we did our country harm. And I think they did." The *they* are the anti-communist liberals. *They,* in turn, were quick to swarm to the counterattack, including Nathan Glazer, Irving Howe, William Phillips, Sidney Hook, Alfred Kazin, and Hilton Kramer (actually, no longer a liberal). Hook wrote a twelve-page indictment in *Encounter.* The opening of Howe's open letter succinctly sums up this view from the liberal Left: "You could not be more mistaken. Those who supported Stalinism and its political enterprises, either here or abroad, helped befoul the political atmosphere, helped to bring totalitarian methods into trade unions, helped perpetrate one of the great lies of the century, helped destroy whatever possibilities there might have been for resurgence of serious radicalism in America. Isn't that harm enough?"[22]

Back in 1948–1949, after the collapse of Wallace's bid for the presidency, the Hollywood members of the CPUSA were still "politically active" in supporting and promulgating the Soviets' version of peace through other means than the Progressive Party. As we've seen, John Howard Lawson and Hellman joined the organizing committee for the Waldorf Peace Conference, held in March of 1949; many joined in. Among the most active was Albert Maltz, whose speeches and articles in this period are once again representative of an intellectual and emotional subservience to the cause, in this case defined in the doctrinaire terms of the current party line on peace. In the spring and summer of 1949, while waiting for legal decisions that would determine prison time or not, Maltz delivered a series of speeches in which he decried the rise of dictatorial fascism in America: "One is destroyed in order that a thousand will be rendered silent and impotent by fear. Through fear and hysteria Americans are to be forced to give up their rights as free citizens." If these oppressions were to continue, he averred, "then there will be no need to look with scorn at the barbaric Nazis."[23]

But in line with the emphasis of the current "peace" crusade, Maltz regularly tied these oppressions to warmongering and the need to stand up, speak out for Peace. At the El Patio Theater in Hollywood, for one example, on May 25: "Henry Wallace has been called a traitor; and anyone who dare advance the ideas of socialism is called a traitor; and all those who speak for peace today are called traitors by those who seek war. Only *they—they* are the patriots."[24]

With the invasion of South Korea by North Korea in June 1950, much of the antiwar activism turned to the alleged United States aggressions there—once again allowing the Cominform to draw attention away from a whole spectrum of aggressions by the Soviets; this time throughout Central and Eastern Europe. For those in Hollywood and the nation who continued to follow the party line, the Korean War brought a new spur for action. For them and such organizations as the Cominform's World Peace Council and its American subsidiary, the American Peace Crusade, the focus was not on protesting the invasion by North Korea, but condemning the U.S. "invasion" of Korea.

The American Peace Crusade organized a pilgrimage to Washington on March 15, 1951. The *Daily Worker* reported that two thousand attended. Among others, there was a Peace on Earth Rally in New York City in December 1952. Present, and speaking, at many of these was one of the most active American peace activists, Willard Uphaus, whose organizations, World Fellowship and the American Peace Crusade, drew numerous Hollywood supporters. At prayer vigils to stop the war, his standard position was that the United States was allied "with British and French Imperialists, expending blood and treasure, in a futile effort to stop the onward march of the colored people to freedom and independence." In the Soviet Union, on the other hand, there was "cooperative living and social justice, with economic plenty, education, health and cultural fulfillment."[25]

In a public letter to his organization, Uphaus called for the United States to cease its aggression against the "normal revolution" taking place in Korea. The letter was reprinted in the *Daily Worker* and distributed widely. In support of this position, Uphaus went on to state that "Dr. James G. Endicott believes there is indisputable evidence that American Armed Forces are guilty of using germ warfare." This claim was supported by the noted scientist and author of numerous books on science in China, Joseph Needham.[26]

Not all on the left believed that claim, but the specter of germ warfare was spread by the party and many did believe, as illustrated in statements by Maltz, Alvah Bessie, and Lester Cole. But beyond this extreme kind of claim, there was widespread agreement on the party-controlled Left, and among others on the periphery of their influence, that America was the aggressor in the war. For many with this belief, the American aggression in the Korean War was only one aspect of a larger pattern of oppression in American policy and life, dangerous oppression at home by the HUAC and other anti-Communist organizations, whether reasonable or not—the first stages of what was frequently called the rise of political "terror." And in the world, the dangerous and aggressive policies that were an increasing threat to peace, and the Soviet Union, even the threat of atomic warfare.

The Hollywood Arts, Sciences, and Professions Council at this time was one of the configurations of the political groups controlled by the CPUSA throughout the country. It distributed a booklet called *The Truth about Korea* through the mailing lists of industry guilds and unions and other organizations. The booklet had as its premise that the United States was the aggressor and had attacked North Korea. Typically, Albert Maltz told Edward Dmytryk at this time that he could not trust the American press, and so he had discussed the war with lawyers of the CPUSA, and they had confirmed the "truth" of the matter. There was no doubt that "the Americans and the South Koreans had invaded the North." North Korea was "only striking back."[27]

Others, including Michael Wilson and Howard Fast, defined the Korean War within this same constellation of elements of a broader American "fascism."

Wilson saw American movies during the war as using the war for deeper propaganda purposes and warmongering. In an article in the short-lived *Hollywood Review*, he saw their danger as fostering "concepts required of the Korean War: blind obedience, the killer instinct, sacrificial death. . . . [They] inculcate a martial spirit that would not fade away with any cessation of hostilities in Korea."[28]

In his memoir *Being Red*, Howard Fast so many years later still provides a revealing depiction of the interaction of several beliefs held by the committed Left in determining a position about the Korean War. It was a position that was indeed the policy of the Soviet Union and the CPUSA, and one that had unintentionally served to widen the breech between the Hollywood Reds and any potential allies of the liberal Left. Fast held fast to the belief of the fifties that the war was the inevitable continuation of the American "campaign of terror"; the only people who stood against that campaign were those who called for peace in such events as the Waldorf Peace Conference. The conference had "brought home to the Truman administration that its carefully orchestrated campaign of terror had not yet reduced everyone to the point of abject cowardice and indifference." If the "peace movement" had been attacked as "a tool of the Soviet Union" that was because it was a tool "of the people of good will the world over. Peace was the only hope of mankind in the new atomic age, and when the Korean War began, the hope of peace crumbled. The government that put me and other political prisoners in jail was a government bereft of all common sense." It was thus a government and a war that could lead into "the beginning of World War Three, the beginning of the great crusade into Communist China that had been pushed for so long by elements of the media." But most of all the war was a sign that "the terror continued" in the United States.[29]

13

The Time of Trials: The Smith Act, the Rosenbergs, and Alger Hiss

These years were also the time of trials. Even through their own travails, other trials and other investigations were a particular point of interest for the Hollywood Reds and their followers, who saw direct parallels between these other actions and the investigations and trials that beset them. As the Communist Party of America (CPUSA) and Soviets mounted campaigns of protest and denial over these other trials, the Hollywood loyalists once again were organized to join the choruses arranged by the party. One center of attention was the series of Smith Act trials of leaders of the CPUSA; another was the trial of Julius and Ethel Rosenberg; and a third the case of Alger Hiss. Protests against these cases drew many of the same responses— and enlisted many of the same protestors—as did those investigations and trials that directly affected the movie industry. From the perspective of the Hollywood Left, the investigations in Hollywood were merely a segment of the fascistic anti-Communism that was enveloping the country. Through the years since, the Left, whether the old or the new, has continued to stress this pattern: the unjust witch hunt of the Hollywood Reds was an inevitable consequence of the oppressive political climate that produced the unjust witch hunts of these major trials.

There is a complexity, a paradox, in this claim. On the one hand, the hearings and the blacklisting were clearly part of an impetus, a national crusade against Communism. But the typical distortion enters with the claim of a total parallel between the two kinds of investigations and legal actions: of seeing the injustice of the attacks on the Hollywood Reds as the equivalent and consequence of the injustice of these other investigations. In this equivalence, there was no basis for any investigations of Communists, no basis for any actions to define the important difference, in the terms of

Sidney Hook, between heresy and conspiracy; that it was all, and equally, an infringement on the right of free speech and normal political association, and in the case of the parallel of the Rosenbergs to the Hollywood group, a Nazi-like surge of anti-Semitism.

The first group of Communist Party leaders was convicted on October 15, 1949, under the Internal Security Act, known as the Smith Act, for belonging to an organization dedicated to the overthrow of the American government. This was several months after the appeals court had upheld the convictions of the Hollywood Ten and the Soviets had exploded their first atomic bomb. It was several months after Senator Joseph McCarthy had delivered his first diatribe about Communists in the State Department.

A central organization for many of these protest campaigns was the Civil Rights Congress (CRC), formed earlier by a Communist splinter group within the National Negro Congress in 1946. Through these years the Civil Rights Congress mounted protests against the House Un-American Activities Committee (HUAC) and other anti-Communist programs, and then organized a campaign to protest the indictment and then conviction of the party leaders. The protests and campaigns organized by the CRC drew the participation of many among the Hollywood Left over a span of several years and several trials. Dashiell Hammett was on the executive board of the CRC and was joined on petitions and open letters by Albert Maltz, John Howard Lawson, Howard Fast, and others. As late as 1953, two typical events for the Smith Act defendants were a "Freedom Festival" and an entertainment fund-raiser, "Culture Fights Back, 1953," songs by Pete Seeger.[1]

The Smith Act trial and the protests against such trials, investigations, and security programs occurred at the time when those investigations had been strikingly successful in revealing the close connection between the CPUSA and the extensive networks of Soviet espionage in the United States. These investigations produced the virtual collapse of those networks; numerous Soviet documents attest to this connection and this collapse. By the time of the first HUAC hearings in Hollywood in 1947, for example, Moscow was informing its new Washington station chief that, despite his desperate pleas, it could not help it maintain intelligence efficiency: "Unfortunately, in the current conditions of counterintelligence measures against us and a bitter anti-Soviet campaign in the country, we cannot thus far give you our agents and let you use them to fulfill present tasks. Reestablishing connection with important American agents can lead to fatal consequences."[2]

By 1948 the new chief, Alexander Panyushkin, was pleading, "Since we have connections now only with a very small number of masters [agents], I ask you to re-examine our network of old masters in order to determine the possibility of resuming contact with some of them." Later in the year Moscow complained that "the stations in the U.S. in 1948 didn't recruit any valuable agent. Moreover, no station acquired prospective talent-spotting for later work with them." Panyushkin, somewhat contradicting his previous position, replied, "To continue the work old agents and talent spottings in such conditions gives American counterintelligence an opportunity to cultivate even more deeply our connections and ourselves. . . . We can cause great damage to our country by striving to get information from old agents who, as experience shows, are exposed."[3]

In a strikingly candid document, in March 1950, Sergei Savchenko, then head of the NKVD intelligence department, summed up the collapse of the previously extensive American network (a collapse that he related also to the defection of Igor Gouzenko in Canada). According to Savchenko, the damage occurred with

> American intelligence intensifying their work against us, managing to inflict serious blows to our Agent network in the U.S. . . . The most tangible blow to our work was inflicted by the defection of our former group-leading agent [Elizabeth Bentley], who gave away more than 40 most valuable agents to American authorities. The majority of agents betrayed by [Bentley] worked at key posts in leading state institutions: the State Department, organs of American intelligence, the Treasury Department, etc. . . .
>
> Besides [Bentley's] treachery, at the same period of time—i.e., since the end of 1945—there were failures of four agent groups . . . that followed testimony given to the Federal Bureau of Investigation. . . . There were more than 30 valuable agents in these four groups. . . .
>
> The last link in this chain of failure was the arrest of [Valentin] Gubitchev and [Judith] Coplon . . . and their trial. . . . Thus, as a result of all these failures, we lost our agent network that had been in operation for many years and was a source of valuable political and economic information for us.[4]

In October of 1950 Panyushkin was still complaining that he could not recruit any new agents because of the "current fascist [*sic*] atmosphere in the U.S. . . . We work here in an atmosphere . . . of almost 50 agents exposed long before us."[5]

Subsequent campaigns of the CRC were conducted to protest the indictment of "second-string" party officials, including V. J. Jerome. In Los Angeles efforts began to focus on the cases of the California party leaders. After the convictions of the national leaders in 1949, twenty-one officials were arrested in Los Angeles. Hollywood Reds contributed the pamphlet *It's You They're After* to the CRC defense campaign. Its opening line carried clear echoes of the testimony of the Ten: "This is the story of political persecution and developing fascism in the United States." In response to further legal action in 1951 and 1952, supporters formed the California Emergency Defense Committee. Ben Margolis, the lead attorney at the HUAC hearings, represented the California party leaders and conducted an appeal that after five years resulted in the Supreme Court overturning the earlier verdicts. His brief was one of the most logical and reasonable of the legal documents he framed during the period. It emphasized that individuals had to be judged separately, that they did have the ability to disagree with the party and so could not be treated as a solid single unit. The Court decided that the government had not adequately provided evidence that each individual had *knowingly* participated in the illegal activities attributed to the party.[6]

During this appeal period, Dalton Trumbo in 1956 contributed a pamphlet for the Defense Committee, *The Devil in the Book*, reprinted with no changes in 1972 as one of three essays in his *The Time of the Toad*. He insisted that the party and its members stand "committed to peaceful coexistence between the two world systems of socialism and capitalism. They demand the abolition of colonialism and imperialism and the prohibition by all nations of atomic weapons [etc., etc.]." In his view, in the Cold War "absolute virtue resided with neither side."[7]

The CRC was also active in the campaign to "Save the Rosenbergs," right down to the series of execution night vigils on June 19, 1953, held across the nation to rally the faithful. At the vigil in downtown Los Angeles, screenwriter Michael Wilson and others of the Hollywood Left spoke. At the New York City vigil at 17th Street and Union Square, Howard Fast, standing on the sound truck platform with CRC leader William J. Patterson, announced the fatal climactic moment. Moaning and crying spread through the throng as a chorus sang "Let My People Go."[8]

Novelist and committed Socialist James T. Farrell commented, "But I wonder—what demonstrations were there when millions were killed in Russia, for Trotsky, Zinoviev, Kamenev, and many others."[9]

The CRC and all other Communist-controlled organizations and publications—and the Hollywood Left—had paid little attention to the case of Julius and Ethel Rosenberg after their arrest for espionage in July 1950. The Soviets, the CPUSA, the *Daily Worker*, the ardent followers of the party line in Hollywood and throughout the country initiated no protests, marches, or rallies. They started no organizations or campaigns; circulated no petitions; published no pamphlets, open letters, or calls. Indeed, they paid no or little attention in official party-oriented print from the time the Rosenbergs were arrested until some very limited attention was paid after they had been found guilty in March 1951. Even then, the few *Daily Worker* articles were brief and mild, mainly news reports on the basic facts of the trial, as in the April 6, 1951, piece reporting on the death sentences imposed. Further coverage did not begin until July, some four months after they had been found guilty.[10]

It was, however, the *National Guardian*, a publication associated with the satellite American Labor Party, that was the first to initiate the major campaign, in a series of articles, not initiated until August 1951. The publisher and coeditor of the *National Guardian* was Cedric Belfrage, an old friend of

Otto Katz, who had been in Hollywood on and off for years helping Katz and others do party business. Documents show Belfrage's espionage activities for the Soviets during World War II. His chief investigative reporter William A. Reuben, never one to let the facts get in the way of an ideological argument, produced a series of seven articles, with an opening editorial that proclaimed from the start, "We are convinced of the overwhelming probability that the Rosenbergs are completely innocent."[11]

In their authoritative *The Rosenberg File*, Ronald Radosh and Joyce Milton conclude that the Reuben series "is memorable for the very paucity of evidence brought forward to support these sweeping conclusions." They note as well the inaccuracy of his key "revelations," such as the claim that the Julius referred to by Elizabeth Bentley was Klaus Fuchs because his middle name was Julius, even though Fuchs was not in the United States until after the events described by Bentley. Reuben's claims were repeated in his book *The Atom Spy Hoax*. They were used by blacklisted screenwriter John Wexley in his *The Judgment of Julius and Ethel Rosenberg*, which, so many years later and despite all the evidence to the contrary, Larry Ceplair and Steven Englund still claimed "carefully and thoroughly destroyed the government's case." In turn, in the decades since, both books have played their part in the building of the myth of the pogrom and the sacrifice of the innocents. Much of the material of these early claims of innocence, for example, was used in a distorting PBS broadcast in 1978, which (as reported in the *New York Times*) twenty-five years after their executions treated them as innocent martyrs, victims of the Cold War.[12]

On April 14, 1951, there is a known cable from the NKGB in New York to Moscow discussing the American party's concern to "organize a powerful campaign [for the Rosenbergs] on our own and equally the foreign press." But there was no follow-up by the CPUSA at that time because no approval was given by Moscow.[13]

No major campaign was actually initiated, funded, and organized by the party until 1952—after approval and planning were finally worked out by the Cominform. As former Communist Party official John Gates looked back: "the signal from the international movement" had finally come. In America the response to this signal was a set of articles in the *Daily Worker*, starting with a small article on page 3 on January, 3, 1952, more on February 28, then increasing as the National Committee to Secure Justice in the Rosenberg case was formed and initiated its fund-raising and propaganda campaign—and with a very strong and meaningful emphasis on anti-Semitism. The headline on a typical pamphlet read, "People Rallying to Save Rosenbergs. Religious and Other Leaders Protest Death Sentence of Young Jewish Couple." At a rally on October 23, 1952, Elaine Ross, an official of the sponsoring CRC, proclaimed, "Every Jew knows in his heart that the Rosenbergs have been convicted because of anti-Semitism."[14]

In Europe the international Rosenberg Defense Committee was not formed until late 1952, December 3, in France. In the month before, however, Howard Fast had published an article in *L'Humanité* claiming that the Rosenbergs were Progressives, "but they were not Communists to the best of anyone's knowledge." Asserting the anti-Semitism implication, he said they "have been judged by Jews" and "sent to death by other Jews"—which he saw as "exactly the old technique of the old Jewish Tribunal employed by Hitler." In Europe the repeated echo was that the Rosenbergs were "victims of American Fascism."[15]

Why the delay in the crusade?

There are several cogent hypotheses. Unclear as to what the Rosenbergs might do or say, the Soviets, in control of the whole process, waited to be sure that they could count on their continued denials and silence before associating with their cause. In turn, once the Rosenbergs were convicted, and sentenced to death, and still remained steadfast, loyal, and silent, they were now useful for a much stronger campaign than merely claiming that they were not spies. They were now victims and martyrs; they could be used as horrendous examples, and Jewish examples, of the evil injustices of the United States.

But especially in Europe, the final intense interest and intensely orchestrated campaign was also used as a mask, a distraction from events in the Soviet sphere at the time. Central among these was the trial of Rudolf Slansky and other party leaders in Czechoslovakia. The Slansky group, the majority of whom were Jews, were arrested in December 1951—just before the American campaign for the Rosenbergs was started. They were tried in 1952, and executed on December 3, 1952—the very day the European campaign was started. In an odd, but defining response to some criticism, Jacques Duclos in Paris set the party line: "The conviction of U.S. atom spies Julius and Ethel Rosenberg was an example of anti-Semitism, but the execution of eight Jews in Czechoslovakia last week was not." Why not? The latter, he pointed out triumphantly, had confessed their guilt as traitors! This theme was developed and spread by acclaimed left-wing historian Herbert Aptheker in a series of articles and books.[16]

By 1957, however, Guy Endore, who had been an active pamphleteer for cause after cause, was seeing it differently, at least in private. He wrote Trumbo that the party's late entry into the Rosenberg case was suspect: "World attention concentrated on the Rosenberg trial, missed the horror of the Prague trials. . . . Was that the pupose of the Communist move into the Rosenberg case?" He no longer wanted to "play politics with the lives of others," to be used "as a decoy, a smoke-screen . . . brother, we've been played."[17]

As we have seen, at this time there were also other trials of "terrorists" throughout the Soviet bloc. During this period of widespread purges, there was an extreme intensification of arrests, tortures, imprisonments, and executions of Jews (traitors, Zionists, Trotskyists, American lackeys) in the Soviet Union and throughout Eastern Europe. During the very spring in which the Rosenbergs were executed, arrests of Jews accelerated, camps were being built for the eventual deportation of Jews, a process Anastas Mikoyan termed "the voluntary-compulsory eviction of Jews."[18]

As the Save the Rosenbergs campaign accelerated, there was increased emphasis in the United States on the claim that the persecution of the Rosenbergs was part of an *American* epidemic of anti-Semitism. As the *Daily Worker* raged in a particularly hysterical editorial, "The Rosenberg case is a ghastly political fraud. It was arranged to provide blood victims to the witch hunters, open the door to new violence, anti-Semitism and court lynching of peace advocates and Marxists as 'spies.'" Their executions, the paper claimed in June 1953, were "to channel the hatred of the American people against the working class vanguard, the Communists, the Negro and Jewish people, the labor and progressive forces generally." The purpose was to institute a "pro-fascist reign of fear in the United States, to brutalize the population, and get it to accept the further fascistization of the U.S. without resistance." Four years earlier Albert Maltz had made similar claims about the persecution of Hollywood writers and intellectuals.[19]

Many years later, in his memoir, screenwriter Walter Bernstein did concede that evidence "indicated" that Julius had "been part of a spy ring," but he still emphasized and insisted that "the trial was corrupt, the evidence fabricated, and the nightmare real." He still sounded the ritual Jewish note: "It [the trial] was a Jewish nightmare come true, as if they were all acting out some archaic, self-destructive ritual for the benefit of the goyim."[20]

All through the time span of the widespread purges and pogroms in the Communist bloc, the campaign to save the "victims of American Fascism" was built and spread, implemented in great part by the party-line proclamations of the American writers and intellectuals who remained so silent about the Soviet terror. Among the Hollywood Reds, Maltz, Lester Cole, Ring Lardner Jr., John Wexley, Herbert Biberman, and Michael Wilson were among the most active participants.

In his 1981 memoir *Hollywood Red*, Cole, for example, looked back on the case: "Darkness had fallen, and with it Julius and Ethel Rosenberg were gone. Their courage was as great as their cause was just, and I vowed I would never betray it."[21] (In contrast, in the 446 pages of his book, there is not one word about the millions killed and imprisoned by the Soviets.)

Howard Fast, even years later, could see "no reasonable way they could have had anything to do with the Soviet development of the bomb. . . . If two people in these United States could be so deliberately framed, then we are no longer a nation of law." And, of course, the Hitlerian tag still: "Indeed, the Rosenberg case had been orchestrated to an anti-Communist frenzy that matched the exuberant hysteria of the Nazi horror."[22] (See chapter 9 for the facts on the Rosenberg espionage ring.)

In 1983 in *The Nation*, Victor Navasky attacked Radosh and Milton's *The Rosenberg File* and them personally for assuming the Communist Party "was in fact a spy recruitment agency," attacked Radosh for his "obsession with the Communist Party as evil," scoffed at these "self-advertised lefties" who arrogantly "had found the Rosenbergs guilty," and allowed the Right to claim "there was an internal Red Menace after all."[23]

In 1978 Navasky had done the same thing in defense of Alger Hiss, attacking both Allen Weinstein and his book, *Perjury* (and later his *The Haunted Wood*), with demeaning personal invective, faulty logic, elevating quibbles over details to major fallacies, refusing to confront the thorough and balanced total pattern of evidence Weinstein presented. Weinstein had actually started the book with the intention of proving Hiss's innocence, and so his turning "informer" made him even more eligible for character assassination.[24]

Navasky's campaigns to defend Hiss and the Rosenbergs and his vituperative attacks on those who disagreed with him bracketed in time the period he was developing and publishing his book *Naming Names* on the blacklist and its victims and villains. The book, so influential through the years in defining the terms and judgments of the period, rose from the same ideological zeal and controlling vision as his denial of the truths about espionage in the United States and his insistence on the vicious indecent motives of those who "testified" about those truths.

The Hiss case had evolved from grand jury hearings in March 1948, initiated on the basis of testimony by Elizabeth Bentley. At these hearings Hiss testified he was not a Communist and did not know Whittaker Chambers. The confrontation between the two occurred at HUAC hearings in August, at which Hiss said he thought he might have encountered Chambers under another name. Chambers' release of the so-called Pumpkin Papers, copies of government documents passed to him by Hiss, in December precipitated a second grand jury hearing, after which Hiss was indicted for perjury. The first trial in May of 1949 resulted in a hung jury (eight to four to convict); the second produced a conviction in January 1950. In both trials the government's case was again negatively affected by its refusal or inability to produce translated Venona documents.

These Venona documents and documents released from Soviet archives fully substantiate the testimony of Bentley and Chambers and provide even further proof of Hiss's participation in both espionage and the attempt to influence the conduct of foreign policy. In one period at the State Department, Hiss would bring documents home at weekly or ten-day intervals, Chambers would photograph them, and Hiss would return them to their files. After Chambers, Hiss was controlled for the NKVD by Boris

Bazurov and Jacob Golos (who used Bentley as a courier), but he then became involved in work for the GRU, the Russian military intelligence service. Since fewer GRU cables are included in the small percentage of cables translated in Venona, there are less mentions of Hiss than might be expected, but some very crucial ones. When correlated with other known facts and documents, these, and especially a long cable of March 30, 1945, clearly establish his identity, and indicate that his service to the Soviets continued at least until 1945.[25]

Immediately after the conviction, the *Daily Worker* of January 24, 1950, set the formula for the defense of Hiss—and complementary attack on the United States:

> There is a new way to spell Franklin D. Roosevelt. Now they spell it H-I-S-S. In going after the youthful New Dealer Alger Hiss, they are out to drive their daggers into the reputation of Roosevelt's administrations. . . .
>
> Will our country let itself be tricked into police state suppression of all opposition to the "cold war" conspiracy? Will we let the confessed perjurer Whittaker Chambers be the Judas goat to lead the nation into the same trap into which the dope fiend and degenerate Van der Lubbe helped Hitler push the German nation?[26]

Despite such hyperbole, and the usual analogies to Nazi Germany, the Hiss case and clear implication of espionage through the perjury conviction did not arouse the intensely emotional fervor of the Rosenberg campaign. It has, however, maintained its own momentum through the decades. As Guenter Lewy sums up the impact of "the revisionist reexamination of the past by New Left scholars": "Books and film documentaries that argue for the innocence of Hiss and the Rosenbergs are praised, no matter how flimsy their factual base."[27]

Lester Cole and Howard Fast are typical of those who made clenched-fist claims resolutely held onto in later writings and memoirs. Fast, in *Being Red*, claims, "Alger Hiss, whose name I had never heard until his trial began, and who seemed to me as unlikely and improbably a Communist as the President himself, was imprisoned in a case so ridiculous that it might have come straight from the pages of *Alice in Wonderland*." Cole, in *Hollywood Red*, states, "Alger Hiss (who, thirty-five years later, is still fighting in the courts to prove that he was framed) . . . Hiss was and is a gentle but determined man. Some might think his thirty year fight to prove his innocence is in vain. Not I. He hasn't lost. You can't lose as long as you keep fighting."[28]

The vagueness and looseness—and disregard for facts—of the rosy remembrances of the Communist past are illustrated in a passing reference Cole makes to Judith Coplon while discussing Hiss: "Judith Coplon (who shortly thereafter was proven innocent and exonerated by the court)."[29]

Coplon was not *proven innocent* or *exonerated*. She had been convicted of being an espionage courier, but on appeal the conviction was overturned on a technicality because of the government's refusal and inability (again) to reveal its interception of Soviet cables. Thus, they could not substantiate the basis, the probable cause, for their wiretapping, and the conviction was overturned on that legal point about the wiretapping. However, even the appeals court judge stated officially that the evidence proved she was, indeed, guilty of the charges against her. Since then, there has been much documentation of her complete participation in espionage. Nonetheless, through the years, and despite early and then additional documentation, not only has the truth of the testimony of Chambers and Bentley been denied, but their character and even mental health have been impugned.

In looking back at the Hiss case, Lillian Hellman's version of the past was even more extreme in its avoidance of both fact and logic. In *Scoundrel Time* she saw the Hiss case as part of "the sly, miserable methods of McCarthy, Nixon and colleagues, as they flailed at Communists, near-Communists, and nowhere-near-Communists." While attacking the "psychotic inventions" of Chambers, she proudly displayed the "logic" and "facts" that she believed demolished the prosecution's case. "Facts are facts—and one of them is that a pumpkin, in which Chambers claimed to have hidden the damaging evidence against Hiss, deteriorates—and there never had been a chance that, as [Lionel] Trilling continues to claim in the *New York Review*, Chambers was a man of honor."[30]

By the time of Hellman's memoir, it had been extensively reported for years that Chambers had placed the microfilm in the pumpkin for only several hours on the very morning of the day he turned them over to the HUAC. Hellman also continued an earlier claim "that most of the frames were unreadable"—while it had been widely publicized that only one roll was illegible and that the two key State Department strips were totally readable. Similar was her claim that all the rolls "contain nothing secret, nothing confidential. They were, in fact, non-classified, which is Washington's way of saying anybody who says please can have them." Again, the "facts" are that all the material on the State Department rolls, the crucial evidence, *was* classified.[31]

In an article in the *New York Times* that responded to the Hellman book, Hilton Kramer (then the *Times'* art critic and soon to be editor of the *New Criterion*) generalized about the "cultural chic" that Hellman represented, the falsifying "climate of amnesia" about the real Communist past. This view of the past, he felt, was being given greater momentum, and honor, because of disillusionment over Watergate and the Vietnam War.

A new wave of movies, books, and television shows is assiduously turning the terrors and controversies of the late 1940s and 1950s into the entertainments and best-sellers of the 1970s . . . to persuade us that the Cold War was somehow a malevolent conspiracy of the Western democracies to undermine the benign intentions of the Soviet Union. . . . The point, it seems, is to acquit 60s radicalism of all malevolent consequence, and to do so by portraying 30s radicalism as similarly innocent, a phenomenon wholly benign, altruistic, and admirable . . . the myth of total innocence must be upheld even where it is contravened by the acknowledged facts.[32]

One of the chief sources for the continuing assertions of the innocence of Alger Hiss was a ten-year crusade in *The Nation*—a total of twenty-seven articles, including two whole special issues, from 1952 to 1962. Other articles defended the innocence of the Rosenbergs, Morton Sobell, Harry Dexter White, and others. *The Nation's* editor through those years, Carey McWilliams, was a longtime and respected liberal journalist and activist in California, particularly interested in and involved in labor and minority issues. He had written about, supported, and in some instances helped to shape and define many of the causes that the Hollywood Left had taken part in. McWilliams had participated in many of the organizations the Hollywood Communists were active in, spoke at meetings and rallies. He was particularly active in the Wallace campaign and the fight against the HUAC "witch hunt" and the "plague" of the blacklist, as he defined them. He entitled a book *Witch Hunt* (1975). McWilliams had become more radicalized and focused on foreign policy and peace during the Cold War and had taken on the editorship of the Soviet-supporting *The Nation* when insistent ideologue Frieda Kirchway had stepped down.[33]

In his 1978 memoir, McWilliams sums up his view of the total basis of the Cold War in this way:

After World War II, the situation was similar in some respects but different in others. The Russian Revolution was by then firmly [sic] established. But the Stalin regime, an ally in the war, had suffered catastrophic losses; in 1945 it could not be regarded as a military threat. . . . Nevertheless, the possibility of revolutionary or socialist regimes coming to power was regarded as sufficiently imminent so that policy-makers felt it imperative to launch a world-wide ideological crusade against "Communism" under cover of which American capitalism might expand to the far corners of the earth. . . . [And so] the public had to be whipped into line by measures far more repressive and ingenious than those used in the "red scare" after World War I.[34]

For McWilliams and *The Nation* the cases against Hiss and the others were part of this whipping into line. What *was* actually "ingenious" was the many ways the articles maintained the crusade by manipulating various facets of the voluminous data, while ignoring the clear-cut total pattern and countering data. These arguments and others are countered and refuted in Allen Weinstein's *Perjury*.

The "climate of amnesia" typified by books such as McWilliams' and articles such as those in *The Nation* have influenced more than other left-wing polemics and polemicists. They have become the basis of the commonly accepted assumptions promulgated by the popular media and standard research sources, in much the same way as the unexamined assumptions about the blacklist and its protagonists.

An important case in point is the distorted use of statements by General Dimitri Volkogonov, a Soviet military historian and author of probing, factually, objectively critical biographies of Lenin, Stalin, and Trotsky. In 1992 he was asked by John Lowenthal to look through Soviet archives to help exonerate this framed innocent. Lowenthal was a longtime active promoter of Hiss's innocence; his documentary *The Trials of Alger Hiss* is itself a prime example of the continuing use of and distortion by bits of evidence that have already been refuted or superseded by more accurate versions. After what he later admitted was a search of only two days, Volkogonov was then persuaded to release a statement proclaiming that he had found no evidence that Hiss had been involved in espionage. The statement was instantly and widely spread through all the popular press and media.

When confronted, Volkogonov retracted these claims, insisting that he had been misinterpreted and misquoted. Attempting merely for humanitarian reasons to help the aging Hiss who "only wanted to die peacefully"—he had meant to make clear only that he had found nothing in his brief search of several files. He pointed out that there were many other files, indeed many other whole archives he had not researched, and that, further, since it was claimed Hiss had worked for the GRU for many years, their files were extremely secret and not available to him, if they even still existed.

After the wide distribution of and emphasis on Volkogonov's original statement, no television networks and only three of the major newspapers carried the retraction, and then with less emphatic length and placement. More importantly, it is the original statement that has been passed on in the years since. For example, the 1995 edition of the widely used *Concise Columbia Encyclopedia* changed its previous entry on Hiss to state, "In 1992 a high-ranking Russian official [which he wasn't] said he had found no evidence in the archives of the former USSR that Hiss had been a spy." In turn, this is then found word for word in the encyclopedia program carried on Microsoft Windows 95. When Hiss died, the Associated Press story and obituary—used, in its turn, by many other media sources—stated that Hiss "proclaimed that [vindication] had come finally in 1992, at age eighty-seven, when a Russian general in charge of [which he wasn't] Soviet intelligence archives declared that Hiss had never been a spy, but rather a victim of Cold War hysteria and the McCarthy Red-hunting era." Note that the Associated Press does more than ignore Volkogonov's subsequent retraction.

In his initial letter he had not talked about "Cold War hysteria" or "McCarthy Red-hunting." And he had not said Hiss had never been a spy.[35]

In his 2005 memoir, *A Matter of Opinion*, Navasky finally expresses doubt about the innocence of Julius Rosenberg, but he says he is still waiting for "a reasoned assessment of the evidence" before allowing any doubts about Alger Hiss.[36]

In striking contrast, through the years of this vehement protest and condemnation of the unfairness and threat to liberty of these trials and investigations in the United States, trials were spreading and intensifying the assault on the freedom and life itself of the peoples of Russia and Eastern Europe. The Slansky trial in Czechoslovakia, as noted, was only one instance in the Soviet sphere of "a Jewish nightmare" in which real anti-Semitism was part of an attack on dissidents. Jews, of course, were not the only victims of these nightmare events. In Czechoslovakia from 1948 to 1950 a broad campaign against the democratic left led to more than three hundred trials of opposition leaders. In one set of thirty-five trials in the rural provinces, there were 639 sentences handed down—including 10 executions, 48 life imprisonments, and a total of 7,800 years of prison allotted. By 1954, some two hundred thousand people had been held in 422 camps and prisons, many of them not even allowed a trial.[37]

And through these years, and in the decades since, the protestors, like Navasky, either did not remark about these events at all, or when, like Navasky, some finally did, they did so still in limited, obfuscating, rhetorically (and psychologically?) evasive terms.

The complicated mixture of these contradictions can be seen, with his own grandiose style, in some of the later comments of Dalton Trumbo. Years later, Trumbo was to claim, in one variation of his many renditions of his own history, that he had joined the CPUSA in 1944 and left in 1948. Why? "On the grounds I should in the future be too busy to attend its meetings, which were, in any event, dull beyond description; and about as revolutionary as Wednesday evening testimonial services in the Christian Science Church." He said that he had not joined again until 1954, and then only because he wanted to protest the injustice of the convictions of the California party leaders under the Smith Act, and left again in 1956. But his "Time of the Toad" was printed in twenty-one installments in the Communist-controlled New York *Compass* in the spring of 1950. According to a letter of February 1954, soon after he returned from Mexico (years after he claimed he left the party) he gave three party-sponsored speeches.[38]

By 1956, Trumbo in private letters was expressing pride in his knowledge, even before the Khrushchev speech, of transgressions and injustices committed by the Soviets. He bragged to John Bright, for example, about all the anti-Communist literature he was familiar with. He told Bright that what he discovered was not agonizing for him "because I never believed in the perfectibility of man nor the perfection of the Soviet Union." In 1958, in an article he submitted to *Mainstream* he criticized the CPUSA at great length. The article was not accepted. He focused particularly on the fallacy of insisting on secrecy of membership and activities. "The question of a secret Communist Party lies at the very heart of the Hollywood blacklist. . . . [Hollywood Reds] should have all been open Communists, or they should not have been members at all." He felt that "all we can be certain of is that secret membership did destroy them." In a typical combination of admission and evasion, Trumbo wrote that "those who embraced the Communist mystique . . . though they were not more innocent of evil than their opponents, their efforts at least produced immeasurably less of it." So, still, the evils of the United States are somehow "immeasurably" greater than anything done in the name of Communism.[39]

Throughout these years, however, Trumbo's pronouncements that were released to the public continued to focus only on the evils of the United States—as seen, among other examples, in his pamphlet for the California party leaders in 1956, *The Devil in the Book*, and his essay for the one hundredth anniversary of *The Nation* in 1965, "Honor Bright and All That Jazz." In the latter, eleven years after his break with the party, Trumbo was still employing the extreme invective of traditional party-line pronouncements. In looking back on the Cuban missile crisis and our decision not to bomb the missile sites, Trumbo wrote, "The danger that we might kill a Cuban child wasn't discussed. It wasn't relevant. . . . If in fighting communism we find it necessary to kill a child, we will surely kill it. We have killed them already in substantial numbers . . . . We will continue to kill them as long as the word 'Communist' triggers hatred and steels us to murder."[40]

The typical level of extravagant hyperbole of this rhetoric about America warrants a juxtaposition with some of the staggering realities of the treatment of *children* in the world of the Soviets, never faced up to by Trumbo or others.

During the Spanish Civil War, thousands of children aged five to twelve were sent to Russia and eventually to Siberia. In one center, 2,000 of the 5,000 children imprisoned died. Out of all those deported, only 1,500 had eventually returned to Spain by 1956.

Following the Civil War in Greece, the Soviets controlled the deportation of 28,296 (a low estimate) children (ages three to fourteen) to Albania, Bulgaria, and Yugoslavia, and then on to further satellites and Soviet republics. Kept in "children's villages," the children had to perform arduous (and killing) manual labor, such as the reclamation of marshes in Hungary, and underwent intensive prison-camp indoctrination programs.

Within a period of forty-eight hours in May of 1948, in Lithuania 36,932 men, women, and children were deported. In the Baltic states in 1949, over a period of two months, 27,084 children under the age of sixteen were deported as part of the mass deportation and imprisonment of "elements who are hostile and dangerous to the Soviet regime."

In the increase of the population of the Gulag from 1948 to 1953, the number of children in what were called "infant houses" increased from 22,815 to 38,000.[41]

The postwar imprisoning (and in substance subsequently of killing) of children was not without its horrific precedents. Robert Conquest has pointed out that a "decree of April 7, 1935, extended all penalties, including death, down to twelve-year-olds." A further decree directed the "treatment of children of enemies of the people. Those over fifteen were to be tried like their mothers. 'Socially dangerous children' were to be sent to labor camps or colonies or 'children's homes of special regime.'" Conquest cited a Soviet report on the Gulag that actually compared the infant mortality rate in the Soviet Union of nonprisoner mothers—0.47 percent—to the rate of infants of mother-prisoners—41.7 percent. In recounting the oppressions of the forced famine and dekulakization in the early thirties, Conquest concludes there were some 3 million deaths of children in the famine years and at least an additional million in the dekulakization campaigns—"mostly the very young."[42]

14

Robert Rossen: Testing of a Moral Life in Hollywood and in Films

In these times of trials and turmoil, and contradictory choices and dilemmas, the journey of Robert Rossen through the political and moral maze can again illuminate the complexity of motives, of choices, and actions within the period's moral challenges and contradictions. It can in his case illuminate as well the interesting relationship between the ambiguities of motives and moral choice in an artist's life with the central moral issues of his work: What are the motives—definable and ambiguous—for one's choices and actions, what impels them, what are their consequences on one's self and on others? What are the complex human and social motives and forces that lead to the corruption of ideals, the many levels of betrayal? Rossen's two films of this period—*All the King's Men* (1949) and *The Brave Bulls* (1951)—can illustrate the way that life influences the work and that the work—consciously or not—reflects the tests and trials of the life.

After the first hearings, Rossen's place and path in the movie industry amidst the upheavals of belief and career were clearer than most, at least for the time being, and more secure due to his strong connection to Harry Cohn. Cohn was the tough, garrulous and famously foul-mouthed, fiercely independent, and surprisingly loyal head of Columbia Pictures. He had long recognized the skill of Rossen's screenplays for Warner Bros. and had given him his first opportunity to direct *Johnny O'Clock* (1947). Cohn had been pleased with *Johnny O'Clock*, and the minor profit it had made, and pleased to see that *Body and Soul* (1947) had also made money for Enterprise. Cohn did love good movies, but he also loved making money and anyone who could make money for him. After *Body and Soul*, Rossen was one of the first writer-directors to form his own production company, Rob-

198

ert Rossen Productions. He and Columbia signed a deal for the studio to finance and release three of his films.

Still, in 1948 when Cohn and Rossen turned to thoughts about their next movie, the realities of the time did begin to intrude on Cohn's kind of Hollywood, as they would now do with more and more regularity. Several years before, when Cohn had been advised by legal counsel to get rid of that Commie John Howard Lawson, he had refused. Now even he knew the times had changed, though he continued to go his own renegade way as much as he could. By some accounts, he was known to urge compliance with some of the formalities; but whether truthfully or not was beside the point. As for a while he was able to do with others in his employ, Cohn reached a modus vivendi with Rossen. Rossen would write a private letter to Cohn attesting to the fact that he was not at that date a member of the Communist Party. Rossen did,[1] but what he meant or what the literal truth at that point was is as conflicted as were his feelings about and dealings with the party at the time. He had left, or was in the shifting process of leaving the party in his heart. When he, or others, would literally or officially cross the line was not a matter of one clear, definite, and absolute step.

The result was *All the King's Men*. Rossen had been attracted by the Robert Penn Warren novel, and its central character, Willie Stark, so clearly a Rossen character—let alone a spirit much like himself and his new mentor, Harry Cohn. Rossen had thought of purchasing the rights himself, but when the novel won the Pulitzer Prize early in 1948, the price was beyond him. He urged Cohn to buy the rights. Others at Columbia agreed it would be a fine prestige picture, and Cohn agreed to buy it, envisioning (rightly, as it turned out) a prestigious major award winner. He agreed as well not only that Rossen would write and direct it, but that under the terms of their releasing agreement, Rossen would also act as producer. It was one of the earliest instances of that kind of complete control by a Hollywood film-maker—writer, director, producer. Complete, of course, within the parameters of Hollywood at the time, and those set by a mogul like Harry Cohn.

While hard at work on *All the King's Men*, Rossen was still active in some left-wing functions, particularly those meetings, functions, organizations related to the House Un-American Activities Committee (HUAC) and its consequences. Like so many on the Hollywood Left, Communist or not, he was attracted by the campaign of Henry Wallace for president. As he later testified about leaving the party, "And this doesn't mean, you know, I still don't contribute money to certain things I believe in. For instance, I contributed to the Wallace campaign. Well, I thought it was a pretty good idea to have a third party in this country, and one doesn't go—at least, I don't, or I can't change—go from being a member of the extreme left to being a member of the extreme right."[2]

Although Rossen believed in the Wallace campaign, in 1948 (and after the campaign in 1949) his political activities were limited. His name was used on some documents for activities of the Progressive Citizens of America, for example; he also attended an occasional rally and some fundraising events for causes, like Wallace, that he still believed in. But he had begun to hold back on paying party dues.

In these times of shifting loyalties and heightened suspicion of betrayals even the matter of paying dues could become a focus point of moral judgment. Comments about Rossen's paying dues and making contributions are typical of the distorting invective (and distortions of memory) about him and others who testified. On arriving in Hollywood, screenwriter Walter Bernstein got his first job as an assistant to Rossen. When interviewed by Paul Buhle for *Tender Comrades*, he claimed that "Rossen hadn't paid and sometimes he still didn't pay. You could tell that there was something slippery about him." He expanded on the topic in his memoir, *Inside Out: A Memoir of the Blacklist*, published in 1996: "On the other hand, he was always failing to pay his Party dues, and I [after just arriving in Hollywood!] was assigned to get them from him. Rossen would promise, but rarely pay. Instead, he would get me to box with him in the office."[3]

Screenwriter John Wexley embellished this line in an interview in the nineties. He distorts some sarcastic remarks by Rossen at a fund-raising event, prompting Wexley to pledge big money because "you won't have to really pay." Rossen, he claimed, insisted he never paid. "And it was true. He told that to the House Committee when he testified, because they asked about all those pledges and contributions and he said, 'I never gave a cent, you know.'" As the documents show, during his testimony Rossen discussed in some detail how he did make contributions of more than forty thousand dollars.[4]

As noted earlier, Rossen was still active in the Screen Writers Guild, for both party and personal motives. *All the King's Men*, however, was his chief focus, and it became his way of responding to and sadly, painfully commenting on the world of politics and all its avid proclaimers and proclamations, corruptions and betrayals. The film is one of the first from the Hollywood industry that reflects the influence of the Italian postwar film renaissance, the development of neorealism. In an interview in the French film journal *Cahiers du Cinema*, Rossen expressed his admiration for the Italian movement: "*Open City, The Bicycle Thief*, and so on, marked me deeply, and I even thought, when I became a director, that was the true way of making films." It was a matter of style—episodic, character-focused, loosely structured, like life itself, naturalistic, even raw, in look and performance—and a matter of vision. "It seemed to me that the whole Hollywood system was condemned if people did not finally decide to look at life with a clear gaze, with a cold eye. Which does not exclude emotion, sensibility. It means only that life represented must be as we see it and not as we wish it to be. We have to say what is out of joint in our time." As he said in his praise of the French director Jean Renoir, "His style, consciously or not, comes from, is about life."[5]

After some ten drafts, consulting frequently with Warren, he found his way into the life that was in the novel and found the style for his film in the neorealist vision. And so he discarded much of the screenplay he had been labouring on—creatively rewriting his own screenplay. As production began, he began to respond freely to the immediacy of the moment on location, mainly in Stockton, California—changing and developing the script as they progressed, using natural light and all kinds of weather conditions. He used many nonactors, marshaled as many as ten thousand people in crowd scenes, shooting with four cameras, often when the extras were unaware.

Before going on location and discovering these new decisive moments, Rossen had submitted the requisite "final" draft of the script to the Columbia executives in charge of the production. When the daily rushes were being viewed back at the studio, there was consternation—this was not the script or the polished look that was expected. Harry Cohn was informed. He passed on their "notes" to Rossen. Rossen sent back an angry telegram.

Cohn telephoned him. As Cohn later liked to tell the story, the conversation went,

Cohn: So what you're saying is, "Go fuck yourself!"

Rossen: You're goddamned right!

Cohn: So, okay, what the hell, do the picture.[6]

While the film extends and expands Rossen's consistent themes, in the context of the burgeoning blacklist it coalesces as a symbolic centerpiece of the paradoxes of idealism and corruption, choice and betrayal, the personal tensions and dilemmas in the real-life political moment in Hollywood. Political "advisers"—in this case, capitalists, not Communists—use the campaign of a "naïf," an idealistic candidate, for their own ends, knowing he will lose. The character Willie Stark, unlike Henry Wallace, does win on his second try. But he betrays all those noble words, all those promises of a new better world for the people, the proletariat, as did, in Rossen's view, the Communist Party. Willie—like the Soviets or right-wing extremists—for his own purposes, conducts secret investigations into the personal lives of people, does what he thinks he has to do to destroy his enemies, the "wreckers." His political opponents, for their own purposes, conduct a blatantly public investigation of him, a hearing on a grand scale, an impeachment. All those around him, affected by him, are caught in the dilemma of choosing to acquiesce in his power and corruption or to act—in one way or another to "testify" or not.

One, Judge Stanton, is even driven to suicide. The judge, honored in the community, is about to come out to advocate the impeachment of Willie. Jack Burden, an alienated idealist, is caught between turning against Willie or continuing to act on his instructions, his party line, for the future good that Willie can do. Burden really knows that Willie is betraying the very ideals he had believed Willie could make a reality, but he betrays his own ideals, and his better self. He still supports the oppressor. He investigates, finds the dirt in the judge's past, but doesn't reveal it. He shares the information with the judge's wealthy niece, whom he has loved since childhood, who is now Willie's lover. She betrays the judge and informs Willie, who attempts to blackmail the judge. It is a powerfully articulated scene, an early example of Rossen's mastery of the visual image—patterns of people, camera angles, editing. The scene and the patterns capture Willie's power, but also pattern physically the position of Jack—caught between the two, wavering in his loyalties, but impaled. The judge himself cannot choose his course of action—to testify will reveal his own flaws; to remain silent will betray his ideals. He cannot choose and kills himself.

The film's implications for the tests and traps of the time have another, deeper implication. The personal betrayals, the forsaking and loss of one's true self, have public and political consequences; personal corruption and the corruption of the power structure of society are linked, interact in a destructive embrace. One cannot evade his complicity in the consequences of actions—whether the intellectual Jack Burden or the political leader Willie Stark. A rough and beaten-down "redneck" himself, Stark finds his calling, the source and energizing of his own unformed, undiscovered power, in connecting with the "hicks," the common people of the state, in their own voice, on their own terms. In his first losing campaign, when he has been set up by the political bosses as a sucker candidate so that their man will win, he finds that common voice in anger and protest and the true needs he sees in the people.

> There's no need for my telling you what the state needs. You are the state and you know what you need. . . .
> Now listen to me, you Hicks. Yeah, you're Hicks, too, and they fooled you a thousand times, just like they fooled me. . . . But I'm on my own now and I'm out for blood.

The cheers of the energized, thrilled crowd erupt, but he silences them, already in total control: "All right, listen to me, listen to me." Already, he (and they) who claim to act for the "people" begin to dominate.

Like the fated and painful closing of a bitter circle, the brilliant climax of the film is like a corrupted crescendo of an echo of the promise and the betrayal already revealed. Outside of the statehouse at the hearings to impeach Willie, a giant banner of Willie's face looms as tall as the building. Willie has brought in the hicks from all over the state. Busses disgorge them to join the masses waiting and cheering, waving banners, ordered regularly over a loudspeaker what to do. The people, the proletariat, are complicit in the corruption of the power structure that controls them. The loudspeaker blares: "All right now. Everybody . . . that means everybody . . . let's let Willie know we're here! All together, WE WANT WILLIE. WE WANT WIL-LIE." The people pick up the chant, the drum beats, the troopers struggle to hold firm against the excited press of the mob, straining to get as close as possible. Dissolve to later in the day, and the crowd remains. The loudspeaker: "Attention, please . . . This is a special announcement from Willie Stark to you people out there. He doesn't want any of you to leave. . . . He wants you to stay in front of the state Capitol until the fight is over . . . stay where you are, stay where you are!" The camera pans up to the engraved plaque above the entrance: "THE PEOPLE'S WILL IS THE LAW OF THIS STATE—GOVERNOR STARK." The people cheer.

Once he has become governor, money is the lever of Willie's political power, and the corrupting force in the governing of the state; but it is the power itself, more than all the accoutrements it can buy, that is the corrupting force within him. Rossen thought that Willie's belief that he was helping people had another side, shared something that was innate, and dangerous, in all politics and politicians, whether Communists or Democrats. Actions that, at least at their beginnings, are for good *causes* can have destructive consequences, "because the drive toward power never permits itself to be naked and always needs a rationale. . . . It needs it because it cannot face the fact that the need for power becomes primarily a subjective need."[7]

All the King's Men received the widest acclaim of any of Rossen's films, as well as some thirty awards, including the New York Film Critics award for Best Picture (though Best Director went to Carol Reed for *The Fallen Idol*) and Best Actor (Crawford); the Screen Directors Guild award for Best Direction; the Foreign Language Press Film Critics Circle award for Best Film, Best Screenwriting, Best Direction, and Best Production; the *Look* Achievement Award for Best Screenwriting; and seven Academy Award nominations. The *Los Angeles Daily News* said it "rates all the Oscars for the year." Crawford again won for Best Actor, Mercedes McCambridge for Best Supporting Actress. Al Clark and Robert Parrish lost the Best Editing award to the boxing movie, *Champion*, while Burnett Guffey's technically innovative and artistically impressive photography had been unfairly denied a nomination. Rossen lost both Best Screenplay and Best Director to Joseph Mankiewicz for the sentimental *A Letter to Three Wives*, but won for Best Picture of 1949. The New York University Center for Research awarded it as "one of the decade's most distingushed films in the field of human relations."[8]

Newsweek praised its "considerable distinction and singular dramatic force." John McCarten in the *New Yorker* found that it "didn't lose its nerve when dealing with the facts of American politics and faced up to Lord Acton's conclusion about the corrupting influence of power." For Bosley Crowther in the *New York Times*, the film had "a quality of turbulence and vitality that is the one [impression] it most fully demonstrates . . . it has a superb pictorialism which perpetually crackles and explodes . . . bears witness to the boundless potential of the screen."[9]

Following the release of *All the King's Men*, Rossen was already busy working on his next project. He was determined to develop his career as a director before the next expected intrusion into his career and life by the HUAC; he, like everyone else, thought the next hearings would be sooner than they turned out to be. The tremendous success of *All the King's Men*—artistic, popular, economic—and his relationship with Harry Cohn allowed him to forge ahead more readily than others of the Nineteen or the circles beyond.

He had begun development on his own next film, *The Brave Bulls*, adapted from the popular novel by Tom Lea. In the novel he had seen the potential for the dramatization of his basic themes and concerns, and a central character who was another variation on the man with a gift, an élan, who, when facing a crisis of courage and honor, betrays that gift and himself. Again, there are echoes of the current real-life dilemmas of Rossen and the others. But there was a strong second motive for his interest in filming the novel. Going to Mexico would allow him to avoid or at least delay the next subpoena. Harry Cohn agreed with Rossen's estimate of the strength of the book. Bullfighting pictures were then still popular—*Blood and Sand* (1941), *The Bullfighter and the Lady* (1951), and *The Sun Also Rises* (1957) among the major versions. Cohn also agreed on the value of the location shooting, mainly for the kind of authenticity that had been achieved, and praised, in *All the King's Men*. He again also wanted Rossen to produce as well as direct the picture.

Still busy at first with *All the King's Men* and then with the hectic and complicated work of producing a movie in a foreign county, Rossen assigned the screenplay to John Bright, an old friend from the early Warner days and Communist colleague, with whom he had never actually worked before. *The Brave Bulls* was Bright's first movie of any note for many years. As was his regular method of working, Rossen worked closely with Bright on the screenplay and continued to adapt material and scenes as the production got underway, but he took no screenplay credit.

Years later, Bright told Bruce Cook, "I was the first person to land in Mexico City. At the time I got there only Gordon Kahn was around, and he was in Cuernavaca. I registered in the Imperial Hotel down there, and one by one, they all came, and everybody on the blacklist, I swear, passed through the Imperial Hotel. . . . Let's see, John Wexley was there, Maltz—until he moved to Cuernavaca—Ring Lardner, Trumbo—until he moved to something grand—Ian Hunter, later, and, well, just all of them."[10]

A good number of Rossen's former comrades found their way to Mexico, a good many to Europe (as did he eventually). For many, the cheaper cost of living in Mexico was a further motive beyond avoiding subpoenas or other legal dangers. It allowed them to live quite well while making much less money writing on the blacklist black market. Some left the country in the period between hearings, already blacklisted or knowing that they would be; some wanting to leave before being subpoenaed, some after they appeared at the series of hearings that began in 1951 and were blacklisted. Some members of the Ten left after their release from prison. Mexico City drew many of the central figures in the Hollywood Communist community as they established the kind of close-knit communal spirit and style of living—on much less money—that they had had before. Money and the lack of it was a central problem; in facing it, they acted communally, loaning each other money, paying certain bills as each could afford it, paying back what one could. In his extensive letters, Trumbo frequently refers to money he has loaned that is being repaid or money others have loaned, or even money that can't be loaned or just given because he or someone else hasn't enough right then or is being besieged by tax demands, and so on. He is also quite careful to see that payments that he needs to make and payments due him are kept as regular as possible.

In a letter to his wife, Cleo, while he was in custody, Trumbo says, "Get in touch with Earl and tell him we haven't forgotten him, and intend to begin repaying him (in driblets, of necessity) early next year. . . . Do John's payment continue? (Note: I paid off the Katz loan in full, so we don't have to think about *that* one.)"[11]

John was John Bright, who later commented on his financial dealings with Trumbo. "Dalton Trumbo is one of the softest touches in the world. If anyone's ever got any trouble, they turn to him. . . . I myself was beneficiary of several legs up from Dalton. . . . I helped support his family when he was in prison. But I was just paying him back money I owed him—money he never asked me for."[12]

Once out of prison, Herbert Biberman was one of those who did not emigrate. As might be expected, he began to organize activities, including a production company, Independent Production Company, to create socially conscious films. When he asked Trumbo to participate, Trumbo wrote him a long letter explaining why he couldn't. At its core: "I sired these kids of mine, and I've got to support them. . . . I am, from today on and for some time in the future, not interested in pamphlets, speeches, or progressive motion pictures. I have got to earn money—a considerable sum of it—very quickly."[13]

Trumbo had sold his home—as many did—and he and his family went to Mexico City in tandem with Hugo Butler and his family in November 1951. Butler had been in Ensenada in Baja California since the spring of 1951, just after filming was completed on the movie he had written for John Garfield, *He Ran All the Way*. He had been an active Communist member on the executive board of the Screen Writers Guild, had worked on screenplays for a number of popular, though minor, movies—*The Adventures of Huckleberry Finn* (1939), *Lassie Come Home* (1943), *Edison the Man* (1940), and *Young Tom Edison* (1940)—as well as drafts on Jean Renoir's *The Southerner* (1945) and Joseph Losey's *The Big Night* (1951) and *Eva* (1962). Bright, as noted, was already in Mexico City. Gordon Kahn had been living nearby in Cuernavaca since the summer of 1950.

Lester Cole considered Mexico, but chose to go to New York City. After five years he returned to Los Angeles and began to get some uncredited rewrite and television jobs. In subsequent years he was in Europe a lot, not only England, but Czechoslovakia as well as other East European countries and Russia itself.

Among the others who were in or near Mexico City at this time were Albert Maltz, John Wexley, Ian Hunter, Ring Lardner Jr., John Howard Lawson, and Howard Fast. Hunter and Lardner soon moved on to New York City, joined there by Abe Polonsky and Millard Lampell, among others. Trumbo stayed on in Mexico until January 1954, Butler remained there the longest, along with a close friend, producer George Pepper. As Bright had remarked, the Imperial Hotel became a kind of clubhouse for the group, as did the nearby Bounty Bar. A letter from Trumbo to Michael Wilson, after Wilson had visited in the fall of 1953, recounts several nights of drinking adventures there and elsewhere around town. When Fast first arrived, he stayed near Kahn at the Hotel Latino Americana in Cuernavaca; then he, like a number of others, moved to an apartment near Chapultepec Park. Some rented houses.[14]

In a letter to Butler in June 1951, Trumbo described the living arrangements of Maltz, already in Mexico at that time and living in the Mexico City suburb of San Angel: "Maltz tells me he pays $147.00 per month for an enormous house and grounds and pool—much larger than his family needs—furnished, of course, and that he pays 80 pesos a week, which is above the average for two servants."[15]

Maltz, and others, of course, would give the maids and their families, and friends, extra money and food, so that they actually attracted people to wait outside their houses. Hunter's wife pointed out that "Trumbo attracted the biggest crowd of all of us—not surprising because his was the biggest house. [in the Colonia Cuauhetemoc district]." "He [Trumbo] always did things on a bigger scale than anybody else," Hunter said. "In an odd way, he always seemed to be in competition with everybody on practically everything."[16]

Among those who emigrated to Europe, Edward Dmytryk went to London immediately after the first hearings, returned again after serving his prison time. One of the earliest to move there was Donald Ogden Stewart, who never returned to America. "Forty-nine, it was forty-nine," he later recalled. " I was asked to come into the [MGM] office. And it was suggested that I clear myself . . . and give names and so forth. And that was the end of that beautiful contract."[17] By the early fifties, Carl Foreman and Joseph Losey were also in London. After New York City, Lardner moved on to Switzerland and Paris at one point. Wilson, Paul Jarrico, Jules Dassin, and Ben Barzman were among those in France. Wilson had a country house near Paris, at which the Wilsons, Dassins, Jarricos, Berrys, and Barzmans would get together. Somewhat later, Adrian Scott was in Paris before moving on to London. Ben and Norma Barzman also were in Italy at one point, but, after having an apartment in Paris, bought a house replete with swimming pool and tennis court on the French Riviera. With his wife, Sue, and three children (ages fourteen, twelve, and five), Rossen later tried Mexico again, then New York and then moved on to Europe, settled in Italy, where Leonardo Bercovici also settled and wrote there for twelve years. Besides Biberman, others stayed in Hollywood: Sam Ornitz, who was ill; Jarrico; Wilson; and Scott, who stayed for some time before emigrating. Alvah Bessie worked in both Los Angeles and San Francisco, but not in the movie business. Lawson returned from Mexico to work on his books and articles for the Communist media.

Bright remained one of the firmest hard-liners of the old Hollywood Left, even prompting later "old friends" disputes with Dalton Trumbo. Pointedly missing from his reminiscence about who was in Mexico City—one might say whitewashed or white-listed out—was his reason for going to Mexico City at that exact time: Robert Rossen and his work with Rossen on *The Brave Bulls*. Rossen and Bright had both been there early in 1950, before Kahn, and Rossen began actual shooting on the picture in the spring of 1950. Final editing was done in October, after which Rossen went to Europe with his family. *The Brave Bulls* was released on April 19, 1951.

In *The Brave Bulls*, the destructive cycle of betrayal is different, but still intense, still resonant of the tensions in Hollywood. The central figure Luis Bello, the matador—an echo of the artist, the filmmaker—is betrayed by others, but betrays no one but himself. Under the pressures of the *business* of bullfighting, he betrays his dedication to his calling, his art, has surrendered to the fear of failing, the fear of dying. He has lost his nerve and his style: "I'm afraid of the horns," he admits when drunk and at his lowest ebb. In the world of bullfighting, as in the world of making movies, the fickle crowd, the public, turns on you, their fickleness incited and manipulated by the arena and radio announcers, by the press. The bosses, the promoters (producers) are disloyal, fearful themselves, concerned only with what they think the public will buy. It is not only the money men, the bosses and owners, who make the sport, the art, of bullfighting a corrupt business. The betrayals wrought by money work on many levels, have many and varied guises and disguises: Raoul, Luis's longtime colleague, his comrade, his friend and manager who controls Luis's money, lives on the money Luis can make; Luis's family lives on that money. The old bullfighters he knows and reveres are living and dying penniless. As Luis, furious at his family, shouts at them, "Everybody asks me for money. You ask for money in my dreams. I pay for everything. With my flesh—the flesh I expose to the bulls while you get ripe with fat."

But Luis too betrays himself with his money, spends his money—and so always needs more money—beyond the bounds of the dedicated matador, living high with his sleek convertible; large, luxurious home in the city; house in the country; servants; parties and tours of the clubs and restaurants; celebrity's wardrobe and movie star's sunglasses. He needs the money, now most of all, because of his love for the blonde actress, the false, betraying kind of love and woman who is in love with the excitement, the glamour, the power of the matador, of the money that bullfighting can buy. Luis, unlike Charlie and Willie, does not betray his friend; it is the friend who betrays him with the actress. Despite all, there is still the spark of his strength and skill within him, though still there is the clutch of fear on his heart. Holding this all together, feeling his unity with his brother the bull in the ritual of life and death, he makes a last good fight. He finds the moment of truth—and regains his better self—as he goes up and over the horns.

While working on the film, Rossen himself could not escape the nagging fear of losing one's career, one's life work, of losing one's personal way. His world was not that different than the bullfighting world of Luis Bello. In his world of Hollywood, there are the moguls and the press and the fickle public; there are fear, the threatening intrusion of the HUAC, the pressures of membership in the party, the nagging counter-pulls of loyalty and independence, of integrity and success, of the spreading, confused alarms of betrayal. There is an unease in the film—not only in its plot and emotions, but in a certain haste and unevenness, a jaggedness, in the telling and ordering of the material. It is more than just a matter of working in a foreign country with mainly foreign staff. It is as if Rossen feels in himself the pressures on Luis Bello, the uncontrollable contradictions—to perform and meet your own needs and the demands of others, to make money while you can; and yet get it done right, with style and honor. And yet, in Rossen's own life, with the fear, the need to get it done *now*, before it is too late.

Just as *The Brave Bulls* was released, Rossen had to face his own moment of truth, his own test at the horns of the bull—as would many others. The second round of HUAC hearings had begun.

15

The Time of Turmoil, 1951 and After: The Hearings Resume, the Real Blacklist Begins

Early in March of 1951, while Robert Rossen was putting a few last finishing touches on *The Brave Bulls* before its release in mid-April, eight subpoenas were served in Hollywood. It was the minor beginning of a major new series of hearings of the House Un-American Activities Committee (HUAC). Within weeks, more subpoenas were served, pouring down with the reverberating impact of hail on echoing metal roofs. By April and May—when the Ten were completing their prison terms—dozens of people had been served and began to appear before the committee. The hearings were held through those two months and into September, then renewed in 1952.

By this time, four years after the first hearings, many had been struggling with the dilemmas of personal choice, loyalty, and career. But for many the options had been reduced; the formula had hardened as to what was morally acceptable, what would be the basis of the conventional assumptions on into the next century.

In these preceding years of turmoil, threat, and hostility, however, some shift of the basic ground in the government's investigations had indeed occurred. There had been a change in the HUAC's assumptions and procedures, and its personnel. Citations for contempt were no longer a consistent weapon of the committee—issued now on some occasions, mainly in response to hostile appearances. There were signs that the committee's own formula of insisting on naming names could be sidestepped for some, especially behind the scenes. But there were now loud and forceful nongovernmental organizations on the right exerting insistent, intimidating pressures on the industry and even on the HUAC. The chances of forming a liberal coalition were gone. And there was still the shouting level of hostility of those on the left and right that left those

in the middle trapped in a tight corner (a *Dark Corner*, in the title of one
of the film noirs of the time) of limited moral and legal options. There
were continuing, and even increasing, behind-the-scenes actions, but the
chances of acting on a less absolute definition of what was acceptable
in public or private responses, of facing a less absolute insistence on the
ritual naming names were dimmed. By 1951, the momentum—the land-
slide force of the pressures of the Right and the crass fears of the leaders
of the industry—was too great to be stopped, or deflected.

In 1951 the first eight summoned were actors Gale Sondergaard, Larry
Parks, Howard Da Silva, and Sterling Hayden and writers Richard Collins,
Paul Jarrico, Waldo Salt, and Robert Lees. When Sondergaard petitioned
the Screen Actors Guild for help and was not only rejected but soundly
rebuked, it was clear that the political and public relations climate had
changed in Southern California. The Left and the Right had intensified their
positions; the liberal and moderate center was left adrift. It was the beginning of a greatly expanded and solidified blacklist.

A number of the Hollywood Left, fearing subpoenas, had left the country before they could be served. But a greater number—Communists and
former Communists, close fellow travelers, progressives, and others on the
fringe—were served and appeared before the committee in 1951–1953, the
great majority in the first two years. About half of those who appeared did
testify, but there were varying degrees of compliance; the main distinctions
involved reservations about what categories of people and circumstances
they would testify about. Many of those who testified, and many who had
not been called but had been otherwise implicated, still had to pursue various behind-the-scenes rehabilitation procedures before having a chance to
work. Among those who refused to testify, citing the Fifth Amendment
(sometimes joined still by the First) was now the strategy of choice. In most
cases, those following these strategies were not cited for contempt, but in
most cases they were blacklisted.

Some who cited the Fifth and refused to testify refused to answer anything, giving 1947-style speeches. Some, with careful consultations with
attorneys, answered some questions, but generally refused to answer questions about political affiliation. In the innovative strategy known as "the
diminished Fifth," one did talk about some political affiliations. One even
talked about being a member or not within certain time frames, but, with
variations, still invoked the Fifth about other time periods, certain organizations or specific events, and declined to talk about other people.

Robert Rossen was one of those who tried this saving middle way.
When he received his subpoena, he told Harry Cohn his plan—just as *The
Brave Bulls* was being released. Cohn said, "You're a goddamned fool. All
of you are!"[1]

It was a tough spring and summer for Cohn, too. Since he had not cared
to delve into the politics of his employees, Columbia had many people

caught in the HUAC hunt, more movie stars and major figures than any studio at that time. Included were two of Cohn's hottest screen talents— Larry Parks, who was not quite yet a star after his Jolson portrayals, and the bonafide star Judy Holliday. Parks's painful and confused testimony won no awards, and he was left to drift into oblivion. Holliday, never a party member, played her good-natured naïf screen persona and kept her career, and its profits, untouched. But also threatened was a close friend and one of Cohn's most trusted producer-writers, Sidney Buchman, whose work he admired and made money for him and whose company he liked to keep outside of business hours, as he did with Rossen. He had, for example, introduced Rossen to the intricacies of playing the horses on visits to Santa Anita and Hollywood Park, often along with Buchman.[2]

Cohn liked to tell a story, with himself as the butt of the joke, that when Rossen had followed a tip and bet on a twenty-to-one shot, he had asked him, "How much did you bet?"

"Twenty dollars on the nose."

"You're a goddamned idiot," Cohn had told him. But the horse won.

This time he was being an idiot, Cohn was afraid, in a much more serious way, and Cohn couldn't help him. Though he found the growing blacklist a distasteful *blackmail*, he reluctantly went along with the advice—the de-mand—of Nate Spingold, his longtime liaison with the corporate bosses in New York. Those who refused to cooperate with the Committee would have to be fired.[3]

Rossen had told Cohn he would admit to having been a Communist since 1937, but was no longer a member of the party. He would testify about himself only. However, what he did do when he testified on June 25 followed a more restricted strategy; it was designed to show his coop-eration, yet defend his Fifth Amendment right to not state anything that had the possibility of incriminating himself. It was the kind of reasonable strategy that might have had a different outcome *if* the words and deeds of the preceding four years had not been so monumentally unreasonable. A big *if*. At his hearing Rossen stated that he was not a member of the party at that moment, but did not answer questions about whether he had been a member yesterday, last month, last year, or even before he walked in the door. And he refused to discuss anybody but himself. He said, "I should like to emphatically state that I am not a member of the Communist Party. I am not sympathetic with it or its aims." Several times he stressed, "There is no question of my loyalty to this country or my opposition to any kind of divided loyalty, especially to the Soviet Union."[4]

When asked, for no apparent reason, if he would want his children to ever join the party, he said, no, "because I don't believe in it. . . . [It] leads only to one thing . . . dictatorship. . . . It opposes freedom of religion, freedom of speech, and it basically is against the dignity of the human in-dividual. . . . I believe in the democratic way of life."[5]

On the one hand, when asked why he withdrew from the party "as of the time you walked into the room," he insisted, "I did not state that I had ever been a member of the Communist Party." But, on the other hand, he was open to discussing his opposition to the Communist movement in general. When asked if he agreed that "the Communist movement is dedicated to the overthrow of other constitutional forms of government," he answered, "In my opinion, I would have to agree to the extent that unquestionably the Communist Party of either this country or any other country would be dedicated to imposing upon the other country or this country a Soviet form of government, which in and of itself would mean a new kind of constitution, a new kind of system of government."[6]

In defining the dilemma at the core of his belief about the Communist Party he quoted a letter from John Foster Dulles to Representative Nixon. It is a statement that defines as well the dilemma that many faced in choosing how to act: "Those who accept the iron discipline of the party are in a very real sense the agents of foreign principals and hold doctrines which partake of treason. On the other hand, many others are finding in the Communist Party an outlet for a sense of grievance. But they are not in reality either agents of the foreign principal, nor do they entertain treasonable plans. The difficulty is how to distinguish one from the other. That is the difficulty which I do not see clearly how to solve."[7]

It was a narrow path to follow, more than a twenty-to-one shot, and this time the horse wouldn't win. Reluctantly, Cohn released Rossen from his contract.

Then it was Buchman's turn. He had written and produced many films since the first days of talking pictures. His most notable work was on such films as *Theodora Goes Wild* (1936), *Lost Horizon* (1937; though uncredited), *The Awful Truth* (1937), *Holiday* (1938), *Mr. Smith Goes to Washington* (1939), *Here Comes Mr. Jordan* (1941), *The Talk of the Town* (1942), *A Song to Remember* (1945), *The Jolson Story* (1946), and *Jolson Sings Again* (1949). His encounter with the HUAC was the most difficult, even painful, for Cohn—as well, of course, for Buchman. It was also one of the oddest of the blacklist scenarios, and again shows the kind of legal ambiguity that had evolved. When he first appeared, Buchman stated he had left the party because Communism was "stupid, blind, and unworkable for the American people" (not, apparently, because of any evils or horrors it had perpetrated). He would not discuss anyone else and he would *not* invoke the Fifth Amendment. At that point Congressman Donald Jackson left the hearing room and thus left the hearing without a quorum. Buchman's lawyer then called for the end of the hearing, and his demand had to be granted. But Buchman was left in limbo. Cohn was troubled, but unable to help. Buchman evaded a second subpoena, then twice attempted to have the courts invalidate the summons on the grounds that it was "arbitrary, harsh, discriminatory, unnecessary"—unnecessary, he claimed, because he had already testified. The district court didn't agree, but it was not until 1953 that the House of Representatives indicted Buchman for contempt and he was found guilty. He was fined a mere $150 and his one-year sentence was suspended. He had achieved a kind of victory legally, but had to go abroad to be able to continue working in the movie business. After a lost decade, Buchman was able to continue his career with such major films as *The Mark* (1961), *Cleopatra* (1963), and *The Group* (1966). Cohn missed him, and, it was said, would remark when faced with difficult decisions, "Dammit, I wish Sidney was here!"[8]

More painfully disturbing—and more revealing of the desperation felt by many in facing the dilemma of testifying—was the appearance of Rossen's old friend and colleague John Garfield. While Garfield was probably not a member of the party, he had taken part in person and with his signature and money in a myriad of party-controlled activities and organizations, had been involved with numerous party members in business, politics, and social life. When he appeared before the HUAC on April 23, he did not want to take the First or Fifth Amendment, but he did not want to incriminate himself or anyone else. His strategy—or, more accurately, his confused, contradictory, and harassed lack of strategy—was to profess his extreme disapproval of Communism and the Communist Party; but he also attempted to claim his total, and totally unlikely, inability to recall his involvement with anybody who was a Communist or his participation in any of the organizations, meetings, incidents, publications and petitions presented to him.

> *Wood*: Let me ask you categorically, have you any knowledge of the identity of a single individual who was a member of the Communist Party during the time you were in Hollywood?
>
> *Garfield*: No, sir.

And later,

> *Jackson*: I am still not convinced of the entire accuracy of what you are giving this committee. It is your contention you did not know, during all the time you were in New York affiliated with the Group theater . . . you contend you did not know a Communist during all that time in New York?
>
> *Garfield*: That is right.
>
> *Jackson*: And that during the years you were in Hollywood and in close contact with a situation in which a number of Communist cells were operating, with electricians, actors, and every class represented . . . the entire period of time you were in Hollywood you did not know of your own personal knowledge a single member of the Communist Party?
>
> *Garfield*: That is absolutely correct, because I was not a party member or associated in any shape, way, or form.[9]

Neither the committee nor anyone else was satisfied. The *Daily Worker* attacked Garfield for betraying the cause by disowning all he had claimed to believe in. Archer Winsten, in the liberal *New York Post*, said *nobody* could have lived in New York in the thirties and not have known a single Communist. On May 23 *Variety* ran a story quoting unnamed sources that not only was HUAC considering recalling him, but Congressman Jackson was urging an FBI investigation of possible perjury. Friends, both Communists and not, turned on him.[10]

Three months after Garfield testified, his last movie was released. Despite his intense and appropriately troubled, even desperate, characterization, it is unfortunately a redundant, clichéd version of his old themes—of what could have been the motto of his own life, *He Ran All the Way* (1951). It was produced by Bob Roberts, directed by Jack Berry, written by Hugo Butler and Guy Endore (and Dalton Trumbo), from a novel by Sam Ross. All but Ross were among the Communists he had never known. For the next year, he struggled even more desperately with the dilemma of testifying or not. By all accounts he was beginning a strategic reversal of his previous position through non-HUAC channels—based on the premise that he had been "used" by the Communists—when he died of a heart attack in May of 1952.

Why this deluge of subpoenas and the return of the committee at this time, after a lapse of more than three years? The reasons were international and national, as well as rising from forces, needs, and situations within the industry itself.

International tensions, and dangers, had intensified. The Soviets had the atomic bomb. It was a time of television glimpses of construction of bomb shelters in suburban backyards, bomb drills in schools, horror movies with allusions to A-bomb destruction. The Soviet's blockade of Berlin had lasted for many months and lingered longer in minds. A new terror had spread through Eastern Europe, spawning government takeovers, purges, trials, deportations, labor camps, and executions. Strong actions were needed, and taken, to prevent Communist takeovers in Greece and Turkey. The Marshall Plan and Truman Doctrine were hailed in the West and vilified in the East and in international Communist circles. China had fallen to the Communists. The Korean War had begun; it was not ended quickly as hoped and escalated dangerously in the winter of 1950 with the entrance of the Chinese and with sudden devastating impact on American troops just below the Chinese border, all graphically depicted on television.

All this exacerbated fears of Communism, at home and abroad, and encouraged more aggressive anti-Communist actions, and feelings, within the country, where internal events had also contributed to this momentum. The Hiss and Rosenberg cases, the Klaus Fuchs international spy case, and other revelations of espionage in the United States raised the public awareness of and hostility toward Communists. Right-wing organizations and demagogues and a wide segment of the press, especially the Hearst newspapers, heightened, manipulated, and promoted the hostility and fears of the public with insistent ranting about Communist threats and dangers. The public furor was fed, of course, by the wilder claims and "investigations" of Senator Joseph McCarthy in the several years after his Wheeling speech early in 1950. His distorting crusade was given exaggerated emphasis and prominence in the Hearst press (as it has be given, conversely, by many historians and popular histories ever since); but it played a minor role in any actual effective and realistic actions against Communist propaganda and infiltration. Truman's loyalty program had broader consequences and was hotly debated at the time—as did, and as was, the McCarren Internal Security Act of 1950. The McCarren Act expanded legislation that had been instituted several years earlier. It called for all "Communist-action" and "Communist-front" organizations to register with the attorney general and for officers of those organizations to do so if the organization did not comply. President Truman had vetoed the bill, but the veto was overridden. Controversial and argued in the courts in subsequent years, it was generally upheld and finally upheld by the Supreme Court in 1961. Much earlier than that, convictions under the Smith Act were being upheld by the courts. Organized labor, led by Walter Reuther, also took strong steps against Communist influence at this time, calling for reforms and expelling a number of Communist-controlled unions.

The HUAC was also encouraged to go ahead full speed with renewed hearings by the government's knowledge of the impact that earlier hearings, investigations, and court cases had had on the Communist Party of America. By 1951, the government was aware that the party had set up a security program and had basically gone underground, influential people meeting in groups of five or less, suspect and "weak" people being weeded out.[11]

Despite the success of the actions taken by the Truman administration, the Republicans used anti-Communism as a battle cry in the November 1950 elections, branding the administration as "soft on Communism." The Republicans gained seats in both houses of Congress, but especially in the House of Representatives.

In Hollywood the conservative Motion Picture Alliance and its action arm, the Motion Picture Industry Council, both basically under the direction of Roy Brewer, were already calling for stronger steps to show the public that the movie industry was not being "soft on Communism." In September 1951, a new coalition was formed between the alliance and a national organization called the Crusade for Freedom. Years earlier, when the alliance was first organized, the Crusade for Freedom's Hollywood chairman Walter Wanger had criticized the alliance for making "unsupported charges of Communism in the motion picture industry." Now, in a public letter,

Wanger asserted "that time and history have proven the correctness of the judgment of the Motion Picture Alliance and its foresight in recognizing the Communist menace. Gladly, I accept your assurance of support in the great task of our lives: that of tightening ranks here and everywhere in defense of freedom and against our proven enemies—Communism and all those who espouse or support it."[12]

After the first set of 1951 hearings, Ronald Reagan wrote a guest column in the *Hollywood Citizen News*, "Reds Beaten in Hollywood." His fervent tone reflects the extreme passions of the time, and the pride of winning in a righteous battle—this time from the Right:

> They [the Reds] tried every trick in the bag, but the actors, led by the Board of Directors of the Screen Actors Guild, out-thought them and out-fought them. We fought them on the record and off the record.
>
> We fought them in meetings and behind the scenes.
>
> Our Red foes even went so far as to threaten to throw acid in the faces of myself and some other stars, so that "we never would appear on the screen again." I packed a gun for some time and policemen lived at my home to guard my kids.
>
> But that was more than five years ago and those days are gone forever, along with the deluded Red sympathizer and fellow traveler. . . .
>
> And any American who has been a member of the Communist Party at any time but who has now changed his mind and is loyal to our country should be willing to stand up and be counted; admit, "I was wrong," and give all the information he has to the government agencies who are combating the Red plotters.[13]

In addition to anti-Communist activists within the industry, a strong influence on them, on the committee members, and on the public was the growing power of nonindustry organizations and publications devoted to fighting Communism for a variety of reasons—from idealism and zealous ideology to commercial gain. The Catholic church and the American Legion were the leading major organizations calling for more action, while new groups such as Aware, Inc., and Crossfire began strident and public campaigns to bar suspected entertainment people from employment. With or without the HUAC, the momentum to implement a more stringent and widespread blacklist was building. The HUAC hearings gave that momentum its focus, its public forum and governmental justification; but as the procedures and actions developed and spread beyond the hearings, more people were caught in the web than those who appeared before the committee.

And, meanwhile, there was no unity or concerted action among the liberals and the Left; voices were random, unfocused, unsure—as much in conflict with each other as with the rampant din of voices on the right.

The hearings themselves also took on a new and paradoxical tone. The new chairman, John S. Wood, and the members were less controversial and more aware of past criticism of the committee's methods. Most of those who appeared, even those who refused to testify, did so less theatrically and aggressively than the Hollywood Ten had done. So that overall the hearings themselves had a strangely calm decorum—despite occasional outbursts, despite the heated anti-Communist climate of the period, and despite the increasing damage being done to the lives of those who had been called to testify. The hearings grew calmer; the blacklist merely grew.

More than one hundred were summoned in this series of hearings. Among those called in 1951 were John Garfield, Gale Sondergaard, Howard Da Silva, Robert Lees, Richard J. Collins, Waldo Salt, Paul Jarrico. Abe Polonsky, Edward Dmytryk (who requested an appearance), Budd Schulberg, Harold J. Ashe, Martin Berkeley, Carl Foreman, Frank Tuttle, Sidney Buchman, Larry Parks, Judy Holliday, Sterling Hayden, Jose Ferrer, Leo Townsend, Pauline Townsend, David Lang, Leonardo Bercovici, and Robert Rossen.

Among those summoned in 1952 were Elia Kazan, Lillian Hellman, Michael Blankfort, Edward G. Robinson, Clifford Odets, Abe Burrows, Lloyd Bridges, Lucille Ball, Isobel Lennart, J. Edward Bromberg, Roy Huggins, Meta Reis Rosenberg, Harold Hecht, Leopold Atlas, Melvin Levy, Michael Wilson, and Millard Lampell.

Lewis Milestone and Howard Koch, among the original Nineteen, were never called to appear. Koch had been one of the writers of the wartime pro-Soviet film *Mission to Moscow* (1943), which had become a center of controversy after the war. He was one of the main writers of *Casablanca* (1942) and numerous other successful movies. Oddly, considering Francis Faragoh's longtime activities within the Screen Writers Guild and the Hollywood party, he did not appear until 1953, as did Jerome Robbins, Lionel Stander, Lee J. Cobb, and Robert Rossen (who requested an appearance).

By 1951 court precedents had established the strict legal acceptance of the Fifth Amendment, though the moral and theoretical validity of its use in these circumstances was subject to much debate. After one of the many evocations of it, Chairman Wood responded, "If you say the question would incriminate you, it leaves one conclusion in my mind and in the mind of every fair-minded person within sound of your voice. Now, if in fact, you are not a member of it [the Communist Party], then your statement that it would tend to incriminate you isn't a true statement."[14]

The Association of Motion Picture Producers did more than express its displeasure at the constant use (for them "misuse") of the Fifth Amendment. It announced that under the provisions of its 1947 Waldorf Statement, producers would now take action against all those who took the Fifth Amendment.[15]

Brewer's Motion Picture Industry Council placed a parallel statement in the record of the HUAC hearings on September 17, 1951: "The country is engaged in a war with Communism. Eighty-seven thousand casualties leave little room for witnesses to stand on the First and Fifth Amendments, and for those who do we have no sympathy. . . . In time of crisis, we believe that the demands of American patriotism make necessary that witnesses respond to the call of their country, as represented by your Committee, and give you all the information necessary to the success of your objective."[16]

While Brewer would not accept the Fifth Amendment as a patriotic answer, he also would not accept what he considered the actions of extremists as a patriotic campaign. By May 15, 1952, Brewer felt he could declare that not one who "hid behind the Fifth Amendment" was working in the industry. In the same speech, however, he also insisted that the only "list" that should be used was that found in the reports of the HUAC. He complained that publications like *Red Channels* gave ammunition to what he scornfully called "amateurs," who actually were harmful to the just and proper conduct of the investigations and distort the public's perception of them. They contribute, he averred, to shifting the focus from Communism to "persecution." For "one of the by-products of this problem is that we make heroes out of guys who are not heroes, and enemies out of people who ought not to be enemies. People who have social consciences are penalized, and guys who never helped anybody are way out in front. It was only the people who were trying to help others who got involved. And they ought not to be punished." By the mid-fifties, Brewer was deeply concerned about the impact of Senator McCarthy's wild claims and actions upon his own crusade in Hollywood. "The McCarthy hearings," he had decided, "so confused the American people that there was no way to buck it. They created the impression you could not isolate the Communist influence without destroying democracy."[17]

The path followed by Carl Foreman through this ambiguous thicket of testifying and not testifying, of public and private maneuvers and disputes, was more complicated than most; but nonetheless it is illustrative of the pressures on many, the strategies contemplated by many, acted on by a good many. Foreman's actions prompted a good deal of controversy on both the left and the right. When he was given his summons, he was working on the completion of *High Noon* (1952). He was the key screenwriter (*Champion* [1949], *Home of the Brave* [1949], *Cyrano de Bergerac* [1950], *The Men* [1950]) for the Stanley Kramer Company, which at that time was negotiating a contract with Columbia and Harry Cohn to affiliate the independent production company with the major studio and thus allow it to set bigger budgets for its quality films. Under the Kramer Company provisions, Foreman, like other associates, was a limited partner in the company. Thus, much was being placed in jeopardy by his appearance.

Across the divide, even the Communist Party was concerned. They sent an envoy to discuss the matter with Foreman and insist that he take a totally anti-HUAC stand. The envoy was party loyalist Eddie Huebsch, who was working with Lester Cole on rewrites and television jobs at the time. After consulting with lawyer Sidney Cohn (no relation to Harry), Foreman chose a unique path through the minefield. He would testify about the present (he claimed to have left the party in 1942) and, step-by-step, certain individual years in the past before invoking his Fifth Amendment rights. Foreman's performance in 1951 did not please the committee, Harry Cohn, Columbia, or Kramer. His contract was revoked and he emigrated to England (and one of the most successful careers among the blacklisted).

In the ironic aftermath, the Kramer Company alliance with Columbia proved a disaster emotionally and financially, though it did produce a number of good small-scale films with a distinct liberal tone and social perspective. Ten films in a row failed to recoup their investment, topped by *The 5,000 Fingers of Dr. T* (1953), a musical fantasy that grossed $249,000 against a cost of $1,631,000. The subsequent success of *The Caine Mutiny* (1954; directed by Edward Dmytryk) compensated for the previous losses and allowed a graceful public parting, though not an amicable one. Cohn continued to protest that Kramer lost him money.

Foreman's later dealings with the committee were also unique. Though they continued to be controversial, they give an indication of the kind of alternative procedures and maneuvers that might have been more widely acted upon by this time. After Foreman's work on the major British film *The Bridge on the River Kwai* (1957), Sidney Cohn advised him that Columbia was interested in him and would be helpful in getting him back to work in the United States. In 1956, in negotiations that have been the subject of much debate (including unfounded rumors of money being passed), Foreman was allowed to appear in a one-man closed executive session with Congressman Francis E. Walter. Harry Cohn was already ill, but was helpful in arranging the session. The deal with Cohn and Columbia was apparently based on Foreman's not taking the Fifth Amendment, and apparently (the testimony has never been released, but has been read by others) he did not, though there are those like Stanley Kramer who believed he did. Foreman testified about himself, but still evaded, one way or another, talking about the membership of others, at least directly. Foreman was cleared. Walter was roundly criticized and allowed no such private sessions after that.[18]

Those who took the Fifth, and the committee members as well, were generally more courteous and subdued than at the first hearings. The more active and ideologically committed party members, like Jarrico, Wilson, and Polonsky, were among the minority who vehemently and dramatically still went on the attack against the HUAC in the confrontational style of the Ten, while this time still invoking their Fifth Amendment rights. Their attacks also brought in the usual rhetoric about "peace" that as a constant aspect of the Left's criticism of the committee, and all investigations.

After the usual litany of Fifth Amendment claims, Polonsky, for example, did answer, while actually evading, a question about whether he would defend America against the Soviet Union if there was a war. "I do not believe that by committing ourselves to a war we can get peace. I do not think that is the way to get peace." After some further evasions, he said, "I believe if we prepare for war constantly, we will surely have it."[19]

Wilson took the Fifth and went on with the usual phraseology, as established at the first hearings in 1947: "and in so doing I wish also to protect the rights of every American citizen to the privacy of belief and association. . . . I think that subversion is what is being committed against the Bill of Rights here today." Wilson had already written a script for *Friendly Persuasion*, which Frank Capra was to produce, but didn't—for reasons that have long been debated. Wilson brought that into his testimony and told the committee, "I feel that this committee might take the credit, or part of it at least, for the fact that *The* [sic] *Friendly Persuasion* was not produced, in view of the fact that it dealt warmly, in my opinion, with a peace-loving people." The film was made by William Wyler and released in 1956.[20]

Jarrico, too, brought in the current peace crusade when asked if he knew of any organization that "advocates the forceful overthrow of the constitutional form of government." He did not, of course, directly answer and say he did not believe the Communist Party advocated that. Rather, he took the usual well-trod path: "By your definition, sir, every organization that has stood for decency and progress, the New Deal, against discrimination, for peace, and so on—these organizations are all allied with an organization which advocates the overthrow of the government."[21]

In 1943 Jarrico had coscripted *Song of Russia* with his close friend Richard J. Collins. While an understandable wartime gesture to an ally experiencing tremendous destruction, it goes beyond valid sentiment and turns its Soviet farm and farm workers into a light opera fantasy world of noble and courageous peasants, joyous communal work and clean living. In 1951, Collins testified, and included Jarrico in his testimony. For one thing, he testified that Jarrico had called him to urge him not to testify. When he, Collins, had asked Jarrico why he was still supporting the Soviet Union, Collins testified that Jarrico said he still believed "the Soviet Union is devoted to the interests of all the people and peace-loving as well." Jarrico, in his appearance, and for years afterward, denounced Collins, as well as others. In defending his stance in the *New York Times* of March 24, 1951, Jarrico said, "If I have to choose between crawling in the mud with Larry Parks or going to jail like my courageous friends of the Hollywood Ten, I shall certainly choose the latter."[22]

As usual, Lillian Hellman's performance was more expertly staged, designed for maximum promotion of her image, while safely slipping past the legal danger zone. Her counsel, Joseph Rauh, managed to get the committee to accept her prepared statement, a polite letter to Chairman Wood. It included her much-publicized statement, "I cannot and will not cut my conscience to fit this year's fashions" (except, of course, when the fashions were directed by the Soviet Union and the Communist Party). When the letter was moved to be included in the record, Rauh proceeded immediately to hand out prepared copies to the press. It was the letter, not her actual testimony, that was widely publicized in the press. The headline in the *New York Times* the next day read: "Lillian Hellman Balks House Unit," not "Lillian Hellman Takes the Fifth."

In the letter Hellman offered to talk about "my own opinions and my own actions, regardless of the risks or consequences to myself . . . if your Committee will agree to refrain from asking me to name other people."[23] The committee said it did not negotiate with witnesses, and the questioning began. Hellman took a confused version of the "diminished Fifth," but it made no difference.

Tavenner: Are you now a member of the Communist Party?

Hellman: No sir.

Tavenner: Were you ever a member of the Communist Party?

Hellman: I refuse to answer, Mr. Tavenner, on the same grounds [the Fifth Amendment].

She then invoked her rights in refusing to answer a series of questions. Except one:

Wood: Were you two years from this time?

Hellman: No, sir. [Not, as expected, "I refuse to answer."][24]

Was it purely a careless slip or was there some more direct conscious or unconscious reason? That she knew she could only say she had not been a member from 1949 on? Despite many, many later words, Hellman afterward did not discuss this one two-word answer.

Despite all the extensive hearings of 1951, the American Legion and others were not satisfied. In December 1951, the Legion magazine published an article by J. B. Matthews, "Did the Movies Really Clean House?" The answer of course was no, they had not gone far enough. The American Legion then distributed a list of some three hundred names to the major studios—compiled from other sources, not original investigation, and containing former Communists and non-Communists alike. The submission included a request for the studios sending "such reports to us as you deem proper." With no clear opposition from the liberals or Left in the game, the producers panicked. They met with legion officials on March 31, 1952, supposedly to arrange a procedure by which people could clear themselves. They ended up capitulating to all the legion's demands, agreeing to investigate the employees listed by the legion, cooperating in a procedure of letter writing for those named to clear their names.[25]

The American Legion (as did other organizations) also organized public demonstrations to protest the distribution of films with alleged Communist participants. For example, on December 23, 1952, they organized a mass of pickets at the premiere of *Moulin Rouge* as a protest against its star, Jose Ferrer, and even its outspoken liberal director, John Huston. This did not halt the attendance of prominent Hollywood people at the premiere or the subsequent distribution of the film.[26]

The American Legion continued to maintain close contacts with the organizations in Hollywood that were now, at least partially, in control of the implementation of the blacklist (still never defined as such) and the rehabilitation procedures. Roy Brewer and his chief assistant, Howard Costigan, were active at both ends of this spectrum—denying work, opening the door to resume work. A number of lawyers, including Sidney Cohn, had open relations with them in attempting to work out procedures for various individuals, while maintaining their independence from the system itself. Martin Gang worked effectively with Costigan, an ex-FBI agent, and Brewer, whom he called a "voice of sanity" and a "decent, honest man." (Historians Larry Ceplair and Steven Englund refer to Brewer as "the fanatical anti-communist.")[27]

Gang himself became the object of much vilification in the standard Left narrative of the period. He believed that people who were not Communists but who were afraid to testify to that because of the climate of the "moral blacklist" that had been created—that these people should have a way of maintaining their livelihood. He was instrumental in both convincing many to seek this kind of "rehabilitation" and guiding them successfully through the process outside of the hearings. Hearst columnists George Sokolsky, Victor Reisel, and Frederick Woltman were directly involved. Sokolsky worked closely with Brewer in attempting to lead people back into the fold.[28]

As the blacklist was accelerated, in part because of the much-publicized pressure of private organizations with special (and commercial) interests, these organizations, who claimed they represented the public and its welfare, became even stronger sources of pressures on all the entertainment industries. American Business Consultants was one of the first with its publications *Counterattack* and *Red Channels*. By 1953 the most influential, and most connected to Hollywood forces, was Aware, Inc., which published *Confidential Notebook*. Its founder, Vincent Hartnett, became one of the central clearance agents, as did James O'Neil, publisher of the American Legion–connected *Firing Line*. The Wage Earners Committee, in their *National*

Wage Earner, named "subversive" films, protested by organizing picketing and distributing circulars.[29]

In the latter half of the decade, the fervor on both sides began to dissipate. The blacklist, the unofficial regulations and decisions, the rehabilitations had become a tawdry status quo. Most of those who were to be affected had been affected, one way or another. The fervor, the clamor, the desperate activity had waned, but the monolith stayed in place, unchanging, yet beginning to show signs of softening into tired old news, and not in the long run good for business. The business of making movies, not its politics loomed larger. Compromises, deals, more and more maneuvers were attempted; but it was still years, at the turn of the decade, before there was any substantial and symbolic breaking of the blacklist, and before many, though not all, not ever, could breathe a sigh of relief and get back to business.

It was, perhaps, fitting that Albert Maltz and Dalton Trumbo participated in the publicized sequence of the symbolic breakthrough. In 1958, it was revealed that blacklisted writer Nedrick A. Young, as Nathan Douglas, was one of the writers nominated for an Academy Award for the script of Stanley Kramer's *The Defiant Ones* (1958). Trumbo had initiated a letter-writing, telephoning campaign; the script won. Frank Sinatra was then encouraged to deal with Albert Maltz for the screenplay of *The Execution of Private Slovik*. After the contract was announced, the American Legion and others protested, and Sinatra backed down. It was up to Trumbo. On January 19, 1960, Otto Preminger announced that Trumbo would write the script for his epic film *Exodus* (1960). Trumbo had already been working on a major rewrite of the script for Howard Fast's novel, *Spartacus* (1951). Kirk Douglas then announced that the screenplay for his film *Spartacus* (1960) was being written by Dalton Trumbo.

In 1955, Adrian Scott had provided a summary of the blacklist in an article in the Left-wing *Hollywood Review*. By his count, 214 of what he termed "studio employees" had been blacklisted—106 writers, 36 actors, 11 directors. Later appraisals of the total vary and are usually higher; there is no single exact source. By several estimates, the Screen Actors Guild total was more than one hundred. The totals of Scott, and several others, appear to be based on those who took the Fifth Amendment, which leaves out all those who never appeared and were blacklisted. On the other hand, many who were on some lists did go through "rehabilitation" and then worked; so totals on any of the lists are a complicated problem. Reports issued by the HUAC had about 325 people by 1954; the American Legion had more than 300, but not all of those were denied work. The most common figure cited is that by the end of the decade, somewhat above 300 were blacklisted and denied work forever or for some period of time.[30]

16

What Is Behaving Decently?
Those Who Testified and
Named Names

Of those who testified before the House Un-American Activities Committee (HUAC) from 1951 to 1953, those who had been members of the party were the most controversial then and have been so ever since. These former members named names. Among the most prominent were Robert Rossen, Elia Kazan, Edward Dmytryk, Budd Schulberg, Clifford Odets, Lee J. Cobb, Martin Berkeley, and Richard Collins. For more than half a century they have been scorned, both in political and extremely personal terms, their work belittled and even ignored in the Left-influenced history and criticism of the period. Within this absolutist moral dichotomy, they have been allowed no principled motives, their statements, however thoughtful, seen as deceitful. They are only immoral stool pigeons, informers, betrayers, driven only by cowardice, greed, even petty spite.

Early on, Albert Maltz wrote Herbert Biberman: "The new Hollywood business is very grim, very savage. I watch it with an inner sickness. . . . Oh, the moral horror of this parade of stool pigeons, what a sickness it spreads over the whole land."[1]

A typical later interview exchange, in this case between Paul Buhle and Walter Bernstein, beginning with the typically loaded question:

Buhle: Is Dmytryk the lowest category of informers for you? Or does Kazan rival him with his own qualifications?

Bernstein: I hate to quantify, although Dmytryk would definitely be among the lowest of the low for me. Why give him [Kazan, on being given a Life Achievement Award in 2001] an award? . . . But any official award given by an official body would be given to someone who disgraced the profession.[2]

If one grants that those who testified did act on principle, they still paid the price—as in all difficult dilemmas—of a kind of betrayal, of both principle and people. They named the names of others as members or former members of the party, and so they became complicit in the actions of the committee and enforcers of the blacklist; because of this, were complicit to some degree in the consequences for those who were named. The nature of this betrayal, however, is further complicated by the fact that in almost all cases the names were already known. Their act of naming them did not actually, directly determine whatever consequences ensued for other people.

Such complexities of motive, action, and consequences are not taken into account by those who did not testify, nor by those who have supported and glorified them. Victor Navasky epitomizes the moral zealotry of the orthodox position in this hyperbolic summation: "The blacklist savaged private lives, but the informer's particular contribution was to pollute the public well, to poison social life in general, to destroy the very possibility of a community; for the informer operates on the principle of betrayal and a community survives on the principle of trust." Walter Bernstein's comment on Rossen is representative of the judgments made on individuals through the years: "Rossen had no real belief larger than his ego. He saw informing as pure survival, without any of the justifications other informers found necessary to give"—ignoring the many pages of analysis and documentation in Rossen's testimony.[3]

As Kazan bluntly phrased his very personal experiencing of this moral arrogance, "I became an easy mark for every self-righteous prick in New York and Hollywood."[4]

There *have been* those who have questioned the absolute duality of this conventional wisdom of the Left—that has been promulgated widely in academia and the media. While Ted Morgan in *Reds* sees the difficult dilemma of testifying, he is stern in his basic response to the silence: "Why could they not tell the truth? The answer given was that if you admitted membership, you would have to name others, which made you a stool pigeon. But between the posturing cardboard heroes who took the fifth and those who named names, the former were cowards afraid of admitting their allegiance, while the latter were doing their duty as citizens under oath before a congressional committee. Some of the latter were opportunists trying to avoid the blacklist, but others had left the party and felt it was proper to expose its underhandedness."[5]

"One would not know from seeing films such as *The Front* or reading books like [Vivian Gornick's] *The Romance of American Communism* that the heroes in them were apologists for Stalin's death machine," writes historian William L. O'Neill, no defender of the HUAC's excesses, in *A Better World: The Great Schism—Stalinism and the American Intellectuals*. For O'Neill the other side of the coin of these evasions, as typified by Lillian Hellman, was to see any breaking of the silence as the result of cowardice or greed. "There was to her no chance that anyone might be anti-Stalinist on principle. It had to be a pretext for doing the comfortable thing."[6]

In 1953 the historian Alan F. Westin argued, "The cause of freedom is best served not by silence but by free speech. Witnesses should answer the question about their organizational memberships or actions and then defend their current political position before the committee and thus before the public." Not testifying, he wrote, created "in the minds of most well-intentioned people simply the image of one more Communist . . . cloaking his activities in the disguise of an appeal to civil liberties. . . . Those who refused to testify helped the Communist Party which wanted all witnesses to choose silence in order to camouflage the activities of the Party."[7]

And so, to place Victor Navasky's aggrandizing phrase in this different context—just what are the complexities of *behaving decently* that are revealed in the testimony of those who turned against the party—and also named names?

Here is a cross-section view of the kind of testimony that is not adequately or accurately presented and is given no credence in the orthodox judgments of the period and its people.

The testimony of Budd Schulberg in 1951 focused in great detail on the infringements on freedom by Communism and the Soviet Union—censorship of writers in America, oppression in the Soviet Union. He later commented, "My guilt is what we [the party] did to the Czechs, not to Ring Lardner. I testified because I felt guilty for having contributed unwittingly to intellectual and artistic as well as racial oppression."[8]

Robert Rossen testified on May 7, 1953, about his beliefs and principles, his membership in the party, his reasons for leaving the party and for testifying, and his knowledge of some he knew as members, though very little about them. Before testifying, he wrestled with his own conscience in attempting to answer for himself that question about behaving decently.

Carey McWilliams recalled intense conversations he had had with Rossen at that time (when the progressive activist was editor of *The Nation*):

> I knew and liked Robert Rossen, the director, who was on the next list of those to be summoned after the Hollywood Ten. I spent hours listening to him as he agonized over the decision he had to make, and I was not surprised when he finally decided to testify. Unless he could make films, life had little meaning for him. . . . Back in 1946, the two of us had served as co-chairmen of a committee which raised more than $20,000 to aid some CIO strikers who were having a rough time of it. So I had reason to know something about his basic social views and sympathies.[9]

In his testimony, Rossen himself stressed the complicated issue of conscience:

> The decision that I arrived at in 1951 was an individual decision. I wasn't a member of the Communist Party at the time, as I stated. I felt that the position I had taken at the time was a position of what I considered to be a position of individual morality. I felt it was a matter between me and my own conscience. . . . I did a lot of thinking. I don't think, after 2 years of thinking, that any one individual can ever indulge himself in the luxury of individual morality or pit it against what I feel today very strongly is the security and safety of this Nation.[10]

In amplifying his view of the Communist Party and its relation to the crises in the world that affected the security of the nation—crises that called for a social as well as an individual morality—Rossen emphasized several major issues that he believed he had to take a stand on. One (as touched on briefly earlier) was the Soviet and CPUSA duplicity about Jews—proclaiming official recognition and support while murdering, repressing, imprisoning, and torturing.

In his 1953 testimony, Rossen provided examples from the party press that illustrated the consistent duplicity. In one example from a crucial series of articles and editorials in September of 1939 (during the Nazi-Soviet Pact), the *Daily Worker* proclaimed in one, "For National Freedom and World Peace,"

> As Hitler's hordes advanced further into Poland, the atrocities against the Jewish people and other minorities exceeded some of fascism's goriest deeds.
> In this situation the Soviet Government sent in the Red Army, an army of liberation, to protect the Ukra[i]nian and White Russian minorities, after the semi-fascist Polish government had ceased to exist [!] and had left them to the ravages of war and fascist enslavement. More than a million Jews living in Western Ukraine and Western Belo Russia [i.e., eastern Poland] are now beyond the pale of fascist anti-Semitism.[11]

The *Worker* did not discuss why the Soviet government had to deport several hundred thousand Poles, including many Jews, to Siberia, and also invade the three Baltic states and Finland. Rather, he testified, that as a result of the party's claims, "the important part of the Nazi-Soviet pact, to me, personally, was the [alleged] fact that it saved over a million Jews from being destroyed by Hitler." He now knew this to be a terrible falsehood, but, he said, it was the party's rationale. "It was always necessary at that time to get a rationale. In other words, practically my whole life in the Party, as I reflect upon it, is one of rationales." Since then, he went on, he had seen many examples of the Soviet's cynical, and brutal, hypocrisy on "the Jew-ish question." Recent events, such as the attacks on Jewish intellectuals and doctors and the Slansky trials, had convinced him that Communist claims of supporting minorities were an immoral lie:

> And the Soviet Union was very well aware, knowing Communists as I have—
> no action is taken without the awareness of the consequences of that action.
> The Soviet Union knew that by raising the word "Jew" and raising the word
> "traitor" it was specifically inciting the people of these various countries, which
> had been hotbeds of anti-Semitism for hundreds of years, to anti-Semitism;
> and I think the act was done deliberately, and all of the good intentions, the
> avowed, professed interests of the Soviet Union in Jews as a minority was
> thrown overboard completely. . . .
>   And I think that is one of the most evil, immoral, and corrupt acts that has
> occurred in my lifetime—something I feel very deeply about, very strongly
> about—and I think if there was any illusion, any more, in terms of the feeling
> of the Soviet Union toward minorities—I think this act must expose to any-
> body that this is all an illusion and it has no basis in fact. . . .
>   . . . to the extent that it [the American Communist Party] supports Soviet
> policy in this—to the extent that it supports these trials—to the extent that
> it does not denounce the equation of the word "Jew" to traitor that has been
> made—to that extent, whether by conscious intent, or whatever it is—to that
> extent, it must be anti-Semitic.[12]

This testimony clearly is based on the thinking and rethinking that he had been doing in January 1953, when he brought his thinking on the Jews into focus with the composition of a letter to the *New York Times*. In that letter he had written, "For if ever a theme [that "absolute power breeds absolute corruption"] has been completely proven by an action, the official sanction of the incitement to anti Semitism, contained in the recent purges and trials occurring behind the Iron Curtain, is that action. Of all the cyni-cal and corrupt acts committed in the name of saving the land of socialism, this is the most cynical, the most corrupt, the most immoral."[13]

Recent events and revelations had also convinced him that other pro-claimed goals and ideals of the Communist Party were equally illusory. He learned that "the same reasons why you go into the party are the same reasons which make you go out, which is ultimately the discovery that the idealism that you were looking for, the fighting for the ideas that you want, are just not in the party."[14]

Rossen had, he said, experienced Communism's infringement on freedom on a personal level, as a writer. "Now at this point the Party is no longer in-terested in this man as a creative artist. . . . At this point the Communist Party position says, 'Oh, no, now you are a Communist; you will accept Com-munist Party discipline.'" He was, for example, present at the 1943 meeting when Albert Maltz was "told his first function was to be a Communist."

I think this was a common thing in my experience in the Party, and naturally you begin to see all of these things in different lights; you begin to get the feeling that, in a sense, where you always felt you were using people, you know, trying to convert them and so forth; you began to suddenly see you were being used; that the Party respect for you, the Party veneration of the masses, which is a wonderful word—its so-called feeling for the masses, for people—somehow or other never really expressed itself in terms of its feeling for the individual. There was quite a separation between the word "masses" and the word "person" and that—it didn't equate itself at all.[15]

Whatever the political and ideological reasons, there were certainly personal needs and motives behind his reasoning and internal debate that must remain conjectures, but several likely possibilities can be cited. For one, Rossen's sincere and intense interest in America, as evidenced in the distinct American flavor of most of his serious work, might well have had two effects. The first can be seen as a growing optimism about the possibilities of the nation, an attitude that would support his change of stance toward the committee, an attitude reflected in this statement from his testimony:

What this country really can become is still something to be believed in very firmly, very strongly, with great conviction. . . . I wouldn't like to see young people today believe what I believed in. I wouldn't like to have them feel there is no growth left in this country: there are no horizons; we have reached our apex, and that it's a dead society. It's not a dead society. It's a young society, it's a growing society; it's a healthy society. It needs a lot of corrections of course, and all societies do, but it needs the corrections, and can get the corrections and realize its hope only in terms of the system of government that's been devised.[16]

A second implication of his concern for American subjects is a more personal one. For Rossen, making movies was a passion, a need, a driving force, and two years of inactivity had left him deeply frustrated. With the kind of particularly American subjects he was most interested in, and handled best, he would find it more difficult than had others (like Joseph Losey, Carl Foreman, and Jules Dassin) to work effectively abroad. And one cannot discount, either, within the conflicting pulls of Rossen's character, the need and drive for success, which as in the case of his characters seemed an essential part of his own will to power.

The nature of the testimony about others that he was called upon to give provides another mitigating factor. He was asked to comment only on those names already compiled from research and voluminous files, names that had also been mentioned time and time again in the six years of testimony preceding his own final appearance. How, then, would the refusal to provide this kind of redundant, and in some ways inconsequential, testimony be worth the sacrifice of a career? That was the kind of question Rossen and others had to answer, each in his or her own way.

What was unusual in his case was that the moral dilemma he faced was like a personal dramatization of the central issues of many of his films. For in the films, the definition and fulfillment or the corruption of one's true self, one's élan, one's gift became more and more intricately entangled with the troubling ambiguities of motives, and the paradoxical varieties of betrayal.

Whatever the combination of motives, the decision and the long ordeal before and after had a lasting effect on Rossen and his work. The actress Jean Seberg, who starred in Rossen's final film, *Lilith* (1964), captured this perceptively in a 1966 article: "He was a very complicated man, agonized even, who continually asked himself questions about himself. Perhaps one must seek out the cause of this anguish in the great McCarthy trauma, in which his world had literally toppled. . . . Rossen had been on the blacklist for a long time. . . . I think the moral shock of this affair changed him deeply. He was led to withdraw into himself, to live a little apart with his family, to take things into consideration more, to examine the secret motivations of people."[17]

Whatever the final effects on Rossen, the immediate result in 1953 was that he was able to work again, although he never again even visited Hollywood.

Two years earlier, during the hearings of 1951, others, including Edward Dmytryk, also emphasized the dilemma involved in defining and acting upon conscience, and the crucial issue of the freedom to speak and act based on one's sense of conscience. His appearance, he said, was "dictated by my own conscience, absolutely."[18] Since Dmytryk had been one of the Ten and had served his sentence, his speaking out, refusing any longer to remain silent, might have been seen as a sincere and difficult reaching for the truth. Instead, within the tangles and twists of the moral fabric of the period, he was seen then (and portrayed ever since) as an even more flagrant betrayer because he now said that he had been *wrong* in defending the party—and so he was a betrayer on several levels and could not be doing it because he believed what he said.

In his testimony, Dmytryk discussed the reasons for his disillusionment in the party in both general and personal terms, and presented his reasons for testifying after refusing to do so during his first appearance in 1947. In a later TV interview, he said, "Defending the Communist Party was worse than naming names. I did not want to remain a martyr to something that I absolutely believed was immoral and wrong." What had brought about this change of heart and conscience? On a personal level, one thing, he said in an article in the *Saturday Evening Post*, "that got me was the way the Ten were being turned into martyrs. . . . When I left, it had basically been a good civil liberties case. Now it was being used as a spearhead against all attacks on Communism. . . . The hardest thing I had to live with was the realization that they were trying to protect Communism in this country by invoking the constitution and civil liberties."[19]

On the world scene, Dmytryk testified, "There is a great deal of difference between 1947 and 1951, as far as the Communist Party is concerned, or at least as far as my awareness of what is going on is concerned." Among the differences was the intensification of the Cold War "beyond the freezing point" due to Soviet aggressions and the CPUSA (Communist Party of America) defense of the Soviet actions. Another was the increase in statements by party leaders, members, or followers that they would refuse to fight for America in a war against Soviet Russia. Related to this in his mind was the deceit of the peace campaigns and his realization that the Communists were not sincere in talking about peace when North Korea invaded South Korea: "I think any intelligent person must realize that the North Koreans would not have attacked the South Koreans unless they had the backing of very strong forces. . . . I believe those forces are Communist China and Communist Russia. This, too, disturbed me tremendously, and made me realize there is a Communist menace and that the Communist Party in this country is a part of that menace." A key factor was the exposure of extensive Soviet espionage in the spy trials: "These people are doing it for love of the Party. This is treason. I think the party that has used them is treasonable also. I don't say all members of the Communist Party are guilty of treason, but I think a party that encourages them to act in this capacity is treasonable. For this reason I am willing to talk today."[20]

In the *Saturday Evening Post* article, Dmytryk continued, "The Hiss conviction, the Judith Coplon trial, they all show that no matter how small a fraction of the party is guilty of espionage, the responsibility is of the whole party, and anyone who supports it."[21]

When he had refused to testify in 1947, he had already broken with the party over its insistence on following the party line and on party discipline that infringed on his freedom of thought and speech—despite the claims made in those hearings to the contrary. In his testimony, Dmytryk recounted a number of instances in which insistence on following the party line was illustrated, including the major response to the Duclos letter and the personally revealing incident in which Herbert Biberman "made a very powerful speech, impassioned speech" one day and "an equally impassioned speech in direct contrast" when the new party line came down. His main personal experience of the party's infringement on freedom of speech and thought concerned meetings held over his film *Cornered* (1945, as discussed in chapter 11). "I had never gone along with any kind of thought control, and before that actually I had never myself experienced any such

instances. The fact that they tried to tell us what to do, that others got together and tried to tell us what to do, shocked me very deeply."[22]

Elia Kazan testified twice in 1952, both times in executive sessions. His
testimony at the January hearing has not been made public, but he has
stated that he had evaded and equivocated at that session. By his April
appearance Kazan had made up his mind. In the released testimony of
that session and his prepared statement, he admitted his membership
in the Communist Party for just under two years from the summer of
1934 to the spring of 1936. In addition to party functionaries like V. J.
Jerome, he named several people he knew as party members in the Group
Theater during that limited period. Kazan's declared reasons for testifying
also were a mixture of his rebellion against infringement on freedom of
thought and speech and his revulsion at the actions of the Soviet Union
and the CPUSA. Certainly his well-known driving need to work, create,
express himself and his gifts, even to triumph, was a personal component
of his decision. He had decided not to sacrifice himself for something he
abhorred. In his statement to the committee, Kazan said, "I have come
to the conclusion that I was wrong to withhold these names before, because secrecy serves the Communists, and is exactly what they want. The
American people need the facts and all the facts about all aspects of Communism in order to deal with it wisely and effectively. It is my obligation
as a citizen to tell everything I know."[23]

In a full-page ad in the *New York Times*, Kazan amplified the point:

Liberals must speak out.
   I think it is useful that certain of us had this kind of experience [dictatorial]
with the Communists, for if we had not, we should not know them so well.
Anyone who has is not to be fooled again. Today, when all the world fears war
and they [Communists] scream peace, we know how much their professions
are worth. We know tomorrow they will have a new slogan. . . .
   . . . We must never let the Communists get away with the pretense that they
stand for the very things which they kill in their own countries.[24]

Kazan's decision was not without its soul-searching anguish, as he
described in his autobiography, *A Life*. After his January appearance, his
disgust with the committee grew, for he felt that its main purpose was to
conduct "a degradation" ceremony in which people were forced to give information that was already known. But he was convinced as well that "there
was no way I could go along with their [the Communists'] crap that the
CP was nothing but another political party, like the Republicans and the
Democrats. I knew very well what it was, a thoroughly organized worldwide
conspiracy."[25] Still, he refused to sign a letter proposed by Spyros Skouras
of Twentieth Century Fox because they were afraid of a boycotting of his
film *Viva Zapata!* (1952). He still refused when Darryl Zanuck urged him,
"Name the names, for cris-sake. Who the hell are you going to jail for?

You'll be sitting there and someone else will sure as hell name those people. Who are you saving?" Kazan talked to Arthur Miller, writing in his diary that despite their differences, Miller told him, "Don't worry about what I'll think. Whatever you do will be all right with me. Because I know your heart is in the right place." He talked with Clifford Odets, who was caught in the same dilemma. He talked to Lee and Paula Strasberg.[26]

Kazan even talked with Lillian Hellman, who had been a friend but immediately, "silent as a coiled snake," made him an enemy, "someone to hate." As several later "historians" quote as gospel (without any acknowledgment of her well-known track record regarding the truth), Hellman later reported that Kazan had admitted it was all about money; he had, she alleged, bragged to her, "I earned over $400,000 last year from theater. But Skouras says I'll never make another movie if I don't go along." Kazan's version of their meeting is that he told her what he had told Miller: that he did believe he wouldn't work again if he didn't testify, but could "get along okay" without the film work; that he was in conflict over giving up a career for something he did not believe in and detested. Afterward, as he began to deal with the viciousness of the reactions to his testimony, Kazan realized that "she had the sharpest knife of all for me. Still I would tell people that I rather liked her, when the fact was that I knew damned well what she was: a liar for one thing and an enemy for sure."[27]

Kazan questioned himself. As he later said, "I did what I did because it was the more tolerable of two alternatives that were, either way, painful, even disastrous, and either way wrong for me. That's what a difficult decision means. Either way you go, you lose."[28] His summary of that introspection reveals the dilemma faced by many. A sampling:

> Wasn't what I'd been defending up until now by my silence a conspiracy working for another country? Hadn't I watched my "comrades" staggering through political switch after political switch by instructions not written in this country?
>
> For a start, why didn't all of us in the Group now name each other? Wouldn't that clear the air, if everyone admitted to everything . . . reduce the issue of Communists in the Group Theater to its proper scale? . . .
>
> Why had I tried so hard and for so long to stay in good with my old comrades when I no longer believed in anything they stood for?
>
> . . . Didn't I have to break into the stealth? I'd been letting the Party fellows get away with what I hated most. . . . Shouldn't they be forced out into the general light? I'd never dared think anything like that before . . . the worst of it: I'd censored my own thinking. . . .
>
> Why had I taken so long to even consider telling the country—that's what it amounted to—everything I knew? Was it because of the moral injunction against "informing," which was respected only depending on which side you were on? If the situation were reversed, wouldn't the "comrades" protect themselves without hesitation and by any means? Including naming me [as Communists had done throughout the world in Party trials].

And so he concluded

> that this committee, which everyone scorned—I had plenty against them too—had a proper duty. I wanted to help break open the secrecy. . . .
>   The "horrible, immoral thing" I would do, I did out of my true self. Everything before was seventeen years of posturing. The people who owe you an explanation (no apology expected) are those who, year after year, held the Soviet blameless for all their crimes.

And yet he faced the other, more intimately revealing side of his motives, the need, the drive to do his work: "I began to measure the weight and worth of what I was giving up, my career in films, which I was surrendering for a cause I didn't believe in. What was I if not a filmmaker?"[29]

For this kind of thoughtful self-analysis, these sincere statements and actions—and accurate appraisal of the world—he was immediately branded a liar who didn't believe anything he said. As Kazan documented later, "A well-organized campaign branding my act as shameful" was conducted. An early rumor, without any basis in fact yet repeated through the years in books and articles, was that, as prearranged, he had signed a contract for five hundred thousand dollars the day after he gave names to the HUAC. (Similarly, after Dmytryk testified, the story was spread that he signed a contract for five thousand dollars a week; the fact was he got a job with King Brothers for a *total* of five thousand dollars.)[30]

Almost fifty years later when, far too late, Kazan was given a Lifetime Achievement Award at the Academy Awards, there still were protests from the expected quarters that can serve as an exemplum of the entrenched strength of the Left's conventional moral dualism. When the honorary Oscar was first announced, a group of still surviving blacklistees, and some of their children and academic and industry supporters, mounted a nostalgic campaign. The group included such familiar names as Norma Barzman, Jean Butler, Robert Lees, and Abe Polonsky. They conducted fund-raisers, published ads in the *Hollywood Reporter*, gave speeches and interviews. A full-page ad in the *Daily Variety*, for example, recruited some new signators like Sean Penn and attacked Kazan and the award, claiming he had given the HUAC its creditability and that his testimony (naming eight people in 1952) had "validated the blacklisting of *thousands* [emphasis added]." They demonstrated outside the event itself, a sparse picket line—including the ailing but insistent, and consistent, Polonsky—a tawdry echo of the passionate picket lines at the Conference of Studio Unions strike of fifty years before. Afterward, almost instinctively, they lied about what happened. In her memoir, for example, Barzman claims, "A big demonstration greeted Oscar-goers, most of whom did not stand or applaud Kazan." In fact, it was a small demonstration. But more important, most—probably 99.5

percent—of the Oscar-goers did stand and applaud. All except a few, positioned strategically in the first rows, who nobly refused to stand with the rest of the thousands in the hall to allow the ill and aging master filmmaker a last deserved honor for his art.[31]

Equally revealing were the institutional events in the aftermath of the presentation to Kazan. The Academy itself was pressured into "righting the balance" with a retrospective of films by blacklistees. At UCLA the senior class in screenwriting held a protest Lifetime Achievement Award ceremony for all blacklisted screenwriters, whatever movies they had written, partly written, or claimed to have written.

The case of Kazan supplies a revealing example of the manner in which the distortions of the passionate Left become the accepted, and unexamined, parlance of the popular media. When Kazan died in September of 2003, the emphasis in an editorial in the *Philadelphia Enquirer* was not on his amazing accomplishment on both stage and screen, but on how his reputation was "tarnished by his betrayals." Moreover, a news article actually drew a parallel between Kazan and the German director Leni Riefenstahl, associating him—on no logical or factual basis whatsoever—with the artful propagandist who, the reporter neatly defined, glorified "the perverted ideals of Nazism."[32]

Clifford Odets testified in 1952. In his much reviled testimony, usually distorted when commented upon, Odets made an interesting and useful comment on the contrast between remaining silent and speaking out. He referred to it in two ways. He pointed out that in the past to speak out about injustices, to not remain silent about them, often had found him allying himself on certain important issues with Communists "because the lines of liberalism and the lines of left thought frequently cross each other." But now he knew that "one of the elements that made me leave the Communist Party was their secrecy. I see no reason now to be conspiratorial in the United States." And so not remaining silent in the present world crisis meant making a difficult decision to oppose the conspiratorial "secrecy" of the Communist Party. In regard to the difficult courses of action, he concluded, "I see that one must do one of two things: One must pick one's way very carefully through the mazes of liberalism and leftism today or one must remain silent. Of the two, I must tell you frankly I would try to pick the first way, because . . . the little that I can contribute to the betterment or welfare of the American people could not permit me to remain silent."[33]

The analysis was articulate, but as both friends and foes alike have described, for Odets the real-life decision to cooperate with the HUAC was shattering. "The sad fact is," Kazan wrote, "that what was possible for me hurt Clifford mortally. He was never the same after he testified. He gave away his identity when he did that; he was no longer the hero-rebel, the fearless prophet of a new world."[34]

The core of the testimony of screenwriter Leo Townsend in 1951 was very articulate, but his personal response much different, measured and resolute. In both his conscience and his testimony he was clear and certain that his testifying, including naming names, was right and necessary. He wrote years later, "My informing was a matter of conscience for me. I had discovered that I had made a terrible mistake in joining the Communist Party; Stalin had been responsible for as many deaths as Hitler."[35]

In his testimony, Townsend stressed the need to expose the evils of the Soviet system, and the refusal of many on the left to do so: "The Communists who decry the lack of freedom in this country haven't given thought to the amount of freedom allowed the people of the Soviet Union." At one point he quoted Peter Viereck: "This kind of liberal tends to avoid the real fact of Soviet Russia, such as the enormous aid given to Germany during the Hitler-Stalin Pact; the Stalinist purge of all Lenin-Marxist associates; the postwar anti-Semitic drive in the Soviet Union; the slave labor camps; increasing class lines and pay differentials between Soviet rich and poor."[36]

He believed, further, that "the Communists in a large sense have destroyed the liberal movement in this country," that they are still "misguided liberals . . . living in an age of innocence." But more personally, he stated, "Also I feel that since the American Communist Party in the last four years hasn't openly and honestly stated its aims and goals and has evaded the issue of its allegiance to the Soviet Union, I think that the American people have a right to know which people have not made up their minds . . . [to speak out about their allegiances]."[37]

He was concerned that "today there is a section of people who shut their eyes to Soviet fascism [and its consequences] . . . and if what I say here and what this Committee does here can help these people, I think this will show a large measure of success." For, he believed, exposure of the Soviet oppressions and the people who have one way or another supported them can force the Soviets to restrict its violations—whether espionage or the imprisonment and slaughter of innocent people. He, too, was particularly concerned about the extreme anti-Semitism in the Soviet Union, and its consequences: that many Jews were arrested and killed, Jewish institutions and culture destroyed.[38]

Frank Tuttle was a veteran director of more than seventy movies, yet he had found time through the years to be a regular presence at party functions and an active part of the Communist cell in the Screen Directors Guild. In his testimony in 1951, Tuttle looked back at the abrupt turn in the party line at the time of the Duclos letter, and the expelling of Earl Browder, as a major shock, and the start of his deciding to leave the party. That change, as directed by "someone from abroad" was, for him, an intimation of a new policy that promoted "violent revolution" around the world. He now believed in the need to expose the combination of Soviet repressions and Communist aggressions, but he focused more on the difficulty of the moral dilemma that had to be faced and his reasons, nonetheless, for choosing not to be silent: "All decent people, who share this dislike for informers, if they think about this carefully, will agree with me that at this particular moment [the Korean War, Soviet expansionism] it is absolutely vital [to testify] . . . for with ruthless aggression abroad in the world, the aggressors are as ruthless with their own people as they are with those they consider their enemies."[39]

Screenwriter Roy Huggins was a man of intensely held beliefs, whatever the turn of his belief at a particular time. His lengthy testimony on September 29, 1952, was knowledgeable and thoughtful on the flaws and fallacies of Marxism, the Soviets, the Comintern, the CPUSA; yet the attacks on him were virulent, even questioning his mental stability.

"It was," he said," a terrible thing when you finally realize the great gap between grim realities and your vision of an ideal future." He traced the destructive fallacies that led to these "grim realities" to the central doctrines of Marxism, and particularly to Marx's theory "of the withering away of the state" once the classless society was achieved.

> In fact, the contrary has been proved by the Soviet Union, where I don't believe they do have any classes, they have just one class, but they have a state in the Soviet Union, and that state is getting more and more powerful and more tyrannical every year. . . .
>
> I realize, like all closed systems of thought, once you find a hole in it, then you realize that it is all wrong, because that is the nature of a closed system of thought. You must either accept it all without question, or you do not accept any of it, and this is understood by the Communists. . . .
>
> A man cannot think for himself in the Communist Party. He must abrogate that privilege, and do it willingly on some theoretical ground.[40]

The CPUSA as a whole acts on this principle, he believed, and insists that all of its members do as well, in accepting all of the dictates and positions, the theoretically proven "truths" of the organization, such as the current positions on foreign policy:

> Soviet foreign policy turns about, or Soviet propaganda, let us say, which is the basis for the Communist Party line here, [and so the CPUSA also] turns everything that this country does upside down. We aid democracy in Europe, and it is called warmongering. We come to the aid through the United Nations of the South Koreans, and we are called warmongers, and the world is even told that the South Koreans started the war . . . and we are just trying to put a yoke on the peoples of Asia. . . .
>
> One of the things that disturbed me deeply about the Communist Party is that they do not believe in individual freedom, and yet they shout to the housetops in defense of individual freedom in all of the democratic countries in which they exist. They become champions of complete political freedom. The moment they get power, they will destroy [it].[41]

While he opposed the party and its obedience to Soviet aggressions, he, nonetheless, was concerned to tell the committee at some length that such hearings were intruding on liberty: "That would be a terrible thing if we are anti-communist because we fee that Communists destroy liberty, and in fighting communism, we destroy individual freedom and liberty."[42] In later years, Huggins became quite cynical about all political activity; it was all, he declared, on all sides, a "refuge of scoundrels." In the late seventies, he told Victor Navasky he regretted his decision to cooperate with the committee: "The naming of names was probably the most unspeakable and heinous aspect of the Un-American Activities Committee. To cooperate with it in that aspect, even though the names had already been mentioned, was, I believe, the wrong thing to do. And that's the only part of my part in this thing that I really regret."[43]

Edward G. Robinson was probably the most famous of a different, and larger, category of people who testified: those who were caught in the middle, whose difficulties and dilemmas had been shaped by the extreme positions taken by the Communists and influential anti-Communists. These were the people who had not been party members or even avid followers, but had taken part in or merely given their name (and money) to a number of party-affiliated functions, campaigns, and organizations. For these people clearance was in some ways easier (often through behind-the-scene channels), but in another way more difficult. Their practical dilemma was that they could claim that they "didn't know." However, within the hardened patterns that had developed about cooperation, this kind of claim, whether truthful or evasive, was frequently seen as a failure or refusal to cooperate. In 1952, after other methods had failed to clear his way, Robinson requested an appearance, "to put to rest," he said, "the ever-recurring innuendoes concerning my loyalty. Surely there must be a way for a person falsely accused of disloyalty to clear his name once and for all." For, Robinson told the committee, "innocent, sincere people were used by the Communists to whom honesty and sincerity are as foreign as the Soviet Union is to America."[44]

The main emphasis of his prepared statement was not the evils of the Soviet Union, but the evil of those who had never told him they were Communists. His testimony has been mocked; it is extreme, and very likely hypocritical. However, even with its self-exculpating rhetoric, this further excerpt does illustrate the web that many were caught in. And so by indirection it illustrates how public exposure can curtail the effectiveness of the party's using secrecy and deceit in its campaigns; and how, conversely, the maintenance of this secrecy places others in jeopardy because of their misguided sympathies.

The revelations that persons whom I thought were sincere liberals were, in fact, Communists has shocked me more than I can tell you. That they persuaded me by lies and concealment of their real purposes to allow them to use my name for what I believed to be a worthy cause is now obvious. I was sincere. They were not. I bitterly resent their false assertions of liberalism and honesty through which they imposed upon me and exploited my sincere desire to help my fellow men. Not one of the Communists who sought my help or requested permission to use my name ever told me that he or she was a member of the Communist Party. My suspicions, which should have been aroused, were allayed by the fact that I had been falsely accused of Communist sympathies, and I was, therefore, willing to believe that other accused persons were also being unfairly smeared.[45]

Martin Berkeley and Richard Collins, former party members themselves, were two of the most controversial "friendly" witnesses. Berkeley named more names than anyone else. Collins, a sincere and thoughtful student of Marxism and an idealistic and active participant in many party functions, surprised and angered his former "tender comrades." They denounced his selfish, greedy betrayal; he saw his testimony as a truthful and principled breaking of the silence.

Berkeley, a screenwriter of middling, though often successful, productions like *My Friend Flicka* (1943), had been an active party member from the mid-thirties. In his testimony he recalled a meeting at his home in 1937 to recruit new members. Party professionals V. J. Jerome and Harry Carlisle and "star" members Alan Campbell, Dashiell Hammett, Lillian Hellman, Dorothy Parker, and Donald Ogden Stewart were there to charm the potential recruits. In the late thirties he was on the board of the Motion Picture Defense Committee as it moved far to the left under Communist influence and eventually imploded. After he broke with the party, in 1946 Berkeley was a leader in organizing the All-Guild Slate in the Screen Writers Guild (SWG) that successfully destroyed Communist control of the guild's executive board. From then on, Berkeley was an active, fervent anti-Communist. He testified on September 19, 1951, and in his overzealous crusading poured out the names of 162 (some say 154) Hollywood people as party members, based on lists and diaries he had maintained for years. While the bulk of his testimony proved to be accurate, in a number of instances it was based also on brief and long-past memberships, on some coincidental and loose connections, and even in a few instances on misidentifications. Even committee investigator William Wheeler later said that the quantity was unnecessary and excessive, that it interfered with getting across in the media the Communist strategies and practices that he wanted to see emphasized.[46]

Collins, in contrast, had been one of the original Nineteen. During those first hearings, he joined with blacklistees Cole, Lardner, and Kahn in writing a rebuttal to SWG President Emmett Lavery's testimony before the HUAC; but even then he was beginning to question himself and his allegiances. He was already disillusioned with the party's denial of artistic freedom and creativity and with its slavish obedience to the Soviet Union. He was, he later said, to all intents and purposes out of the party by then, but out of loyalty to the others would have refused to testify if called to appear. By the time of his testimony on April 12, 1951, Collins felt that "there has been a marked change in the world situation since 1947, and there has been as great a change in me. It is hard to tell where one thing begins and the other ends." In his testimony he said, "Now, because of the worsened conditions [in the world], no one can be on the side of the United States and the Communists at the same time."[47]

Collins commented, "So it was not for me a matter of, 'Well, I'm going to bounce back and go to work.' It turned out that that's what happened finally, but that was not the primary consideration. The primary consideration was that I thought it was ridiculous to go through life as a member of the Party—which taking the Fifth in effect said publicly you were doing—when I wasn't." His strategy, as worked out with Meta Rosenberg, was to name as few people as possible (though he claimed he knew at least three hundred), focusing on three categories: people who were dead, who had already appeared before the Committee, and who had left the party years before after only a brief membership. He felt later that he was sorry that the third group, who he thought would be safe, were hurt more than he thought they would.[48]

Isobel Lennart, a screenwriter who had worked on many successful and joyful films, especially musicals such as *Anchors Aweigh* (1945) and, later, *Funny Girl* (1968), was a close friend of Collins. She was a party member from 1939 into the postwar period, when she broke with the party over its militant allegiance to Soviet aggressions. She testified in 1952, careful, she said, to name only those who had been named earlier because she knew how people could be harmed. But she did also believe that "a person cannot be a member of the Communist Party without doing harm, because by being a member you are lending your moral assistance and your aid to those . . . who are out to do harm. . . . You can't be as irresponsible as to think what you specifically are doing is all there is to it. You have to see how this ties in with what other people are doing, and you have to consider yourself a party to it, and that is why I did not want to be in it." Nonetheless, she was anguished over the dilemma of speaking out against what she now opposed, but thus having to name names. She hated the committee for forcing her to do so. Even though she had been careful to name only those who had been named before, for the rest of her life she regretted having done so.[49]

Lennart knew that Collins was caught in the same harsh bind. But in a later interview she (unlike so many of his former comrades) honored the integrity of his decision. "Dick Collins didn't testify out of fear [or greed] . . . and he was much hated in this town for a long time. . . . Three, four years before he testified, he turned violently against the Communist Party for the most honest reasons. He testified out of conviction. . . . Dick was a very rigid man and a fanatic [about what he believed in]."[50]

The fanaticism of others would, loudly, continue to deny Collins, and others, the merest morsel of integrity. But it would keep them silent about so much else.

17

What Is Behaving Decently?
Those Who Did Not Testify,
Attacked, and Remained Silent

In his autobiography *Take Two*, Philip Dunne, an early supporter of the original Nineteen and an early active opponent of the strategy and posturing of the Ten, felt he needed to puncture the "virtual deification" of the Hollywood Ten and others. For him they were never "reliable champions of civil liberties"; they took up causes "only to serve their own political purposes."[1] Dunne's criticism points up the central moral paradox of those who refused to testify—and of the conventional history about them ever since.

They were morally strong (whatever their mix of motives) in attempting to defend their rights, and their beliefs, at the risk and cost of losing their (often lucrative) livelihood. But their moral stance was ambiguously entangled with, weakened and compromised by the destructive righteousness of their crusade that often betrayed truth—and betrayed those who were led to support and emulate them. Their righteous zeal led to denials and evasions of the immensities—and human cost—of the betrayals of their ideals by Communism and the Soviet Union, other Communist nations, and the Communist Party of America (CPUSA); to evasions of any personal complicity, responsibility, or regret.

On the other hand, whatever the mix of *their* motives, the testimony (in great part) of those who did testify—and thus named names—contained thoughtful principles and beliefs. This testimony was accurate about the state of the world and took place after painful inner debates about having to name names within the circumscribed world of choice that had been created. But their moral stance was ambiguously entangled with righteous crusades of anti-Communism that also betrayed the ideals for which they testified. The complications and contradictions within their choice—its moral paradoxes—however, received only loud and absolute condemnation. Those who called for, indeed demanded and received, sympathetic understanding of their own choices and behavior consistently heaped personal invective upon those who had testified—a litany of vilification carried forward by others.

Here are some emblematic and symptomatic samples of being mind-blind to the complexity of the motives and behavior of others—and to the possibility of realities beyond one's own righteous bias and resentment, of the slightest glimmer of any allowance of weaknesses in one's own motives and behavior.

Ring Lardner: "But most of the stool pigeons were terrorized into it, by economic and other pressures, went through the ritual with self-loathing, and sooner or later came to wish they hadn't done it." Or more succinctly in a letter to Albert Maltz in October of 1977, "The choice we faced was between being 'heroes' and being complete shits."[2]

Lardner on Robert Rossen: "He had just started a new career as a director when he was subpoenaed for the second time and decided to preserve that career at the expense of his former values."[3]

Paul Buhle interview of Walter Bernstein:

> *Buhle*: Abe Polonsky related to me the feeling he always had that Rossen was never to be trusted. Was that at all in your mind?
>
> *Bernstein*: Yeah, I felt that there was something essentially corrupt about him on a personal level. . . . The first time he [Rossen] testified, he only gave the Committee the Fifth Amendment [not accurate] and was excused. The second time he gave them a lot of junk, rationalizations about why he was testifying now. I felt the same as I did while rereading Kazan's testimony: the two of them didn't believe anything that they were saying.[4]

Bernstein refused to allowed any credence for Rossen and Kazan's thoughtful and meaningful statements.

For Lester Cole, all those who testified were the "scum of the industry." As he saw it, "Informing on his friends was not enough [for Elia Kazan]. With Budd Schulberg, fellow stoolie, to write it for him, he directed *On the Waterfront*, a film designed to justify stoolpigeons and slander trade unionism [neither of which it did]."[5]

"The fact of the matter," Abe Polonsky judged, was that "all he [Kazan] had was a disagreement politically with some people," and so he should have merely had more arguments with them. What Kazan did, Polonsky insisted, "was something else. This was, Who goes to the concentration camp? Do I go with you or do you go by yourself?"[6]

On Richard Collins, Polonsky's attack added a novel element, a double betrayal: "Collins is interesting because his role is more complex than the normal informer who went before the Committee and did his thing and then tried to forget it. He was reporting to the FBI while he was still ostensibly a member of the Party."[7]

The fact of the FBI matter, as Collins attested, is that when he had decided to cooperate, but had not yet decided what to do about naming people, he talked to Mark Bright at the FBI. He wanted to get some idea of what records they had about him and others, of what he might be asked to talk about. That was the reality of his "reporting to the FBI."[8]

For Cole, Edward Dmytryk was "so morally degenerate it is almost impossible to comprehend."[9]

On several occasions Maltz wrote about the blow to him of what Dmytryk had done. After a Richard English–Dmytryk article in the *Saturday Evening Post* of May 19, 1951, Maltz wrote the magazine an "open letter" that was printed in the *Hollywood Reporter*. "He has not now made peace with his conscience," Maltz wrote, "he made it [his testimony] with his pocket book and career." He went on:

> It is nauseatingly ugly when someone you have known, someone who fought by your side, went with you into prison—became such an eager wretch, such a fawning informer. . . .
> He has lied and befouled others with his lies; he has traduced the good principles for which he once stood; and now he buys his way back into the film industry by trampling the careers of thirty others. Who but the blind, the stupid, and the prejudiced will believe anything he says?[10]

Bernstein told Buhle, "I can happily despise someone like Edward Dmytryk." So much so, that some thirty years after Dmytryk's apostasy, at the Barcelona Film Festival of 1988, Bernstein, surprised to find Dmytryk in attendance, called him "garbage" from the stage.[11]

Denunciations of those who testified took some unique turns, beyond the usual basis of greed, deceit, cowardice. These were assaults on those who supposedly had been driven by more exotic immoralities, psychological flaws and warps, had acted out of personal spite and resentment, more perverse motivations.

As Paul Jarrico said about Collins, his former writing collaborator, "He was a nice guy, and he became a shit. . . . I carried him [on a writing assignment]—which was why, I guess, he knifed me. As I've said before, he wanted to stand on his own two knees." For him, "The most painful betrayal was that of Collins."[12]

On Collins, Polonsky, referring to the time that Collins was going through a difficult divorce, talked about his "welching" on his child-support payments and debts. "When the people from whom he had borrowed money tried to get it back, he claimed the statute of limitations had run. . . . *More* than the statute of limitations had run; the statute of all limitations had run."[13]

Bernstein analyzed Kazan's motivations: "He was extremely insecure about himself in that regard [women]. . . . The fact that his wife was a Protestant with three names tells us something. He was insecure about his entrance into American proper society. Refusing to testify would amount to another instance of being cut off, or cutting himself off, making himself rejected, lumping himself willingly with the undesirables. Not to do that was of primary importance to him."[14]

Jules Dassin twisted any reasonable interpretation of Kazan's behavior even in the years after he had testified: "You look for forgiveness, you try to understand, but I can't manage it with Kazan. What he did was diabolical. And what he did afterward was diabolical—to try to reach and offer work to blacklisted people. He tried to corrupt them by giving them work and by so doing make them accept him."[15]

For Joan LaCoeur Scott, Dmytryk's testimony was a result of his *size*: "He was an antsy-pantsy guy. If he'd had a couple more feet on him, he might have been more confident. As it was, he was just this little man always trying to impress."[16]

Cole saw personal spite and resentment behind those who had named him. He claimed Melvin P. Levy had violated a business arrangement between them. While Cole was in prison, he claimed, he had included Levy in a writing assignment to help during Levy's financial troubles. Levy had then named him "five times" because Levy was "guilty" over "having stolen weeks of my wife's rightful share of the salary coming to me." He claimed that Berkeley had named him because he (Cole) had demanded his expulsion from the party at a 1940 party "hearing."[17]

Early on, for Trumbo, it was primarily a matter of money. In a letter to Guy Endore in 1956, Trumbo told him, with his usual epistolary flourish, that if you look at someone who has informed "on friends who have harmed no one, and who thereafter earns money he could not have earned before, . . . I will show you not a decent citizen, not a patriot, but a miserable scoundrel who will . . . if the price is right, betray not just his friends but his country itself."[18]

Michael Wilson's remark to Victor Navasky in 1978 might sum it all up: "My attitude toward informers has remained from the start unforgiving. . . . I don't defend my attitude in terms of principles. . . . I just don't like the fuckers."[19]

The converse of the absolutism of these attacks was the self-righteous complacency, the moral blindness of not coming to terms with or even allowing for any degree of evil in what the Hollywood Reds had supported and defended, any complicity of their own in their years of support and defense.

This form of testimony, this contrasting "silence" about Communism and the Soviet Union—and themselves—took several forms. One was the restrictive (and false) focus on the madness of Stalin as the basis for any cause for one's disillusionment. For many this was the far boundary of their admission of any flaw in their understandings and declarations about the Soviet Union.

It was the famous, but generally misreported and misinterpreted speech by Nikita Khrushchev in 1956 that provided the basis for this kind of admission that was itself a self-protective evasion of the immensity of the truth. At the Twentieth Congress of the Communist Party of the Soviet Union, the Khrushchev speech itself contained three significant evasions of the truth—which influenced responses and commentaries for years to come. First, it has generally not been noted or taken into account that Khrushchev spoke only of (rather limited) offenses against *party members*, who were far, far fewer in number than the victims who were not party members. Second, the speech placed blame only on Stalin, evading any reference to the Soviet system, referring in a euphemism only to "*abuses* [emphasis added] committed under Stalin." And third, Khrushchev, of course, did not refer to roles played by himself and any of the other leaders in the room in the crimes against fellow Communists or in the mass murders and deportations that he and they organized and managed. In fact, the speech was thus, at least in great part, a denial of his own complicity in evil. It was a strategic maneuver to deflect attention from his own past brutalities, errors, or lies (for one, blatant lies about there being no famine in the Ukraine when he was party boss there) at the time of his own battle for domination in the Communist Party. It was, by indirection, a defense of himself and the others, and of the system that was still being enforced.[20] (We've looked at the actions of these Soviet leaders in previous chapters.)

As the writers of *The Black Book of Communism* state, "Carried out under the direction of a Stalinist, Nikita Khrushchev (who, like all other leaders of his generation had played a major role in the worst acts of repression, such as dekulakization, purges, deportations, and executions), de-Stalinization could afford to condemn only certain excesses of the 'cult of personality.'" The writers go on to condemn those who have, despite all the significant revelations made by others, thus defended all that he did not reveal: "Most of the time, however, the witness statements and the work carried out by independent commissions . . . have been buried beneath an avalanche of Communist propaganda, aided and abetted by a silence born of cowardice and indifference. . . . Regrettably, it was most tenacious in Western societies whenever the phenomenon of Communism came under the microscope. Until now they have refused to face the reality that the Communist system, albeit in varying degrees, possessed fundamentally criminal underpinnings. By refusing to acknowledge this, they were co-conspirators in 'the lie.'"[21]

Khrushchev's false, partial admission was for many devastating enough. Nonetheless, it led most of the true believers, even some who broke with the party over it, to an equally false evasion, to the new formula, the new rationale, the new basic lie about the Soviet Union: that whatever had gone wrong was due to Stalin's *craziness*, not to Lenin or the basis of the system. If only Lenin had lived, if only Stalin had not gone mad, Communism in Soviet Russia would have achieved the workers' paradise after all.

For example, Howard Fast wrote in 1990: "An inner contradiction that drained the strength from Communism, which had been defined by Lenin as the correct path to Socialism. . . . But under Stalin, it did not work."[22]

As for some actual statements and principles of Lenin himself:

- In 1918: Lenin ordered local authorities to use "merciless mass terror against kulaks, priests, and White Guards."[23]
- In 1918: when Stalin was conducting a purge of suspected counter-revolutionaries in the Caucasus, Lenin ordered him to be "ever more merciless and ruthless." Stalin replied, "Be assured our hand will not tremble."[24]
- In 1920: "We will go forward for ten-twenty versts and hang the Kulaks, priests, landowners."[25]
- In 1922: "The greater the number of the representatives of the reactionary bourgeoisie and reactionary clergy we will manage to execute the better."[26]
- In 1922: "It is a mistake to think that the NEP [New Economic Policy] has put an end to terror. We shall return to terror and economic terror."[27]
- In 1922: "The Court must not eliminate terror; to promise that would be self-deception or deception. It [terror] must be grounded and legalized in principle, without duplicity and embellishment."[28]

For Lenin, "A revolution without firing squads is meaningless," for "Bolshevism is a social system based on blood-letting." And so he ordered authorities "to shoot plotters and waverers [*sic*] without asking anyone and without idiotic red tape."[29]

Similarly, it was Lenin who first, and repeatedly, established the basic policy and goal of worldwide conquest and revolution. In 1918 he was already calling for "an army of three million" to lead an "international workers' revolution." By March of 1919 he announced, "Our Congress is convinced that the time is not far off when Communism will be victorious throughout the world. . . . Long live the international Communist Republic!" By March of 1920, he gave the Comintern a "guarantee that the victory of the Communist revolution is inevitable . . . and that it is not too far off."[30]

Simon Sebag Montefiore, in his thorough study *Stalin: The Court of the Red Tsar*, sums up this point neatly: "This [putting all the blame on Stalin] is demonology, not history. It has the effect of merely indicting one madman and offers us no lesson about either the danger of utopian ideas and systems, or the responsibility of individuals . . . because systematic murder started soon after Lenin took power in 1917. . . . The responsibility lies with the hundreds of thousands of officials who ordered or perpetrated the murders . . . and they usually killed more than they were asked to kill."[31]

A parallel to the reiterated refrain that it was all the "abuses" of mad Stalin was the claim through the decades that we didn't know, had no way of knowing, couldn't trust what we might have heard anyway—despite the prevalence through these same decades of reports, documents, books, personal testimony of the realities of Soviet Communism.

> Maltz: "There was very little available knowledge of the USSR, and those who claimed to know were not sympathizers, hence were suspected of being part of the two decade-long capitalist crusade against the lone socialist state." On another occasion, he said, "a decade-long fabric of lying and intervention on the part of world capitalism against the single socialist state."[32]
>
> Dassin: "The strength of the propaganda against us was so overwhelming and so easily sold to the American people that we just couldn't deal with it very well."[33]
>
> Fast: "We had no way of winnowing out the truth about Russia and Stalin from the mass of manufactured indictments of communism. . . . I don't believe our leadership lied to us; I think they knew as little as we did."[34]

Even after the "revelations" by Khrushchev that staggered many, there were still those who continued to find ways to evade the truth.

In the late eighties, Lionel Stander also held to the belief that "the anti-Soviet, anti-Communist hysteria, it isn't based on reality . . . on the face of it is ridiculous."[35]

By that time, Rapf had become the director of the film studies program at Dartmouth. He was still one of the most extreme in his denials of any need to see any flaw in his consistent defense of the Soviet Union or any need to admit any flaw in himself or the history of Communism: "I don't argue about what happened in the Soviet Union, because I don't know what happened in the Soviet Union." He had split with his old friend Budd Schulberg even before Schulberg had testified because Schulberg had come under the sway of anti-Soviets like Arthur Koestler and the PEN organization, who, Rapf claimed, were "basically Trotskyites. They hate the Communist Party, and they hate anybody who was associated with it. They think we should all get down on our knees and repent. I refuse to do it."[36]

For a greater number there was a basic contradiction in the new configuration of their moral and intellectual position that they had been forced to allow. Within limits, they could admit that there were some flaws, even horrors; but they, the American Communists, had been, and were still, without moral stain or tarnishing in the idealism—the purity—of their beliefs.

In an interview in the nineties, Dassin recognized what he called the "naïveté" of the Hollywood Reds, but looked back fondly at it, with no context of its consequences: "They certainly were the best citizens. They really cared. They were the purest most idealistic of the lot. They were going to make a better world. That was the naïve, idealistic dream they all had. . . . They were pure to the point of naïveté."[37]

The terms of Jarrico's admissions were stronger, go further than most, but still he reserves a space for the sanctity of *us*. For example, "When the Khrushchev report came along in 1956, even the slowest of us realized that the accusations *against Stalin and Stalinism* [emphasis added] had been true—though we had denied they were true—and that we had been defending indefensible things." But in America "the Communist Party was not a revolutionary organization." He had, he admitted, maintained an "illusion" about the Soviet Union, but "the illusion didn't make me disloyal; it made me a fool."[38]

In the late eighties, Martin Ritt was more euphemistic and complacent, allowing for "certain mistakes" in his political life. There were, he admitted, "certain *excesses* [emphasis added]. But I don't feel I have anything to be ashamed of."[39]

Lardner, too, admitted he had been "losing what remained of my illusions about *Stalin and his excesses* [emphasis added], yet it still seemed to me that the Soviet leaders were more serious than ours about wanting peaceful relations." Under Stalin the Soviet state, as he evasively phrased it, "would wither into the moral and social *rigidity* [emphasis added] that lasted."[40]

In his memoir, *Inside Out*, in 1996, Bernstein, like so many others, held to this same double standard. After the Khrushchev speech, Bernstein remarked, "What he said was shattering—a detailed attack on the dead Stalin as despot and dictator . . . all that our enemies had been saying about *him* [emphasis added]." Bernstein would leave the party and he "would not miss the dogma or the unthinking obedience to the Soviet Union." However, he also said, "I had left the Party but not the idea of socialism, the possibility that there could be a system not based on inequality and exploitation [as he goes on to still claim exists in America]."[41]

Cole continued to be even more morally smug and blindly proud: "For myself, if I had to do it over again, I would do just the same. . . . I don't feel I was betrayed, or misled, or bamboozled. I knew just what I was doing, and I don't regret any of it." For "to reach those goals [brotherhood and equality] required organization, and the Party, whatever its strengths or weaknesses at any given time—and I was aware of both—remained the only viable organization through which to make the struggle."[42]

Maltz continued to exhibit the unshakeable grip of these moral and intellectual contradictions, the hold likely strengthened by the intensity of his feelings about the injustices of the blacklist and the culpability of those who testified. In later interviews and statements he allowed for partial admissions, recognized that "mistakes" had been made by "Stalin" and some of his leaders, but insisted he could not have known any of that earlier. As was typical, he particularly talked about the unfair purges and "trials" of *party* members. In an interview by Victor Navasky, Maltz did briefly refer to the treatment of farmers; yet here he still spoke of them as those "who wouldn't accept collectivization."[43]

By the seventies and eighties, Maltz could criticize the CPUSA "for its slavish refusal to think for itself or to take any political position not advocated by the Soviet Union." He could criticize the Soviet Union for its "serious distortion [*sic*] of the socialist dream . . . [through] thought control and government tyranny." Nonetheless, he still believed the Soviets were on the "right side of history," had made the "tremendous social advances" he had spoken of through the years. He still believed the United States had started the Korean War, had even used germ warfare. As for himself, he admitted none of the destructive consequences of his innocent blindness to reality—or any complicity in these consequences. He looked back only at the romanticized idealism:

> We were starry-eyed and innocent. . . .
> . . . I felt that the Communist movement represented that force in the United States—and internationally—which was the best hope for humanity . . . the force which moved the world toward brotherhood.
> It [the Communist Party] actuated a passion for social justice which cultivated one's own innate passion and decency.[44]

In 1956 Trumbo, with a usual moral flourish of self-satisfaction, wrote Guy Endore to sum up what, as he put it, "had happened." As he saw it, "I look back on two decades through which good friends stood together, moved forward a little, dreamed that the world could be better and tried to make it so, tasted the joy of small victories, wounded each other, made mistakes, suffered much injury, and stood silent in the chamber of liars."[45]

In commenting on one writer's lauding of Dalton Trumbo as a man "to whom principle and honor are not just words but integral parts of his being and way of life," historian Guenter Lewy commented, "One need not become a defender of the blacklist . . . in order to wonder how a man of 'principle and honor' could become a champion of Stalin's policies that caused the death of millions and the loss of liberty to many more."[46]

Being Red, the 1990 memoir of Howard Fast, presents a valuable cross-section of the extreme contradictions—intellectually and emotionally—

that many could not resolve, however strong their later condemnation of aspects of the world of the Soviet Union and the CPUSA.

In the memoir, Fast expresses the shock and pain of his disillusionment in both the CPUSA and the Soviet Union in novelistic terms, trying to capture the way he—often expressed as "we"—felt then as well as now. This tends to blur the exact way he feels now, exactly what he is now admitting. He conveys deeper sorrow and pain than most of the others about the destruction created by the Soviet Union *under Stalin* and the "rigid, mindless Party leadership" of the CPUSA.[47]

In describing the stages of his rebellion against the party, Fast at one point enumerated an odd and revealing equivalence of consequences. Because of the leadership, "My writing would suffer, but this party to which I had pledged my wits and my energy would suffer even more, and throughout the world, millions would suffer." He did not go on to explain this connection of party bureaucracy to the causes of the tragedy of the millions. As for us, the members, "we were brave, uncorruptible, and led by stupid rigid men whose orders we accepted without demurral. . . . Rigidity, insensitivity, stupidity—we were guilty of all of these. But cruelty, harm to other human beings—never, and in all the years of our existence we had fought to organize working people, to build trade unions, to increase wages, to prevent evictions of the poor—and in Spain we had fought and died to stop the fascists." But the next stage—what responsibility *we* have *now* for what has been revealed—is not discussed. "We had," he still insists, "no connection to the Russians; we asked nothing from them and received nothing from them."[48]

The revelations that affected Fast are mainly derived from the Khrushchev speech and its indictment of Stalin. He felt betrayed by Stalin as the cause of the "horror stories that were told against Russia, the stories of imprisonment and injustice and total disregard for the rights of anyone who opposed Stalin, stories unhappily proved true," with no reference to the millions who did not oppose Stalin at all and yet were imprisoned or killed. In one strong passage, he dramatized the stages of his response—from denial to rage and "total despair"—to information about the "horrendous" persecution and killing of Jews, "all this under the benign rule of Josef Stalin." While referring again and again to Stalin as mad, Fast did make several brief and undefined references to "the manner of organization that gave him the passport to power."[49]

Despite his "total despair" over the revelations, Fast, along with many others, repeatedly carried on the rhetoric and mind-set of moral equivalence between the Soviets and the Americans. He used, for example, the word "terror" equally to refer to both countries, though he actually used it more in talking about the United States. Among a number of such comments about the United States are the following: "the miasma of terror and hatred"; "its carefully orchestrated campaign of terror"; "the terror was not slackening."[50] At one point he compares the apathy of the people in not standing up to the "spreading, creeping terror" of fifties anti-Communism to the way that "the German people did not rise up in anger when Hitler put 500,000 members of the German Communist Party to death [a distortion in itself], and why should we doubt that the same thing could happen here?" At another point, he says, "The punishment was not, as in Germany [note: not, as in Russia], death and the concentration camp; it was instead loss of one's job, blacklist in one's profession . . . and the result was the kind of *terror* [emphasis added] this country had never seen before or since."[51]

Despite Fast's (partial) recognitions, it was still America that was the land of terror. He could still state about America's Communist Control Act of 1954, "There is no law extant in any country in the entire world as all-embracing and as terrifying."[52]

A frequent proponent of this kind of equivalence is Abraham Polonsky, as in this statement in 1956, writing about the role of art in promoting "a truthful life, to be shaken up, to be disturbed, to be awakened, even from the dream of the American or Soviet Paradise." For "the tendency in social commitment is uniformity, as in the United States and in the Soviet Union."[53] Thusly, Soviet *terror* is obfuscated down to *uniformity* and made the equivalent of some American problem.

In *The Black Book of Communism*, French historian Stéphane Courtois defines the kind of silence that is the false use of words to mask evil:

> When the tyrants could no longer hide the truth—the firing squads, the concentration camps, the man-made famines—they did their best to justify these atrocities by glossing them over. . . . Perhaps the single greatest evil [in this propaganda campaign] was the perversion of language. As if by magic, the concentration-camp system was turned into a "re-education system," and the tyrants became "educators" who transformed the people of the old society into "new people." The *zeks*, a term for Soviet concentration camp prisoners, were forcibly "invited" to place their trust in a system that enslaved them. In China the concentration-camp prisoner is called a "student.". . . Perverted words are situated in a twisted vision that distorts the landscape.[54]

Arthur Miller, in his autobiography *Timebends*, portrayed his own questioning of the moral absolutism when he was considering having Kazan direct his play *After the Fall* in 1964: "As for morals, perhaps it was just as well not to cast too wide a net; for one thing, how many who knew by now that they had been supporting a paranoid and murderous Stalinist regime had really confronted their abetting of it?"[55]

Here there is still the ubiquitous focus on Stalin, not the system. The deeper troubling irony here, however, is that Miller's play *The Crucible*

(1953) continues to have tremendous impact and influence in maintaining the opposite viewpoint to his recognition of the complex issue of complicity. Within the potent drama of the play's invalid historical parallel, it is still one of the most iconic, reductive means of codifying the conventional "witch-hunt" formula of the absolutist moral definitions of the time. In addition to its myriad productions, in book form *The Crucible* has sold more than 4.5 million copies.

18

Hearings and Filmmaking: The Denial of Value and the Record on Film

A corresponding chord to the denunciations of individuals who testified has been sounded in the repeated Cassandra cry that the period was a time of total darkness and emptiness in the making of movies. That the "witch hunt"—the blacklist, the censorship, the Fascism, the McCarthyism—had produced a total dearth, a famine of intelligent and meaningful social, political, or even mature films for more than a decade. The real world—this time of movies, not Communist actions—exposes the hyperbole of this claim as being as false and distorting as were the major ideological proclamations about the nature of Communism, the Communist Party, the Soviet Union, and the United States.

Embodying the tone for this defiance of movie reality was Adrian Scott's 1955 article in the *Hollywood Review*. In it he bemoans what was lost in the contrast between pre- and post-blacklist movies. He displays the paradigm for this distortion of history: "Few if *any* of the films made . . . since 1947 have dramatized the humanist, democratic, and antifascist values that illuminated [the films] in the Roosevelt era."[1]

By 1948, in his early paean to the Hollywood Ten, Gordon Kahn (one of the first Nineteen) was already lamenting, "The prospects are that pictures like *Grapes of Wrath*, *Gentleman's Agreement* and others with force and meaning—the kind in which writers, actors, and directors can take pride—will be strangers to the screen of America."[2]

The comments are not only indicative of the standard claim, but also of the refusal to see that times had changed—and movies needed to change, and would. The depression was over as were the particular economic structures and injustices of that time; the war was over, there were new areas, new ways of life to deal with, new kinds and degrees of conflicts. The old forms and formulas, structures and sentiments, icons and injustices, even overt forms of corruption and betrayal were not only outdated artistically; they were out of date, out of step with the realities of the times. That they were lost, no longer central was understandable, expected, inevitable. These were new times, and films did respond to them, often in quite valuable artistic and social ways: with effectiveness, with insight, artistry, sophistication beyond the themes and standard paradigms and structures, the legacy of the protest theater of the thirties, of those films "in the Roosevelt era," all so fondly remembered.

During the Korean War, Michael Wilson, nevertheless, saw only Fascist warmongering and thought control in the films of the time. They had "a pervading anti-intellectual quality, an absence of ideas, a disdain for rational motive. . . . Why do informers have to make themselves out as idiots?" Wilson saw even so-called "escapist" films as "propaganda films expressing the doctrines of Manifest Destiny, the American Century, and white supremacy in gaudy technicolor." The typical American hero in adventure films was "an inhuman killer" who prefers "violence to debate." In the same year, 1953, Dalton Trumbo argued that the committee's purpose was "to remove progressive content of films. . . . I think the content of films was better in 1943 than in 1953." Earlier, screenwriter Leonard Spiegelgass, in a legal deposition, had cried that from the Waldorf resolution in 1947 on there had been an "effect upon this industry of stifling the creation of original stories which might 'probe the dark corners and dark places of our society'; . . . a fear of writing and creating those materials."[3]

The Jarricos, Paul and Sylvia, joined the chorus. In 1955 Paul saw "a direct relation between the blacklist and the increasing emphasis on pro-war and *anti-human* [emphasis added] themes. We have seen more and more pictures of violence-for-the-sake-of-violence, more and more unmotivated brutality on the screen as the blacklist grew." Sylvia, one of the editors of the *Hollywood Review*, in an essay titled "Evil Heroines of 1953," even saw the blacklist as one of the forces in a male-dominated industry used to fight against the emerging role of women in postwar America: "The complacent theme that submission is the natural state of women has given way to the aggressive theme that submission is the *necessary* state of women."[4]

Years later, Joseph Losey was still proclaiming that "[in Blacklist America] the intellectual core of Hollywood disappeared virtually overnight. Within a few years any kind of really strong intellectual freedom of thought, let alone expression, disappeared in the United States."[5]

Repetitions of the same themes and judgments have continued ever since—locked in by ideology and anger, even by romantic nostalgia. In his memoir of 1996, *Inside Out*, writer-director Walter Bernstein continued to sound the refrain. Even after half a century had passed, for Bernstein anything but a straight-jabbing, straight-on, surface attack on the capitalist system was still a sellout. "The new movies [of the fifties] were different. They were becoming glossier. They were also becoming emptier. Psychology was in, social criticism was out [Either-or. No allowance that one can reflect, enhance the other]. . . . People were bad because they were bad. . . . It was easier to blame it on Mom and Dad than on some kind of system."[6]

In an interview with Patrick McGilligan, actress Karen Morley was typical in her frozen-in-time vision: "The movie just got worse. Movies have always been fairly violent, but in the old days writers tried to express human values. . . . All that kind of treatment pretty much went by the board during the blacklist. Now violence became an art, a cult, and with it came the passive women . . . the 'hate the ladies movement.'. . . The treatment of minorities simply disappeared, I would say, in movies of the 1950s. The issue simply wasn't treated at all."[7]

Director Martin Ritt, whose career was just beginning in the fifties, agreed with interviewer McGilligan that "the blacklist was really a form of censorship," that films had become "bland, smug, repressed." For Ritt, many decades later, "Oh, the fifties were probably the worst decade of the century."[8]

The promoters of the mythic history of the forces of light against the forces of darkness—such as McGilligan, Buhle, Ceplair, Englund, Navasky, and others—carried on the same message. Buhle and McGilligan provide a cogent summary of this unchanging vision of a destroyed golden era in the introduction to *Tender Comrades*: "The films of the 1930s and 1940s [were] stories suffused with feeling for people and their ordinary concerns. . . . They [the writers of the Left] believed in the power of storytelling to illuminate social contradictions. . . . The blacklist robbed them and us. America's iron curtain rang down on an era. Hollywood movies took a giant step backward; the humane traditions that the leftists had brought with them to Hollywood were jettisoned. The outrage over prejudice disappeared. Violence, which had always been a part of film, would become ritualistic. The roles for actresses grew passive and cartoonish."[9]

Not only do Ceplair and Englund (in their much-quoted *Inquisition in Hollywood*, 1979–1983) proclaim that "the studios withdrew before the lengthening shadows of HUAC and McCarthy and the distorted confines of patriotic conformity and circumscribed creativity. . . . Controversial and social subjects . . . were no longer countenanced as story materials." They also insist that whatever content there *was*, was reactionary: "Hollywood films of the fifties did not lack *any* political or social content, however; they contained a conservative, vindictive, troubled content which betrayed [*revealed?*] the new forces and attitudes at work in the industry. . . . Nearly everyone noticed sooner or later the ice age which had descended on Hollywood."[10]

The contrast with reality is immense. These distorting claims of a "dark ages" for Hollywood films of this era are readily exposed by an easily gathered set of films of the period, ranging from good to fine, that did deal with social, political, cultural, and psychological themes; films that were deeply, significantly humane, and some that were just plain innovative or high-quality movies, some of the best ever made. In the main these were films that had a deeper view of and sharper focus on the true inner consequences—and their human complexities and ambiguities—of "lived-in" social and economic structures, pressures, and forces. They often displayed a fuller, more artistic sense of the ways visual, dramatic, verbal—that a film builds and conveys meaning, a sense of the possibilities of the poetry of film form.

In the "initial" blacklist period, 1948–1950, these included the following films:

All the King's Men	*The Brave Bulls*
Gentleman's Agreement	*Pinky*
White Heat	*The Treasure of the Sierra Madre*
The Asphalt Jungle	*Knock on Any Door*
Intruder in the Dust	*All about Eve*
The Glass Menagerie	*The Gunfighter*
The Men	*The Heiress*
Broken Arrow	*No Way Out*
Home of the Brave	*Lost Boundaries*
In a Lonely Place	*Sunset Boulevard*
Champion	*Twelve O'Clock High*

In the "high" blacklist period, 1951–1959, these included the following films:

On the Waterfront	*Viva Zapata!*
East of Eden	*A Face in the Crowd*
A Streetcar Named Desire	*Baby Doll*
Alexander the Great	*They Came to Cordura*
Island in the Sun	*Sweet Smell of Success*
Bad Day at Black Rock	*Blackboard Jungle*
Rebel without a Cause	*Giant*
The Searchers	*The Strange One*
Patterns	*Twelve Angry Men*
The Big Heat	*The Diary of Anne Frank*
Death of a Salesman	*Cat on a Hot Tin Roof*
Marty	*High Noon*
The Red Badge of Courage	*From Here to Eternity*
The Caine Mutiny	*The Bridge on the River Kwai*
Friendly Persuasion	*Paths of Glory*
Edge of the City	*The Defiant Ones*

The Big Carnival | The Rack
Attack! | A Place in the Sun
Some Like It Hot | Hud
Detective Story | Carrie
Apache | The Big Knife
The Wild One | Vertigo
The Man with the Golden Arm | Cry, the Beloved Country
On the Beach | Touch of Evil
The Member of the Wedding | The Night of the Hunter
The Steel Helmet | The Wrong Man
The Harder They Fall | Clash by Night
The Young Lions | The Sun Also Rises
The African Queen | Odds against Tomorrow
No Down Payment | A Hatful of Rain
The Day the Earth Stood Still | Magnificent Obsession
Written on the Wind | All That Heaven Allows
Imitation of Life | The Cobweb
The Left-Handed Gun | Bend of the River
The Bad and the Beautiful | Picnic
Tea and Sympathy | Come Back, Little Sheba
Peyton Place | The Long, Hot Summer
Invasion of the Body Snatchers | The Lawless
Trial | The Rose Tattoo
Bright Victory | The Young Stranger
Shane | Kiss Me Deadly

In the transition period into the sixties, 1960–1961, these included the following films:

The Hustler | Wild River
The Misfits | Son and Lovers
The Apartment | Suddenly, Last Summer
The Manchurian Candidate | The Fugitive Kind
A Raisin in the Sun | Spartacus
Judgment at Nuremberg | Sergeant Rutledge
Winchester 73 | Home from the Hill
Summer and Smoke | The Dark at the Top of the Stairs
The Unforgiven

In more substantive detail, we can look at some films of the period that are significant memorable representatives of the very categories that the left has held up as signs and symptoms of the deplorable consequences of oppression and fear.

One of the frequent claims is that there were no films of insight, impact, and interest that dealt with themes of blacks and other minorities. In reality, the imposing contrast is that there were more such films than in any period until then—whether directly, or indirectly in genre films. Among the earliest were *Pinky* (1949), *Lost Boundaries* (1949), and *Gentleman's Agreement* (1947). The films with Sidney Poitier alone probably outnumbered the total released earlier—and certainly equaled or excelled any in quality and insight. Whatever the plot or emphasis—the carriage, the sense of inner poise, the diction, the dignity of Poitier brought a kind of freedom, an opening in the thinking of many about the nature of blacks ("negroes"). His films of this period included *No Way Out* (1950); *Cry, the Beloved Country* (1951); *Blackboard Jungle* (1955); *Edge of the City* (1957); *The Defiant Ones* (1958); *Porgy and Bess* (1959); and *A Raisin in the Sun* (1961). No one span of films by an individual actor—and certainly by a "negro" actor—had ever done as much to break the stereotype and start to forge a new, more accurate image, of a minority group than the films of Poitier in this period. And it is certainly arguable that it equals, or surpasses, the impact and value of any since.

James Edwards had strong roles in some twenty films in a ten-year span, not all of them in films of substance. But these did include meaningful roles, for example, in *The Set-Up* (1949), *Home of the Brave* (1949), *The Steel Helmet* (1951), *The Member of the Wedding* (1952), *The Joe Louis Story* (1953), *Bright Victory* (1951). The latter also starred Dorothy Dandridge, who also starred in *Porgy and Bess*, *Carmen Jones* (1954), and *Island in the Sun* (1957), and a number of films of lesser worth. Harry Belafonte also starred in *Bright Road* (1953), *Carmen Jones*, and *Island in the Sun*. He was interested in promoting more unusual, imaginative development of racial themes and helped produce two thrillers that developed themes of racial issues within genre plots: *The World, the Flesh, and the Devil* (1959); and *Odds against Tomorrow* (1959).

In this period, some of the films concerning racial prejudices and injustices were among the films in the standard commercial genres that were structured to convey or imply the kind of social themes appropriate to the fifties that Robert Rossen and others had embodied, for example, in gangster films of the earlier period. A breakthrough in more sophisticated Westerns with psychological and social implications found a number of Western films—such as *Broken Arrow* (1950), *Devil's Doorway* (1950), *Apache* (1954), John Huston's *The Unforgiven* (1960), and the modern-day *The Outsider* (1961)—dramatizing meaningful racial issues—as did John Ford's *Sergeant Rutledge* (1960) and *The Searchers* (1956), the latter considered by many critics to be his finest film. Another, deeply *human* revisionist depiction of American Indians, Ford's *Cheyenne Autumn* (1964), was to follow in the early sixties.

In the genre of science fiction films, Don Seigel's *Invasion of the Body Snatchers* (1956) set an influential pattern in dealing with contemporary social issues. Within its "thriller" narrative, its central metaphor is structured to capture the paranoia of the Cold War period, its fears whether warranted or propagandized. The oppressive combination of conformity, apathy, and betrayal is morphed into the relentlessly producing giant pods taking over individuals, groups, communities. As one character says, they are like "a malignant disease spreading throughout the country." In the iconic *The Manchurian Candidate* (1962), literal brainwashing is fancifully exaggerated into a satirical metaphor of conformity within a political structure of ambiguous corruption.

Bad Day at Black Rock (1955) was a unique modern use of the structure of the Western, a milestone treatment of contemporary bigotry—this time directed against Japanese Americans—seen as but one aspect of oppressive control of a small town in the West. It is a convincingly personalized clash of democratic good and fascistic evil in modern terms, building tension and insight with quiet power and without "capitalized" straining for standardized "social" meaning. A valuable but forgotten film of the time (never mentioned by writers on the left) was *Trial* (1955), directed by Mark Robson. *Trial* takes an iconoclastic view of a situation involving the persecution of young Mexican Americans in a case modeled on the Sleepy Lagoon trial. It focuses on the cynical use made of the situation by a Communist organizer. He (like Ben Margolis?) is concerned with the party's ideological and financial benefits, not with the saving of an innocent boy—while a liberal lawyer (like those who testified?) is painfully disillusioned by what he sees and so rebels against the party line. A similar mature treatment of the paradoxes, ironies, and betrayals of revolutionary zeal in Mexico has brought Elia Kazan's powerful *Viva Zapata!* (1952) the scorn of critics on the left.

Wilson's claim about war films is definitively challenged by such Korean War films as *Attack* (1956) and *The Rack* (1956) and by one of the greatest antiwar films of any period, Stanley Kubrick's *Paths of Glory* (1957) in which the dictatorial, and devastating, oppressions of wartime command are potently drawn in parallel to the injustice and inequalities of the political system. It is no evasion of impact or meaning that the narrative surface is a story of the French army in World War I or that the oppressive injustice of military justice in Fred Zinnemann's *From Here to Eternity* (1953) is part of a full view of human and system frailties and virtues in the American army in World War II.

Robson also directed, among other strong and meaningful films, *Champion* (1949), *Home of the Brave* (1949), *Bright Victory* (1951), *The Harder They Fall* (1956), and *Peyton Place* (1957). Several of Robson's films were produced by the Stanley Kramer Company, which, among other new independent producers, dealt with the distortions of self, the corruptions and betrayals that false values and social pressures produced in individuals, and still with some allusions to the capitalist system. Other Kramer Company films with social and moral implications—and excellent cinematic qualities—included *The Sniper* (1952), *Eight Iron Men* (1952), *The Juggler* (1953), *The Caine Mutiny* (1954), *Champion, Home of the Brave, Cyrano de Bergerac* (1950), and *The Men* (1950).

It was the time of the flowering of the genre of film noir—much admired, discussed, minutely analyzed and subdivided in categories and meanings—with varying degrees of expertise, artistry, cynicism (whether truly felt or genre influenced), indirect social criticism. The epitome is Billy Wilder's *Double Indemnity* (1944) as Walter Neff tells his dictation machine, "I did it for the money, and I did it for the woman. I didn't get the money and I didn't get the woman."

The psychology maligned by Bernstein *was* present in films as they responded to the ambiance of the times. The filmmakers were responding to new interpretations of social issues, the complex interaction of individual psychology—needs and desires, weaknesses, motives—and social pressures. It was not a time of the bedrock fears of poverty and unemployment; the new momentum of the zeitgeist and the new fears were caught up together in upwardly mobile possibilities of a dream of success, a detached ranch-style house with a two-car garage, and yet an emptiness, an inner displaced fear and sense of loss, an alienation.

Many films of the period dramatized in many ways the dangers of conformity and repression, the new pressures in a new society—as experienced in man-woman relationships, families, groups, and within dogmatic communities. *Repression* was prevalent in films of the fifties; but it was not, as claimed, *of* the films; it was *in* the films—an echo on film of the times. This constellation of themes has been recognized in such major "serious" films as Kazan's *East of Eden* (1955) and *Splendor in the Grass* (1961) and Nicholas Ray's *Rebel without a Cause* (1955). Another of Ray's strong dramas of the period, *In a Lonely Place* (1950), has a taut, and oddly, disturbingly controlled intensity. In its depiction of the implacable, volatile inner tensions of an ostensibly liberal screenwriter, it captures the alienation and unfocused resentment that are so central in the sociological commentary of the time. Yet it is not bound by psycho-sociological theorizing, maintains a sense of uncertainty, undefined ambiguity.

But it was also indicative of the times, the new times, that the fifties were also the *anni mirabili*, the coming of age, of the genre of meaningful, diamond-faceted domestic melodramas, as exemplified in the films of Douglas Sirk and the dramas of Vincente Minnelli. The best of these films display an understanding of the potent, fascinating grammar of visual meaning, a language of film beyond dialogue and plot.

A noted exponent of semiotic film theory and criticism, Thomas Elsaesser insisted that the domestic melodrama was

> at its best perhaps the most highly elaborated, complex mode of cinematic signification . . . because of the restricted scope for external action determined by the subject, and because, as Sirk said, everything happens "inside" . . . a sublimation of dramatic values into décor, colour, gesture and composition of frame, which in the best melodramas is perfectly thematized in terms of the characters' emotional and psychological predicament . . . by the function of the décor and the symbolization of objects. The setting of the family melodrama almost by definition is the middle-class home, filled with objects, which surround the heroine [or hero] in a hierarchy of apparent order that becomes increasingly suffocating.[11]

Sirk and Minnelli, at the forefront of this development, are both masters, in the defining phrase of film historian Thomas Schatz, "of formal artifice and expressive décor."[12] Their repressed and dominated characters, particularly women, are "caught" in the oppressive vise of a variety of social institutions. The counterpoint between the normal, complacent surfaces of their lives and their inner torment and turmoil is regularly captured in the ironic treatment of their physical surroundings, the décor of their well-appointed, comfortable imprisonment. So that, especially in Sirk's films, décor and color schemes, often richly elaborate and overripe—even a changing spectrum of cocktail dresses, or heavy window drapes and curtains, or the shining shapes of automobiles—could be seen as part of the drama, emblems of the society in which character was developed, contributing to thematic implication, which was often left ironic and ambiguous. This kind of irony seems to remain invisible to the politically committed.

In his films Sirk, an émigré, is in tune with the dominant themes that were developing in postwar philosophy, particularly existentialism, and modernist art: isolation and loneliness, uncertainty, alienation. And within the bright neatness of his mise-en-scène and tightly wound plots, he exhibits, in his own wry way, the burgeoning sense of *irony* in the serious art of the period: the way artists of the time began to welcome contradictory impulses, mixing control with intuition and even accident; relishing ambiguity and contradiction, elusiveness, finding a saving joy in accepting and living with paradox. As one critic wrote of the paintings of Willem de Kooning in the fifties, there is no "slighting of the essential unresolved clutter of experience." Critics have seen how de Kooning's heated, passionate, explosive, even ferocious paintings "capture the dissonant social rhythms of the twentieth century, encompassing a time of displacement, dislocation."[13]

Sirk's cool, dispassionate irony, his calm, classical distancing convey other echoes of this dissonance. His film world is tightly controlled, yet elusive in its implications; he is devious, equivocal in his evaluations. He captures, often by indirection, the flaws of this world—the pain and loss caused by the inhibiting and even destructive restrictions, the immovable power and value structures of society, the self-defeat of dependence. Yet he eschews the pat answers of the Left. He leaves unresolved the slippery ambiguities and paradoxes of these social structures—families, wealth and power, the relations of men and women, rich and poor, black and white. The traditional progressive demand of a work of art—as typified in the folk-song refrain, "Which side are you on, boys, which side are you on"—is not a good template for viewing his world on film.

It seems appropriate for the paradoxes of Sirk's films that Rock Hudson was one of the stars in four of the films. The Rock Hudson image, his very size and solidity, was the iconic surface balance, the saving source of independence in these films. Yet—like the draperies and furnishing of the rooms of the wealthy and seemingly self-content—his solid surface still somehow carried in the stiffness of his controlled presence a sense of the hidden presence of his own inner complexities and demons. Hudson was in *The Magnificent Obsession* (1954), *All That Heaven Allows* (1955), and *Written on the Wind* (1956)—which are the core of this series of films—as well as the peripheral variation, *The Tarnished Angels* (1958). The fourth film at the center of this series is *Imitation of Life* (1959), which interestingly blends the ambiguous tensions of race and the paradoxical connections between theater and reality with Sirk's usual thematic concerns: the pressures and repressions of family, power, community.

These films are often defined away as women's films, "weepies"; they *are*, indeed, women's films in their repeated narrative and thematic emphasis on the plight of women: women caught in the décor and decorum of their tightly ordered world, the discordance and dislocation of their inner lives weighted down under the ironically smooth veneer of their everyday lives, in the richly furnished homes in which they are not really at home. Feminist critic and theorist Laura Mulvey, in an essay on Sirk's films, goes so far (too far?) as to see how *All That Heaven Allows* exposes the impossibility of female desire under a patriarchal order. The wealthy widow, Jane Wyman, is not "allowed" to express, and fulfill, her desire for a younger man, Hudson, who is also a Thoreau-like individualist, a representative of pure nature, whose life among plants and trees is outside of the artificially furnished world in which she lives. For Mulvey, she is caught in "the lived contradictions and repression of women in a phallocentric [*sic*] order." That is, she has internalized her society's rules and biases and contributes to the betrayal of her own desires—until, and not without a good deal of irony, an accident immobilizes Hudson and she is able to take care of him, "mother" him, and so can finally free her love and herself.[14]

Schatz has caught the significant link between Vincente Minnelli and Sirk, defining Minnelli's characters as also framed in "a filmic world—at once familiar and yet lavishly artificial and visually stylized."[15] In Minnelli's melodramas his repressed and dominated characters are seen "caught" in a variety of circumstances; his films, however, are given more definite, and non-ironic, resolutions than are Sirk's. As a character in *The Cobweb* (1955) says, "In all institutions, something of the individual gets lost." These individuals must fight to find or rediscover their true selves. In *The Cobweb* the institution is a mental hospital, in which there are conflicts within an actual family and the supposedly benign "family" of the hospital—and between them. In *The Bad and the Beautiful* (1952), there is a parallel between the pressures of an actual family (father and daughter) and the greedy and cruel domination of the father-figure, the power- and success-hungry movie producer (Kirk Douglas) in the perverse "family" of Hollywood filmmakers. Lana Turner is the woman at the center of these forces, as she was in Sirk's *Imitation of Life*. Family conflicts and sexual desires and contradictions are enacted within the tight system of a college campus in *Tea and Sympathy* (1956) and in another Hollywood story, *Two Weeks in Another Town* (1962), are displaced (as is the central character, this time a male) to the production system of a film being made in Europe. One can find in both of Minnelli's Hollywood stories, and their relentless producers, definite echoes of the depredations of the blacklist and the pressures of money and success. In *Home from the Hill* (1960), the parallel between destructive discordance in the family and in the community is given a definite economic interpretation. The dominating father figure, Robert Mitchum, not only seeks to control his sons, but the whole town, much of which he owns.

It is interesting to note that through this same period, Minnelli, the consummate blend of artist and professional, was making such masterful and iconic musicals as *An American in Paris* (1951), *The Band Wagon* (1953), *Brigadoon* (1954), *Kismet* (1955), and *Gigi* (1958). In this supposedly barren decade of filmmaking, he was not alone in fashioning masterpieces of the musical genre. Others included *The Pirate* (1948), *Easter Parade* (1948), *Words and Music* (1948), *Take Me Out to the Ball Game* (1949), *On the Town* (1949), *Annie Get Your Gun* (1950), *Royal Wedding* (1951), *Silk Stockings* (1957), and *Singin' in the Rain* (1952). And these were only those produced by Arthur Freed.

This was the period also of the filmed versions of plays by Tennessee Williams and William Inge, the masters of repression and warping, of destructive conformity, of devastating families—works that are far from empty or merely full of evasive psychology. The screened plays by Williams were *The Glass Menagerie* (1950), *A Streetcar Named Desire* (1951), *The Rose Tattoo* (1955), *Cat on a Hot Tin Roof* (1958), *Suddenly, Last Summer* (1959), *The Fugitive Kind* (1960), and *Summer and Smoke* (1961). Those by Inge were *Come Back, Little Sheba* (1952); *Picnic* (1955); *Bus Stop* (1956); and *The Dark at the Top of the Stairs* (1960). In *America in the Movies*, Michael Wood speaks of *Picnic's* "persistent, insidious hysteria that reflects ironically the repressed pain of alienation and loneliness." Such "popular movies," he believes, "permit us to look without looking at things we can neither face fully nor entirely disavow."[16]

It was the period of powerful and varied films by John Huston, possibly the strongest series of works of his career, including *The Treasure of the Sierra Madre* (1948), *The Asphalt Jungle* (1950), and *The African Queen* (1951). In these years the masterful director William Wyler created a series of films that also may be the strongest, most meaningful set of his long career. These included probing, echoing psychological and socially analytical films, both intelligent and emotional, like *The Heiress* (1949), *Detective Story* (1951), and *Carrie* (1952), as well as the idealistic *Friendly Persuasion* (1956) and the magnificent epic *Ben Hur* (1959). As in all of his best work, these beautifully wrought films had a visual sophistication and artistry—particularly in the development of the signature aspects of his style, shots of deep focus and long duration—as changing patterns of movements and physical relationships captured and heightened the emotional relationships and psychological conflicts of the characters.

It was the period of major big-budget films of substance and skill, among them George Stevens' American trilogy of *Giant* (1956), *Shane* (1953), and *A Place in the Sun* (1951); Otto Preminger's *The Man with the Golden Arm* (1955); and varied and inventive approaches to genre such as *High Noon* (1952), *The Gunfighter* (1950), *The Left-handed Gun* (1958), and *Hud* (1963), or Orson Welles' flamboyant, eccentric "crime" film of inevitable human weakness and corruption, *Touch of Evil* (1958).

The decade was also the richest period for Alfred Hitchcock—including, among others, *Strangers on a Train* (1951), *Rear Window* (1954), *Vertigo* (1958), *North by Northwest* (1959), and *Psycho* (1960). *Vertigo*, one might argue (as others have), is the finest film of the period, not only for its visual poetry, but for its ironic, tragically witty admission of the paradoxes of being human. Within its structure as a mystery—a conventional structure that it consistently bends and explodes—it visually, dramatically, emotionally exposes the limits of logic and reason and control. Its "private eye" is not only unable to understand what he is investigating; more dangerously, and finally destructively, he is unable even to understand himself. Subtly, by both quiet stealth and sudden extremity and in the midst of constant beauty, the film lays open the ambiguities of motivation, of love, passion and commitment, and most poignantly and meaningfully for its period—of the unresolved regions of betrayal. There is more exposed in *Vertigo* about the relations of men and women than in the whole panoply of movies whose loss Karen Morley grieved over.

This period was certainly not the "worst decade" for the irrepressible Billy Wilder. His irreverent films, like whirling pinwheels, cast out more sardonic, satirical sparks of exposure of repression, conformity, social manipulation, and false symbols of personal identity and fulfillment than most films considered "meaningful" by the conventional wisdom of the Left, and definitely with more bright sparks of wit and flourishes of personal style. From 1950 to 1960 they were *Sunset Boulevard* (1950), *Ace in the Hole/The Big Carnival* (1951), *Stalag 17* (1953), *Sabrina* (1954), *The Seven Year Itch* (1955), *The Spirit of St. Louis* (1957), *Love in the Afternoon* (1957), *Witness for the Prosecution* (1957), *Some Like It Hot* (1959), and *The Apartment* (1960). It is an awesome sequence of work. Similarly, the notable émigré director Fritz Lang made *twelve* movies in this period. Though they were of varying degrees of seriousness and too often made under pressures of time and commercial demands, a Fritz Lang film was never without some worthy degree of artistic originality and of insight, often bleak and ironic, into the frailties of human beings and the societies they create and are trapped in.

About those who denigrated such achievements, Wilder commented on the "Unfriendly Ten," as they were referred to at the time, with his usual mixture of mockery and seriousness. "Only two," he said, "were talented—the rest were just unfriendly."[17]

19

Testifying and Filmmaking: Attacks on Individuals and the Record on Film

Not only has it been consistently proclaimed that the industry suffered through a "dark ages." Within the rigid moral dichotomy established by the committed Left, a parallel repeated refrain has sounded, and with more personal venom: that the work of individual filmmakers who testified suffered, the moral stain debilitating the whole man, the later works a betrayal of his talents, marred by his moral and ideological betrayals.

This has been especially true in the treatment of the films of Elia Kazan and Robert Rossen, the most significant of the filmmakers who testified and the most maligned. Comments by noted liberal director Martin Ritt capture the essence of this consistent approach—indicating as well how ideology and long-held resentment can blind an accomplished director to the real accomplishments of others:

> And I knew a lot of guys who behaved badly, and who have not really realized themselves as artists or human beings since that time. . . .
>
> They [Rossen, Kazan, Dmytryk, others] made a wrong move. They violated themselves. I think [their] work suffered. . . . I think Kazan's work suffered. I don't think he ever realized his great talent. I think his films before the testimony were better than afterward.[1]

Abe Polonsky commented on the work of both Rossen and Kazan with the peculiar mix of moral righteousness and artistic evaluation that is central to this "genre" of criticism: "He [Rossen] was talented, but like Kazan he also had a rotten character." After they testified, the films of both were "marred by bad conscience."[2]

Walter Bernstein agreed: "So informing compromised Kazan, and his cultural contribution lessened in the 1950s."[3]

Kazan's *Boomerang!* (1947), *Panic in the Streets* (1950), and *A Tree Grows in Brooklyn* (1945) are safe, solid films, showing developing skills; *Gentleman's Agreement* a safe, solid, neatly limited treatment of anti-Semitism. They have nowhere near the cinematic verve and human probing, the engrossing, revealing emotionality, the personal artistic excitement, of his later films, risk-taking and a bit ragged. The actual result of this "lessening" and "suffering" was that in the decade or so following his testimony in 1952, Kazan produced an amazing and important body of work, both on the screen and on the stage. Of the films done before, the only equals were the film of Tennessee Williams' *A Streetcar Named Desire* (1951) and *Viva Zapata!* (1952), and both of these were worked on during the period of his intense soul-searching over his rebellion against his previous silence.

On the Waterfront (1954) humanized and modernized, raised to a new level the Left's traditional agitprop pattern of the plays of the thirties, such as *Stevedore* and *Marching Song*. In this traditional pattern, events and other people help raise the consciousness of an uncommitted young man (Marlon Brando as Terry Malloy) who then stands up to the oppressors of the workers and leads the community to a new level of consciousness and living. As in the plays of the thirties, it is gangsters, and their goons, who are the face of capitalist evil, but this time it is corrupt union gangsters, and their goons, who provide the factual contemporary slant. They talk about themselves as businessmen, but through threats of violence and acts of violence they intimidate the union members, the workers, into a resigned and fearful silence. Terry, an ex-boxer, has been complicit in perpetuating the mobsters' control. Influenced by his brother Charley (Rod Steiger), the mob's unofficial legal arm, he does their petty dirty work.

The movement of his consciousness, and spirit, toward social awareness and redemption is convincingly developed within the film's full texture of strong personal emotions, of conflicted and conflicting feelings, intensely expressed. These are human beings, even if still figures in the morality play, seen within the social context of the corrupting force of greed and apathy. As Terry realizes he loves, realizes he *can* love the young woman (Eva Marie Saint) whose brother has been killed, he realizes she is right. He must change his life and act; but he fights against the realization, is torn within. The stages of his path toward redemption are orchestrated in beautiful, landmark scenes: On a cold day in a park (as he tellingly tries to put his large hand into the glove she has dropped). In a bar (where, fresh from the convent, she is having her first drink, along with her first love) he haltingly tries to tell her what he has never expressed before, even to himself, and she reaches across the small bar table and tenderly touches his cheek.

In the tight confines of her family's apartment, where, both screaming, he fights against what she demands of him. And the famous scene in the taxi (where it is often forgotten that Charley is supposed to talk him out of testifying or take him to a beating or even death), when Terry pours out his recognition that the mob had sold him out, that he had sold himself out for a few bucks, his cri de coeur, "I coulda been somebody," echoes more than a championship lost in the "fix." It is his manhood he knows he lost, his true self.

The film is consistently undervalued by the Left, misinterpreted, even misdescribed. Ceplair and Englund, for example, have Kazan exculpating his own immorality with a film that "glorified the hero's decision to testify against his former *friends* and union *comrades* [emphasis added]." Not really knowing much about movies, they probably got that idea from a phrasing by Victor Navasky: "*On the Waterfront*, in which Terry Malloy comes to maturity when he realizes his obligation to fink on his fellow hoods." Navasky reduces the film to merely a dishonest defense of informing, not granting that there *are* things that one should not remain silent about. In his angry piece in the *Hollywood Review*, Adrian Scott sees the deceitful *On the Waterfront* as really a disguised attack on trade unionism—"theme: courageous stool pigeon frees sheeplike long-shoremen from tyranny of corrupt union." He fails *Viva Zapata!* too because it demeans the ideals of revolution; he sees no value, or truth, in what he claims is reductive and reactionary in its time-proven theme: "power corrupts revolutionaries."[4]

Budd Schulberg, who had testified in 1951, wrote the screenplay. He also wrote *A Face in the Crowd* (1957) for Kazan, a strong, innovative blend of satire and emotionality that foreshadows the mixed tones of sixties films. It is prophetic in its exposure not only of the dangerous power of the media (then nowhere near as ubiquitous and dominant as it was to become) and its domineering personalities, but also of the dangerous alliance of the manipulative capabilities of the media with political agendas and manipulation of "the people." It focuses on the rise of a down-and-out "hick" who, somewhat like Rossen's Willie Stark, rises to the top on the basis of his connection to the common people as well as his cynical manipulation of them—this time in the world of small-town and then network radio and television. Reveling in his new sense of power, he allies himself and his down-home influence on his public with conservative political forces; he is used by them as he thinks he is using and controlling them. The film traces his rise and moral and emotional fall with strong and often satiric scenes and images: From the humble local successes of his frank and fresh salesmanship, folklore, folk songs, and humor; to the false folksy network shows with his "friend," the senator; to the grandiose emptiness of his success. In the bizarre final penthouse scene he is caught, lost in his own media world, image and sound blaring in the apartment, alone with the luxurious furnishings he cares nothing about, crying out at a world that he thinks has deserted and betrayed him. Dusty Rhoades betrays not only the public, but himself, his own particular knack, and the woman who loves and believes in him. For the politicians he has thought he could control, he has been just one more new mass media source, like a cigarette ad. Some fifty years later, this undervalued film has as much vivid life and pertinence as it had in 1957. Schulberg wrote another strong social film in this period, *Wild across the Everglades* (1958), as well as working with the filmmakers in bringing his novel *The Harder They Fall* to the screen in 1956.

A third work in Kazan's trilogy of directly social films is *Wild River* (1960). More sober and measured than the other two, lacking some of their electricity, it is as David Thomson noted, an example of "the concerned American thinking and feeling in unison . . . subtle in its situation, its colouring and acting."[5] It is interesting in the absence of a real villain. It poses moral and human dilemmas in making choices, in the conflict between opposing positions that are, in their ways, both right and just—electrification of a rural area to help the many with a dam that will flood the homes and livelihood of some. As in the previous two films, the dilemmas, and the emotional costs and gains, are played out on both the public level and the personal level. And it is the living level of personal feelings, of shared sympathy that is finally seen as the true basis for public action, not ideology alone. As the government agent (Montgomery Clift) interacts with the old woman (thirty-seven-year-old Jo Van Fleet!) who is "obstructing progress," his ideological certainty is loosened, if not shattered. He becomes aware of human ambivalence, compassion, even opens himself to the stirrings of love for a young local widow.

Kazan's other films in this period are a rich spectrum of approaches, tones, and experiments in dealing with personal relationships and conflicts—but always with an underlying sense of the impact of society and its pressures on both the emotional possibilities and the psychological disfigurements of individuals. *Baby Doll* (1956) nicely and flamboyantly captures the bizarre yet oddly tender gothic humor of Tennessee Williams' treatment of the vagaries of the path of love in the corrupting culture of the South. In contrast, *East of Eden* (1955), based on sections of John Steinbeck's novel and for many the best movie of this sequence, dares full-throttle emotional intensity in immersing the explosive personal drama of twisted family ties in a fully realized sense of the restrictive society around it. Typifying Kazan's skill and intuitive force in bringing out the best, and most intimate, in actors is the amazingly exposed performance by James Dean. A similar intense emotionality pervades *Splendor in the Grass* (1961) as the dogmatic restrictions of another time and place in American society distort and destroy not only family relationships, but the possibilities of loving—and even living—of a teenage couple. Again, Kazan draws special performances from the society-crossed young lovers, Natalie Wood and Warren Beatty. David Thomson's comment on the film is worth noting: "the most extreme instance of Kazan's emotional involvement with his characters, the source of all that is most vital and alarming in his work."[6]

A unique, loosely structured personal odyssey, a modern *Pilgrim's Progress*, marks a fitting closing note to this period of his work. In *America, America* (1963), Kazan depicts the yearning while in Greece and the initial promise and disappointment on his arrival in America of a young man much like himself who seeks a new life in a new world.

It hardly seems possible, but through this same decade, Kazan shaped and directed the initial production of these major stage plays: *Camino Real* (1953), *Tea and Sympathy* (1956), *Cat on a Hot Tin Roof* (1958), *Dark at the Top of the Stairs* (1960), *Sweet Bird of Youth* (1959), and Arthur Miller's *After the Fall* (1964), which actually has a character said to betray his friends by testifying.

In delineating the falsifying, damaging nature of the process of historical and critical distortion, we can again point to Robert Rossen as an illustrative figure. Walter Bernstein's comment is representative of the denial of value: "It's important, too, what informing did to his [Rossen's] work." Polonsky insisted that "Rossen [and his work] seemed diminished in his own eyes by his decision." The decision to testify—wrenching and painful—did mark Rossen for the rest of life, but it did not diminish him or his work. Paradoxically, it opened paths to deeper, disturbing levels of feeling and insight, and as a result to more humane and artistic work.[7]

After he testified, Rossen's struggle to regain the artistic control that he needed for his best work was more complex and difficult than Kazan's. The later films followed a somewhat erratic course, but the solid record on film shows an increase in complexity and ambiguity in theme and character, in the creation of visual correlatives to embody this deepening sense of human possibilities and frailties. But for all their differences, the films in this sequence, directly and indirectly, not only reflect Rossen's responses to his own inner turmoil; while never about the blacklist, they reflect as well the moral and political conflicts and themes that were given such sharp and wrenching definition in the lives of those caught in the period of the blacklist and the end of Communism in Hollywood—the painful paradoxes of power, of motives and choices, of trust and betrayal.

While in Italy, Rossen worked on *Mambo* (1954), one of several movies produced by Dino De Laurentiis for his wife, Silvana Mangano. A melodramatic tale, it did touch on his typical themes: at the center, for example, a young person of talent (this time a woman dancer) is seeking the true nature of her identity as she tries to break away from the trap of her life and a destructive lover. But the film got caught in the complications and compromises of its production, with constant controlling interference by De

Laurentiis, especially in protecting the image of his wife and thus blurring the truth of the character. Rossen directed and worked on the screenplay with the three original Italian screenwriters. At first, he later commented, he "got involved, took it seriously, but it didn't come off." Finally, he "just didn't believe it."[8]

By the time *Mambo* was released, he was deep into the production of *Alexander the Great* (1956), which he wrote, produced, and directed. It might seem an odd choice on which to base Rossen's comeback, but we can trace the reasons for his years of interest (even obsession) and work on the project. It was for him, an epic, even Shakespearean expansion (if sometimes grandiose in the doing) of his dominant themes and concerns. He felt a personal affinity for the driving power, the striving hubris of Alexander. As Rossen commented, Alexander was "a man born before his time, a catalytic agent, he emerged from an era of warring nationalisms to try for the first time in history to get the peoples of Asia and Europe to live together. But he became a destructive force and in the process of destroying other people while attempting to unify them, he destroyed himself."[9] The epitome of Rossen's core concerns—an unformed young man of power, energy, and will; the ineffable human stain of corruption and betrayal.

There is also a contemporary political dimension to the narrative pattern: the destructive failure of professed political ideals (such as Communism) as they become twisted and distorted by the corruptions of power and the weakness of men. When Alexander (Richard Burton) forces out his father and takes over the army, his first act is to kill the "traitors" within. As he pushes on into Persia, more traitors are purged, whole villages are burned, and "enemies of the people" are killed because of alleged treacherous activities. Thus, any act, however cruel and bloody, becomes justified by ideological fervor—especially when that ideology is tainted by an obsessive lust for power.

Although still a long film, *Alexander* is marred by severe postproduction cutting. It remains an unsettled mixture of epic spectacle, powerful personal confrontations, and dialogue both sharp and provocative, and too often declamatory. Still, it is a film more fulfilled and meaningful than most of its genre. Burton felt that it was originally the best script that he had ever read, before commercial pressures had interfered. After *Alexander*'s disappointing reception, Rossen accepted two offers to work as what he saw as a "director for hire." In 1956 he directed *Island in the Sun*. Working with producer Darryl F. Zanuck's concept and under his control, Rossen was not able to forge a final unity out of the splintered script's four separate, though related, narrative strands—four love relationships influenced by family and society. Two of the relationships are interracial—with a pat contrast between them. Dorothy Dandridge marries John Justin, who gives up his position in the government for love. Harry Belafonte breaks off his relationship with Joan

Fontaine because of his anger at and resentment of the white community and because of his zealousness in his role as a leader in the black community. Rossen is not able to establish any clear attitude toward the contrasting situations, including the possible ironies and limitations implicit in these two decisions.

The compromises and confusions on *Island* were disappointing; the compromises, conflicts, and artistic defeats on *They Came to Cordura* (1959) were deeply painful. This was a project that Rossen believed in, saw himself and his true concerns in. But this belief was betrayed in the actual production, the course of which brought conflicts with producer William Goetz over casting, script and dialogue decisions, and postproduction editing. Goetz's final cut reverses the kind of balance Rossen wanted between the development of characters and their interactions and action sequences. As Rossen saw it, the basic material posed provocative questions that resonated personally for him: Who are heroes, and why? What is courage, and what is honor? What is betrayal?

The ironies of the narrative (from the best-selling novel by Glendon Swarthout) do pose provocative questions about rigid moral judgments, but are based on too neat a pattern of character reversals. Unfairly branded as a coward after an earlier military engagement, Major Thorn (Gary Cooper) acts with honor and courage to bring the five supposed heroes to Cordura to be honored. On the difficult trek through the western desert, the flawed motives for the "heroic" actions of each are revealed. In a series of intense confrontations against a backdrop of harsh desert settings, each reveals even worse traits of viciousness and betrayal, threatening Thorn, even planning to kill him to keep him from taking them to Cordura. In a parallel thread, the supposedly immoral woman being taken to Cordura as a traitor (Rita Hayworth) acts with courage and compassion, giving herself to the worst of the five to allow Thorn to get some much needed rest without being murdered in his sleep.

The treatment of the ambiguous nature of character and the paradoxes of moral choice reaches a level of fulfillment in *The Hustler* (1961) and *Lilith* (1964), which reflect with fascinating indirection the pain of the conflicts and betrayals of the blacklist period.

The Hustler was a breakthrough on Rossen's part, a film of deeper understanding and sympathy, which extended the limits of his earlier kind of social realism, deepened even further his use of setting, décor, and visual character patterns and movements as a means of expressing the inner lives of his characters. Rossen produced and directed the film and wrote the screenplay, along with Sidney Carroll (in a drastic reworking of the Walter Tevis novel). Fast Eddie Felson (Paul Newman) is the complex, most enigmatic of Rossen's young seekers, wandering from town to town, pool game to pool game, hustle to hustle. He has the élan, the craft, but he has an obsessive need for the power felt in winning. It not only mars him as a human being, warping his ability to love, to connect; it even distorts the very act of attempting to win, betrays his knack, his gift. It is not a desire for money; he just *needs* to win, to show them all.

For he is a hustler, and hustlers are out there on a risky ride of illusory bravado—you must control or be controlled; that's the equation. And so he loses control of himself, goes too far, one way or another, hustles others or himself. And so he loses, gets his thumbs broken, betrays, and destroys. The film is certainly not directly about the period of Communism, investigations, testimony, and blacklist in Hollywood. And yet in its deepest emotions and implications it resonates with the wounds and woundings of that time. This young seeker echoes some of the same conflicts that Rossen had been living through himself—both political and commercial. In this parable of the artist in Hollywood, all are merely, utterly human, all are hustlers. They *need*—to win, to be right, to believe. The artist strives too much to hustle and win, to be a success; the party member goes beyond reason to hold on to his beliefs, his sainted dreams. The more either (or both in one) hustles and strives, the more he undercuts, betrays his gift, his élan; betrays his ideals and dreams of a better world. And the more he ends up placing himself in the hands of the moguls, who not only want to control the products, but, like the gambler Bert Gordon, want to own and control the people who *create* for them; or in the bloody hands of the political leaders, who, too, must control all in ways that have much more dire consequences.

In this parable of destructive needs and power, the figure of the gambler-promoter Bert Gordon (George C. Scott) is no longer the standard symbol of the corruption of capitalism. He is a man of both satanic power and human weakness. There is in him the need for possession and violation of other human beings as objects of one's ego, a drive for power rising from an ego that is paradoxically both strong and uncertain. It is reflected as well in sexual lust warped into the same terms of domination and violation. Bert is the Hollywood power broker, the congressional committee member, the Communist Party manipulator, the insatiable totalitarian dominator. He is one of those who will use you, break your spirit, or your thumbs, if he has to. To win—in whatever way he needs.

The woman in the power struggle over the soul of Fast Eddie, Sarah (Piper Laurie), is more fully developed than any of Rossen's previous female characters. She is a potential artist, a writer; she is sensitive to the possibilities of love. But she *needs* so strongly, and yet is so resigned to lose what she needs. It is true that she is physically crippled (lame), while the others are emotionally crippled, but she herself does not escape psychic crippling. Sarah is complicit—drinking too much, surrendering—in the defeat that with cruel relish Bert inflicts on her during the painfully ironic pleasantries and excitement of Derby Week in Louisville. Broken in spirit by Eddie's betrayal of her, punishing herself, hating herself and life, Sarah gives in to Bert's need to conquer her sexually, to break her in body and soul, even after he has defeated her; then kills herself.

But, still, even after the most careless and brutal of betrayals, Rossen sees, hopes to see, some enduring possibility of redemption. Eddie's redemption is not in his final winning; it lies in why he wins, in what he recognizes and accepts within himself and his actions. And so he refuses to go along and play their game any more—standing up to the Bert Gordons, the dominators of the world, sacrificing his career in what he loves best for what he thinks is right.

When Rossen was asked about his tendency to speak of disability in his last films, his answer seemed to reflect the painful dilemmas of the time of the blacklist, as well as the state of the world that he explicitly refers to: "It is because if I look at the world in which we live, if I think about this world of today, I cannot keep from seeing in it a great number of cripples, and I cannot speak of them as if it were a matter of contemptibly depraved beings. I want to speak of them with sympathy, to try to understand them."[10]

This concern for understanding the complexity of the fully, the utterly human, even the "crippled" in whatever form is even more deeply embedded in *Lilith*—his misunderstood and undervalued final film. It could not be further away from a film of political or social realism; yet in its complex web of emotion and desire, idealism and corruption, fulfillment and betrayal, it captures the plight of many caught—as Vincent is in Lilith's alluring and destructive web—in the many kinds of choosing and acting, of behaving decently. Frequently derided in America, when it was noted at all, in France *Lilith* won high placement on the *Cahiers du Cinema* yearly listings and received such high praise as Jean-Andre Fieschi's "incontestable masterpiece." Fieschi called it (along with Hitchcock's *Vertigo*) "the most complete realization in cinematographic form of the indefinable, the inaccessible, which the coupled plays of beauty and illusion shape into a sumptuous and fatal mirage."[11] As in the admirable visual patterns and imagery of *The Hustler*, Rossen was aided by the creative and lyrical cinematography of Eugen Shuftan, which made the settings—a tawdry downtown, a gloomy old residence, a luxurious mental clinic set in paradisical grounds, the web-like patterns of Lilith's room, the calm and turbulent currents of a stream, the sunlit peace of an open field—made them evocative, paradoxical "objective correlatives" for the shifting, evanescent emotions of the characters.

Despite the title, the central character, the moral center, of the film is Vincent (Warren Beatty). He is Rossen's loneliest, most isolated seeker of himself. There is this time a sympathetic sadness in Rossen's treatment of the forces that lead to betrayal and destruction. Seriously ill and in pain throughout the making of the film, affected by the years of tension and conflict over his testifying, Rossen seems to be recognizing with a rue-ful regret the inevitability of human frailty. For Jean Seberg, who played Lilith, Rossen "knew, in this last film, how to go beyond appearances, towards something very beautiful, in which all his personal unhappi-nesses were buried."[12]

Vincent is not driven by desire for money and success or power or the illusory dream of a better world and universal peace. He only knows he wants something more, though not even why. All he can recognize is that he wants to "help people directly." Troubled himself, he is drawn to those who are troubled and insane, mad. The tragic irony of his betrayal is that his helping, and finally his loving, end up hurting, killing, destroying. For someone like Vincent, for anyone, Lilith is an irresistible call to passion and love: artistic, lovely, spontaneous, joyful—in the words of her doctor, full of rapture. But trapped in the welter of her own emotions, her madness, she is also selfish and cruel, beyond any moral restraint. She is driven to control and dominate, to hurt—all within the passion that is, beyond her control, wonder and her danger.

Lilith's passions, her whole warring syndrome of desires, cannot be contained. Vincent's love is driven, both by her and something uncon-trollable within himself, to possess her, jealously, zealously. Obsessed, he deceives and thus betrays the trust of the gentle, fragile young man, Stephen (Peter Fonda), whom Lilith has begun to torment him with as her next lover. Stephen kills himself. Vincent is unable to bear what he has done. Within the web-like patterns of her room, he demands that she admit her complicity in Stephen's death and drives her into a living death of complete catatonic isolation. It is the final betrayal depicted in Rossen's films—and the most painful. Yet it is followed by a moment of shared recognition and compassion—an almost wordless, aching requiem.

Vincent flees across the rolling lawns of the asylum. But he stops and returns, retraces the path of his very first visit, when he had first come to try to "help people directly." He again stops at the door of the asylum, before the same social worker who had at that earlier time asked, with mere for-mality, "Can I help you?" As he walks slowly into a close-up of his anguish, he says, "Help me."

In *Lilith*, Rossen's most lyrical and tragic work, we are beyond political cant and pompous pride about behaving decently. Why we do what we do, as we seek to define ourselves, find our truest selves, how we may betray even as we seek to love, is left an awful, if sometimes strangely beautiful, mystery.

There is a final irony, a final intrusion of ideology into the world of Rossen's filmmaking. *Lilith* was named as the official American entry at the 1964 Venice Film Festival, but days before the opening of the festival, the organizing committee chairman, Luigi Chiarini, leaked a devious and unofficial pronouncement that, however, was widely circulated. It was a singular and unprecedented polemic against the film. Chiarini was a longtime advocate and historian of Italian neorealism and its political implications. An ardent defender of the faith, he had previously turned against those like Federico Fellini and Luchino Visconti whom he felt had betrayed their principles of objective realism by moving into the realms of evanescent subjectivity, the ambiguities of the inner life. Although never a member of the Communist Party, he was equally firm in his defense of the true causes of the Italian Left. For Chiarini, Rossen's venture into that other reality of the slippery, paradoxical inner life was a shock, an unacceptable betrayal. And so too—maybe even more galling—was Rossen's betrayal of the cause by *testifying*. Rossen demanded Chiarini's resignation; instead, *Lilith* was withdrawn from competition.[13]

Rossen died of a coronary occlusion on February 18, 1966, a month before his fifty-eighth birthday.

Two other important targets for the demeaning refrain—the moral stain debilitating the whole man and especially his talent and work—were Edward Dmytryk and Clifford Odets. The movies of Edward Dmytryk—except for *Salt to the Devil* (1949)—were never as meaningful, personal, or artistic as those of Rossen and Kazan. But he was a skillful, efficient director of standard fare—often with some social context and theme. His films were certainly the equal of those on which the "unfriendly" worked, and no more commercially oriented. Still, his work has been treated with disdain.

Buhl and Wagner comment on Dmytryk: "*Mirage* (1965), the most interesting of the mainly dreadful features that Dmytryk made after his friendly testimony." Even his pre-testimony films were suspect. If there was any social validity to these (such as *Cornered* and *Crossfire*), in them "the shrewdly self-promoting director . . . expertly fitted themes [for commercial possibilities]. . . . Even better-timed for box-office effect was *Crossfire* (1947)." In another reference, Buhle demeans *Crossfire*'s theme of anti-Semitism as "the suddenly salable issue of anti-Semitism."[14] Dmytryk was overall an expert craftsman, who after World War II moved up from B movies to a series of film noirs, *Murder My Sweet* (1944), as well as *Cornered* (1945) and *Crossfire*. While awaiting sentencing, he had directed his most meaningful and artistic film, *Salt to the Devil*.

After his testimony, Dmytryk directed several of the idealistic, humanistic small films that Stanley Kramer produced: *The Sniper* (1952), *Eight Iron Men* (1952), *The Juggler* (1953), and the one Kramer Company commercial success, *The Caine Mutiny*. In the same year as *The Caine Mutiny* (1954) he also directed a distinctive Western, *Broken Lance*, with a strong sense of personal and social corruption and an interesting, noir-like flashback structure, and he directed a solid version of Graham Greene's important novel *The End of the Affair*. He moved on to large-scale movies, mainly based on successful novels, polished and often too slick, but full of strong emotions. These included *Raintree County* (1957), *The Young Lions* (1958), *Warlock* (1959), *Walk on the Wild Side* (1962), *The Carpetbaggers* (1964), and *Where Love Has Gone* (1964). It is certainly not a career to be met with unwavering disdain.

Salt to the Devil was made in England while Dmytryk and the rest of the Ten were awaiting the outcome of their appeals and while he, alone among the Ten, was beginning his painful inner debate about the decent course of action for someone who opposed what circumstances, and troubled loyalty, had forced him to defend. The film was written for the screen by an unbending Hollywood Red, Ben Barzman, who moved to Europe before he could be subpoenaed, lived well in Paris and on the French Riviera, wrote a number of major commercial movies, and never wrote a screenplay as meaningful, emotionally full, and true as *Salt to the Devil*. It is an expert translation into film of Pietro di Donato's powerful short novel; but it is infused with the tensions and doubts, dilemmas of need and betrayal that were roiling within Dmytryk, and imbued with a visual poetry that Dmytryk was never to express again. It has been rarely seen since its production, rarely even discussed within the patterns of film history established by the aftermath of the blacklist period. It has also been known (when known at all) by its British title, *Give Us This Day* and by the title of the novel, *Christ in Concrete*, for a reissue on compact disc in 2003 (after long-standing legal issues were settled). It is indicative of the generational seepage of the vendetta against Dmytryk (and others) that in the DVD package, David Kalat of All Day Entertainment, who produced the disc, praises the film but says, "To rescue his Hollywood career, Dmytryk defected from the Ten and testified, naming names, betraying all those who had hailed him as a martyred hero." And so, he concludes, "*Christ in Concrete* suffered from his part in its creation."[15]

By whatever title, and within the best traditions of the dramas and films of the Left, it probes the "dark places" in capitalistic values *and within* human beings—the complexities of desire, choice, and feeling that can lead even a good man into betrayal and destruction of his better self. In this, and in its artistic value, it affords a striking and significant contrast to *Salt of the Earth* (1954), created by several others of the Hollywood Ten.

Salt to the Devil follows the rise and fall of an immigrant, Geremio (the blacklisted Sam Wanamaker), who, through dramatically developed and understandable needs and flaws of personal character, is corrupted. He betrays himself and his friends by going along with illegal and unsafe building practices. The *Salt* title is a reference to a folk ritual among Italian peasants, casting salt in the corners to ward off the devil and evil when a family moves into a new home, as they are seen doing in the film. They have brought their traditional life, its rituals and routines, its social reinforcements to their new, bleak world. It gives them the strength to endure, but ironically its salt is cast in vain, cannot keep evil from the home of the central couple, the home that is not really theirs. In *Salt to the Devil*, the workers are not depicted as propagandistic symbols, mere class victims. With a humanly flawed dignity, they attempt to endure an existence that is as tough and harsh as the bitter cold of the New York winter that is rendered so palpably by the inspired black-and-white cinematography. The imagery's solid, locked-in dramatic shadings of classical chiaroscuro are heightened by the stronger dramatic contrasts and camera angles of American film noir: the somber black of plain wool coats and hats against the pervasive gray of tenement buildings and unrelenting sky; occasional, fugitive areas of cold light; somber, serious faces caught in all of this, surrounded by it; beset, but holding still onto diminished hope.

In the noir fashion that Dmytryk had been working in, we open at a point of climactic tension in the central story, and then go back to the story's beginnings. An embittered wife, Annunziata (Italian actress Lea Padovani), slams the door on her unfaithful husband, Geremio, sending him back to his Irish-American mistress. But he goes back to Kathleen in guilt and pain. He has hit Annunziata; then, while steam rises from the vents of the sewers on the shadowed street, he bangs his hand down on the spike of the iron railing of the tenement steps. As Kathleen bandages his hand, their dialogue has the lyricism that is typical of the tone of the film—heightened, but still personal and emotional, not didactic.

> *Geremio*: Where is the beauty that once was in my life? Why did I come to this? How did it happen?
>
> *Kathleen*: You always wanted a little more, why couldn't you take life as it came?
>
> *Geremio*: Who wants life as it comes?
>
> *Kathleen*: Well, what do you want?
>
> *Geremio*: I knew once, I thought I knew.

In the flashback that becomes the main narrative, in the early 1920s Geremio realizes how alone he is in this new world of America. He arranges for a wife to be brought from the Abruzzi, a woman he has known only in a photograph. Within the tradition of the Abruzzi, her father insists he must have a home in which to establish their marriage. And so, even for a life-affirming purpose, begin the lies and corruptions. When she arrives, he must lie and tell her he owns the house that they stay in after the wedding. In contrast, the wedding itself is captured beautifully with all the hope of the moment, the closeness, the joyfulness, the true camaraderie of the people. In the joyous tumult, the shy Annunziata rises. They are silent as she speaks: "I didn't know what I would find when I came here. Now I know. I am among my people." She looks down. Geremio rises and they kiss. A friend, Luigi, enters the shot: "Let's devour!" We cut to a giant pig being cut up, and the devouring, and more drinking and laughing, begin.

The wedding night house in Brooklyn, in which they find they love with each other, becomes a receding dream. They *will* own it one day, plan and hope for it, but never can. In their tenement on the Lower East Side, through the years of hard work and little gain, they mark their painfully slow progress toward owning the house by notations on the kitchen wall and the births of children. Especially after the stock market crash, the marks on the kitchen wall are mocking reminders of the defeat of the receding dream, not only for the couple, but their friends. They all want to band together, be as "one"; but life is not that easily mastered.

At work, they are forced to speed up and compete with each other. In one offer, only one of them will get the extra hundred dollars, the one who lays the most bricks. Luigi proposes they all split it, anyway: "We've always been like five sticks in the bundle." Geremio agrees, but he insists that the winner (knowing it will be him) gets more. Luigi responds, "It already begins—one against the other."

As the depression and the cold winters hit harder, their closeness and their conflicts, their quiet dignity and their human weakness are all heightened. Their plight and their emotions are captured in one brilliant ensemble sequence.

In their black overcoats, the men stand, as somber as at a funeral, around the grey stone steps of their tenement. The slightest touch of cold sun is only on the gray wall of the building behind them. Merton, their foreman, tells them he has work for one man, for half a day! Who will it be? In a brilliant series of shot patterns and terse yet poetically revealing dialogue, they debate and present their cases. By the end of the sequence, we see, they all know, that Geremio is already separated from them, visually and emotionally. Giulio has said, "In the house of Giulio the air has become hunger. Stomachs have become wounds. In the house of Giulio, the children's hearts have become swollen vessels." The others agree he should get the work. Geremio first says the foreman must choose, knowing he will be chosen, but then he relents. He goes along, but turns away. The others leave; he is left alone. Things will never be the same.

A man is justified in wanting to get ahead, buy that house for his family, even get work for his friends, isn't he? But the very desperate need to do so leads to betrayal. Geremio works his way up to be foreman, but loses his moral center, even in a love affair that is an escape from his conflicts and contradictions, is both true and betraying. He feels more and more isolated, alone. A final desperate dilemma typifies the contradictions of his work and within himself. The jobs of his men, his friends, are threatened unless costs can be cut—a demand by the owners that is partly based on necessity, but also based on greed. Geremio goes along with the contractor; he cuts corners on construction materials and methods—for their jobs and for the little extra money it brings him.

His closest friend, Luigi, falls through a floor that has not been properly supported, is crippled. We are back to the opening sequence. Geremio runs from what he knows he has done, but when his lover, Kathleen, wants him to go away with her, he says (in a motif echoed in so many of the Left's dramas and films), "No. A man must not live for himself alone. There must be more than that. . . . There is something more."

He will work together now with his friends, work together to shore up the work site more securely. But it is already too late to break the chain of consequences that defeat all of his efforts, both the good and the bad. In the climactic and symbolic series of images, a wall collapses onto a floor that collapses, loosening some shoring, and Geremio is knocked off a ledge. Above, a giant vat of concrete tips and the concrete begins to pour out, unstoppable, inexorable as his fate. He has fallen into a mooring box, with rods sticking out and up. He is trapped, impaled, as concrete begins to pour over him. He yells for help as the concrete keeps pelting down on him, covering him. Above, the last of the concrete seeps out. But below, it is hardening over him, only part of his face still above it, as he cries, "Annunziata, forgive me. I tried!" His face sinks and the concrete closes and hardens over him.

Salt to the Devil is a true and proud example of what the Left could create, a film of great force and deep true feeling, of human dignity and social conscience in the time of the blacklist—even if not in the memory of the Left. When Dmytryk died in 1999, the obituary in the *Los Angeles Times* was headlined "Director Edward Dmytryk Dies; Testified in Blacklist Era." The article did not mention *Salt to the Devil.*

The bitter consequences of judgments rising from ideology are clearly, and unfortunately, caught in sharp focus in the differing conventional treatments and histories of Dmytryk's *Salt to the Devil* and the Hollywood Ten's film *Salt of the Earth.* Symptomatic, dramatically symbolic, of the Left's myopic view of film history has been the glorifying of the retrograde, blatantly propagandistic *Salt of the Earth*—as if the unfair and difficult circumstances under which it had to be made thus made it a worthy and exalted film, while ignoring Dmytryk's film and its value.

Salt of the Earth was produced in 1953 and shown first, and intermittently, in the spring of 1954. Through the years it has been lauded as the martyred film, a revelatory example of all that was lost when that alleged "iron curtain" fell on American movies and culture. It has been lauded as well in regularly promoted showings on college campuses and at progressive film festivals and seminars. Paul Buhle and David Wagner encapsulate the litany, seeing it as an example of what the Left could produce—even under difficult circumstances and persecution—when free of the chains of the Hollywood system: "the one unfettered creation of Hollywood's 'victims.'" For Larry Ceplair and Steven Englund, it was the sainted example of the kind of "stunning" films we had lost: "the proudest cinematic event in the Left's experience."[16]

This *Salt* was the creation basically of three members of the Hollywood Ten. Paul Jarrico was the producer, Herbert Biberman the director, and Michael Wilson (and "the people," as it was claimed) wrote the screenplay, a script strikingly below the quality of his commercial screenplays. In one indicative sidelight that suggests the retrograde nature of the enterprise, the basic plot and structure echo the scripts that Wilson as a young screenwriter and ardent propagandist wrote in a B movie series involving the Western hero Hopalong Cassidy. In one, titled (with conscious irony?) *Colt Comrades* (1943), Hoppy recruits others and leads them in destroying a cruel banker's monopoly on cattle raising in the region. In the almost prophetic parallel of another, *Border Patrol* (1943), an evil owner of a silver mine, with the help of cowboy-style "goons," oppresses the Mexican workers. At the climax, Hoppy delivers a rousing speech to the workers to unite and free themselves from this (capitalist and racist) oppression. With a new solidarity, they rise up and overthrow the tyranny of the owner and his brutal lackeys.

Salt of the Earth was financed by—and glorifies—the International Union of Mine, Mill, and Smelter Workers. The union had been ejected from the Congress of Industrial Organizations (CIO) in 1950 because, as the CIO formally declared, "The Communist Party is in direct control of the union's leadership and dictates to that leadership the policies it shall adopt." Those policies, the CIO had determined, had in turn been carried out to the detriment of the union's membership on a number of occasions.

Based on an actual specific strike by Mexican mineworkers conducted by Mine, Mill, the film reduces the reality of these people to tired symbols of the oppressed workers of the capitalistic world—and spouters of inflated clichés. Whatever their slight individual coloration, they are types, deep down noble, courageous—except of course for the obligatory stool pigeon, the defector who must be made to see the light. Even when the plot demands that they disagree or argue, they are pure in heart still, always preaching to each other, always willing to learn from each other. Ultimately, of course, they are energized by the women as in a number of thirties dramas and films. Their collective consciousness is raised and they rise up in solidarity against the oppressive capitalists, the bosses and their goons, and the police. In turn, their regeneration spreads, and in the final sequence and images of the film, they are joined in a last protest by workers from all over the area. This ideological pattern and images are clearly reminiscent of such thirties plays as Biberman's production of *Roar, China* (1936); John Howard

Lawson's *Marching Song* (1937); and even Clifford Odets' *Waiting for Lefty* (1935)—and with even more direct echoes of Soviet films such as Sergei Eisenstein's *Battleship Potemkin* (1925) and *The General Line* (1929) and V. I. Pudovkin's *Mother* (1926) (and even Robert Rossen/Lewis Milestone's *Edge of Darkness* [1942]). As the voice-over narrator solemnly tells us, "They came as many and left as one."

It is didactic and manipulative. Not only a simplistic, hollow echo of thirties labor idealism and left-wing agitprop, but a formulaic development of the principles of cultural Zhdanovism that the Soviets were promulgating during the Cold War. There is always an ideological elbow prodding one's ribs. No blatant propagandistic cliché is refused. A worker is proud of a new radio; the sheriff takes the radio. Someone looks proudly at a photo of Benito Juarez; the photo is destroyed. A candlelit christening party is being held; the sheriffs break in. The leading woman, Esperanza, is giving birth; shots of her and her birth pangs and screams are stridently intercut with shots of her husband being punched in the stomach by a sheriff. Food is delivered to the miners; the truck is driven by a black man, a shot capturing the moment of the handshake between his hand and a miner's. When we see a montage of envelopes, in voice-over Esperanza refers to the contributions in obsolete proletarian clichés, "messages of solidarity and the crumpled dollar bills of working men." When the miners are joined by other workers at the end, one shouts, "Hey, the guys from the open pit! The guys from the mill!"

At the conclusion of her detailed, devastating critique, the grande dame of film critics, Pauline Kael, summed up the intersection of filmmaking and ideology that this *Salt* represents: "A film like *Salt of the Earth* is so ridiculously and patently false that it requires something like determination to consider that those who make it believe in it. They serve a higher truth—and, of course, they have a guiding thread for their beliefs, a lifeline which directs them through the maze of realities and symbols."[17]

The playwright, screenwriter, and sometime director Clifford Odets did seem to lose *his* way after he testified, but then he was troubled and unsure of himself and his way before that day in 1952. As a young man, he had been the genius, the golden boy, of the radical thirties theater, but then his subsequent work began to flounder; even when successful, it was always compared to the golden days of his youth. He turned to writing screenplays, but continued to be torn between being a success in the Hollywood that he knew was corrupting his soul and working in the theater for which it became harder and harder to write. These inner tensions and the fearful sense of corrupting pressures are portrayed, quite differently, in the two plays he wrote during the early blacklist period (and before he decided to testify): modulated indirectly in *The Country Girl* (1951) and directly, passionately, in *The Big Knife* (1949). In the latter, he transposes the pressures of the blacklist to a more timeless pattern of power and corruption. The unscrupulous, unrelenting Hollywood producer breaks the spirit, and the last vestiges of withered integrity, in the already corrupted actor by blackmailing him to force him to continue the work that he knows betrays his ideals. Both plays were then done as movies.

Before his untimely death in 1963, Odets finished only one more play, *The Flowering Peach* (1954), a compassionate, humorous, and benign parable of conflict and regeneration within a family that stands for all mankind. An optimistic adaptation of the biblical tale of Noah and the ark, it is a kind of heartfelt, harmonious wish fulfillment for all the idealistic causes he had believed in, and for himself, transcending with whimsical folk poetry the unresolved tensions within him.

In the major films that he wrote during this period, Odets was far more bitter. *Sweet Smell of Success* (1957), the script sharpened by Ernest Lehman and wonderfully directed by Alexander Mackendrick, has its own bleak kind of harmony in mixing bitter satire and intense interpersonal drama, the poetics of Odets' signature heightened dialogue and the harsh realism of the dishonorable jungle of New York show business. Much in the manner of Rossen and Kazan in exposing the destructive synergy of personal and public betrayal and corruption, its unscrupulous force is a newspaper and radio columnist turned political force (Burt Lancaster). To do his dirty work, he uses would-be gossip columnist Sidney Falco (a beautifully slippery, jittery performance by Tony Curtis), who will do anything or betray anyone to get ahead. Both finally get their comeuppance, but even that is kept controlled and modulated at the end. *Story on Page One* (1960), which Odets wrote and directed, is a straightforward depiction of the unjust, destructive influence of the scandal-mongering media on the trial of a woman (Rita Hayworth) indicted for murder. It is nowhere as distinctive or memorable as *Sweet Smell*, which is one of the unfairly ignored unique films of this unfairly maligned period.

20

The Moral Crusade in Its Broader Context: The Myth of Total McCarthyism

Those among the blacklisted who were the most vituperative toward those who testified and those who through the years have shaped the view and judgments of that period spoke, wrote, and acted within a more significant enduring ideological crusade that has been carried forward in political history, not merely in Hollywood history. The distortions in the Left's, and particularly in what has been called the New Left's, writing of the history of Hollywood can best be understood by placing them in this broader sustaining context: the Left's insistent equation of the whole area, and era, of anti-Communism with "McCarthyism," its deformed dark corner. The distortions of truth and moral justice in the history of the Hollywood world were given sustenance and continued justification by this broader crusade—the panoply of distortions of fact, assumptions and judgments encapsulated in the use of the term "McCarthyism."

The basis of this broader campaign is that McCarthyism is not only the symbol but the alleged factual nature of all anti-Communism activity of the postwar and Cold War period. This position is in most instances correlated with the claim of generalized fascistic tendencies in U.S. history, policies, actions—of which McCarthyism is but one manifestation, or indeed a calculated tactic within the general capitalist strategy of oppression. These claims about the McCarthyite Fascist tendencies in America diminish or even deny any basis in threat, evil, or violation by any Communist entities that might have caused or justified anti-Communist actions. Or, ultimately, when the world of facts becomes too demanding, the fallback positions are a softening use of euphemism and a finding of equivalence, evil, and mistakes on both sides, with the United States still generally tipping the balance. And so McCarthyism—despite the actual limited (if demagogically flamboyant) role Senator Joseph McCarthy played in the major anti-Communist actions of the period—becomes a shorthand symbolic term for the alleged fascistic tendencies of these actions; and, in turn, in later years the emblem, the foreshadowing of American policies and actions in the world.

The lasting power of this distorting concordance is defined by Richard Gid Powers in *Not Without Honor: The History of American Anticommunism*:

> But if McCarthyism as a system of repression did not long survive McCarthy's political collapse in 1954, McCarthyism as a stereotype for all anticommunism proved far more enduring. . . .
>
> Real anticommunism—what it had been, what it was, how it mattered—was long forgotten . . . [as were] the reasons why Americans once fought so savagely among themselves over how they should respond to it, or the reasons why Americans sacrificed so much for so long to confront, contain and defeat it. What was recalled instead were the melodramatic excesses of the anticommunist as McCarthyite, militarist, and bigot.[1]

In the course of their study of Communism and anti-Communism in the United States in books "that challenge deeply held beliefs," John Earl Haynes and Harvey Klehr saw that the endurance of the stereotype, and its impact, were not mere happenstance: "We came to see our experience as an illustration of how an alienated and politicized academic culture misunderstands and distorts America's past, and of the crucial role played by historical gatekeepers such as professional journals in misshaping cultural memories to fit the ideological biases of the academic establishment."[2]

For many years, Professor Ellen Schrecker has been a prominent bearer of this banner, an indefatigable apostle of this gospel that all anti-Communism is rightly seen as fascistic McCarthyism in the political history of the era. In a journal article in 1988, she advocated the use of the term "McCarthyism" as the term of choice for the entire "movement to eliminate communism from American life during the late 1940s and 1950s."[3] Ten years later, in her influential book *Many Are the Crimes: McCarthyism in America*, she asserted that this equation is valid because "there is a near universal consensus [*sic*] that much of what happened during the late 1940s and 1950s [i.e., American anti-Communism] was misguided or worse"; that "cold war liberalism did not, in fact, get it right." For "the left-labor coalition that McCarthyism destroyed might have offered an alternative to the Cold War and provided the basis for an expanded welfare state." In the revised edition of the book she claimed that "the recent disclosures from the archives of the former Soviet Union [that there were, indeed, the spies who she had previously denied existed] reinforce the main thesis of this book—that the political repression it describes was unnecessary," since the government actions (which she had previously denounced) had taken care of the danger.[4] Any criticism of her position showed "that the political agendas that fueled Mc-

Carthyism still resonate today." Anti-Communism, she contended, "tapped into something dark and nasty in the human soul."[5]

In an example of the influence of Schrecker (among other New Left academics) in defining the terms for interpreting and judging the era in the popular media: In a 1998 article in the *New York Times*, "Rethinking McCarthyism, If Not McCarthy," Ethan Bronner discussed a debate among scholars over recently released Soviet archival material. The article posed as equally valid claims that the material was accurate or inaccurate, meaningful or insignificant, and used as a key quote, and in a favorable context, Schrecker's statement that "whatever harm may have come to the country from Soviet-sponsored spies is dwarfed by McCarthy's wave of terror."[6]

Other academic historians have proclaimed the threat of McCarthyite anti-Communism in even more extravagant terms. These terms have emphasized the reign of terror of the United States, internally and abroad. Norman Markowitz has often used the conventional connection to the Nazis: "primal anti-Communism is generally associated with Vichy collaborators and Nazi occupiers. . . . The purpose of primal anti-Communism was to suppress all forms of critical thought." Blanche Wiesen Cook finds that because of anti-Communism "everything fine and creative in American thought has been splattered and smeared." Joel Kovel, Alger Hiss Professor of Social Studies at Bard College, ventures further into the realm of vitriolic hyperbole in a typical passage that ties McCarthyite anti-Communism to worldwide U.S. aggression: "[It] works hand-in-glove with racism, and as a philosophy of killing has generated corpses beyond imagination." In *Red-Hunting in the Promised Land* (1994), Kovel sees this result of this American "terror": "millions of innocents lie dead, whole societies have been laid to waste, a vigorous domestic labor movement has been castrated, and the political culture of the United States has been frozen in a retrograde position." The United States has become "the enemy of humanity." The typical rhetoric of University of Michigan professor Alan Wald is similar: "United States capitalism and imperialism remain absolute horrors for the poor and people of color of the world, and ultimately hazardous to the health of the rest of us."[7]

One of the earliest models for this predilection for finding fascistic evil in America was a pamphlet distributed by the Communist Party of the United States of America (CPUSA) in 1949, titled *The Deadly Parallel*. It introduced the term "paranoia" to the discussion of anti-Communist activities and established the parallel between America and German Fascism. It featured prominently the juxtaposition of two sets of photographs. One set showed Nazis rounding up Jews and shipping them to Auschwitz, concluding with a photo of the concentration camp. The other set depicted U.S. marshals escorting American Communists to their Smith Act trial, concluding with the photo of a detention center. The caption labeled the center "concentration camp."[8]

As the party developed its campaign of criticism of the American government's actions, in 1951 Philip Frankfield, a CPUSA official, submitted a position paper for consideration by the party hierarchy. He advised focusing on Truman and Trumanism as the objects of the party's propaganda campaign, rather than McCarthy and McCarthyism, because, he argued, it was the president who had done the most damage and McCarthy was irrelevant. And so the party should "direct its main blows against Trumanism as the main enemy of the American people today." The party leaders rejected the idea; McCarthy was the best target for the demonizing of an opponent. "McCarthyism" became the banner for the crusade. Frankfield was expelled from the party.[9]

By the end of the sixties the party strategy had spread beyond the true believers. The model was picked up by more than left-wing historians. The idealistic American Friends Service Committee (the Quakers) published *Anatomy of Anti-Communism*, which defined anti-Communism as a strategy "that fights not only Communism, but neutralism and democratic revolution as well. It is based on antipathy to social change and a defense of the status quo. . . . These consequences of a blind, emotional anti-Communism pose the most critical problem that American society presently confronts." As David Caute agreed in *The Great Fear*, still widely quoted despite its factual flaws, we had entered a McCarthyite reign of terror where "the wealthiest, most secure nation in the world was sweat-drenched in fear."[10]

Mocking this misuse of "terror," Irving Howe wrote, "In a reign of terror, people turn silent, fear a knock on the door at four in the morning, flee in all directions: but they do not, because they cannot, talk endlessly in public about the outrage of terror."[11]

The enduring outcries over the investigation of espionage are a salient clue to and symptom of the enduring definition of *all* anti-Communism as McCarthyism.

The issue of the guilt of Julius and Ethel Rosenberg—and of their executions—has precipitated a continuing emotional outpouring of words, demonstrations, and memorial events—tied to the continuing manifestations in the political-culture wars over McCarthyism. The pattern is consistent. Frequently, it is not only their innocence that is proclaimed; it is the claim that their trials—as well as all the others—were the result of witch-hunting American Cold War oppressions. In the Hollywood world of the 1990s, for one, John Wexley was still adamant that the assertions in his earlier book (still much praised on the left) on the innocence of the Rosenbergs were true without a doubt. Their case was "the high point of the McCarthy era. . . . They couldn't prove espionage—they had no evidence like that—it had to be hearsay."[12]

Left-wing historians Walter and Miriam Schneir were among the most insistent on the Rosenbergs' total innocence and their trial strictly a witch hunt, as in *Invitation to an Inquest* in 1965. In their view, crusading anti-Communism included FBI forgeries, false confessions, and perjuring witnesses. As counterevidence mounted, however, they began to equivocate and back off. But it wasn't until more than thirty years had passed that the Venona transcripts finally caused them to admit that "what these messages show, briefly, is that Julius Rosenberg was the head of a spy ring gathering and passing on non-atomic defense information." Thus, they still insisted that "the messages do not confirm key elements of the atomic spying charges against him." In further articles they still attacked those who attempted to use the new evidence to vindicate McCarthyite anti-Communism.[13]

For a committed anti-anti-Communist like Professor Bernice Shrank, their limited admissions were mistaken apostasy, a "premature capitulation." The only reason for their "inexplicable failure of nerve" that she could find was "the right-wing drift of American domestic policy to read indeterminate texts of unverified provenance as proof positive of extensive Cold War Communist subversion." Schrank refused to consider the Venona transcriptions as part of a collation of sources, and in several articles claimed that she was destroying their validity or at least any *determinate* meaning. Haynes and Klehr have convincingly demonstrated the inaccuracy, illogic, and cryptological incompetence of her arguments regarding Venona. Yet her statements are regularly cited and flourished. Schrank even accused the United States of immorality in daring to intercept and translate messages of "its ally in World War II."[14]

When forced to, Schrank joined the ranks of the euphemism users in admitting that Julius did *something* that was not really espionage; it was merely "unauthorized technological transfer" of standard materials to a friend and ally. When Professor Schrecker had to concede that "it is clear that some kind of espionage took place during the 1930s and 1940s," she nonetheless found that "it is important to realize that as Communists these people did not subscribe to traditional forms of patriotism; they were internationalists whose political allegiances transcended national boundaries. They thought they were 'building . . . a better world for the masses,' not betraying a country."[15]

Denials of the guilt of Alger Hiss have been even more entrenched in both the academic and popular worlds. In the 1998 edition of the *Encyclopedia of the American Left*, the entry is written by William Reuben. Haynes and Klehr call it "a decision akin to choosing a Holocaust denier to contribute to an encyclopedia of Jewish history." In his essay, Reuben not only denied that Hiss was a spy, but denied as well that Whittaker Chambers was ever a Communist. The Reuben entry is symptomatic of the consistent and extreme bias of the entire *Encyclopedia*, which was recommended by both *Choice* and the *Library Journal* as one of the ten best reference books for libraries.[16]

For her part, Professor Schrecker, editor of the prestigious journal of the American Association of University Professors *Academe*, for years claimed "the case remained problematic in many ways." But when she had to concede that there had been espionage, she still insisted that the real evil was that "the sixty citizens, most of them Communists" were being used "as a rationalization for the most widespread and longest-lasting episode of political repression in our nation's history." Indeed, the *New York Times* editorial of October 23, 1998, in responding to information on newly released Soviet archival material on espionage, agreed with Schrecker that it was the consensus of opinion that it was McCarthyism that "was a lethal threat to American democracy."[17]

That the guilt of the Rosenbergs or Hiss was still "debatable" has filtered down into popular culture and the unquestioned assumptions of our day. In the widely distributed, widely praised general history *Grand Expectations: The United States 1945–1974*, James Patterson (not a "die-hard Party loyalist") in discussing the "red scare" of the McCarthy era, passed on the popularized view that "whether Hiss was innocent remained a much-disputed fact years later." In the 1999 edition of the standard library source, *American National Biography*, the assignment on the entry on the Rosenbergs was given to Norman Markowitz! He starts by stressing their Jewish orthodoxy (which, in fact, both abandoned early on for Communism) and then moves to the "anti-Semitic subtext" of their trial. He insists (in 1999) that the only people who believed them guilty were "conservatives and anti-Communist or Cold War liberals" whose "unquestioning belief in the Rosenbergs' guilt" was "a kind of loyalty oath." Upholding their innocence, he avers still, was "the most significant expression of resistance to the spread of the domestic Cold War." In New York in 2001, the New York Historical Society held an exhibit entitled "The Rosenbergs Reconsidered: The Death Penalty in the Cold War Era" that again illustrates the unexamined acceptance of the Left's mantra in popular treatments of history. The society does accept the fact of their espionage, but has found rationalizations for it. A typical sentence in the exhibit's materials that emphasizes this nostalgic romanticizing of the actions of Communists in their material: "They [the Rosenbergs] imbibed the values of the Communist Left that were prevalent in New York City politics at the time and eventually were recruited by the Soviet Union to fight fascism and help the cause of beleaguered workers."[18]

The *National Standards for United States History* is a government-funded guide for history teachers. Its references to any actions of the Rosenbergs and Hiss are couched in vague neutral terms; however, their trials and investigations and trials of others are emphatically connected to the rampant destructive spirit of McCarthyism. In one instance, teachers are coached to stress how the cases "contributed to the rise of McCarthyism." McCarthy and McCarthyism get extensive negative discussion (in twenty separate references), but there is not a single mention of the Communists (beyond the persecuted Rosenbergs and Hiss, who are not discussed as such), in and out of the government, who spied for the Soviets.[19]

An instructive example of how these unreconstructed mythologies permeate popular culture and wisdom is the career, as well as the legacy, of John Lowenthal in promoting the innocence of Alger Hiss. Lowenthal, a former law professor, came to prominence with a 1979 documentary film *The Trials of Alger Hiss,* which not only defends his innocence but also attacks the McCarthyite, witch-hunting corruption of the prosecution case against him. At that time it was praised by Vincent Canby in the *New York Times* for displaying "an appreciation of the uses of history that is rare in a documentary movie and virtually non-existent in most of our contemporary fiction films." When Lowenthal died in 2003, the *Times* laudatory obituary, syndicated to newspapers large and small across the country, repeated that praise and summed up as untainted truth the key original claims made by Lowenthal's documentary without a single word about any of the contrary information about Hiss, espionage, or the film itself that had become available in the twenty-five years between, information and evidence that contradict his arguments and expose his factual inaccuracies and have been cited by others to do just that. In just one example, the obituary baldly presents, with no comment, Lowenthal's central claim of the existence "of an FBI memo asserting that a message supposedly typewritten by Hiss was a forgery [by the FBI]." As has been analyzed and determined for years, most extensively in Allen Weinstein's *Perjury*, the memo in question did not say that, and all accurate tests have definitely tied the typewriter in question to the Hisses. Similarly, the *Times* passed on without criticism and without reference to later refutations Lowenthal's later inaccurate and distorted claims about the findings of Soviet General Dimitri Volkogonov that allegedly "proved" the innocence of Hiss. (See chapter 13.) What is conveyed by the *New York Times* is the death of a heroic fighter against McCarthyism, who stood up to expose the frauds of anti-Communism.[20]

In 1998 CNN aired a lengthy documentary, *Cold War*, accompanied by a book, *Cold War: An Illustrated History, 1945–1991*. Robert Conquest has devastatingly critiqued its consistent pattern of distorting assumptions, interpretations, images, and phrasings such as the repetitions of "possessed with hating Communism," "witch hunt," "paranoia," and "hysterical." Its references to espionage are one category of its general criticism of U.S. Cold War policies and actions. Spies are assigned positive motives: The Rosenbergs were among "a network of spies who felt uncomfortable that the United States was the sole owner of the key to atomic warfare." (Of course, this "network" all actually began spying years before this "key" was developed.) In references to the international sphere, the documentary and book echo the emphasis on American aggressions. In Europe, U.S. troops are "all

threatening the Soviet Union"; the nations of Eastern Europe are "left-lean-
ing governments" (not Soviet-controlled and ravaged governments). As for
Hollywood (treated quite extensively in the book *Cold War*), no allowance
for the moral dilemma of testifying or not is introduced. The investigations,
unwarranted and unjust as they were, are exaggeratedly characterized as
part of the McCarthyite "torture by the Inquisition."[21]

From the same quarter of the influential academic world, the corollary
to the derision of all anti-Communism as McCarthyite fascism and a consequence of the imperialism of the United States throughout the world is
defense of the actions of the Soviet Union before and during the Cold War.
A sampling: Answering the liberal claims, Markowitz praised Stalin for his
"consistent strategy . . . to construct Socialism across the huge territory of the
Soviet Union, and to outmaneuver the British Empire, France, Imperial Japan, Nazi Germany, the United States and lesser capitalist states." Theodore
Van Laue found "Stalin's style of leadership, although crude by Western
standards, was persuasive among the disoriented peoples. The sophisticated
design of Soviet Totalitarianism has perhaps not been sufficiently appreci-
ated. However brutal, it was a remarkable human achievement despite its
flaws. . . . [It] promised a glorious communist future to follow." Robert W.
Thurston, as late as 1999, announced that Stalin "was more human than
others have portrayed him . . . reacted, and over-reacted to events . . . did
not plan to carry out a systematic campaign to crush the nation." Thurston was among a number of other academics (including Jerry F. Hough,
J. Arch Getty, and Alfred Reiber) who fought the battle against documented
revelations of the immensity of the Terror. They regularly had to increase
their minimalist claims about the number of victims, while still denying
the totals reached anything like the levels that had been documented and
while still claiming that the large numbers they finally admitted (tens of
thousands, many thousands, even [by Getty] a million) did not constitute
a totalitarian Terror. As Van Laue reluctantly allowed, "Mistakes had been
made." In typical euphemistic terms, Leslie Adler and Thomas Patterson
denied any similarity to Nazi totalitarianism because Soviet communism
was a "system proclaiming a humanistic ideology" that had seen its efforts
"fail to live up to its ideals."[22]

The writings of Schrecker also provide a cross-section view of this international aspect of symbolic McCarthyism—the connection between American aggression at home and abroad. In *Many Are the Crimes* she concludes,
"McCarthyism can be seen as the home front of the Cold War." In the Cold
War the two sides were equivalent, equally suspicious of each other: "The
Cold War escalated as both the United States and the Soviet Union took
ostensibly defensive actions that looked ever more threatening to the other
side." The United States failed to understand that "the USSR would control
the area [of eastern Europe] in order to ensure it would never again have

a hostile power on its Western border." For Schrecker, the Soviet Union's oppressions inflicted on the nations of this area were merely a matter of self defense, "largely in order to ensure its own security." A few passing references to Stalinist transgressions are couched in conventional evasive terms like "the worst excesses of Stalin's regime"; "Stalinist rigidity." Across the world, when "the North Korean army *crossed* [emphasis added] the 38th parallel," the U.S. Cold War mind-set caused it to intervene in what was "actually the culmination of a festering civil war."[23]

The writers who have contributed the most to defining and spreading the Left's, and New Left's, romanticized version of the Hollywood blacklist have themselves developed their judgments within this context of this symbolic and symptomatic McCarthyism. The bias of their writing about the blacklist period is shaped by their bias about America and the Cold War. Prominent and representative figures among this group, as we've noted, are Larry Ceplair and Steven Englund, Victor Navasky, and Paul Buhle.

Ceplair and Englund, authors of the frequently quoted *The Inquisition in Hollywood*, have played less of a role in the directly political realm than Navasky and Buhle. Their political views are found mainly in the editions of that book or their other writings about the political history of Hollywood. In their view, the "unfriendly" witnesses were refusing to deny "the achievements of Communists in recent world history: the Popular Front, the successes of the Red Army, the resistance movements in Axis-occupied countries, etc." Three samples of their typical jargon and attitude:

A particularly vicious brand of liberal anti-Communism.

The general structure of the American anti-Communist crusade is familiar to the student of political reaction.

While individual Communists *might* have deplored the *more ruthless methods Stalin employed* in the Russian take-over of Eastern Europe, *none* could have denied that American foreign policy was following an *equally determined* path toward carving out spheres of influence with different but *equally* implacable methods [all emphases added].[24]

As a basis for their own approach to the blacklist period, Ceplair and Englund paraphrase Navasky's crucial question: "Do the informers by virtue of their willingness to cooperate with what were political show trials, bear a significant measure of collective responsibility for a shameful decade in American history?" For Ceplair and Englund only those who testified bear this "collective responsibility," never those who fueled the public fervor by their actions and by supporting the more than merely "shameful" violations of the Soviet Union by remaining silent. Their definition of the sole motive behind testifying is typical: "The aura of pious sincerity, not to say sanctity, which had to suffuse the proceedings was essential to all concerned. How would it have looked, after all, if fifty-eight men and women had stood in the dock and prefaced their candor with the simple admission, 'Mr. Wood, I'm doing this because I don't want to cease earning $50,000 a year'?"[25]

Navasky, author of the era-defining *Naming Names*, has been both editor and publisher of *The Nation*. Over a tested time span, *The Nation*, one critic has noted, ran three times fewer reviews of books on Communist aggression and repression than did conservative journals. Their approach to major books that could not be ignored—books that reveal monstrous horrors—was to criticize them for being rabble-rousing exploiters. The authoritative *The Black Book of Communism* was said to be performing a "service to capitalist elites"; for by writing it, the authors "exploit a tragedy." Anne Applebaum in her valuable *The Gulag* was "exploiting the Gulag" for political reasons, distorting the real situation by ignoring that "it is no easy matter . . . to separate the innocent from the guilty."[26]

Navasky himself continued to deny the reality of Soviet financial support of the CPUSA. He characterized the Venona project as an attempt "to enlarge post-cold war intelligence gathering capability at the expense of civil liberty." He insisted (as did Schrecker) that Elizabeth Bentley was "notoriously unreliable," despite the full corroboration of her testimony by later documentation. What spying he allowed was merely "a lot of exchanges of information among people of good will, many of whom were Marxists, some of whom were Communists, some of whom were critical of U.S. government policy and most of whom were patriots." He also liked to use equivalence (as did advocates like Professors Athan Theoharis, Bernice Schrank, and Schrecker) in insisting that the spying on "both sides" was the same.[27]

Navasky climbed and re-climbed the barricade in defense of the innocence of Alger Hiss into the new millennium, denying the validity of new and old evidence, even the Venona transcripts, and even the validity of Allen Weinstein's magisterial *Perjury* (1978), along with characteristically personal attacks on Weinstein. In 2001, Navasky was still claiming that the massive and solidly documented body of evidence in Weinstein and Alexander Vassiliev's *The Haunted Wood: Soviet Espionage in America—The Stalin Era* was "at best, inconclusive" and "methodologically challenged."[28]

Those who continued to document Soviet and American Communist Party espionage often were regularly given harsh treatment in Navasky's *The Nation*. Navasky himself claimed they "seem to argue that, in effect, McCarthy and Co. were right all along": "The unseemly and ahistorical rush to reconvict the American Left based on half-baked evidence, suggests the weakness of the new post-cold war red-baiters case, and reminds one of the political hysteria that is supposed to be part of our so-distant-as-to-be-seen-antique past."[29]

When he turned to Hollywood and the blacklist in *Naming Names*, published in 1980, Navasky framed House Un-American Activities Committee's (HUAC's) hearings—and responses to them—within the pattern of these broader ideological premises about America. The HUAC's "assault on Hollywood," typified "the fundamental cold war assumption that to be a Communist was to be an agent of a foreign power." And so "its attempt to cleanse the cultural apparatus can be understood only within the larger framework of the efforts to cleanse the political apparatus. In both of the dubious enterprises, the informer was the nonsecret agent, the instrument of the purge." This agent was "creating a climate of concern and fear. The effect was to create an exact parallel to McCarthyism: namely, the purging of the cultural apparatus of alien forces, just as McCarthyism was the purging of the state apparatus, an exercise in political purification." In this all-encompassing McCarthyism—in which "emblems of the terror were ever on display"—Navasky placed the Hollywood informers within the broader circle of the government's ex-Communist informers, for him all untrustworthy and nefarious. "Our lawmakers relied on, our media magnified, and our internal-security bureaucracy exploited and reinforced the images of Communism unleashed by the most sensational and therefore often least reliable of the ex-Communists." Thus the whole terror apparatus was hinged on these "frustrated, previously anonymous failures." He finds support in quoting sociologist Edward Shils' analysis that these ex-Communists, who have nurtured "fantasies of destroying American society and harming their fellow citizens, having fallen out with their equally villainous comrades, now provide a steady stream of information and misinformation.'"[30]

For Navasky, the moral equation of the Hollywood investigations was equally absolute, either-or: "These were not information-gathering investigations so much as they were degradation ceremonies. Ironically, it was the informer who was degraded, because the informer represented a threat not merely to the person he named but to the community. He was regarded as a polluter—and became a perpetual outsider." In contrast: "Whatever the motive, they [the resisters] did not permit the state to take over *their* values; they defined their own situation, and by risking self and career they emerged as moral exemplars."[31]

As for the motives of the "informers," Navasky insists on the same absolutist duality, allowing none of the complexity of moral dilemmas and the soul-wrenching necessity of making choices between flawed, mixed options. For Navasky, those who testified did not really believe their political or moral statements and were merely testifying to be able to work. At one point he approvingly devoted a page and a half to Abraham Polonsky's version of this motif. Those who testified, Navasky insists, knew they were not doing the right thing—"knew better than to cooperate with McCarthyism"—and thus created rationalizations "to cancel out the basic presumption against informing, to obfuscate the question of betrayal, to overwhelm compunction."[32]

Navasky, however, does not consider the demanding realistic dilemmas of moral choice. One can recognize the problems and pain of what one chooses to do, including its impact on others, can even rather not have to do it; but still have a moral basis for deciding to do it—be truthful and moral in the doing. Thus, if one part of one's motivation is to be able to work, does that make all the other elements in the mix of motives invalid and untrue, and thus the whole enterprise immoral and false? Is it immoral not to want to sacrifice one's work for a cause one opposes and believes is destructive? Cannot one be self-protective and principled at the same time? Be truthful, have integrity, yet recognize one's own mixed motives?

One last segment among the strands of Navasky's argument is revealing of the illogic of its either-or dualism. Navasky states, "The informer's highest claim to virtue is that he told the truth, but we learn that as a class they were involved in a fiction. The informers' particular lie was that they were telling all when they only told some." In other words, it turns out, they lied because they actually did not always name all of those that they could have named (even, apparently, if they did it to protect and help others). And they lied, in one way or another, because they did not admit to taking place in the "charade" that Navasky claimed "name-naming was."[33] And so if they lied in any single instance, literally or figuratively, all that they said was invalidated, could not be accepted as true or spoken with (in one of his favorite terms) "candor," by which he means with any moral standing.

The ubiquitous New Left activist and alumnus Paul Buhle has authored and coauthored more hagiographic books on the blacklisted heroes and their works than anyone. He, however, is also an indefatigable left-wing ideologue, writing frequently for a number of left political journals, including *Radical History Review*. In one article in that journal, he equated Truman with Stalin—"America's Stalin." Indeed, he says, "when the judgment of the twentieth century's second half is made, every American president will be seen as a jerk. After Truman, Nixon yields only to Reagan—another Truman heir—as the jerkiest of all."[34] Beyond his rhetoric, the article, typical of all of his pieces, is flawed by the kind of historical inaccuracies and distortions that have been exposed by Haynes and Klehr, among others. (Many of Buhle's descriptions of movies, in *Blacklisted*, for example, are equally inaccurate.)

A coeditor of *The Encyclopedia of the American Left*, Buhle has written a number of the articles in it. In the entry on the "Communist Party, USA," 1999, written with Dan Georgakas, a main contention is the independence of the American party. For example, they go to great lengths in denying the evidence of the immense Soviet financial support of the CPUSA. While ignoring the bulk of historical data now known, they refer only to certain allegedly *minor* exchanges of money and compare those to the way all immigrants send money back to their homelands, in which process "inevitably, legal niceties were avoided." But that is money *from* America to a foreign country, not the other way around. They claim that "the over-whelming flow of money went from American shores to the Soviet Union, mainly for specific campaigns, such as food support in the early 1920s and war relief in the 1940s."[35] This conjoins faulty logic with careless and/or evasive scholarship. For this is comparing apples and oranges; these were charity donations from millions of people (often encouraged by the party, to be sure), not official party contributions.

As for espionage, in the "Secret Work" entry, Buhle denies the reality that has been substantiated on both sides of the former Iron Curtain. He main-tains that any "trivial espionage episodes" were "known only at the top lev-els of the U.S. Communist Party." And for Buhle, who were these people at the top levels? He dealt at length implicating Jay Lovestone, who broke with the party by the mid-thirties and became a fervent anti-Communist. But in Buhle's smokescreen: "A handful of trade Union officials—most prominent among them, Jay Lovestone, former Communist Party leader and future as-sociate of the Central Intelligence Agency—and some liberal intellectuals ap-parently traded secret communications with the Soviet regime in the 1930s, but the substance of them involved personal information without any great importance or high-level security connections." He insists—against the real-ity of massive documentation—that "as of the late 1990s, documents exam-ined in the Soviet Union or reprinted for scholars offered little that was new in regard to illegal or secret work by Soviet sympathizers."[36]

Buhle's claims and interpretations about the blacklist period and Hol-lywood Reds and their works are an extension of his political and ideologi-cal bias—and his distortions of fact and logic. Indeed, he often discusses the two realms in similar terms. In commenting on a passage in Arthur Schlesinger's *The Vital Center* that criticizes the Hollywood Left, he and coauthor Dave Wagner characterize Schlesinger's argument as a typical component of American Cold War belligerence. They term the book "a totemic document of liberal zeal for the Cold War." Buhle's books about the movies—he has taken part in six to this point—promote the heroism and insights of those who have, he believes, challenged this Cold War op-pression—the "victims who were . . . quietly heroic"—while they spread as well the denigration of the "stool pigeons" and belittling of their works, especially those created after they testified.[37] A passage from the Introduc-tion of *Tender Comrades* conveys the consistent shaping pattern and flavor of his discourse:

> Whether or not to inform was, for those who refused, above all not a question
> of politics but a matter of ethics and morality. . . .

> The "cooperative witnesses" were not all paid agents. They had varied mo-
> tives. Sometimes they testified out of plain fear and confusion, more often out
> of opportunism and the determination to keep their fancy houses and swim-
> ming pools.[38]

This kind of scornful, reductive definition of the moral dilemmas and
complexities of the time has filtered down into the world of popular culture, whether carried forth through ideological zeal or merely as an unexamined premise of the accepted climate of opinion: in documentaries on
PBS and other TV networks; in full-length documentaries such as *Red Hollywood* (1995); in college courses and film festivals; in plays and in films such
as *The Front* (1976), *Guilty by Suspicion* (1991), *The Majestic* (2001), *One
of the Hollywood Ten* (2000), and *The Way We Were* (1973); in articles and
obituaries; in histories and biographies. As a headline in the *San Francisco
Chronicle* proclaims for an article about Brian Dennehy playing the role of
Dalton Trumbo in the popular one-man play, a role first played by Nathan
Lane: "For Dennehy, a chance to play a real-life hero."

The blacklisted martyrs and "real-life heroes" themselves have followed a
similar narrative pattern. They have framed their unjust treatment within this
broader context of McCarthyite fascism in the United States, but also have
continued the "silence"—in many tenors and tones—about the full nature
of the Soviet Union and the Communist crusade. In this narrative of purity
versus immorality, the blacklist is seen to have its major equivalents in the
oppressive policies and actions of the United States, at home and abroad.

In the moral pantheon, Dalton Trumbo may have had a play written
about him and in many ways received the most publicity and popularity
of the Hollywood Reds, but, as we've seen, it is screenwriter and director
Abraham Polonsky who has been elevated to be the serious and mythical
icon of the cinematic, ideological, and moral world of the blacklist period
and its festering aftermath.

For Polonsky, the blacklist pogrom was an extension of American imperialism in the Cold War. He observed to William Pechter in 1962, "The Cold
War was behind the blacklist, and everyone participated from those on the
political right through those who had no politics. It was like collaboration
with the Nazis. And it was like the Resistance."[39]

Among other iterations of the theme, about ten year later Polonsky again
tied the depiction of total McCarthyism, the new mood of fascism in the
United States that was destroying an innocent "social movement," to the
"witch hunt" of the blacklist: "But really and truly, the triumph of Mc-
Carthyism was in effect the cutting-off of a generalized social movement
which began before the war. As the war changed, when it was over, and the
battle was drawn between the two victors, that social movement came to
an abrupt halt as United States policy changed. So the witchhunt against

the Hollywood people was, in a sense, a consequence of that generalized defeat. I would say, and it's gotten a lot of attention because everybody knew who these people were."[40]

In a number of comments, Polonsky again raised the issue to the level of Nazism—of Resistance Fighters versus Collaborators in a "world which was becoming Fascist"—including an analogy he uses to invalidate any claim to truth or principle in the statements of those who testified. It was as if "the Nazis pointed a gun up against his head and said, 'Look, give us some names,' and he says, 'Yeah, I hate those guys anyway. You know I hate those guys.'"[41]

For Polonsky, it was an unbroken skein of oppression. From the thirties and the Spanish Civil War on through the rest of his lifetime, despite all the party's failures, "it was important to be a Communist. In that way, and in that way only, could people overcome what they felt was the major thrust of political action in the world, which was becoming Fascist."[42]

Other central protagonists in this proclaimed battle of biblical dimensions of good and evil defined the blacklist as a consequence and tool of McCarthyite aggression. Walter Bernstein, for example, explained in his memoir that he could see "the structure [of Communism] had begun to show cracks [a typical euphemism], but I plastered them over with my belief in the rightness of the cause, and the reassuring knowledge that at least I knew my enemy. He was right there in my face. The United States had started the Cold War, needed it for imperial purpose, needed the terror of a blacklist to make that war seem necessary. . . . The Cold War continued. . . . Joseph McCarthy died, but he had done his work."[43]

With a more analytical manner, typical of him, Paul Jarrico made the same connection in a late interview: "We underestimated the direct connection between the Cold War abroad and repression at home. Looking back on it now, it seems very obvious. If you're going to call on people to give their lives in a fight against Communism internationally, you can certainly raise logically the question of why we should allow Communists or Communist sympathizers to express themselves domestically, here at home."[44]

For Maurice Rapf, the Cold War aggressions of the United States at home and abroad were the center of injustice in the world: "I believed that World War II started as an imperialist war—and I still do—and that it was intended to be a war against the Soviet Union but got turned around. . . . I still think that the Cold War [that America pursued] was responsible for more mischief in the postwar world than anything else."[45]

Terror was the abiding concern of John Wexley. He saw America during the Cold War as "approaching a police state. . . . The climate of fear was tremendous." He claimed that there was a child custody case in which "the judge gave him [the husband] the child because the woman had been against the Korean War."[46]

Joseph Losey's consistent focus on the evils of America first was even more extreme. At the time of the hearings in the fifties, he wrote that "Fascism begins again [in the United States]. Unmistakably and faster. Also tougher and stronger. . . . Just now the prospects are horrifying."[47]

In a late sixties interview by Tom Milne, Losey insisted, "The most serious thing was that the right of the American people to say what they thought with freedom and to protest against what they thought was wrong, was destroyed. They lived, and they still do to some extent, in an atmosphere of terror."[48]

In 1976, French critic Michel Ciment in an interview suggested to Losey that what had been done in Russia had been "much worse" than what had happened to the blacklistees:

Losey: I doubt if it could have been, maybe worse, but I doubt if it could have been.

Ciment: People were killed.

Losey: Well, they weren't killed in court. . . .

Ciment: No—well they were killed in camps.

Losey: Yes, I know. I know *now* [emphasis added]. They [Hollywood's victims] were also killed in a different way.[49]

Director Martin Ritt, who was just beginning his career at the time of the backlist, saw those who stood up against McCarthyism and Fascism as enabling people like himself "to have any kind of career." For "the country owes an everlasting debt to the people who stood up and were prepared to be counted at that point. Because without that body of people and without that body of thought, perhaps McCarthy would have been able to go a lot farther than he did. And perhaps any Fascist or neo-Fascist would be able to do a lot more than they've been able to do."[50]

Polonsky puts the cap on this ubiquitous emphasis on the purity of "our" cause and actions, and their consequences, in an impure world. In response to what he saw as the oppressions, even from the party commissars, that beset them, he claimed, "We [the Hollywood Reds] didn't give a shit. The cultural leadership obviously didn't know what they were talking about. We ignored them out here, and we did a lot of wonderful things."[51]

This emphasis on righteous actions in the face of an American McCarthyite and Cold War spread of terror is the complementary corollary to the evasion of the context of the realities of Soviet dangers and destructive terror. It is one more facet of the kind of silence that Yevgeni Yevtushenko knew "can be a lie." This silence—by the participants and by those who have written about them in later years—carries its own moral paradoxes. It tarnished, shadowed, and blurred the principled stands taken by these central figures who refused to testify; it belied the heavy burden of years of unjust treatment, the losses suffered. But this silence—along with the loud evasive behavior that was the norm in their fight against the blacklist—did also, to some degree, affect the lives of others in Hollywood. To whatever degree, it helped to supply the mask for the violation of the lives of millions of others. In whatever mixture with principle, it violated truth. In the contrasting pattern of the moral paradox, the naming of names by those who testified did affect, also to some degree, the lives of others in Hollywood. In whatever mixture with other motives and feelings, their testimony stood for the principle of truth. In whatever contributing way, it honored those millions who had been violated, as by breaking the silence it aided in the fight against such massive violations.

The full history of the time can show us that there are many Dantean circles of betrayals in the moral ambiguities of testifying (and to what) and remaining silent (and to what)—of determining just what is it to behave decently. Two final commentaries can point the way toward a fairer, more balanced revision of the morality, of the moral equation, of loyalty and betrayal—one scholarly and harsh; the other personal, heartfelt—both demanding of moral clarity.

The French historian Stéphane Courtois was the chief writer and editor of the magisterial *The Black Book of Communism*. In one passage of his essay in that text, he analyzed the several levels and degrees of complicity. He cited a number of criminal codes in which "crimes against humanity" include, as in the Canadian code, "providing encouragement for de facto complicity." That is, the Communists in power encouraged the complicity of those who believed and followed—those who, in turn, were to some degree responsible. "The complicity of those who rushed into voluntary servitude has not always been as abstract and theoretical as it may seem. Simple acceptance and/or *dissemination* [emphasis added] of propaganda designed to conceal the truth is invariably a symptom of active complicity." Thus, one must judge harshly those in the self-proclaimed

> world party of the revolution . . . those communists and fellow-travelers around the world who warmly approved Lenin's and subsequently Stalin's policies. . . .
>
> Undoubtedly, of course, it was not always easy to learn the facts or to discover the truth, for Communist regimes had mastered the art of censorship as their favorite technique for concealing their true activities. But quite often this ignorance was merely the result of ideologically motivated self-deception. Starting in the 1940s and 1950s, many facts about these atrocities had become public knowledge and undeniable. And although many of these apologists have cast aside their gods of yesterday, they have done so quietly and discreetly.[52]

The esteemed Polish poet and philosopher Aleksander Wat based his judgment on devastating personal experience. Wat spent years in a total of eleven different prisons and camps under Communist rule. His valiant fight for human rights deserves the last word on the subject. For Wat, "Stalinism is Marxism-Leninism as it works out in practice, its culmination. . . . The essence of Stalinism is the poison of the inner man." His most fervent protest is against the betrayal of truth—the lies that were a silence, the silence that was a lie—that accompanied the violence and destruction:

> The loss of freedom, tyranny, abuse, hunger would all have been easier to bear if not for the compulsion to call them freedom, justice, the good of the people. Mass exterminations are not an exception in history; cruelty is part of human nature, part of society. But a new, third dimension had been added that was more deeply and subtly oppressive: a vast enterprise to deform language . . . now any word could mean whatever suited the whims of the usurper of all words, meanings, things, and souls. . . . In this case a coherent set of grandiloquent terms and the opposing monstrous reality were kept side by side. . . . Young enthusiasts sang rapturously: "I know no other land/where a man can breathe so free" while their fathers perished in the camps. . . .
>
> When I was at liberty in Russia, which by then had been pacified until it was like a cemetery, I saw some old people who risked their lives to shout out, if only once, that slavery is slavery and not freedom.[53]

Notes

CHAPTER 1

1. For Maltz article, see, for example, Otto Friedrich, *City of Nets: A Portrait of Hollywood in the 1940s* (New York: Harper & Row, 1986), 323; Mike Gold, *Mike Gold: A Literary Anthology* (New York: International Publishers, 1972), 283–84; Victor Navasky, *Naming Names* (New York: Viking Press, 1980), 288; Robert Vaughn, *Only Victims: A Study in Show Business Blacklisting* (New York: G. P. Putnam and Sons, 1972), 191. The article is reprinted in Kenneth Lloyd Billingsley, *Hollywood Party: How Communism Seduced the American Film Industry in the 1930s and 1940s* (Rocklin, Calif.: Prima Publishing, 1998), 290ff.

2. Zhdanov is quoted in Dwight McDonald, *Memoirs of a Revolutionist* (New York: Farrar, Straus and Cudahy, 1957), 238–39.

3. For Maltz's article and response of others, especially of Sillen and Dennis, see Joseph R. Starobin, *American Communism in Crisis, 1943–1957* (Berkeley: University of California Press, 1975), 136–38. For response by Gold and Sillen, see Gold, *A Literary Anthology*, 283–91; Larry Ceplair and Steven Englund, *The Inquisition in Hollywood: Politics in the Film Community, 1930–1960* (Berkeley: University of California Press, 1983), 233–35; and Robert K. Landers, *An Honest Writer: The Life and Times of James T. Farrell* (San Francisco: Encounter Books, 2004), 279–80.

4. V. J. Jerome, *Daily Worker*, October 20, 1937; quoted in Landers, *An Honest Writer*, 198.

5. Howard Fast, "Art and Politics," *New Masses*, February 26, 1946, 6ff; quoted in Joan Mellen, *Hellman and Hammett: The Legendary Passion of Lillian Hellman and Dashiell Hammett* (New York: HarperCollins, 1996), 173; and Ronald Radosh and Allis Radosh, *Red Star over Hollywood: The Film Colony's Long Romance with the Left* (San Francisco: Encounter Books, 2005), 128.

6. For Bessie quote, see Alvah Bessie, "What Is Freedom for Writers?" *New Masses*, March 12, 1946, 8ff; quoted in Walter Goodman, *The Committee* (New York: Farrar,

Straus & Giroux, 1968), 214. For Lawson quote, see John Howard Lawson, "Art Is a Weapon," *New Masses*, March 19, 1946, 18–20.

7. See "Testimony of Leopold Atlas," in *Communism in the Motion Picture Industry: Hearings before the House Committee on Un-American Activities* [hereafter, *Motion Picture Industry: Hearings*], U.S. Congress, House Committee on Un-American Activities, Eighty-fifth Congress, March 12, 1953, 945–47. Quoted in part in Navasky, *Naming Names*, 290–92; Murray Kempton, *Part of Our Time: Some Monuments and Ruins of the Thirties* (New York: Simon & Schuster, 1955).

8. "Testimony of Leopold Atlas," 946. For Trumbo quote, see Bruce Cook, *Dalton Trumbo* (New York: Charles Scribner's Sons, 1977), 166.

9. "Testimony of Leopold Atlas," 946.

10. Albert Maltz, "Moving Forward," *New Masses*, April 19, 1946; quoted and discussed in Landers, *An Honest Writer*, 281. For quotes from the meeting, see Barbara Zheutlin and David Talbot, "Albert Maltz: Portrait of a Hollywood Dissident," *Cineaste* 8, no. 3 (Winter 1977–1978): 11.

11. Alan Casty, *The Films of Robert Rossen* (New York: Museum of Modern Art, 1969), 21.

12. For Zhdanovschina and the film, see Mira Liehm, *Passion and Defiance: Film in Italy from 1942 to the Present* (Berkeley: University of California Press, 1984), 92–95, 334–35. A salient discussion is in Tag Gallagher, *The Adventures of Roberto Rossellini: His Life and Films* (New York: Da Capo Press, 1998), 278–79. For the World Congress, see, among many, Sidney Hook, *Out of Step: An Unquiet Life in the 20th Century* (New York: Harper & Row, 1987), 385–87; Guenter Lewy, *The Cause That Failed: Communism in American Political Life* (New York: Oxford University Press, 1990), 81ff. For Zhdanov's speech, see Andrei Zhdanov, *Essays on Literature, Philosophy, and Music* (New York: International Publishers, 1950), 25ff; translated in Italy, for example, as *Politica e Ideologia, 1949*; quoted in Ceplair and Englund, *The Inquisition in Hollywood*, 236. For Hook quote, see Hook, *Out of Step*, 556.

13. See Simon Sebag Montefiore, *Stalin: The Court of the Red Tsar* (New York: Alfred A. Knopf, 2004), 541–44. See also Vladislav Zubok and Constantine Pleshakov, *Inside the Kremlin's Cold War: From Stalin to Khrushchev* (Cambridge, Mass.: Harvard University Press, 1996), 110ff; William Taubman, *Khrushchev: The Man and His Era* (New York: W.W. Norton, 2003), 197–99; Amy Knight, *Beria: Stalin's First Lieutenant* (Princeton, N.J.: Princeton University Press, 1983), 44–46.

14. Hook, *Out of Step*, 385; Stéphane Courtois et al., *The Black Book of Communism: Crimes, Terror Repression* (Cambridge, Mass.: Harvard University Press, 1999), 437–38; Zubok and Pleshakov, *Inside the Kremlin's Cold War*, 110–11.

15. Harvey Klehr, John Earl Haynes, and Kyrill M. Anderson, *The Soviet World of American Communism* (New Haven, Conn.: Yale University Press, 1998), 261.

16. Liehm, *Passion and Defiance*, 92.

17. Quoted in Roger Kimball, "Leszek Kolakowski and the Anatomy of Totalitarianism," *New Criterion*, June 2005, 9. For a full and deeply instructive analysis of the context of Marxist-Leninist-Stalinist thought and action, see Leszek Kolakowski, *Main Currents of Marxism: The Founders, the Golden Age, the Breakdown* (New York: W.W. Norton, 2004). In sum, for Kolakowski, Marxist-Leninist doctrine was "a good blueprint for converting human society into a giant concentration camp"; quoted in Kimball, "Leszek Kolakowski," 11.

18. Liehm, *Passion and Defiance*, 92, 93; 334–35.

19. Quoted in Nancy Lynn Schwartz, *The Hollywood Writers' Wars* (New York: McGraw-Hill, 1983), 153.

20. Howard Fast, *Being Red* (Boston: Houghton Mifflin, 1990), 300.

21. See Schwartz, *The Hollywood Writers' Wars*, 152–53. On Sparks, see "Testimony of Richard Collins," in *Motion Picture Industry: Hearings*, April 12, 1951, 252.

22. See Edward Dmytryk, *Odd Man Out: A Memoir of the Hollywood Ten* (Carbondale: Southern Illinois University Press, 1956), 114–15.

23. Quoted in Schwartz, *The Hollywood Writers' Wars*, 170. See also Ring Lardner Jr., *The Lardners: My Family Remembered* (New York: Harper & Row, 1976), and *I'd Hate Myself in the Morning* (New York: Nation Books, 2000).

24. Dmytryk, *Odd Man Out*, 115.

25. Robert Rossen, unpublished letter, January 21, 1953, 1. Property of Sue Rossen.

26. For Bernstein quote, see Patrick McGilligan and Paul Buhle, *Tender Comrades: A Backstory of the Blacklist* (New York: St. Martin's Griffin, 1999), 46–47. For Dassin quote, see McGilligan and Buhle, *Tender Comrades*, 214.

27. Yevtushenko's shocked response to the Khrushchev revelations is conveyed in his long poem "Zima Station," which appeared in a new journal, *Literaturanaya Moskva*, in November of 1956. See Taubman, *Khrushchev*, 307. Yevtushenko's convoluted and erratic relationship to the Soviet powers, especially Khrushchev, is traced in Taubman, *Khrushchev*, 528, 593, 629. See also Pavel Sudoplatov and Anatoli Sudoplatov, *Special Tasks* (Boston: Little, Brown, 1994), 412–13.

28. See Navasky, *Naming Names*.

CHAPTER 2

1. "Testimony of Robert Rossen," in *Investigation of Communist Activities in the New York City Area: Hearings before the Committee on Un-American Activities* [hereafter, *New York City Area: Hearings*], U.S. Congress, House Committee on Un-American Activities, Eighty-third Congress, May 7, 1953, 1456 and 1459.

2. From Kazan's advertisement in the *New York Times*, April 12, 1952, after Kazan testified (and briefly) in an executive session on April 10, 1952. Reprinted in Eric Bentley, *Thirty Years of Treason* (New York: Viking Press, 1973), 484.

3. Quoted in Michael J. Ybarra, "Blacklist Whitewash," *New Republic*, January 5 and 12, 1998, 23.

4. "Testimony of Leo Townsend," in *Motion Picture Industry: Hearings*, September 18, 1951, 1527.

5. Victor Navasky, *Naming Names* (New York: Viking Press, 1980), xii.

6. Yevtushenko poem is quoted in William Taubman, *Khrushchev: The Man and His Era* (New York: W.W. Norton, 2003), 307. See also n. 27 for ch. 1.

7. Stéphane Courtois et al., *The Black Book of Communism: Crimes, Terror, Repression* (Cambridge, Mass.: Harvard University Press, 1999), 26.

8. Quoted in Courtois, *The Black Book*, 741, from V. I. Lenin, *The Proletarian Revolution and the Renegade Kautsky* (Moscow: Foreign Languages Publishing House, 1952), 32–33.

9. Robert Conquest, *The Great Terror: A Reassessment* (New York: Oxford University Press, 1940), 464. The entire section on "Foreign Misapprehensions" is a detailed and cogent indictment of "an extraordinary potpourri of inhumanity and self-deception which a later generation might take to heart" (464–76).

10. For a discussion of the two orders, see Simon Sebag Montefiore, *Stalin: The Court of the Red Tsar* (New York: Alfred A. Knopf, 2004), 228–35; and Robert Conquest, *The Dragons of Expectation: Reality and Delusion in the Course of History* (New York: W.W. Norton, 2005), 117. See also, Courtois, *The Black Book*, 87–88, 249 (on Khrushchev), 252 (on Malenkov), and 250–51 (on Beria and Zhdanov).

11. See Joyce Milton, *Tramp: The Life of Charlie Chaplin* (New York: HarperCollins, 1996), 403ff.

12. Quoted in Larry Ceplair and Steven Englund, *The Inquisition in Hollywood: Politics in the Film Community, 1930–1960* (Berkeley: University of California Press, 1983), 77.

13. Lester Cole, *Hollywood Red* (Palo Alto, Calif.: Ramparts Press, 1981), 9. Walter Bernstein, *Inside Out: A Memoir of the Blacklist* (New York: Da Capo Press, 1966), 255, 137.

14. Hilton Kramer, "The Blacklist and the Cold War," *New York Times*, October 3, 1976, Arts and Leisure section, 1. Phillips is quoted in Kramer, "The Blacklist," 1.

15. For Pauly quote, see Peter Coleman, *The Liberal Conspiracy: The Congress for Cultural Freedom and the Struggle for the Mind of Postwar Europe* (New York: Free Press, 1989), 62–63. Irving Kristol, "Civil Liberties 1952: A Study in Confusion," *Commentary*, March 1952.

16. Quoted in Roger Kimball, "Leszek Kolakowski & the Anatomy of Totalitarianism," *New Criterion*, June 2005, 10. From the title essay in Leszek Kolakowski, *My Correct Views on Everything* (New York: St. Augustine's Press), 2004.

17. Schulberg quote from interview quoted in Navasky, *Naming Names*, 246.

18. Schickel's "The Hollywood Ten: Printing the Legend" and other writings on the period are reprinted in Richard Schickel, *Schickel on Film* (New York: HarperCollins, 1989), quotes on 100, 96.

19. Sidney Hook, *Out of Step: An Unquiet Life in the 20th Century* (New York: Harper & Row, 1987), 334. See his extended development of the concept in *Heresy, Yes—Conspiracy, No!* (New York: American Committee for Cultural Freedom, 1952). On the members of the party, see Hook, *Out of Step*, 506.

20. Philip Dunne, *Take Two: A Life in Movies and Politics* (New York: McGraw-Hill, 1990), 217, 114.

21. Trumbo is quoted in Ronald Radosh and Allis Radosh, *Red Star over Hollywood: The Film Colony's Long Romance with the Left* (San Francisco: Encounter Books, 2005), 220–21.

22. Kazan, *New York Times* ad, reprinted in Bentley, *Thirty Years of Treason*, 484.

23. Farrell is quoted in Robert K. Landers, *An Honest Writer: The Life and Times of James T. Farrell* (San Francisco: Encounter Books, 2004), 28–29.

24. Dunne, *Take Two*, 200.

25. *New York Times* review is quoted in Ron Radosh, "The Real Dalton Trumbo: What *Trumbo: The Movie* Won't Tell You," *Weekly Standard*, July 18, 2008, 24. For Joan Mellen quote, see Joan Mellen, *Hellman and Hammett: The Legendary Passion of Lillian Hellman and Dashiell Hammett* (New York: HarperCollins, 1996), 307.

26. See Bruce Cook, *Dalton Trumbo* (New York: Charles Scribner's Sons, 1977), 308–13, for a full development of the interchange and statements. Also in Navasky, *Naming Names*, 387–401.

27. Richard Gid Powers, *Not Without Honor: The History of American Anticommunism* (New York: Free Press, 1995), 425; Hook, *Out of Step*, 507.

28. Ybarra, "Blacklist Whitewash," 21.

29. Peter Collier and David Horowitz, "McCarthyism: The Last Refuge of the Left," *Commentary*, January 1988, 40.

30. Ted Morgan, *Reds: McCarthyism in Twentieth Century America* (New York: Random House, 2003), 547 and 255; Harvey Klehr, John Earl Haynes, and Fridrikh Igorevich Firsov, *The Secret World of American Communism* (New Haven, Conn.: Yale University Press, 1995), 16.

31. Savchencho's report is quoted in Allen Weinstein and Alexander Vassiliev, *The Haunted Wood: Soviet Espionage in America—The Stalin Era* (New York: Random House, 1999), 297–98.

32. See Eugene Genovese, "The Question," *Dissent* 41, no. 3 (Summer 1994): 371–76; also quoted in John Earl Haynes and Harvey Klehr, *In Denial: Historians, Communism & Espionage* (San Francisco: Encounter Books, 2003), 37.

CHAPTER 3

1. "Testimony of Martin Berkeley," in *Motion Picture Industry: Hearings*, September 19, 1951, 1585. Reprinted in Eric Bentley, *Thirty Years of Treason* (New York: Viking Press, 1973), 535.

2. For information on Tom Mooney, see Paul Buhle and Patrick McGilligan, *Tender Comrades: A Backstory of the Blacklist* (New York: St. Martin's Griffin, 1999), 242–43. For Ornitz's play *In New Kentucky* being praised by John Howard Lawson, see Nancy Lynn Schwartz, *The Hollywood Writers' Wars* (New York: McGraw-Hill, 1983), 35 and 59.

3. Schwartz, *The Hollywood Writers' Wars*, 147–48.

4. Schwartz, *The Hollywood Writers' Wars*, 315.

5. The Bright interview is in McGilligan and Buhle, *Tender Comrades*, 145, 151–52.

6. McGilligan and Buhle, *Tender Comrades*, 145.

7. On Lawrence, see Maurice Rapf, *Back Lot: Growing Up with the Movies* (Lanham, Md.: Scarecrow Press, 1999), 121–22. See also the Schulberg interview in Victor Navasky, *Naming Names* (New York: Viking Press, 1980), 244.

8. On Biberman, see Lester Cole, *Hollywood Red* (Palo Alto, Calif.: Ramparts Press, 1981), 137. On the meetings, see Otto Friedrich, *City of Nets: A Portrait of Hollywood in the 1940s* (New York: Harper & Row, 1986), 304–6. On Bessie quote, see interview in McGilligan and Buhle, *Tender Comrades*, 108. For *Red Rust* and *Roar, China*, see Jay Williams, *Stage Left* (New York: Charles Scribner's Sons, 1974), 102–3. For Lockridge, see Williams, *Stage Left*, 103. See also Harold Clurman, *The Fervent Years: The Story of the Group Theatre and the Thirties* (New York: Hill & Wang, 1957), 25–26.

9. On Pamplona, see Donald Ogden Stewart, *By a Stroke of Luck: An Autobiography* (New York and London: Paddington Press, 1975), 132–33. On the play *Bury*

the Dead, see Stewart, *By a Stroke of Luck*, 222–23. See also Ronald Brownstein, *The Power and the Glitter: The Washington-Hollywood Connection* (New York: Pantheon Books, 1990), 59.

10. See Larry Ceplair and Steven Englund, *The Inquisition in Hollywood: Politics in the Film Community, 1930–1960* (Berkeley: University of California Press, 1983), 58; Ted Morgan, *Reds: McCarthyism in Twentieth Century America* (New York: Random House, 2003), 211; "Testimony of Martin Berkeley," 1584–85. On Katz, see interesting note in Stephen Koch, *Double Lives: Spies and Writers in the Secret Soviet War of Ideas against the West* (New York: Harcourt Brace Jovanovich, 1979), 342, n. 23, and discussion of Katz while he was in Spain, 285–86. Using FBI documents, Alexander Stephan quotes a number of informants, including Erica Mann and Dorothy Thompson, who speak of Katz as a Comintern or Soviet agent: Alexander Stephan, *"Communazis": FBI Surveillance of German Émigré Writers* (New Haven, Conn.: Yale University Press, 2000).

11. Stanley G. Payne, *The Spanish Civil War, The Soviet Union, and Communism* (New Haven, Conn.: Yale University Press, 2004), 4–7.

12. Francois Furet, *The Passing of an Illusion: The Idea of Communism in the Twentieth Century* (Chicago: University of Chicago Press, 1999), 213–14.

13. Koch, *Double Lives*, 15 (Koestler), 20 (Gross), and 19 (Munzenberg). See also Guenter Lewy, *The Cause That Failed: Communism in American Political Life* (New York: Oxford University Press, 1990), 27.

14. Furet, *The Passing of an Illusion*, 219 and 225.

15. See Koch, *Double Lives*, 22–23, 75ff, 222f; Babette Gross, *Willi Munzenberg: A Political Biography* (East Lansing: Michigan State University Press, 1974), 309ff; Theodore Draper, "The Man Who Wanted to Hang," *Reporter*, January 6, 1953, 26–30. Quote on the Comintern is from Stéphane Courtois et al., *The Black Book of Communism: Crimes, Terror, Repression* (Cambridge, Mass.: Harvard University Press, 1999), 295.

16. See John Costello, *Mask of Treachery* (New York: William Morrow, 1988), 295–98. See also Koch, *Double Lives*, 65–67; 22–23; 343, n. 24; 376, n. 57.

17. Koch, *Double Lives*, 104–5; 106–7, passim. Arthur Koestler, *The Invisible Writing: The Second Volume of an Autobiography* (New York: MacMillan, 1954), 247–49; Einstein quote is on 249.

18. For another view of the "counter-trial," see Arthur Garfield Hays, *City Lawyer* (New York: Simon & Schuster, 1942).

19. For data on the creation of the Popular Front, see Payne, *The Spanish Civil War*, 60–66; and Robert C. Tucker, *Stalin in Power* (New York: W.W. Norton, 1999), 338–41.

20. For Dimitrov quote from Seventh World Congress, see Payne, *The Spanish Civil War*, 62–63. See also Furet, *The Passing of an Illusion*, 219–25.

21. Furet, *The Passing of an Illusion*, 283–91. Herbert Lottman, *The Left Bank: Writers, Artists, and Politics from the Popular Front to the Cold War* (Boston: Houghton Mifflin, 1982), ch. 12.

22. Robert K. Landers, *An Honest Writer: The Life and Times of James T. Farrell* (San Francisco: Encounter Books, 2004), 129–36. Joan Mellen, *Hellman and Hammett: The Legendary Passion of Lillian Hellman and Dashiell Hammett* (New York: Harper-Collins, 1996), 109. *Daily Worker*, January 18, 1935.

23. Harvey Klehr, John Earl Haynes, and Kyrill M. Anderson, *The Soviet World of American Communism* (New Haven, Conn.: Yale University Press, 1998), 35–38.

24. Koch, *Double Lives*, 63–64; 350, n. 39.

25. Koch, *Double Lives*, 35–36; 157; 231–33; 373, n. 21. See full details on Hermann and Herbst in John Earl Haynes and Harvey Klehr, *Venona: Decoding Soviet Espionage in America* (New Haven, Conn.: Yale University Press, 1990), 64.

26. On Lowenstein, see Stephen Koch, *Double Lives*, 222–24; and Ronald Radosh and Allis Radosh, *Red Star over Hollywood: The Film Colony's Long Romance with the Left* (San Francisco. Encounter Books, 2005), 48–49.

27. On Katz, see Gross, *Willi Munzenberg*, 310–11; Koestler, *The Invisible Writing*, 209; Koch, *Double Lives*, 222–23; and Salka Viertel, *The Kindness of Strangers* (New York: Holt, Rinehart, and Winston, 1969), 101–2, 211ff. Stewart is quoted in Koch, *Double Lives*, 223.

28. For discussion of Hellman and Katz, see Koch, *Double Lives*, 80, 82, 328; and Mellen, *Hellman and Hammett*, 161. For quotation, see Lillian Hellman, *An Unfinished Woman* (Boston: Little, Brown, 1970), 69.

29. Justin Kaplan, *Lincoln Steffens* (New York: Simon & Schuster, 1974), 321–24.

30. Koch, *Double Lives*, 22–23. Gibarti quoted in Koch, *Double Lives*, 227 and 375, n. 56. Ernest Hemingway, *Selected Letters, 1917–1960*, ed. Carlos Baker (New York: Charles Scribner's Sons, 1981), 120. See also Ella Winter, *And Not to Yield: An Autobiography* (New York: Harcourt, Brace and World, 1963).

31. "Testimony of Martin Berkeley," 1584–85. Reprinted in Bentley, *Thirty Years of Treason*, 535. On Bright, see McGilligan and Buhle, *Tender Comrades*, 145–46.

32. For Jerome's quote on Stalin, see Haynes and Klehr, *Venona*, 335; taken from V. J. Jerome, "The Individual in History," *New Masses*, May 18, 1943, 19. "The Negro in Hollywood" is quoted in Ceplair and Englund, *The Inquisition in Hollywood*, 74 (from *Political Affairs*, June 1950, 65ff).

33. On Schulberg, see Friedrich, *City of Nets*, 75.

34. Healey is quoted in Schwartz, *The Hollywood Writers' Wars*, 153. On the Hollywood writers, see Ceplair and Englund, *The Inquisition in Hollywood*, 70. Jerome quote is from V. J. Jerome, *Intellectuals and the War* (New York: Workers Library Publishers, 1940), 56–58.

35. For the sampling, in sequence, see the following: on John Bright, see McGilligan and Buhle, *Tender Comrades*, 150; on Leech, see Morgan, *Reds*, 211–12; on Lawrence and Carlisle, see "Testimony of Martin Berkeley," reprinted in Bentley, *Thirty Years of Treason*, 535; on Jerome, see "Testimony of Martin Berkeley," reprinted in Bentley, *Thirty Years of Treason*, 535–36; on Tuttle, see "Testimony of Martin Berkeley," 1581; on Tuttle, see "Testimony of Lionel Stander," in *Motion Picture Industry: Hearings*, May 6, 1953, reprinted in Bentley, *Thirty Years of Treason*, 646; on Jerome, see "Testimony of Lionel Stander," in Bentley, *Thirty Years of Treason*, 646; for Lawrence, see "Testimony of Marc Lawrence," in *Motion Picture Industry: Hearings*, April 24, 1951, reprinted in Bentley, *Thirty Years of Treason*, 645–46; on Salka Viertel, see Viertel, *The Kindness of Strangers*, 180–82 and passim.

36. Dorothy Healey, *Dorothy Healey Remembers* (New York: Oxford University Press, 1990), 120.

37. "Testimony of Sterling Hayden," in *Motion Picture Industry: Hearings*, April 10, 1951, reprinted in Bentley, *Thirty Years of Treason*, 365–66. "Testimony of Abe

Burrows," in *Motion Picture Industry: Hearings*, November 12, 1952, reprinted in Bentley, *Thirty Years of Treason*, 560–61.

38. Paul Jarrico: McGilligan and Buhle, *Tender Comrades*, 348.

39. Klehr, Haynes, and Anderson, *The Soviet World*, 36–38.

CHAPTER 4

1. See, for example, Stephen Koch, *Double Lives: Spies and Writers in the Secret Soviet War of Ideas against the West* (New York: Free Press, 1994), 78ff and 355, n. 15; and Babette Gross, *Willi Munzenberg: A Political Biography* (East Lansing: Michigan State University Press, 1974), 309ff.

2. Browder is quoted in Guenter Lewy, *The Cause That Failed: Communism in American Political Life* (New York: Oxford University Press, 1990), 169–70; see also 147, 173.

3. See, for example, Nancy Lynn Schwartz, *The Hollywood Writers' War* (New York: McGraw-Hill, 1983), 83ff; Koch, *Double Lives*, 78; Marion Meade, *Dorothy Parker: What Fresh Hell Is This?* (New York: Random House, 1987), 253–54. On Biberman, see Lester Cole, *Hollywood Red* (Palo Alto, Calif.: Ramparts Press, 1981), 137. On Chaplin, see Joyce Milton, *Tramp: The Life of Charlie Chaplin* (New York: HarperCollins, 1996).

4. Edmund Wilson, *A Literary Chronicle, 1920–1950* (Garden City, N.Y.: Doubleday, 1956), 286.

5. Larry Ceplair and Stephen Englund, *The Inquisition in Hollywood: Politics in the Film Community, 1930–1960* (Berkeley: University of California Press, 1983), 107, 108–9.

6. On the film screenings, see Ceplair and Englund, *The Inquisition in Hollywood*, 115. For the Stander party, see "Testimony of Martin Berkeley," in *Motion Picture Industry: Hearings*, September 19, 1951, 1586. On the four fund-raising dinners, see John Russell Taylor, *Strangers in Paradise: The Hollywood Emigres, 1933–1950* (New York: Holt, Rinehart and Winston, 1983), 118–19; and Salka Viertel, *The Kindness of Strangers* (New York: Holt, Rinehart, and Winston, 1969), 215 and passim for a personal view of the times and events. See also John Keats, *You Might as Well Live: The Life and Times of Dorothy Parker* (New York: Simon & Schuster, 1970). On Malraux's speaking engagements, see Curtis Cate, *Andre Malraux* (New York: Fromm International Publishing, 1998), 255–57. See also Budd Schulberg, *Writers in America: The Four Seasons of Success* (New York: Stein and Day, 1983), 82–83. For Viertel's comment, see Viertel, *The Kindness of Strangers*, 215.

7. Cate, *Andre Malraux*, 256.

8. On Stewart, see Donald Ogden Stewart, *By a Stroke of Luck: An Autobiography* (New York and London: Paddington Press, 1975). O'Hara is quoted in Ronald Brownstein, *The Power and the Glitter: The Washington-Hollywood Connection* (New York: Pantheon Books, 1990), 59.

9. Keats, *You Might as Well Live*, 218–23.

10. See Stanley G. Payne, *The Spanish Civil War, the Soviet Union, and Communism* (New Haven, Conn.: Yale University Press, 2004), 131 and 344–45, n. 70.

11. See Joan Mellen, *Hellman and Hammett: The Legendary Passion of Lillian Hellman and Dashiell Hammett* (New York: HarperCollins, 1996), 128, 165; Brownstein, *The Power and the Glitter*, 60–61; Ceplair and Englund, *The Inquisition in Hollywood*, 112–16; Ronald Radosh and Allis Radosh, *Red Star over Hollywood: The Film Colony's Long Romance with the Left* (San Francisco: Encounter Books, 2005), 57–59.

12. See Payne, *The Spanish Civil War*, 50, 98ff, 123ff, 181, 297, passim; Sarin and Dvoretsky quote is found on 298–99.

13. For Marty quote, see Payne, *The Spanish Civil War*, 184. See also Payne, *The Spanish Civil War*, 226–31.

14. For Marty quote, see Stéphane Courtois et al., *The Black Book of Communism: Crimes, Terror, Repression* (Cambridge, Mass.: Harvard University Press, 1999), 348–49, and executions total, 343. For significant documents about the International Brigades, see also Harvey Klehr, John Earl Haynes, and Fridrikh Igorevich Firsov, *The Secret World of American Communism* (New Haven, Conn.: Yale University Press, 1995), 151–87. A long Andre Marty report is printed in Ronald Radosh, Mary R. Habeck, and Grigory Sevstianov, *Spain Betrayed: The Soviet Union in the Spanish Civil War* (New Haven, Conn.: Yale University Press, 2001), 40–55.

15. Quoted in Joan Mellen, *Hellman and Hammett*, 432. For Orwell's book, see George Orwell, *Homage to Catalonia* (London: Secker and Warburg, 1938).

16. Printed in Klehr, Haynes, and Firsov, *The Secret World of American Communism*, 81–83.

17. Quoted in William Wright, *Lillian Hellman: The Image, the Woman* (New York: Simon & Schuster, 1986), 161; from the *New York Times*, January 20, 1940. See Carl Rollyson, *Lillian Hellman: Her Legend and Her Legacy* (New York: St. Martin's Press, 1986), 149–52.

18. Quoted in Ceplair and Englund, *The Inquisition in Hollywood*, 166.

19. Lester Cole, *Hollywood Red*, 171.

20. See Mellen, *Hellman and Hammett*, 162–66; Rollyson, *Lillian Hellman*, 152.

21. Quoted in Ceplair and Englund, *The Inquisition in Hollywood*, 165.

22. Rapf is quoted in an interview in Patrick McGilligan and Paul Buhle, *Tender Comrades: A Backstory of the Blacklist* (New York: St. Martin's Griffin, 1999), 539. For Stewart quote, see Brownstein, *The Power and the Glitter*, 69.

23. See, for example, Brownstein, *The Power and the Glitter*, 69–72; Lewy, *The Cause That Failed*, 179–80. For "wrecking crew," see Radosh and Radosh, *Red Star over Hollywood*, 69. For MPDC statement and Browder slogan, see Brownstein, *The Power and the Glitter*, 71.

24. These and other activities are described in Schwartz, *The Hollywood Writers' Wars*, 150–51; and Ceplair and Englund, *The Inquisition in Hollywood*, 165–68.

25. Cole, *Hollywood Red*, 171.

26. On Trumbo's novel, see Bruce Cook, *Dalton Trumbo* (New York: Charles Scribner's Sons, 1977), 131. See also Robert Vaughn, *Only Victims: A Study in Show Business Blacklisting* (New York: G. P. Putnam and Sons, 1972), 305. This material and subsequent references in Vaughn are a reprinting of "Information from the Files of the Committee," entered into the record of *Motion Picture Industry: Hearings*, October 1947. For Trumbo's speeches, see Vaughn, *Only Victims*, 306. See also Ceplair and Englund, *The Inquisition in Hollywood*, 166 and 469, n. 29. See discussion

of period in Eugene Lyons, *The Red Decade: The Stalinist Penetration of America* (New York: Bobbs, Merrill, 1941), 344ff. For party background on the lend-lease program, see Lewy, *The Cause That Failed*, 180.

27. On Trumbo, see Vaughn, *Only Victims*, 308–9. On Lawson, see Vaughn, *Only Victims*, 299.

28. See discussion in Irving Howe and Lewis Coser, *The American Communist Party: A Critical History (1919–1957)* (New York: Frederick A. Praeger, 1962), 394ff. See Ceplair and Englund, *The Inquisition in Hollywood*, 174.

29. Radosh and Radosh, *Red Star over Hollywood*, 81–82.

30. For quote by Losey, see David Caute, *Joseph Losey: A Revenge on Life* (New York: Oxford University Press, 1994), 72–73. For the Maltz film, see Milton, *Tramp*, 399. For Lawson's statement, see Vaughn, *Only Victims*, 296.

31. On Chaplin's speaking engagements, see Milton, *Tramp*, 399–405; 402 (New York—Madison Square Garden), 400 (San Francisco), 401 (Los Angeles), and 402–3 (New York—Carnegie Hall).

32. Milton, *Tramp*, 346–50 (on Soviets in the thirties); 378–80, 398–99 (on the Pact and Peace); and 475–76, 485–88 (on postwar politics and U.S. government).

33. Milton, *Tramp*, 346–47, 405.

34. See Koch, *Double Lives*, ch. 11. See also Robert Conquest, *The Great Terror: A Reassessment* (New York: Oxford University Press, 1940), 402; and Gross, *Willi Munzenberg*.

35. On the Spanish Civil War, see Gross, *Willi Munzenberg*, 311–12; and Koch, *Double Lives*, 285–86. On Mexico and Kisch, see Alexander Stephan, *Communazis: FBI Surveillance of Émigré Writers* (New Haven, Conn.: Yale University Press, 2000), ch. 4.

36. Koch, *Double Lives*, 322, 330.

37. Koch, *Double Lives*, 330–31. See also Eugen Lobl, *My Mind on Trial* (New York: Harcourt Brace Jovanovich, 1976).

38. Koch, *Double Lives*, 332 and 390, n. 17.

CHAPTER 5

1. Nancy Lynn Schwartz, *The Hollywood Writers' Wars* (New York: McGraw-Hill, 1983, 15; see also 14–15 and 21 for background. For Faragoh, Lawson, and formation of the club in general, see Paul Buhle and Dave Wagner, *Radical Hollywood* (New York: New Press, 2002), 13–14, 82, 185.

2. "Testimony of Richard Collins," in *Motion Picture Industry: Hearings*, April 12, 1951, 220–21. See also Ronald Radosh and Allis Radosh, *Red Star over Hollywood: The Film Colony's Long Romance with the Left* (San Francisco: Encounter Books, 2005), 44.

3. See Larry Ceplair and Stephen Englund, *The Inquisition in Hollywood: Politics in the Film Community, 1930–1960* (Berkeley: University of California Press, 1983), 65–66. SWG board member lists can be found in Schwartz, *The Hollywood Writers' Wars*, 321–24.

4. Schwartz, *The Hollywood Writers' Wars*, 21, 29. Ceplair and Englund, *The Inquisition in Hollywood*, 28, and see n. 19 on p. 461.

5. Schwartz, *The Hollywood Writers' Wars*, 24, 27–29.

6. See interview "Organizing the Screen Writers' Guild—An Interview with John Howard Lawson," *Cineaste*, Fall 1977, 4–11, 58.

7. Schwartz, *The Hollywood Writers' Wars*, 36–38.

8. John Howard Lawson, "Straight from the Shoulder," *New Theatre*, November 1934, quoted in Eric Bentley, *Thirty Years of Treason* (New York: Viking Press, 1973), 233; see the editors' response on 234.

9. Mike Gold, "A Bourgeois Hamlet for Our Time," *New Masses*, April 10, 1934, 29. Quoted in Gerald Rabkin, *Drama and Commitment: Politics in the American Theater of the Thirties* (Bloomington: Indiana University Press, 1964), 151.

10. John Howard Lawson, "Inner Conflict and Proletarian Art," *New Masses*, April 17, 1934, 30. John Howard Lawson, *With a Reckless Preface* (New York: Farrar and Rinehart, 1934), xvii. See also Rabkin, *Drama and Commitment*, 151–52.

11. John Howard Lawson, "Toward a Revolutionary Theatre," *New Theatre*, June 30, 1934, 6; see also Rabkin, *Drama and Commitment*, 154. John Howard Lawson, "Play on Dimitroff," *Daily Worker*, July 23, 1934, 5; see also Rabkin, *Drama and Commitment*, 155.

12. Lawson, "Straight from the Shoulder." On Maltz, Peters, and Sklar, see Jay Williams, *Stage Left* (New York: Charles Scribner's Sons, 1974), 133–34. On Ornitz's play, see Schwartz, *The Hollywood Writers' Wars*, 59.

13. Harold Clurman, *The Fervent Years: The Story of the Group Theatre and the Thirties* (New York: Hill & Wang, 1957), 174–75. Buchwald is quoted in Rabkin, *Drama and Commitment*, 159.

14. Dos Passos is quoted in Otto Friedrich, *City of Nets: A Portrait of Hollywood in the 1940s* (New York: Harper & Row, 1986), 322–33.

15. "Testimony of Leo Townsend," in *Motion Picture Industry: Hearings*, September 18, 1951, 1523.

16. Beilinson is quoted in Schwartz, *The Hollywood Writers' Wars*, 71. For material on this drastic idea and the conservatives' response, see Schwartz, *The Hollywood Writers' Wars*, ch. 4 and pp. 291–92; Friedrich, *City of Nets*, 74–77; Ceplair and Englund, *The Inquisition in Hollywood*, 41–44.

17. See, for example, Maurice Rapf, quoted in Schwartz, *The Hollywood Writers' Wars*, 79. See later reminiscences by "conservative" John Lee Mahin in Schwartz, *The Hollywood Writers' Wars*, 291.

18. Schwartz, *The Hollywood Writers' Wars*, 96–99 and passim, 123. See also Ceplair and Englund, *The Inquisition in Hollywood*, 44–46.

19. See Ceplair and Englund, *The Inquisition in Hollywood*, 142ff; Schwartz, *The Hollywood Writers' Wars*, 155–57.

20. See treatment of the 1937 strike in David F. Prindle, *The Politics of Glamour: Ideology and Democracy in the Screen Actors Guild* (Madison: University of Wisconsin Press, 1988), 27–31; and Schwartz, *The Hollywood Writers' Wars*, 113–15. Rinaldo is quoted in Schwartz, *The Hollywood Writers' Wars*, 221. For *New Masses* articles and support, see Prindle, *The Politics of Glamour*, 225, n. 41.

21. For Bioff, Kibre, and others, see Prindle, *The Politics of Glamour*, 32–34; Schwartz, *The Hollywood Writers' Wars*, 135 and 220–21; and Prindle, *The Politics of Glamour*, 46.

22. Sorrell quoted in Friedrich, *City of Nets*, 248. See also Prindle, *The Politics of Glamour*, 45–46; Schwartz, *The Hollywood Writers's Wars*, 221–22; John Cogley,

Report on Blacklisting: 1—Movies (New York: Fund for the Republic, 1956), 55–56; "Testimony of Roy Brewer," in *Motion Picture Industry: Hearings*, 1951, 352–56.

23. For overview, see Prindle, *The Politics of Glamour*, 40–50; and Friedrich, *City of Nets*, 247–50. On Brewer versus Sorrell, see Dan E. Moldea, *Dark Victory: Ronald Reagan, MCA, and the Mob* (New York: Viking Press, 1986), 65–70; and Ceplair and Englund, *The Inquisition in Hollywood*, 213–25. For Brewer's comment on the Communists, see Ceplair and Englund, *The Inquisition in Hollywood*, 66–67; and Cogley, *Report on Blacklisting*, 64.

24. Schwartz, *The Hollywood Writers' Wars*, 204–11. "Statement of Principle" in Prindle, *The Politics of Glamour*, 50. Friedrich, *City of Nets*, 167–68. McGuiness quoted in Ronald Brownstein, *The Power and the Glitter: The Hollywood-Washington Connection* (New York: Pantheon Books, 1968), 111. For the Lawson meeting, see Schwartz, *The Hollywood Writers' Wars*, 217.

25. Schwartz, *The Hollywod Writers' Wars*, 250.

26. For discussion of Sorrell, the development of the Strike and relationship to the CPUSA, see Schwartz, *The Hollywood Writers' Wars*, 223–27, 250; Ceplair and Englund, *The Inquisition in Hollywood*, 218; Prindle, *The Politics of Glamour*, 42; Friedrich, *City of Nets*, 248. For Lawson's position and opposition to it, see Schwartz, *The Hollywood Writers' Wars*, 223.

27. Schwartz, *The Hollywood Writers' Wars*, 226–27; Ceplair and Englund, *The Inquisition in Hollywood*, 219–21; Friedrich, *City of Nets*, 248–49.

28. Schwartz, *The Hollywood Writers' Wars*, 228. Bruce Cook, *Dalton Trumbo* (New York: Charles Scribner's Sons, 1977), 167–68.

29. Cook, *Dalton Trumbo*, 227–28; Friedrich, *City of Nets*, 249–50. Radosh and Radosh, *Red Star over Hollywood*, 19. On Roy Brewer, see Bentley, *Thirty Years of Treason*, 198–99. On Lawson, see Schwartz, *The Hollywood Writers' Wars*, 229.

30. Statement in Bentley, *Thirty Years of Treason*, 198.

31. Schwartz, *The Hollywood Writers' Wars*, 229.

32. Schwartz, *The Hollywood Writers' Wars*, 244–50; *Time* quoted on 244. See also Friedrich, *City of Nets*, 276–83.

33. Schwartz, *The Hollywood Writers' Wars*, 248.

34. "Testimony of Sterling Hayden," in *Motion Picture Industry: Hearings*, April 10, 1951, 142–43, 162. See Bentley, *Thirty Years of Treason*, 361–66; and Prindle, *The Politics of Glamour*, 47.

35. Prindle, *The Politics of Glamour*, 47–49; SAG Report on 47. Friedrich, *City of Nets*, 279–80.

36. Friedrich, *City of Nets*, 283.

37. Prindle, *The Politics of Glamour*, 41.

38. See Brownstein, *The Power and the Glitter*, 81–85; and Ceplair and Englund, *The Inquisition in Hollywood*, 225–29; Lawson and Trumbo are quoted on 229.

39. Quotation in Brownstein, *The Power and the Glitter*, 107; see 107–11. Ceplair and Englund, *The Inquisition in Hollywood*, 225–29.

40. See Robert Vaughn, *Only Victims: A Study in Show Business Blacklisting* (New York: G. P. Putnam and Sons, 1972), 308–9.

41. Scott is quoted in Schwartz, *The Hollywood Writers' Wars*, 261. Sperling is quoted in Brownstein, *The Power and the Glitter*, 107. On Sparks and the election, see Ceplair and Englund, *The Inquisition in Hollywood*, 237–39.

42. On the special committee, see Brownstein, *The Power and the Glitter*, 108; and Radosh and Radosh, *Red Star over Hollywood*, 115. On Reagan's recollections, see Richard Gid Powers, *Not Without Honor: The History of American Anticommunism* (New York: Free Press, 1995), 219–20; Moldea, *Dark Victory*, 79; Reagan letter to Hugh Heffner, 1960; and Ronald Reagan, *Where's the Rest of Me?* (New York: Elsevier-Dutton, 1965), 116ff.

43. On Lawson, see Brownstein, *The Power and the Glitter*, 109. Brownstein quote is from Brownstein, *The Power and the Glitter*, 117.

44. See "Testimony of Richard Collins," in *Motion Picture Industry: Hearings*, April 12, 1951, 230–32. Ceplair and Englund, *The Inquisition in Hollywood*, 230–31.

45. Spiegelgass and Stuhlberg are quoted in Schwartz, *The Hollywood Writers' Wars*, 265. See "Testimony of Martin Berkeley," in *Motion Picture Industry: Hearings*, September 19, 1951, 1581–85, 1604.

46. See Schwartz, *The Hollywood Writers' Wars*, 263–66; Ceplair and Englund, *The Inquisition in Hollywood*, 292–96; Friedrich, *City of Nets*, 332 and 378.

CHAPTER 6

1. "Testimony of Robert Rossen," in *Motion Picture Industry: Hearings*, part 3, June 25, 1951, 672, 681, 709.

2. "Testimony of Robert Rossen," in *New York City Area: Hearings*, part 4, May 7, 1953, 1460.

3. Rossen, unpublished statement, 1951, 2. Property of Sue Rossen.

4. "Testimony of Robert Rossen," *New York City Area: Hearings*, 1457–58.

5. "Testimony of Robert Rossen," *New York City Area: Hearings*, 1460–65. See also discussion of Hollywood Writers' Mobilization, pp. 1472ff.

6. Robert Rossen, "The Shakespeare Experience: *Show* Poll #5," *Show*, February 1964, 81.

7. On the telegrams sent, see "Testimony of Robert Rossen," *Motion Picture Industry: Hearings*, 683. On the artists committee, see, for example, Larry Ceplair and Stephen Englund, *The Inquisition in Hollywood: Politics in the Film Community* (Berkeley: University of California Press, 1983), 114–17; and Ronald Radosh and Allis Radosh, *Red Star over Hollywood: The Film Colony's Long Romance with the Left* (San Francisco: Encounter Books, 2005), 54–60. On Paul Robeson, see "Testimony of Robert Rossen," *Motion Picture Industry: Hearings*, 682; Larry Swindell, *Body and Soul: The Story of John Garfield* (New York: William Morrow, 1975), 249.

8. "Testimony of Robert Rossen," *New York City: Hearings*, 1465–70.

9. John Mosher, *New Yorker*, March 1941.

10. Harold Clurman, *The Fervent Years: The Story of the Group Theatre and the Thirties* (New York: Hill & Wang, 1957), 224.

11. "Testimony of Louis J. Russell," in *Motion Picture Industry: Hearings*, October 30, 1947, quoted in Eric Bentley, *Thirty Years of Treason* (New York: Viking Press, 1973), 240–41.

12. On the HDC during World War II, see Ceplair and Englund, *The Inquisition in Hollywood*, 190, 227–28. On the Rossen party, Gorney, and Meyers, see Norma Barzman, *The Red and the Blacklist* (New York: Nation Books, 2003), 3–5, 41, 93. On

Meet the People, see Nancy Lynn Schwartz, *The Hollywood Writers' Wars* (New York: McGraw-Hill, 1983), 164–66.

13. On Harburg, see "Testimony of Robert Lees," in *Motion Picture Industry: Hearings,* 1951, 203; and "Testimony of Robert Rossen," *Motion Picture Industry: Hearings,* 678. On Butler and Tuttle, see "Testimony of Robert Rossen," *Motion Picture Industry: Hearings,* 633 and 635; "Testimony of Larry Parks," in *Motion Picture Industry: Hearings,* 1951, reprinted in Eric Bentley, *Thirty Years of Treason,* 339.

14. Rossen's discussion of his participation in HWM and the Writers' Congress is in "Testimony of Robert Rossen," *New York City Area: Hearings,* 1472–80; and in his unpublished statement, 1951, 5–6. Kanin is quoted in Schwartz, *The Hollywood Writers' Wars,* 190.

15. See Schwartz, *The Hollywood Writers' Wars,* 198–202 and 295, note for 199; and Ceplair and Englund, *The Inquisition in Hollywood,* 187–90.

16. "Testimony of Robert Rossen," *New York City Area: Hearings,* 1476 and 1479–80.

17. On Browder, see "Testimony of Robert Rossen," *New York City Area: Hearings,* 1481–82. For Rossen's speech, see "New Characters for the Screen," *New Masses,* January 18, 1944, 18–19. The speech is discussed with quotations in Paul Buhle and Dave Wagner, *Radical Hollywood* (New York: New Press, 2002), 286–87.

18. Faragoh's speech is quoted in Schwartz, *The Hollywood Writers' Wars,* 189.

19. See Schwartz, *The Hollywood Writers' Wars,* 163–64, 193–94; and extensive note for 193 on 294. On the meeting and Rossen's lecture, see "Testimony of Robert Rossen," *Motion Picture Industry: Hearings,* 683–85.

20. John Houseman quoted in Schwartz, *The Hollywood Writers' Wars,* 189.

21. "Testimony of Robert Rossen," *New York City Area: Hearings,* 1487–90.

22. "Testimony of Robert Rossen," *New York City Area: Hearings,* 1473–74.

23. On Kalatozov's visit, see "Testimony of Lewis J. Russell," in *Motion Picture Industry: Hearings,* 1951, reprinted in Eric Bentley, *Thirty Years of Treason,* 234–35; and "Testimony of Robert Rossen," *Motion Picture Industry: Hearings,* 683.

24. On the Salvameni event, see "Testimony of Robert Rossen," *Motion Picture Industry: Hearings,* 695.

25. "Testimony of Robert Rossen," *Motion Picture Industry: Hearings,* 687–88.

26. "Testimony of Robert Rossen," *New York City Area: Hearings,* 1489.

27. "Testimony of Robert Rossen," *Motion Picture Industry: Hearings,* 682, 686.

28. "Testimony of Robert Rossen," *New York City Area: Hearings,* 1489, 1458–59.

29. "Testimony of Robert Rossen," *New York City Area: Hearings,* 1490. "Testimony of Richard Collins," in *Motion Picture Industry: Hearings,* April 12, 1951, 241–42.

30. "Testimony of Robert Rossen," *Motion Picture Industry: Hearings,* 1951, 697.

31. "Testimony of Robert Rossen," *Motion Picture Industry: Hearings,* 696, 698.

CHAPTER 7

1. John Earl Haynes and Harvey Klehr, *In Denial: Historians, Communism, & Espionage* (San Francisco: Encounter Books, 2003), 112–13.

2. Paul Buhle and Dave Wagner, *A Very Dangerous Citizen: Abraham Lincoln Polonsky and the Hollywood Left* (Berkeley: University of California Press, 2001), 2 and 3.

3. On Buhle's comments on noir, among other variations, see Buhle and Wagner, *A Very Dangerous Citizen*, 1, 3, 101, and 189.

4. Polonsky's obituary is quoted in Buhle and Wagner, *A Very Dangerous Citizen*, 234.

5. Quoted in Buhle and Wagner, *A Very Dangerous Citizen*, 137.

6. "Testimony of Sterling Hayden," in *Motion Picture Industry: Hearings*, April 10, 1951, reprinted in Eric Bentley, *Thirty Years of Treason* (New York: Viking Press, 1973), 365–66. "Testimony of Abe Burrows," in *Motion Picture Industry: Hearings*, November 12, 1952, reprinted in Bentley, *Thirty Years of Treason*, 560–61.

7. "Testimony of Stanley Roberts," in *Motion Picture Industry: Hearings*, May 20, 1952, 3335. On the picket line, see Buhle and Wagner, *A Very Dangerous Citizen*, 251, n. 7.

8. "Testimony of Leopold Atlas," in *Motion Picture Industry: Hearings*, March 12, 1943, 945ff.

9. "Testimony of Stanley Roberts," 3335–36.

10. Patrick McGilligan and Paul Buhle, *Tender Comrades: A Backstory of the Hollywood Blacklist* (New York: St. Martin's Griffin, 1999), 486.

11. Paul Buhle and Dave Wagner, *Blacklisted: The Film Lover's Guide to the Hollywood Blacklist* (New York: Palgrave Macmillan, 2003), 26.

12. McGilligan and Buhle, *Tender Comrades*, 486.

13. Buhle and Wagner, *Radical Hollywood*, 168.

14. Buhle and Wagner, *Radical Hollywood*, 386–87.

15. On being voted best film, see Buhle and Wagner, *Blacklisted*, 9. Buhle and Wagner, *Radical Hollywood*, 387ff.

16. On Polonsky, see Buhle and Wagner, *A Very Dangerous Citizen*, 102 and 108. Polonsky is quoted in McGilligan and Buhle, *Tender Comrades*, 485.

17. Polonsky is quoted in McGilligan and Buhle, *Tender Comrades*, 486. Buhle is quoted in Buhle and Wagner, *A Very Dangerous Citizen*, 113.

18. On Aldrich's reservations, see Tony Williams, *The Cinematic Vision of Robert Aldrich* (Lanham, Md.: Scarecrow Press, 2004), 52. On Rossen and Wong Howe, see Daniel Stern, "An Interview with Robert Rossen," *Art in Society*, Winter 1966, 7; see also Williams, *The Cinematic Vision of Robert Aldrich*, 138. For Aldrich quote on Enterprise's "one hit," see the interview with Pierre Sauvage in Eugene L. Miller Jr. and Edwin T. Arnold, *Robert Aldrich: Interviews* (Jackson: University Press of Mississippi, 2004), 38.

19. Aldrich quoted in Miller and Arnold, *Robert Aldrich*, 42.

20. For Rossen quote on Garfield, see Stern, "An Interview with Robert Rossen," 4; and an interview with Jean-Louis Noames, "Lessons Learned in Combat," *Cahiers du Cinema in English*, January 1967, 26.

21. Larry Swindell, *Body and Soul: The Story of John Garfield* (New York: William Morrow, 1975), 152.

22. Swindell, *Body and Soul*, 153–54.

23. Stern, "An Interview with Robert Rossen," 6.

24. Stern, "An Interview with Robert Rossen," 6.

25. Interview in Miller and Arnold, *Robert Aldrich*, 97.

26. Miller and Arnold, *Robert Aldrich*, 97.

27. Polonsky is quoted in Buhle and Wagner, *A Very Dangerous Citizen*, 115–16. Buhle quote is from Buhle and Wagner, *Radical Hollywood*, 392.

28. Bosley Crowther, "Movie Review: *Body and Soul* (1947)," *New York Times*, November 10, 1947. James Agee, *The Nation*, November 8, 1947, 511; see in James Agee, *Agee on Film* (n.p.: Beacon Press, 1964), 281.

29. Raymond Durgnat, "Ways of Melodrama," in *Imitations of Life: A Reader on Film and Television Melodrama*, ed. Marcia Landy (Detroit: Wayne University Press, 1991), 143.

30. Buhle and Wagner, *Radical Hollywood*, 403.

31. Buhle and Wagner, *A Very Dangerous Citizen*, 176.

32. Described and quoted in Buhle and Wagner, *A Very Dangerous Citizen*, 217–20.

33. See discussion in Peter Kornbluth, *The Pinochet File: A Declassified Dossier on Atrocity and Acceptability* (Washington, D.C.: A National Security Archive Book, 2003). Nathaniel Davis, *The Last Two Years of Salvador Allende* (Ithaca, N.Y.: Cornell University Press, 1985), 170. See also Pamela Constable and Arturo Valenzuela, *A Nation of Enemies: Chile under Pinochet* (New York: W.W. Norton, 1993).

34. Buhle and Wagner, *A Very Dangerous Citizen*, 205–6.

35. Buhle and Wagner, *A Very Dangerous Citizen*, 2, 211.

36. Janet Maslin, "Movie Review: *Monsignor* (1982)," *New York Times*, October 22, 1982.

CHAPTER 8

1. Joseph North, "Crossfire," *New Masses*, November 11, 1947, 3. Further examples in Joseph North, "Torquemada in Technicolor," *New Masses*, November 4, 1947; and Henry F. Ward, "Method in Madness," *New Masses*, November 11, 1947.

2. John Howard Lawson, "Straight from the Shoulder," *New Theatre*, April 10, 1934. Quoted in Bentley, *Thirty Years of Treason*, 233.

3. "Testimony of John Howard Lawson," in *Motion Picture Industry: Hearings*, October 27, 1947, reprinted in Eric Bentley, *Thirty Years of Treason* (New York: Viking Press, 1973), 153–65; quotation on 157.

4. "Written Statement of John Howard Lawson," in *Motion Picture Industry: Hearings*, October 27, 1947, in Bentley, *Thirty Years of Treason*, 164.

5. "Testimony of John Howard Lawson," in Bentley, *Thirty Years of Treason*, 153–65; also quoted in Edward Dmytryk, *Odd Man Out: A Memoir of the Hollywood Ten* (Carbondale: Southern Illinois University Press, 1956), 59–61. And see Robert Vaughn, *Only Victims: A Study in Show Business Blacklisting* (New York: G. P. Putnam and Sons, 1972), 91ff, for Lawson testimony and that of others.

6. See Otto Friedrich, *City of Nets: A Portrait of Hollywood in the Forties* (New York: Harper & Row, 1986), 304 and 310; Nancy Lynn Schwartz, *The Hollywood Writers' Wars* (New York: McGraw-Hill, 1983), 260, 266; "Testimony of Edward Dmytryk," in *Motion Picture Industry: Hearings*, 1951, 427–28, reprinted in Bentley, *Thirty Years of Treason*, 393; Dmytryk, *Odd Man Out*, 53–54; and Patricia Bosworth, *Anything*

Your Little Heart Desires: An American Family Story (New York: Simon & Schuster, 1997), 163–64.

7. The sequence of events, from April to June, is captured in Ceplair and Englund, *The Inquisition in Hollywood: Politics in the Film Commuity, 1930–1960* (Berkeley: University of California Press, 1983), 256–60; for Johnston quote, see 257–58; for Warner quote, see 258; for Johnson and Producers Association, see 259–60; and for Hughes, see 259. For comments by Thomas, see Schwartz, *The Hollywood Writers' Wars*, 254; and Friedrich, *City of Nets*, 303.

8. Quoted in Ceplair and Englund, *The Inquisition in Hollywood*, 260.

9. Maltz quoted in Schwartz, *The Hollywood Writers' Wars*, 259; and Albert Maltz, "The Writer as the Conscience of the People," in *The Citizen Writer* (New York: International Publishers, 1950), 11.

10. For Kenny quote, see interview in Bruce Cook, *Dalton Trumbo* (New York: Charles Scribner's Sons, 1977), 186. Also see Friedrich, *City of Nets*, 305; "Testimony of Edward Dmytryk," 427–28; and Dmytryk, *Odd Man Out*, 38, 53–54. Also see "Written Statement of Roy Brewer," in *Motion Picture Industry: Hearings*, 1947, reprinted in Eric Bentley, *Thirty Year of Treason*, 199.

11. "Testimony of Edward Dmytryk," 427–28.

12. Quoted in Victor Navasky, *Naming Names* (New York: Viking Press, 1980), 303.

13. See Friedrich, *City of Nets*, 304. The ad in the *Hollywood Reporter* appeared on November 26, 1947. Howard Koch, *As Time Goes By* (New York: Harcourt Brace Jovanovich, 1979), 167.

14. "Testimony of Edward Dmytryk," 424. On the Fifth Amendment and Charles Katz, see Ceplair and Englund, *The Inquisition in Hollywood*, 267. On later uses of the Fifth Amendment, see, for example, Ted Morgan, *Reds: McCarthyism in Twentieth Century America* (New York: Random House, 2003), 524; Joseph R. Starobin, *American Communism in Crisis, 1943–1957* (Berkeley: University of California Press, 1975), 208.

15. Katz is quoted in Schwartz, *The Hollywood Writers' Wars*, 269. On the Margolis letter to Kenny, see Morgan, *Reds*, 520. For Margolis' speech, see "Testimony of Robert Rossen," in *Motion Picture Industry: Hearings*, 1951, 696–97. Morgan, *Reds*, 518–19.

16. Schwartz, *The Hollywood Writers' Wars*, 115 and 160.

17. On Sleepy Lagoon case, see Edward Obregon Pagan, *Murder at the Sleepy Lagoon* (Chapel Hill: University of North Carolina Press, 2003); and Kevin Starr, *Embattled Dreams: California in War and Peace, 1940–1950* (New York: Oxford University Press, 2002). Also see Ceplair and Englund, *The Inquisition in Hollywood*, 195–96.

18. Margolis quoted in Walter Goodman, *The Committee* (New York: Farrar, Straus & Giroux, 1968), 313.

19. On Dunne, see Philip Dunne, *Take Two: A Life in the Movies and Politics* (New York: McGraw-Hill, 1990), 197–200, summarized in Guenter Lewy, *The Cause That Failed: Communism in American Life* (New York: Oxford University Press, 1990), 92. See also Lawrence Grobel, *The Hustons* (New York: Charles Scribner's Sons, 1989), 302–3. Lester Cole, *Hollywood Red* (Palo Alto, Calif.: Ramparts Press, 1981), 201.

20. Dunne quoted in Dunne, *Take Two*, 197–200; and Grobel, *The Hustons*, 303. Huston quoted in Grobel, *The Hustons*, 302–3. See also John Huston, *An Open Book*

(New York: Alfred A. Knopf, 1980). See also Friedrich, *City of Nets*, 326; "Testimony of Edward Dmytryk," 427–28.

21. Schary is quoted in Schwartz, *The Hollywood Writers' Wars*, note for 280 on 300. See also Schary speech and Writers Guild meeting on pp. 280–81. Rovere is quoted in Michael J. Ybarra, "Blacklist Whitewash," *New Republic*, January 5 and 12, 1998, 23. Healey is quoted in Cook, *Dalton Trumbo*, 259.

22. Morgan, *Reds*, 520. For Brownstein quote, see Ronald Brownstein, *The Power and the Glitter: The Washington-Hollywood Connection* (New York: Pantheon Books, 1990), 119.

23. Navasky, *Naming Names*, 403. See also 423; Ring Lardner, *I'd Hate Myself in the Morning* (New York: Nation Books, 2000), 119.

24. Tony Judt, "Rehearsal for Evil," *New Republic*, September 10, 2001, 35.

25. Quoted in Schwartz, *The Hollywood Writers' Wars*, note for 280 on 300.

26. The statement is reprinted in Ceplair and Englund, *The Inquisition in Hollywood*, 455. For discussion, see Ceplair and Englund, *The Inquisition in Hollywood*, 328–31; Friedrich, *City of Nets*, 332–34; Gordon Kahn, *Hollywood on Trial: The Story of the Ten Who Were Indicted* (New York: Boni and Gaer, 1948), 182–85. See also Dore Schary, *Heyday: An Autobiography* (New York: Little, Brown, 1979), 165–67. Gabler quote from Neal Gabler, *An Empire of Their Own: How the Jews Invented Hollywood* (New York: Anchor Books, 1988), 373.

27. On Silberberg, see Gabler, *An Empire of Their Own*, 371–74.

28. See Dmytryk, *Odd Man Out*, 94–95; Kahn, *Hollywood on Trial*, 185–88; Schwartz, *The Hollywood Writers' Wars*, 279–80.

29. Lardner's article is reprinted in Bentley, *Thirty Years of Treason*, 189–94, as is Brewer's rebuttal, 195–206.

30. The following excerpts are from testimonies and written statements in *Motion Picture Industry: Hearings*, October 27–30, 1947. See Schwartz, *The Hollywood Writers' Wars*, 267–76; and Ceplair and Englund, *The Inquisition in Hollywood*, 279–87, for discussion of hearings.

31. Lawson's testimony is reprinted in Bentley, *Thirty Years of Treason*, 153–65; and partially in Kahn, *Hollywood on Trial*, 68–77.

32. Lardner's testimony is reprinted in Bentley, *Thirty Years of Treason*, 184–88; and Kahn, *Hollywood on Trial*, 113–17.

33. Trumbo's testimony is reprinted in Kahn, *Hollywood on Trial*, 78–85; see also Cook, *Dalton Trumbo*, 179–81. For Jarrico on Trumbo, see Schwartz, *The Hollywood Writers' Wars*, 185–86.

34. Bessie's exchange is reprinted in Kahn, *Hollywood on Trial*, 92–96.

35. Cole's testimony is reprinted in Kahn, *Hollywood on Trial*, 117–20.

36. Cole is quoted in Kahn, *Hollywood on Trial*, 120.

37. "Written Statement of Alvah Bessie," in *Motion Picture Industry: Hearings*, 1947, reprinted in Kahn, *Hollywood on Trial*, 94.

38. Biberman's testimony and written statement are in *Motion Picture Industry: Hearings*, 1947, reprinted in Kahn, *Hollywood on Trial*, 100–104.

39. Jarrico quoted in Schwartz, *The Hollywood Writers' Wars*, 235.

40. Maltz's written statement and testimony are in *Motion Picture Industry: Hearings*, 1947, reprinted in Kahn, *Hollywood on Trial*, 87–91.

41. "Written Statement of John Howard Lawson," in Kahn, *Hollywood on Trial*, 72–73.

42. Kahn, *Hollywood on Trial*, 137–38.

43. Elia Kazan, *A Life* (New York: Alfred A. Knopf, 1998), 449.

CHAPTER 9

1. Harvey Klehr, John Earl Haynes, and Kyrill M. Anderson, *The Soviet World of American Communism* (New Haven, Conn.: Yale University Press, 1998). Chapter 2, "Moscow Gold," provides thorough details, summaries, interpretations, and actual documents that tell the story of this Soviet system of subsidies. See also Robert Conquest, "Revolutionary High Finance," in *The Dragons of Expectation: Reality and Delusion in the Course of History* (New York: W.W. Norton, 2005), 95–99.

2. Ruthenberg is quoted in Klehr, Haynes, and Anderson, *The Soviet World*, 111. Lovestone is quoted in Klehr, Haynes, and Anderson, *The Soviet World*, 137.

3. On the twenties figures, see Klehr, Haynes, and Anderson, *The Soviet World*, 107–37.

4. On the thirties, see Klehr, Haynes, and Anderson, *The Soviet World*, 142.

5. On Baker and the 1943 report, see Klehr, Haynes, and Anderson, *The Soviet World*, 147.

6. Klehr, Haynes, and Anderson, *The Soviet World*, 149–51, with documents on 152–64. Conquest, "Revolutionary High Finance," 97–98.

7. Klehr, Haynes, and Anderson, *The Soviet World*, 148 and 262.

8. On the Comintern conditions and Lenin, see Stanley Payne, *The Spanish Civil War, the Soviet Union, and Communism* (New Haven: Yale University Press, 2004), 3–6.

9. On the ultimatum, see Klehr, Haynes, and Anderson, *The Soviet World*, 16–17 and 19.

10. See John Earl Haynes and Harvey Klehr, *Venona: Decoding Soviet Espionage in America* (New Haven: Yale University Press, 1990), 9, and appendix B, 371–82.

11. See, for example, Christopher Andrew and Vasili Mitrokhin, *The Sword and the Shield: The Mitrokhin Archive and the Secret History of the KGB* (New York: Basic Books, 1999), 110–11; and on Hiss, 132–33. See also Allen Weinstein and Alexander Vassiliev, *The Haunted Wood: Soviet Espionage in America—the Stalin Era* (New York: Random House, 1999), passim. Also Jerrold Schecter and Leona Schecter, *Sacred Secrets: How Soviet Intelligence Operations Changed American History* (Washington, D.C.: Brassey's, 2002), 26 and 32–35. See documents in Harvey Klehr, John Earl Haynes, and Fridrikh Igorevich Firsov, *The Secret World of American Communism* (New Haven, Conn.: Yale University Press, 1995), 312–17.

12. On Soviet documents and the Silvermaster network, see Weinstein and Vassiliev, *The Haunted Wood*, 165–66; and Akhmerov on Silvermaster, 166. For KGB records, see John Earl Haynes and Harvey Klehr, *In Denial: Historians, Communism & Espionage* (San Francisco: Encounter Books, 2003), 214–15. On the Akhmerov networks, see also Andrew and Mitrokhin, *The Sword and the Shield*, 118.

13. On Glasser, see Weinstein and Vassiliev, *The Haunted Wood*, 170ff.

14. Andrew and Mitrokhin, *The Sword and the Shield*, 109. On Weisband, see Haynes and Klehr, *Venona*, 48–56. On Weisband and the memorandum, see Weinstein and Vassiliev, *The Haunted Wood*, 291–93.

15. Among the many thorough documentations of the espionage and influence of Hiss and White, with particular emphasis on Germany and the United Nations, Teheran and Yalta conferences, see Weinstein and Vassiliev, *The Haunted Wood*, 163–64; Herbert Romerstein and Eric Breindel, *The Venona Secrets: Exposing Soviet Espionage and America's Traitors* (Washington, D.C.: Regnery Publishing, 2000), 47–48, 136–37; Andrew and Mitrokhin, *The Sword and the Shield*, 111–12 and 133–34; Klehr, Haynes, and Anderson, *The Secret World*, 110–18; Haynes and Klehr, *Venona*, 138–50; Christopher Andrew and Oleg Gordievsky, *KGB: The Inside Story of Its Foreign Operations from Lenin to Gorbachev* (New York: HarperCollins, 1990), 335–40.

16. On Currie, see, for example, Weinstein and Vassiliev, *The Haunted Wood*, 161; Romerstein and Breindel, *The Venona Secrets*, 42–43, 167–70, 183–84.

17. Quoted in Schecter and Schecter, *Sacred Secrets*, 39 and 41.

18. On Operation Snow, see Jerrold and Leona Schecter, *Sacred Secrets*, 3–7, 22–32; Romerstein and Breindel, *The Venona Secrets*, 40–44; Karpov quotation on 43–44.

19. Howard Fast, *Being Red* (Boston: Houghton Mifflin, 1990), 178.

20. Ring Lardner Jr., *I'd Hate Myself in the Morning* (New York: Nation Books, 2000), 7.

21. Andrew and Mitrokhin, *The Sword and the Shield*, 107 and 592, n. 30.

22. Among many extensive discussions, see Romerstein and Breindel, *The Venona Secrets*, 231–41; Haynes and Klehr, *Venona*, 295–303, 307–11; Weinstein and Vassiliev, *The Haunted Wood*, 178, 197–210, 222, 327–34; Andrew and Mitrokhin, *The Sword and the Shield*, 128; Pavel Sudoplatov and Anatoli Sudoplatov, *Special Tasks* (Boston: Little, Brown and Company, 1994), 213–17.

23. Andrew and Mitrokhin, *The Sword and the Shield*, 218.

24. On Rosenberg data, see Haynes and Klehr, *In Denial*, 295–303. See also Weinstein and Vassiliev, *The Haunted Wood*, 205–6, 216. Semyonov is quoted in Weinstein and Vassiliev, *The Haunted Wood*, 178.

25. Data is from Schecter and Schecter, *Sacred Secrets*, 52; Haynes and Klehr, *In Denial*, 214–15.

26. Wexley quote is from an interview in Patrick McGilligan and Paul Buhle, *Tender Comrades: A Backstory of the Blacklist* (New York: St. Martin's Griffin, 1999), 717.

27. Ted Morgan, *Reds: McCarthyism in Twentieth Century America* (New York: Random House, 2003), 293.

28. Haynes and Klehr, *Venona*, 7. Andrew and Mitrokhin, *The Sword and the Shield*, 164 and 148.

29. On Bentley and Browder, see Andrew and Mitrokhin, *The Sword and the Shield*, 129; and for the memo, 131. See also the revealing letter to Beria himself, from Commisar of State Security Vsevelod Merkulov, in Schecter and Schecter, *Sacred Secrets*, 49–50.

30. Schecter and Schecter, *Sacred Secrets*, 21, 111 and 122, 104–5. On Nelson and Baker cable, see Haynes and Klehr, *Venona*, 229–32. See also Sudoplatov and Sudoplatov, *Special Tasks*, 187. For Fitin and Zubilin, see Sudoplatov and Sudoplatov, *Special Tasks*, 88.

31. Andrew and Mitrokhin, *The Sword and the Shield*, 108–9.

32. For the 1945 and 1946 memos, see Weinstein and Vassiliev, *The Haunted Wlood*, 302–3, 305–6. For extensive documents on Browder-Soviet connection, see Klehr, Haynes, and Firsov, *The Secret World*, 231–48.

33. Documents and discussion in Klehr, Haynes, and Firsov, *The Secret World*, 270–281.

34. The material on Baker and the Father-Son and Dimitrov Network is based on Klehr, Haynes, and Firsov, *The Secret World*, 83–96, 119–32, and 205–31; Haynes and Klehr, *Venona*, 67–73.

35. Klehr, Haynes, and Firsov, *The Secret World*, 90 (Browder's concern) and 88 (Baker's work).

36. Klehr, Haynes, and Firsov, *The Secret World*, 100. See also 100–104.

37. Klehr, Haynes, and Firsov, *The Secret World*, 212 (Cooper and George) and 209 (Dimitrov). Full discussion in Document 59, 208–12.

38. Andrew and Mitrokhin, *The Sword and the Shield*, 148–49.

39. Klehr, Haynes, and Firsov, *The Secret World*, 326.

40. Caute is quoted and discussed in Haynes and Klehr, *In Denial*, 77. From David Caute, *The Great Fear: The Anti-Communist Purge under Truman and Eisenhower* (New York: Simon & Schuster, 1977), 21.

41. Ellen Schrecker, *Many Are the Crimes: McCarthyism in America* (Boston: Little, Brown, 1998), 166.

42. William Phillips, "What Happened in the Fifties," *Partisan Review*, no. 10 (1976): 338. Quoted in Hilton Kramer, "The Blacklist and the Cold-War Revisited," *New York Times*, October 3, 1976, Arts and Leisure section, 1. See also *New Criterion*, November 1997, 11–16.

CHAPTER 10

1. Reprinted in Dwight McDonald, *Memoirs of a Revolutionist* (New York: Farrar, Straus and Cudahy, 1957), 113.

2. McDonald, *Memoirs of a Revolutionist*, 115.

3. On the Dimitrov-Stalin meeting and consequences, see Francoise Furet, *The Passing of an Illusion: The Idea of Communism in the Twentieth Century* (Chicago: University of Chicago Press, 1999), 321ff. See also Guenter Lewy, *The Cause That Failed: Communism in American Political Life* (New York: Oxford University Press, 1990), 61ff; and Richard Gid Powers, *Not Without Honor: The History of American Anticommunism* (New York: Free Press, 1995), 159. On Dimitrov's comments to Browder, see Harvey Klehr, John Earl Haynes, and Kyrill Anderson, *The Soviet World of American Communism* (New Haven, Conn.: Yale University Press, 1998), 71–80; and Dimitrov document on 81–83.

4. On the Ross document, see Klehr, Haynes, and Anderson, *The Soviet World*, 83–84; and for Minor's speech, 77–78.

5. Klehr, Haynes, and Anderson, *The Soviet World*, 84–85 and 88–91. Quote from *Daily Worker*, September 19, 1939, 73. See also *Sunday Worker* of November 5, 1939.

6. On the pact and its consequences, see Anne Applebaum, *Gulag: A History* (New York: Doubleday, 2003), 423; Simon Sebag Montefiore, *Stalin: The Court of the*

Red Tsar (New York: Alfred A. Knopf, 2004), 306–15, 334, 705. See also Stéphane Courtois et al., *The Black Book of Communism: Crimes, Terror, Repression* (Cambridge, Mass.: Harvard University Press, 1999), 208–13; and John Earl Haynes and Harvey Klehr, *In Denial: Historians, Communism & Espionage* (San Francisco: Encounter Books, 2003), 253.

7. Jarrico is quoted in Patrick McGilligan and Paul Buhle, *Tender Comrades: A Backstory of the Blacklist* (New York: St. Martin's Griffin, 1999), 335.

8. Stander is quoted in McGilligan and Buhle, *Tender Comrades*, 617

9. Boretz is quoted in McGilligan and Buhle, *Tender Comrades*, 120.

10. Lardner quote is from Ring Lardner Jr., *I'd Hate Myself in the Morning* (New York: Nation Books, 2000), 101.

11. Howard Fast, *Being Red* (Boston: Houghton Mifflin, 1990), 219.

12. On Pat survey, see Courtois, *The Black Book*, 319.

13. Powers, *Not Without Honor*, 159.

14. Quoted in Carl Rollyson, *Lillian Hellman: Her Legend and Her Legacy* (New York: St. Martin's Press, 1986), 153.

15. See, for example, Larry Ceplair and Steven Englund, *The Inquistion in Hollywood: Politics in the Film Community, 1930–1960* (Berkeley: University of California Press, 1983), 174; and Lewy, *The Cause That Failed*, 179–80. Dimitrov quoted in Klehr, Haynes, and Anderson, *The Soviet World*, 85–86 and 87.

16. On the earlier league, see Rollyson, *Lillian Hellman*, 146. On the new call, see Rollyson, *Lillian Hellman*, 184. See also Joan Mellen, *Hellman and Hammett: The Legendary Passion of Lillian Hellman and Dashiell Hammett* (New York: HarperCollins, 1996), 169.

17. Klehr, Haynes, and Anderson, *The Soviet World*, 273.

18. Harvey Klehr, John Earl Haynes, and Fridrikh Igorevich Firsov, *The Secret World of American Communism* (New Haven, Conn.: Yale University Press, 1995), 128–32.

19. Klehr, Haynes, and Anderson, *The Soviet World*, 94–97.

20. Klehr, Haynes, and Anderson, *The Soviet World*, 297–301.

21. Klehr, Haynes, and Anderson, *The Soviet World*, 307–17.

22. Letters discussed and quoted in Robert K. Landers, *An Honest Writer: The Life and Times of James T. Farrell* (San Francisco: Encounter Books, 2004), 198; and Lewy, *The Cause That Failed*, 50. See also Ted Morgan, *Reds: McCarthyism in Twentieth Century America* (New York: Random House, 2003), 171. For New York background, see Lionel Abel, *The Intellectual Follies* (New York: W.W. Norton, 1984), 360.

23. For quote on NKVD, see Courtois, *The Black Book*, 190–91. See also Courtois, *The Black* Book, ch. 10, on the Great Terror; ch. 7, on collectivization; and pp. 9–10 for a summary. Stalin is quoted in Montefiore, *Stalin*, 185.

24. For the broader picture of oppression, see Dimitri Volkogonov, *Trotsky: The Eternal Revolutionary* (New York: Free Press, 1996), 405, and for single day, 462.

25. On the fate of writers and clergy, see Courtois, *The Black Book*, 200. See also Montefiore, *Stalin*, 84–85, 90.

26. See summaries in Martin Amis, *Koba and the Dread: Laughter and the Twenty Million* (New York: Hyperion, 2002), 14, 127–29, 147. See summary of statistics in Robert Conquest, *Harvest of Sorrow: Soviet Collectivization and the Terror-Famine* (New York: Oxford University Press, 1986), ch. 16, "The Death Roll."

27. Montefiore, *Stalin*, 46.

28. See Applebaum, *Gulag*, especially summary in "Appendix: How Many?" Also Robert Conquest, *The Great Terror: A Reassessment* (New York: Oxford University Press, 1940), ch. 11, "The Labor Camps;" Courtois, *The Black Book*, ch. 11, "The Empire of the Camps," summary 206–7.

29. Courtois, *The Black Book*, 221–30, 321–23; see ch. 19 on actions in Poland alone. Applebaum, *Gulag*, 411–38. On Gulag, also see Amy Knight, *Beria: Stalin's First Lieutenant* (Princeton, N.J.: Princeton University Press, 1983), 118–19; Montefiore, *Stalin*, 313, 371–79, 394–95, 441, 472–73; Robert Conquest, *The Dragons of Expectation: Reality and Delusion in the Course of History* (New York: W.W. Norton, 2005), 125–29.

30. Lawson is quoted in Otto Friedrich, *City of Nets: A Portrait of Hollywood in the 1940s* (New York: Harper & Row, 1986), 254. Open letter is quoted in Sidney Hook, *Out of Step: An Unquiet Life in the 20th Century* (New York: Harper & Row, 1987), 268; for full discussion of the letter, 264–70. Lardner is quoted in Nancy Lynn Schwartz, The *Hollywood Writers' Wars* (New York: McGraw-Hill, 1983), 39, from Ring Lardner Jr., *The Lardners: My Family Remembered* (New York: Harper & Row, 1976). Polonsky is quoted in Brian Neve, *Film and Politics in America: A Social Tradition* (New York: Routledge, 1992), 203. Rapf is quoted in McGilligan and Buhle, *Tender Comrades*, 539. Robeson quote is from "Testimony of Paul Robeson," in *Motion Picture Industry: Hearings*, 1956, reprinted in Eric Bentley, *Thirty Years of Treason* (New York: Viking Press, 1973), 787.

31. Lardner quote from Lardner, *The Lardners*, 45–46. Seeger is quoted in Ronald Radosh, *Commies: A Journey through the Old Left, the New Left, and the Leftover Left* (San Francisco: Encounter Books, 2001), 37. Hellman quote is from Lillian Hellman, *Scoundrel Time* (Boston: Little, Brown, 1976), 46. Boretz is quoted in McGilligan and Buhle, *Tender Comrades*, 119. Weinstein is quoted in Arnold Beichman, "Out of Gas," *Claremont Review of Books*, Winter 2003, 18.

32. Dassin is quoted in McGilligan and Buhle, *Tender Comrades*, 209. Lardner quote is from Lardner, *The Lardners*, 256. Trumbo quote is from Dalton Trumbo, "The Devil in the Book," in *The Time of the Toad: A Study of Inquisition in America* (New York: Perennial Library, Harper & Row, 1972), 74; first published by the California Emergency Defense Committee, 1956.

33. Conquest, *The Great Terror*, 464.

34. On the Cominform and Zhdanov, see Furet, *The Passing of an Illusion*, 402. Browder is quoted in Klehr, Haynes, and Anderson, *The Soviet World*, 99; see thorough discussion, 95–100, and documents, 101–6.

35. See Klehr, Haynes, and Anderson, *The Soviet World*, 97–98; Lewy, *The Cause That Failed*, 74–75; Foret, *The Passing of an Illusion*, 425; Joseph R. Starobin, *American Communism in Crisis, 1943–1957* (Berkeley: University of California Press, 1975), 103–6.

36. Bright is quoted in McGilligan and Buhle, *Tender Comrades*, 151. Wilson and Lardner are quoted in Ceplair and Englund, *The Inquistion in Hollywood*, 21.

37. "Testimony of Robert Rossen," in *New York City: Hearings*, 1953, 1489.

38. On the first call, see *Daily Worker*, January 10, 1949; quoted in "Testimony of Jose Ferrer," in *Motion Picture Industry: Hearings*, 1951, reprinted in Bentley, *Thirty Years of Treason*, 428. On the second call, see *Daily Worker*, March 8, 1949, 13,

quoted in Bentley, *Thirty Years of Treason*, 662. On the conference and sponsors and attendees, see U.S. Congress House Un-American Activities Committee (HUAC in future citations), *Report on the Communist Peace Offensive*, April 1, 1951, 166. The call and lists are also in *New York Times*, March 24, 1949; David Caute, *Joseph Losey: A Revenge on Life* (New York: Oxford University Press), 102.

39. For Cominform, see Hook, *Out of Step*, 385–86; and Landers, *An Honest Writer*, 306–9.

40. Powers, *Not Without Honor*, 207.

41. For details of Soviet campaign, see HUAC, *Report on the Communist Peace Offensive*, April 1951. See also Lewy, *The Cause That Failed*, 181–83; Hook, *Out of Step*, 382–87. Fast quote is from Fast, *Being Red*, 200.

42. On the HUAC report, see Bentley, *Thirty Years of Treason*, 429–30. See also HUAC, *Report on the Communist Peace Offensive*. The quote by Rahv is from *Partisan Review*, March 1949. On conference and Hook committee, see Lewy, *The Cause That Failed*, 108–14; see also Hook, *Out of Step*, 382–96, quote on 384. See also William Barrett, "Culture Conference at the Waldorf," *Commentary*, May 1949.

43. On Cousins and Hellman, see William Wright, *Lillian Hellman: The Image, the Woman* (New York: Simon & Schuster, 1986), 228; on conference, 225–29.

44. Nathan Glazer, *Commentary*, June 1976, quoted in Wright, *Lillian Hellman*, 359.

45. For quotes from Copland's speech, see Terry Teachout, "Composers for Communism," *Commentary*, May 2004, 61.

46. On Shostakovich, see Teachout, "Composers for Communism," 59–60 and 62.

47. Suslov is quoted in HUAC, *Report on the Communist Peace Offensive*, 6.

48. HUAC, *Report on the Communist Peace Offensive*, 34–41; quote, 41. See also Lewy, *The Cause That Failed*, 183–85. On Seeger, see Radosh, *Commies*, 35.

49. On the signers, see HUAC, *Report on the Communist Peace Offensive*, 34.

50. HUAC, *Report on the Communist Peace Offensive*, 70ff. On Uphaus, see Lewy, *The Cause That Failed*, 184–85. For quote from Uphaus' speech, see Bentley, *Thirty Years of Treason*, 756.

51. Czeslaw Milosz, "A Letter to Picasso," in *Voices of Dissent: A Collection of Articles from Dissent Magazine* (New York: Grove Press, 1958), 381–84; quote on 384.

52. See Courtois, *The Black Book*, 230–38; 379–82; ch. 20, especially 395–99, 405, 415–20, 439–42. Montefiore, *Stalin*, 472–73, 569, 597–601, 611, 617. George Hodos, *Show Trials: Stalinist Purges in Eastern Europe, 1948–1954* (New York: Praeger, 1987), passim. Applebaum, *Gulag*, 454–67. See also Christopher Andrew and Vasili Mitrokhin, *The Sword and the Shield: The Mitrokhin Archive and the Secret History of the KGB* (New York: Basic Books, 1999), ch. 16, "Spying on the Soviet Bloc."

53. "Testimony of Michael Wilson," in *Motion Picture Industry: Hearings*, September 20, 1951, 1677–78.

54. On Trumbo, see discussion of his disputes in Ronald Radosh and Allis Radosh, *Red Star over Hollywood: The Film Colony's Long Romance with the Left* (San Francisco: Encounter Books, 2005), 207ff, based on files in "Dalton Trumbo Papers." Quote used in the play *Trumbo*, quoted in *New Criterion*, October 2003, 45.

55. Wilson quoted in Ceplair and Englund, *The Inquisition in Hollywood*, 421.

56. Robeson quoted in "Testimony of Paul Robeson," reprinted in Bentley, *Thirty Years of Treason*, 787.

57. Hellman quoted in Hook, *Out of Step*, 389.

CHAPTER 11

1. "Testimony of Adrian Scott," in *Motion Picture Industry: Hearings*, October 29, 1947, reprinted in Gordon Kahn, *Hollywood on Trial: The Story of the Ten Who Were Indicted* (New York: Boni and Gaer, 1948), 106 and 108.

2. "Testimony of Edward Dmytryk," in *Motion Picture Industry: Hearings*, October 29, 1947, reprinted in Kahn, *Hollywood on Trial*, 111.

3. "Written Statement of Samuel Ornitz," in *Motion Picture Industry: Hearings*, October 28, 1947, reprinted in Kahn, *Hollywood on Trial*, 98–99.

4. On the Soviet suppression of Jews, see, for example, Robert Conquest, *The Great Terror: A Reassessment* (New York: Oxford University Press, 1940), 337, 401–2; Robert C. Tucker, *Stalin in Power* (New York: W.W. Norton, 1990), 490–91; Stéphane Courtois et al., *The Black Book of Communism: Crimes, Terror, Repression* (Cambridge, Mass.: Harvard University Press, 1999), 302–4, 317–18. On Khrushchev, see Simon Sebag Montefiore, *Stalin: The Court of the Red Tsar* (New York: Alfred A. Knopf, 2004), 545–57; and Pavel Sudoplatov and Anatoli Sudoplatov, *Special Tasks* (Boston: Little, Brown, 1994), 294; see also Amy Knight, *Beria: Stalin's First Lieutenant* (Princeton, N.J.: Princeton University Press, 1983), 173–74.

5. Montefiore, *Stalin*, 546.

6. For Stalin's comment to Khrushchev, see Montefiore, *Stalin*, 546–47. On Khrushchev's comment, see Montefiore, *Stalin*, 609–10. On Zhdanov's new cultural terror, see Montefiore, *Stalin*, 542–44, 559–61. On Abakunov and the others, see Montefiore, *Stalin*, 587–88 and 561. See also Conquest, *The Great Terror*, 462–63; and Knight, *Beria*, 146–50. For discussion of these and all aspects of the Jewish purges, see also Christopher Andrew and Oleg Gordievsky, *KGB: The Inside Story of Its Foreign Operations from Lenin to Gorbachev* (New York: HarperCollins, 1990), 416–21; and Sudoplatov and Sudoplatov, *Special Tasks*, ch. 10, "The Jews: California in the Crimea."

7. See Sudoplatov and Sudoplatov, *Special Tasks*, 296–97; Montefiore, *Stalin*, 573–75.

8. See Courtois, *The Black Book*, 242–49; and on *Pravda* question, 242. On Lubianka and Komarov's comment, see Montefiore, *Stalin*, 588.

9. On the committee, see Courtois, *The Black Book*, 248.

10. On the Doctors' Plot, see Knight, *Beria*, 169–75; Sudoplatov and Sudoplatov, *Special Tasks*, 298–309; Courtois, *The Black Book*, 247–48; Montefiore, *Stalin*, 612–23. On Zhdanov's death, see Montefiore, *Stalin*, 597.

11. For the *Pravda* article, see Andrew and Gordievsky, *KGB*, 418. On evictions and camps, see Montefiore, *Stalin*, 634–35.

12. See Courtois, *The Black Book*, ch. 20, "Central and Eastern Europe," and on the Slansky trial, 248. See also Andrew and Gordievsky, *KGB*, 415–21.

13. Yossi Klein Halevi, *Azure*, no. 17 (2004): 28.

14. Trumbo quote is from Dalton Trumbo, *The Time of the Toad: A Study of Inquisition in America* (New York: Perennial Library, Harper & Row, 1972), 8–9.

15. Halevi, *Azure*, 33.

16. "Written Statement of Dalton Trumbo," in *Motion Picture Industry: Hearings*, 1947, reprinted in Kahn, *Hollywood on Trial*, 84.

17. "Testimony of Ring Lardner Jr.," in *Motion Picture Industry: Hearings*, October 30, 1947, reprinted in Bentley, *Thirty Years of Treason*, 187.

18. "Testimony of Herbert Biberman," in *Motion Picture Industry: Hearings*, reprinted in Kahn, *Hollywood on Trial*, 102.

19. "Written Statement of Edward Dmytryk," in *Motion Picture Industry: Hearings*, October 29, 1947, reprinted in Kahn, *Hollywood on Trial*, 111.

20. "Written Statement of John Howard Lawson," in *Motion Picture Industry: Hearings*, October 27, 1947, reprinted in Kahn, *Hollywood on Trial*, 74.

21. "Written Statement of Albert Maltz," in *Motion Picture Industry: Hearings*, October 28, 1947, reprinted in Kahn, *Hollywood on Trial*, 90.

22. "Testimony of Robert Rossen," in *New York City: Hearings*, May 7, 1953, 1487–88.

23. Elia Kazan, *A Life* (New York: Alfred A. Knopf, 1998), 127–33, and 457. See also "Testimony of Elia Kazan," in *Motion Picture Industry: Hearings*, April 10, 1952, reprinted in Eric Bentley, *Thirty Years of Treason* (New York: Viking Press, 1973), 484–95.

24. "Testimony of Clifford Odets," in *Motion Picture Industry: Hearings*, 1952, reprinted in Bentley, *Thirty Years of Treason*, 514–17. For the party reversal on Odets' plays, see Bentley, *Thirty Years of Treason*, 514–22.

25. Buchwald quoted in Bentley, *Thirty Years of Treason*, 518.

26. Lawson quoted in Bentley, *Thirty Years of Treason*, 518–19.

27. Gerlando is quoted in Bentley, *Thirty Years of Treason*, 521, and Burnshaw on 518.

28. "Testimony of Michael Blankfort," in *Motion Picture Industry: Hearings*, January 28, 1952, reprinted in Bentley, *Thirty Years of Treason*, 464–66.

29. "Testimony of Budd Schulberg," in *Motion Picture Industry: Hearings*, 1951, reprinted in Bentley, *Thirty Years of Treason*, 438–42; see also Robert Vaughn, *Only Victims: A Study in Show Business Blacklisting* (New York: G. P. Putnam and Sons, 1972), 150–52.

30. Nancy Lynn Schwartz, *Hollywood Writers' Wars* (New York: McGraw-Hill Company, 1983), 168.

31. Bentley, *Thirty Years of Treason*, 445.

32. Glenn quoted in Bentley, *Thirty Years of Treason*, 442–45.

33. For Bessie, see Joan Mellen, *Hellman and Hammett: The Legendary Passion of Lillian Hellman and Dashiell Hammett* (New York: HarperCollins, 1996), 173, and for *New Masses* article, 185. For Maltz 1946 article, see William Wright, *Lillian Hellman: The Image, the Woman* (New York: Simon & Schuster, 1986), 209–10.

34. "Testimony of Edward Dymtryk," 416–18, reprinted in Bentley, *Thirty Years of Treason*, 384–86. See also Roy Brewer article, reprinted in Bentley, *Thirty Years of Treason*, 201. Discussed in detail in Edward Dmytryk, *Odd Man Out: A Memoir of the*

Hollywood Ten (Carbondale: Southern Illinois University Press, 1956), 20–23; and Edward Dmytryk, *It's a Helluva Life but Not a Bad Living* (New York: Times Books, 1978), 71–73.

35. "Testimony of Edward Dymtryk," reprinted in Bentley, *Thirty Years of Treason*, 387.

36. For the *Daily Worker* editorial, see Guenter Lewy, *The Cause That Failed: Communism in American Political Life* (New York: Oxford University Press, 1990), 72.

37. Lewy, *The Cause That Failed*, 72–73.

38. For Robeson quote, see "Testimony of Arthur Miller," *Motion Picture Industry: Hearings*, June 21, 1952, reprinted in Bentley, *Thirty Years of Treason*, 810. Robeson's quote was introduced by the HUAC during testimony of Miller.

39. See Robert K. Landers, *An Honest Writer: The Life and Times of James T. Farrell* (San Francisco: Encounter Books, 2004), 191–95; Lewy, *The Cause That Failed*, 49–50; Richard Gid Powers, *Not Without Honor: The History of American Anticommunism* (New York: Free Press, 1995), 142–45.

40. For a succinct summary, see Dimitri Volkogonov, *Trotsky: The Eternal Revolutionary* (New York: Free Press, 1996), 402, 457ff.

41. "Testimony of Dalton Trumbo," in *Motion Picture Industry: Hearings*, 1947, reprinted in Helen Manfull, ed., *Additional Dialogue: Letters of Dalton Trumbo, 1942–1962* (New York: Bantam Books, 1972), 32–41. See also Kahn, *Hollywood on Trial*, 81; Morgan, *Reds*, 519; Bruce Cook, *Dalton Trumbo* (New York: Charles Scribner's Sons, 1977), 181.

42. Interview in Patrick McGilligan and Paul Buhle, *Tender Comrades: A Backstory of the Blacklist* (New York: St. Martin's Griffin, 1999), 479.

43. On Orders 246 and 270, see Montefiore, *Stalin*, 379. For statistics from during the war, see Courtois, *The Black Book*, 230.

44. For statistics at the war's end, see Courtois, *The Black Book*, 320. On Beria and during the war, see Montefiore, *Stalin*, 473. For the postwar report, see Courtois, *The Black Book*, 231. On the Gulag, see Anne Applebaum, *Gulag: A History* (New York: Doubleday, 2003), 463.

45. For further discussions, see also Applebaum, *Gulag*, 128, 436–37, 421–23, 428, 432; Francois Furet, *The Passing of an Illusion: The Idea of Communism in the Twentieth Century* (Chicago: University of Chicago Press, 1999), 372–74; Knight, *Beria*, 126–28; Courtois, *The Black Book*, ch. 11, "The Other Side of Victory."

46. On Khrushchev, see Montefiore, *Stalin*, 600; and William Taubman, *Khrushchev: The Man and His Era* (New York: W.W. Norton, 2003), 195–99. See also Courtois, *The Black Book*, 237. On the decrees, see Courtois, *The Black Book*, 234–35.

47. Courtois, *The Black Book*, 235, 238. Applebaum, *Gulag*, 463–67, quote on 466. Furet, *The Passing of an Illusion*, 408–9. See also Sudoplatov and Sudoplatov, *Special Tasks*, ch. 11, "Final Years under Stalin."

48. Courtois, *The Black Book*, 235–38, 417–35. See George Hodos, *Show Trials: Stalinist Purges in Eastern Europe, 1948–1954* (New York: Praeger, 1987), passim.

49. Applebaum, *Gulag*, 454–55; Courtois, *The Black Book*, 417.

50. Quoted in Morgan, *Reds*, 521. See in Murray Kempton, *Part of Our Time: Some Monuments and Ruins of the Thirties* (New York: Simon & Schuster, 1955). See letter to Kempton in Manfull, *Additional Dialogue*, 409–13.

CHAPTER 12

1. Larry Ceplair and Steven Englund, *The Inquisition in Hollywood: Politics in the Film Community, 1930–1960* (Berkeley: University of California Press, 1983), 345.

2. Ceplair and Englund, *The Inquisition in Hollywood*, 288–89; Nancy Lynn Schwartz, *Hollywood Writers' Wars* (New York: McGraw-Hill, 1983), 260; Otto Friedrich, *City of Nets: A Portrait of Hollywood in the 1940s* (New York: Harper & Row, 1986), 306–7, 320–21. See also David Caute, *Joseph Losey: A Revenge on Life* (New York: Oxford University Press, 1994), 101. See Lawrence Grobel, *The Hustons* (New York: Charles Scribner's Sons, 1989), 300–305; and Philip Dunne's memoir, *Take Two: A Life in the Movies and Politics* (New York: McGraw-Hill, 1990).

3. Ceplair and Englund, *The Inquisition in Hollywood*, 344–45.

4. Ceplair and Englund, *The Inquisition in Hollywood*, 354.

5. For Trumbo, see Helen Manfull, ed., *Additional Dialogue: Letters of Dalton Trumbo, 1942–1962* (New York: Bantam Books, 1972), 115–16. On Cole, see Lester Cole, *Hollywood Red* (Palo Alto, Calif.: Ramparts Press, 1981), 303–8; quote on 307.

6. Trumbo is quoted in Ronald Radosh and Allis Radosh, *Red Star over Hollywood: The Film Colony's Long Romance with the Left* (San Francisco: Encounter Books, 2005), 22; from "Secrecy and the Communist Party," an unpublished document in the Dalton Trumbo Papers.

7. Ceplair and Englund, The *Inquisition in Hollywood*, 339–40.

8. On Sondegaard and 1951 policy, see Ceplair and Englund, *The Inquisition in Hollywood*, 367–68; Walter Goodman, *The Committee* (New York: Farrar, Straus & Giroux, 1968), 300.

9. David E. Prindle, *The Politics of Glamour Ideology and Democracy in the Screen Actors Guild* (Madison: University of Wisconsin Press, 1988), 59 and 60; Friedrich, *City of Nets*, 379.

10. On the SWG, see Ceplair and Englund, *The Inquisition in Hollywood*, 369–70.

11. On the SDG, see Grobel, *The Hustons*, 361–62. Ford is quoted in Tag Gallagher, *John Ford: The Man and His Films* (Berkeley: University of California Press, 1986), 340–41. See also Ceplair and Englund, *The Inquisition in Hollywood*, 368–69.

12. Richard Gid Powers, *Not Without Honor: The History of American Anticommunism* (New York: Free Press, 1995), 219–22. For the announcement, see Ceplair and Englund, *The Inquisition in Hollywood*, 370. On the criticisms, see Powers, *Not Without Honor*, 249. On the Council of Motion Picture Organizations, see Friedrich, *City of Nets*, 379; Goodman, *The Committee*, 300–301. Reagan article is reprinted in Eric Bentley, *Thirty Years of Treason* (New York: Viking Press, 1973), 294.

13. Ceplair and Englund, *The Inquisition in Hollywood*, 345–54; Bruce Cook, *Dalton Trumbo* (New York: Charles Scribner's Sons, 1977), 208–13.

14. On the PCA, see Guenter Lewy, *The Cause That Failed: Communism in American Political Life* (New York: Oxford University Press, 1990), 202–3; Powers, *Not Without Honor*, 200. On Wallace, see Schwartz, *The Hollywood Writers' Wars*, 205–6; Friedrich, *City of Nets*, 168.

15. Wallace is quoted in Ted Morgan, *Reds: McCarthysim in Twentieth Century America* (New York: Random House, 2003), 307. See also Ronald Brownstein, *The Power and the Glitter: The Washington-Hollywood Connection* (New York: Pantheon Books, 1990), 109.

16. On Childs, see Harvey Klehr, John Earl Haynes, and Kyrill Anderson, *The Soviet World of American Communism* (New Haven, Conn.: Yale University Press, 1998), 258–60, 261–62; documents reprinted on 265–71. On the CPUSA, see Joseph R. Starobin, *American Communism in Crisis, 1943–1957* (Berkeley: University of California Press, 1975), 174–77; Lewy, *The Cause That Failed*, 204.

17. McDonald quote is from Dwight McDonald, *Memoirs of a Revolutionist* (New York: Farrar, Straus and Cudahy, 1957), 308.

18. On the Hollywood committee and Dunne's quote, see Grobel, *The Hustons*, 302. On the Wallace campaign, see Morgan, *Reds*, 308–9.

19. Morgan, *Reds*, 309. Murray is quoted in Starobin, *American Communism in Crisis*, 174. See also Lewy, *The Cause That Failed*, 206–8. Wallace is quoted in Lewy, *The Cause That Failed*, 214 and 207.

20. On Hellman's editorial, see William Wright, *Lillian Hellman: The Image, the Woman* (New York: Simon & Schuster, 1986), 212–17.

21. For Hellman on Wallace, see Lillian Hellman, *Scoundrel Time* (Boston: Little, Brown, 1976), 40, 126–32, 154. For "dividend check" statement, see Joan Mellen, *Hellman and Hammett: The Legendary Passion of Lillian Hellman and Dashiell Hammett* (New York: HarperCollins, 1996), 259. This comment was a regular feature of Hellman speeches at "Women for Wallace" luncheons in 1948.

22. For Hellman quote on "sins of Stalin Communism," see Hellman, *Scoundrel Time*, 128. On the counterattack, see Wright, *Lillian Hellman*, 358–62. Howe quote is from *Dissent*, Fall 1976, Nathan Glazer, *Commentary*, June 1976; Sidney Hook, *Encounter*, February 1977; Hilton Kramer, *New York Times*, October 3, 1976; Alfred Kazin, *Esquire*, August 1977; and see Hilton Kramer, *New Criterion*, November 1997.

23. First quote by Maltz is in Albert Maltz, "The Anti-American Conspiracy," in *The Citizen Writer* (New York: International Publishers, 1950), 39–40. Second quote is in Maltz, "Books Are on Trial in America," in *The Citizen Writer*, 47.

24. Albert Maltz, "The Verdict of History," in *The Citizen Writer*, 33–34.

25. Lewy, *The Cause That Failed*, 184–85. "Testimony of Willard Uphaus," in *Motion Picture Industry: Hearings*, May 23, 1956, reprinted in Bentley, *Thirty Years of Treason*, 748 and 756 and subsequent testimony, 756–65.

26. For Uphaus quotes, see "Testimony of Willard Uphaus," reprinted in Bentley, *Thirty Years of Treason*, 748, 756, 758. On Needham, see Simon Winchester, *The Fantastic Story of the Eccentric Scientist Who Unlocked the Mysteries of the Middle Kingdom* (New York: HarperCollins, 2008).

27. On the council, see Ceplair and Englund, *The Inquisition in Hollywood*, 408. Maltz quoted in Edward Dmytryk, *Odd Man Out: A Memoir of the Hollywood Ten* (Carbondale: Southern Illinois University Press, 1956), 124.

28. Wilson is quoted in Ceplair and Englund, *The Inquisition in Hollywood*, 414.

29. Howard Fast, *Being Red* (Boston: Houghton Mifflin, 1990), 202, 263–64, 279.

CHAPTER 13

1. See Eric Bentley, *Thirty Years of Treason* (New York: Viking Press, 1973), 693 and 842. For Hammett, see Joan Mellen, *Hellman and Hammett: The Legendary*

Passion of Lillian Hellman and Dashiell Hammett (New York: HarperCollins, 1996), 281–85.

2. The quote on Moscow is found in Allen Weinstein and Alexander Vassiliev, *The Haunted Wood: Soviet Espionage in America—the Stalin Era* (New York: Random House, 1999), 287.

3. On Panyushkin, see Weintstein and Vassiliev, *The Haunted Wood*, 290 and 296; on Moscow, 293–94.

4. Savchenko is quoted in Weinstein and Vassiliev, *The Haunted Wood*, 297–98.

5. Panyushkin is quoted in Ted Morgan, *Reds: McCarthyism in Twentieth Century America* (New York: Random House, 2003), 375.

6. On the pamphlet, see Dorothy Healey, *Dorothy Healey Remembers* (New York: Oxford University Press, 1990), 118. On the Margolis brief, see Healey, *Dorothy Healey Remembers*, 145–46.

7. Dalton Trumbo, *The Time of the Toad: A Study of Inquisition in America* (New York: Perennial Library, Harper & Row, 1972), 76–77, 116.

8. Larry Ceplair and Steven Englund, *The Inquisition in Hollywood: Politics in the Film Community, 1930–1960* (Berkeley: University of California Press, 1983), 409. Ronald Radosh, *Commies: A Journey through the Old Left, the New Left, and the Leftover Left* (San Francisco: Encounter Books, 2001), 47–48.

9. Farrell is quoted in Robert K. Landers, *An Honest Writer: The Life and Times of James T. Farrell* (San Francisco: Encounter Books, 2004), 335.

10. On the *Daily Worker* articles, see Ronald Radosh and Joyce Milton, *The Rosenberg File: The Search for the Truth* (New York: Holt, Rinehart and Winston, 1983), 323.

11. On Belfrage, see John Earl Haynes and Harvey Klehr, *Venona: Decoding Soviet Espionage in America* (New Haven, Conn.: Yale University Press, 1990), 109–11; Morgan, *Reds*, 445–46. For the editorial, see Radosh and Milton, *The Rosenberg File*, 324.

12. On the Reuben series, see Radosh and Milton, *The Rosenberg File*, 324–25. On Wexley, see Ceplair and Englund, *The Inquisition in Hollywood*, 416. On the PBS program, see Richard Gid Powers, *Not Without Honor: The History of American Anti-communism* (New York: Free Press, 1995), 352.

13. Weinstein and Vassiliev, *The Haunted Wood*, 333.

14. Gates is quoted in Radosh and Milton, *The Roseberg File*, 328. For the pamphlet, see Herbert Romerstein and Eric Reindel, *The Venona Secrets: Exposing Soviet Espionage and America's Traitors* (Washington D.C.: Regnery Publishing, 2000), 249. See their whole discussion, 247–52. Ross is quoted in Radosh and Milton, *The Rosenberg File*, 329. See their full discussion in ch. 23, "The Propaganda War: The Defense Committee," 347ff.

15. Romerstein and Breindel, *The Venona Secrets*, 251; Radosh and Milton, *The Rosenberg File*, 348–51. Fast is quoted in Radosh and Milton, *The Rosenberg File*, 350. On the victims, see Jerrold Schecter and Leona Schecter, *Sacred Secrets: How Soviet Intelligence Operations Changed American History* (Washington, D.C.: Brassey's, 2002), 180.

16. See Schecter and Schecter, *Sacred Secrets*, 179–80; Radosh and Milton, *The Rosenberg File*, 348–51. Duclos is quoted in Romerstein and Breindel, *The Venona Secrets*, 251. On Aptheker, see Radosh and Milton, *The Rosenberg File*, 349–50.

17. Quoted in Ronald Radosh and Allis Radosh, *Red Star over Hollywood: The Film Colony's Long Romance with the Left* (San Francisco: Encounter Books, 2005), 224.

18. Mikoyan quoted in Simon Sebag Montefiore, *Stalin: The Court of the Red Tsar* (New York: Alfred A. Knopf, 2004), 635; full discussion, 559–87, 610–33. See also Stéphane Courtois et al., *The Black Book of Communism: Crimes, Terror, Repression* (Cambridge, Mass.: Harvard University Press, 1999), 247–49, 434–46; Christopher Andrew and Oleg Gordievesky, *KGB: The Inside Story of Its Foreign Operations from Lenin to Gorbachev* (New York: HarperCollins, 1990), 413–21; Robert Conquest, *The Dragons of Expectation: Reality and Delusion in the Course of History* (New York: W.W. Norton, 2005),139.

19. Schecter and Schecter, *Sacred Secrets*, 180. Editorial, *Daily Worker*, June 23, 1953; and see Radosh and Milton, *The Rosenberg File*, 420–21.

20. Walter Bernstein, *Inside Out: A Memoir of the Blacklist* (New York: Da Capo Press, 1966), 228–29.

21. Lester Cole, *Hollywood Red* (Palo Alto, Calif.: Ramparts Press, 1981), 349.

22. Howard Fast, *Being Red* (Boston: Houghton Mifflin, 1990), 283, 278.

23. Navasky quoted in Radosh, *Commies*, 162.

24. See, for example, Haynes and Klehr, *In Denial*, 142, 150. See also useful review and context in Neil Rosenthal's essay on Navasky's memoir *A Matter of Opinion*: Neil Rosenthal, "State of the 'Nation,'" *Commentary*, September 2005, 81–84.

25. In addition to Allen Weinstein, *Perjury: The Hiss-Chambers Case* (New York: Alfred A. Knopf, 1978), and extensive treatment throughout Weinstein and Vassiliev, *The Haunted Wood*, valuable discussions include Haynes and Klehr, *Venona*, 167–73, with the March 30 cable on 171–72; Romerstein and Breindel, *The Venona Secrets*, passim; interesting background on the initial case in Powers, *Not Without Honor*, 221–25.

26. Weinstein, *Perjury*, 456.

27. Guenter Lewy, *The Cause That Failed: Communism in American Political Life* (New York: Oxford University Press, 1990), 121.

28. Fast, *Being Red*, 318. Cole, *Hollywood Red*, 346.

29. Cole, *Hollywood Red*, 351.

30. Lillian Hellman, *Scoundrel Time* (Boston: Little, Brown, 1976), 83–85.

31. Discussion of Hellman's memoir in Weinstein, *Perjury*, 489; William Wright, *Lillian Hellman: The Image, the Woman* (New York: Simon & Schuster, 1986), 357–58.

32. Kramer quoted in Weinstein, *Perjury*, 489–90.

33. See Weinstein, *Perjury*, 459.

34. Carey McWilliams, *The Education of Carey McWilliams* (New York: Simon & Schuster, 1979), 311.

35. For encyclopedia and Associated Press, see Weinstein, *Perjury*, 6; See also Haynes and Klehr, *In Denial*, 165–69; Romerstein and Breindel, 139–41.

36. On Navasky, see discussion in Neil Rosenthal, "State of the 'Nation,'" 83.

37. On Czechoslovakia, see Courtois, *The Black Book*, ch. 20.

38. See Helen Manfull, ed., *Additional Dialogue: Letters of Dalton Trumbo, 1942–1962* (New York: Bantam Books, 1972); quotation is on 459. See also 299.

39. Discussion of the article and its context is available in Radosh and Radosh, *Red Star over Hollywood*, 218–21; letter to Bright on 218.

40. Dalton Trumbo, "Honor Bright and All That Jazz," *The Nation*, 1965, reprinted in Trumbo, *Time of the Toad*; quote on 152.

41. All statistics are from Courtois, *The Black Book*: Spain, 350–51; Greece, 330; Lithuania and Baltics, 236; Gulag, 234.

42. Conquest, *The Dragons of Expectation*, 115–16. On famine and dekulakization, see Robert Conquest, *Harvest of Sorrow: Soviet Collectivization and the Terror-Famine* (New York: Oxford University Press, 1986), 296–97.

CHAPTER 14

1. Bob Thomas, *King Cohn: The Life and Times of Harry Cohn* (New York: G. P. Putnam and Sons, 1967), 299 and 262–65. See also "Testimony of Richard Collins," in *Motion Picture Industry: Hearings*, April 12, 1951, 240.

2. Bob Thomas, *King Cohn*, 263. "Testimony of Robert Rossen," in *New York City Area: Hearings*, 1953, 1490.

3. Bernstein interviewed in Patrick McGilligan and Paul Buhle, *Tender Comrades: A Backstory of the Blacklist* (New York: St. Martin's Griffin, 1999), 46–47. From Bernstein's memoir, Walter Bernstein, *Inside Out: A Memoir of the Blacklist* (New York: Da Capo Press, 1966), 7.

4. For Wexley, see McGilligan and Buhle, *Tender Comrades*, 716–17. On Rossen's contributions of forty thousand dollars, see "Testimony of Robert Rossen," 1463.

5. Robert Rossen, "Lessons Learned in Combat," interview by Jean-Louis Noames, *Cahiers du Cinema in English*, January 1967, 23 and 25. Translated from *Cahiers du Cinema*, April 1966, 36.

6. Thomas, *King Cohn*, 262–65.

7. Robert Rossen, "An Interview with Robert Rossen," interview by Daniel Stein, *Arts in Society*, Winter 1966–1967, 47.

8. Alan Casty, *The Films of Robert Rossen* (New York: Museum of Modern Art, 1969), 21.

9. *Newsweek*, November 21, 1949, 91. John McCarten, *New Yorker*, November 12, 1949, 64. Bosley Crowther, *New York Times*, November 9, 1949, 37; and see also *New York Times*, November 13, 1949, sec. 2, 1.

10. Bruce Cook, *Dalton Trumbo* (New York: Charles Scribner's Sons, 1977), 226.

11. For Trumbo's letter to Cleo, see Helen Manfull, ed., *Additional Dialogue: Letters of Dalton Trumbo, 1942–1962* (New York: Bantam Books, 1972), 145–46.

12. Bright is quoted in Cook, *Dalton Trumbo*, 92.

13. For Trumbo's letter to Biberman, see Cook, *Dalton Trumbo*, 224. Letters through this period that are reprinted in Manfull's *Additional Dialogue* have many discussions of money and schemes to make it.

14. For Trumbo's letter to Wilson, see Manfull, *Additional Dialogue*, 283ff.

15. For Trumbo's letter to Butler, see Manfull, *Additional Dialogue*, 212ff.

16. Hunter and his wife are quoted in Cook, *Dalton Trumbo*, 232–33.

17. Stewart is quoted in Larry Ceplair and Steven Englund, *The Inquisition in Hollywood: Politics in the Film Community, 1930–1960* (Berkeley: University of California Press, 1983), 363.

CHAPTER 15

1. Bob Thomas, *King Cohn: The Life and Times of Harry Cohn* (New York: G. P. Putnam and Sons, 1967), 300.

2. For Parks, Holliday, and Buchman, see Thomas, *King Cohn*, 299–302.

3. Thomas, *King Cohn*, 189–90.

4. "Testimony of Robert Rossen," in *Motion Picture Industry: Hearings*, June 25, 1951; on strategy, see, for example, 677, and quotation on 676.

5. "Testimony of Robert Rossen," 702.

6. "Testimony of Robert Rossen," 704, 707.

7. "Testimony of Robert Rossen," 713–14.

8. Buchman is quoted in Thomas, *King Cohn*, 301–2. For background, see also Larry Ceplair and Steven Englund, *The Inquisition in Hollywood: Politics in the Film Community, 1930–1960* (Berkeley: University of California Press, 1983), 382–83.

9. Garfield is quoted in Larry Swindell, *Body and Soul: The Story of John Garfield* (New York: William Morrow, 1975), 251; Garfield's testimony reprinted extensively on 241–53.

10. Swindell, *Body and Soul*, 254–55.

11. See Joseph R. Starobin, *American Communism in Crisis, 1943–1957* (Berkeley: University of California Press, 1975), 217–23; Dorothy Healey, *Dorothy Healey Remembers* (New York: Oxford University Press, 1990), 104; Ted Morgan, *Reds: McCarthyism in Twentieth Century America* (New York: Random House, 2003), 300–301, 319–20.

12. See Ceplair and Englund, *The Inquisition in Hollywood*, 370. On Wanger, see background and sequence of public letters in Eric Bentley, *Thirty Years of Treason* (New York: Viking Press, 1973), 292–93.

13. Ronald Reagan, "Reds Beaten in Hollywood," *Hollywood Citizen News*, reprinted in Bentley, *Thirty Years of Treason*, 293–95.

14. Wood is quoted in Walter Goodman, *The Committee* (New York: Farrar, Straus & Giroux, 1968), 298.

15. Goodman, *The Committee*, 300.

16. Quoted in Goodman, *The Committee*, 301. From "Testimony of Roy Brewer," in *Motion Picture Industry: Hearings*, September 17, 1951, 1416.

17. Quoted in Richard Gid Powers, *Not Without Honor: The History of American Anticommunism* (New York: Free Press, 1995), 249. For Brewer's quote on McCarthy, see Ronald Brownstein, *The Power and the Glitter: The Washington-Hollywood Connection* (New York: Pantheon Books, 1990), 138.

18. See detailed discussion in Victor Navasky, *Naming Names* (New York: Viking Press, 1980), 156–64. See also Ceplair and Englund, *The Inquisition in Hollywood*, 396–97.

19. "Testimony of Abraham Polonsky," in *Motion Picture Industry: Hearings*, April 25, 1951, 405.

20. Wilson is discussed and quoted in Joseph McBride, *Frank Capra: The Catastrophe of Success* (New York: Simon & Schuster, 1992), 586–87.

21. "Testimony of Paul Jarrico," in *Motion Picture Industry: Hearings*, April 12, 1951, 276 and 280.

22. See "Testimony of Richard Collins," in *Motion Picture Industry: Hearings*, April 12, 1951, 255. The *Times* comment is quoted in Walter Goodman, *The Committee*, 301.

23. "Testimony of Lillian Hellman," in *Motion Picture Industry: Hearings*, May 21, 1951, discussed and quoted in William Wright, *Lillian Hellman: The Image, the Woman* (New York: Simon & Schuster, 1986), 244–54. For Hellman's letter to the committee, see Wright, *Lillian Hellman*, 246–47.

24. "Testimony of Lillian Hellman," quoted in Wright, *Lillian Hellman*, 251–52. For Hellman's version of the trial, see Lillian Hellman, *Scoundrel Time* (Boston: Little, Brown, 1976), 93 ff.

25. David F. Prindle, *The Politics of Glamour: Ideology and Democracy in the Screen Actors Guild* (Madison: University of Wisconsin Press, 1988), 57. Ceplair and Englund, *The Inquisition in Hollywood*, 392–94; Brownstein, *The Power and the Glitter*, 116; Powers, *Not Without Honor*, 246.

26. Lawrence Grobel, *The Hustons* (New York: Scribners, 1989), 398.

27. Navasky, *Naming Names*, 87ff; Ceplair and Englund, *The Inquisition in Hollywood*, 388ff.

28. On Gang, see Navasky, *Naming Names*, 98–109; Navasky, *Naming Names*, 390–92. On Brewer, see Navasky, *Naming Names*, 389.

29. See Robert Vaughn, *Only Victims: A Study in Show Business Blacklisting* (New York: G. P. Putnam and Sons, 1972), 202–6; Goodman, *The Committee*, 381–82; Prindle, *The Politics of Glamour*, 55–58; Ceplair and Englund, *The Inquisition in Hollywood*, 386–88; Navasky, *Naming Names*, 88–89, passim.

30. On Scott, see Helen Manfull, ed., *Additional Dialogue: Letters of Dalton Trumbo, 1942–1962* (New York: Bantam Books, 1972), 307; Prindle, *The Politics of Glamour*, 61. On the HUAC and the American Legion, see Otto Friedrich, *City of Nets: A Portrait of Hollywood in the 1940s* (New York: Harper & Row, 1986), 379; and Powers, *Not Without Honor*, 246. Both use figures from John Cogley, *Report on Blacklisting: 1—Movies* (New York: Fund for the Republic, 1956).

CHAPTER 16

1. Maltz letter is quoted in Larry Ceplair and Steven Englund, *The Inquisition in Hollywood: Politics in the Film Community, 1930–1960* (Berkeley: University of California Press, 1983), 376.

2. Buhle interview of Bernstein is quoted in Patrick McGilligan and Paul Buhle, *Tender Comrades: A Backstory of the Blacklist* (New York: St. Martin's Griffin, 1999), 54.

3. Navasky quote is from Victor Navasky, *Naming Names* (New York: Viking Press, 1980), 347. Bernstein quote is from Walter Bernstein, *Inside Out: A Memoir of the Blacklist* (New York: Da Capo Press, 966), 8.

4. Kazan is quoted in Ted Morgan, *Reds: McCarthyism in Twentieth Century America* (New York: Random House, 2003), 524.

5. Morgan, *Reds*, 522.

6. William L. O'Neill, *A Better World: The Great Schism—Stalinism and the American Intellectuals* (New York: Simon & Schuster, 1982), quoted in Guenter Lewy, *The

Cause That Failed: Communism in American Political Life (New York: Oxford University Press, 1990), 124.

7. Alan F. Westin, "Do Silent Witnesses Defend Civil Liberties?" *Commentary*, June 1953, 541ff, quoted in Guenter Lewy, *The Cause That Failed*, 96–97.

8. Schulberg is quoted in Navasky, *Naming Names*, 242.

9. Carey McWilliams, *The Education of Carey McWilliams* (New York: Simon & Schuster, 1979), 137.

10. "Testimony of Robert Rossen," in *New York City Area: Hearings*, May 7, 1953, 1456.

11. "Testimony of Robert Rossen," 1467.

12. "Testimony of Robert Rossen," 1465 and 1470.

13. Unsent letter to the *New York Times*, dated January 31, 1953, 1. Property of Sue Rossen.

14. "Testimony of Robert Rossen," 1458–59.

15. "Testimony of Robert Rossen," 1487–89, and see 1490.

16. "Testimony of Robert Rossen," 1491.

17. Jean Seberg, "Lilith and I," *Cahiers du Cinema in English*, January 1967, 35.

18. "Testimony of Edward Dmytryk," in *Motion Picture Industry: Hearings*, April 25, 1951, reprinted in Eric Bentley, *Thirty Years of Treason* (New York: Viking Press, 1973), 398.

19. TV interview with Tristram Powell is quoted in Navasky, *Naming Names*, 238. Richard English, "What Makes a Hollywood Communist?" *Saturday Evening Post*, May 17, 1951, 30ff.

20. "Testimony of Edward Dmytryk," 410–11.

21. English, "What Makes a Hollywood Communist?" 30.

22. On Duclos and Biberman, see Bentley, *Thirty Years of Treason*, 397. On the film *Cornered*, see Bentley, *Thirty Years of Treason*, 396.

23. "Written Statement of Elia Kazan," *New York City Area: Hearings*, April 10, 1952, reprinted in Bentley, *Thirty Years of Treason*, 485; full statement on 485–95.

24. *New York Times* ad reprinted in Bentley, *Thirty Years of Treason*, 484. See also discussion in Morgan, *Reds*, 523–24.

25. Elia Kazan, *A Life* (New York: Alfred A. Knopf, 1998), 449.

26. On Skouras, see Kazan, *A Life*, 451. For quote by Zanuck, see Kazan, *A Life*, 455. On Miller's comments, see Kazan, *A Life*, 460–61. On Odets and Strasbergs, see Kazan, *A Life*, 462–64.

27. Quoted as fact in Ceplair and Englund, *The Inquisition in Hollywood*, 377. The authors trace it to Stefan Kanfer, *A Journal of the Plague Years* (New York: Atheneum, 1971), 173. Kazan discusses the conversation in Kazan, *A Life*, 461–62, and the "sharpest knife" comment on 592.

28. See Michel Ciment, *Kazan on Kazan* (New York: Viking Press, 1974), 84.

29. Kazan, *A Life*, 458–60.

30. Kazan, *A Life*, 465–70; see also 566. On Dmytryk, see Bentley, *Thirty Years of Treason*, 398.

31. For the *Variety* ad, see Morgan, *Reds*, 524; and Ronald Radosh and Allis Radosh, *Red Star over Hollywood: The Film Colony's Long Romance with the Left* (San Francisco: Encounter Books, 2005), 240. For details of the campaign, see Norma

Barzman, *The Red and the Blacklist* (New York: Nation Books, 2003), 442–43; Barzman quote is on 442.

32. Editorial, *Philadelphia Enquirer*, September 20, 2003; and *Philadelphia Enquirer*, October 4, 2003, quoted in Radosh and Radosh, *Red Star over Hollywood*, 240.

33. "Testimony of Clifford Odets," in *Motion Picture Industry: Hearings*, May 19–20, 1952; Odets' comments on secrecy are reprinted in Bentley, *Thirty Years of Treason*, 526–27. His comment on being silent is reprinted in Bentley, *Thirty Years of Treason*, 531.

34. Kazan, *A Life*, 463. For later further discussion of Odets, 664–66.

35. See footnote in Ceplair and Englund, *The Inquisition in Hollywood*, 374.

36. "Testimony of Leo Townsend," in *Motion Picture Industry: Hearings*, September 18, 1951, 1527.

37. "Testimony of Leo Townsend," 1511.

38. "Testimony of Leo Townsend," 1527.

39. "Testimony of Frank Tuttle," in *Motion Picture Industry: Hearings*, May 24, 1951, 644, 646. See also Morgan, *Reds*, 522; Robert Vaughn, *Only Victims: A Study in Show Business Blacklisting* (New York: G. P. Putnam and Sons, 1972), 22.

40. "Testimony of Roy Huggins," in *Motion Picture Industry: Hearings*, September 19, 1952, 4269 (on the gap), 4270 (on classes), 4271 (on systems).

41. "Testimony of Roy Huggins," 4278 (on Soviet foreign policy) and 4279 (on individual freedom).

42. "Testimony of Roy Huggins," 4280.

43. Interview in Navasky, *Naming Names*, 263–64.

44. "Testimony of Edward G. Robinson," in *Motion Picture Industry: Hearings*, April 30, 1952, reprinted in Bentley, *Thirty Years of Treason*, 497.

45. "Testimony of Edward G. Robinson," 498.

46. See Vaughn, *Only Victims*, 155. For examples of detailed testimony of Berkeley (as used with other witnesses), see Bentley, *Thirty Years of Treason*, 535, 646, 712. For Wheeler's comments, see Navasky, *Naming Names*, 317–18.

47. On the first hearings, see Ceplair and Englund, *The Inquisition in Hollywood*, 294. For Collins' testimony, see "Testimony of Richard Collins," in *Motion Picture Industry: Hearings*, April 12, 1951, 257–58.

48. Collins is in Navasky, *Naming Names*, 229. On Collins' strategy, see Navasky, *Naming Names*, 229. For the general discussion and interview, see Navasky, *Naming Names*, 225–32.

49. Navasky, *Naming Names*, 254. For full discussion, see 252–56. On regrets, see Navasky, *Naming Names*, 257.

50. On Collins, see Navasky, *Naming Names*, 257.

CHAPTER 17

1. Philip Dunne, *Take Two: A Life in Movies and Politics* (New York: McGraw-Hill, 1990), 205–6.

2. Interview in Patrick McGilligan and Paul Buhle, *Tender Comrades: A Backstory of the Blacklist* (New York: St. Martin's Griffin, 1999), 405. Letter to Maltz from Oc-

tober 28, 1977, quoted in Victor Navasky, *Naming Names* (New York: Viking Press, 1980), 406.

3. McGilligan and Buhle, *Tender Comrades*, 405.

4. Bernstein quotes are from interview in McGilligan and Buhle, *Tender Comrades*, 47.

5. Lester Cole, *Hollywood Red* (Palo Alto, Calif.: Ramparts Press, 1981), 351–52.

6. Polonsky is quoted in Navasky, *Naming Names*, 279.

7. Polonsky is quoted in Navasky, *Naming Names*, 227.

8. On Collins and the FBI, see Navasky, *Naming Names*, 231.

9. Cole, *Hollywood Red*, 346.

10. Albert Maltz, *Hollywood Reporter*, May 29, 1951, reprinted in Eric Bentley, *Thirty Years of Treason* (New York: Viking Press, 1973), 400–405.

11. Quoted in McGilligan and Buhle, *Tender Comrades*, 53.

12. Jarrico is quoted in McGilligan and Buhle, *Tender Comrades*, 339, 345.

13. Polonsky is quoted in Navasky, *Naming Names*, 227.

14. Bernstein quoted in McGilligan and Buhle, *Tender Comrades*, 51.

15. Dassin is quoted in McGilligan and Buhle, *Tender Comrades*, 215.

16. Scott is quoted in McGilligan and Buhle, *Tender Comrades*, 591.

17. On Levy, see Cole, *Hollywood Red*, 350, and also 320–21. On Berkeley, see Cole, *Hollywood Red*, 354, and see also 174–75.

18. Helen Manfull, ed., *Additional Dialogue: Letters of Dalton Trumbo, 1942–1962* (New York: Bantam Books, 1972), 389. This is in long letter to Endore, December 30, 1956, 378–93. See also Trumbo's correspondence with Endore in Ronald Radosh and Allis Radosh, *Red Star over Hollywood: The Movie Colony's Long Romance with the Left* (San Francisco: Encounter Books, 2005), 222–24 and n. 31 and 32, 287.

19. Navasky, *Naming Names*, 379.

20. See Stéphane Courtois et al., *The Black Book of Communism: Crimes, Terror, Repression* (Cambridge, Mass.: Harvard University Press, 1999), 18, 23–26, 185, 255. Pages 192ff contrast what was talked about and all that was not. See also William Taubman, *Khrushchev: The Man and His Era* (New York: W.W. Norton, 2003), ch. 11.

21. Courtois, *The Black Book*, 255 and 26.

22. Howard Fast, *Being Red* (Boston: Houghton Mifflin, 1990), 274.

23. Robert C. Tucker, *Stalin in Power* (New York: W.W. Norton, 2003), 27.

24. Simon Sebag Montefiore, *Stalin: The Court of the Red Tsar* (New York: Alfred A. Knopf, 2004), 33.

25. Martin Amis, *Koba and the Dread: Laughter and the Twenty Million* (New York: Hyperion, 2002), 25.

26. Amis, *Koba*, 29.

27. Amis, *Koba*, 29.

28. Amis, *Koba*, 33.

29. Amis, *Koba*, 33.

30. For quotes on worldwide conquest, see Amis, *Koba*, 90, 91, 95. See also Tucker, *Stalin in Power*, 33–34.

31. Montefiore, *Stalin*, xx and 230–31.

32. Maltz is quoted in Larry Ceplair and Steven Englund, *The Inquisition in Hollywood: Politics in the Film Community, 1930–1960* (Berkeley: University of California Press, 1983), 239.

33. Dassin is quoted in McGilligan and Buhle, *Tender Comrades*, 211.

34. Fast, *Being Red*, 138.

35. Stander is quoted in McGilligan and Buhle, *Tender Comrades*, 489.

36. Rapf is quoted in McGilligan and Buhle, *Tender Comrades*, 510–11.

37. Dassin is quoted in McGilligan and Buhle, *Tender Comrades*, 209.

38. Jarrico is quoted in McGilligan and Buhle, *Tender Comrades*, 336, 347, 348. See also Ceplair and Englund, *The Inquisition in Hollywood*, 408.

39. Ritt is quoted in McGilligan and Buhle, *Tender Comrades*, 563.

40. Ring Lardner Jr., *I'd Hate Myself in the Morning* (New York: Nation Books, 2000), 113, 45.

41. Walter Bernstein, *Inside Out: A Memoir of the Blacklist* (New York: Da Capo Press, 1966), 254–55.

42. Cole, *Hollywood Red*, 209, 369–70, 9.

43. Maltz quoted in Navasky, *Naming Names*, 296.

44. See interview by B. Zeitlin and David Talbot, *Cineaste* 8, no. 3 (1978): 2–24. See also Ceplair and Englund, *The Inquisition in Hollywood*, 176; Radosh and Radosh, *Red Star over Hollywood*, 172, 233; Navasky, *Naming Names*, 296; Ceplair and Englund, *The Inquisition in Hollywood*, 235 and 77.

45. Trumbo quoted in McGilligan and Buhle, *Tender Comrades*, xxi.

46. Guenter Lewy, *The Cause That Failed: Communism in American Life* (New York: Oxford University Press, 1990), 125.

47. Fast, *Being Red*, 299.

48. Fast, *Being Red*, 138, 324, and 343 (pages in same sequence as quotes).

49. Fast, *Being Red*, 134, 345, and 344 (pages in same sequence as quotes).

50. Fast, *Being Red*, 202, 278.

51. Fast, *Being Red*, 182 and 145.

52. Fast, *Being Red*, 397.

53. Abraham Polonsky [signed as Timon], "The Troubled Mandarins," *Masses and Mainstream*, August 1956, 46. Quoted in Paul Buhle and David Wagner, *A Very Dangerous Citizen: Abraham Polonsky and the Hollywood Left* (Berkeley: University of California Press, 2001), 171.

54. Courtois, *The Black Book*, 19.

55. Arthur Miller, *Timebends: A Life* (New York: Grove Press, 1987), 529.

CHAPTER 18

1. Scott is quoted in Victor Navasky, *Naming Names* (New York: Viking Press, 1980), 339.

2. Gordon Kahn, *Hollywood on Trial: The Story of the Ten Who Were Indicted* (New York: Boni and Gaer, 1948), 3.

3. Wilson is quoted in Larry Ceplair and Steven Englund, *The Inquisition in Hollywood: Politics in the Film Community, 1930–1960* (Berkeley: University of California Press, 1983), 414–15. Trumbo is quoted in Nancy Lynn Schwartz, *The Hollywood Writers' Wars* (New York: McGraw-Hill, 1983), 286. Spiegelgass is quoted in Ceplair and Englund, *The Inquisition in Hollywood*, 423.

4. Paul and Sylvia Jarrico are quoted in Navasky, *Naming Names*, 336.

5. Losey is quoted in Tom Milne, *Losey on Losey* (Garden City, N.Y.: Doubleday, 1968), 42.

6. Walter Bernstein, *Inside Out: A Memoir of the Blacklist* (New York: Da Capo Press, 1966), 284.

7. Morley is quoted in Patrick McGilligan and Paul Buhle, *Tender Comrades: A Backstory of the Blacklist* (New York: St. Martin's Griffin, 1999), 478–89.

8. Ritt is quoted in McGilligan and Buhle, *Tender Comrades*, 564.

9. McGilligan and Buhle, *Tender Comrades*, xx, xix.

10. Ceplair and Englund, *The Inquisition in Hollywood*, 422.

11. Thomas Elsaesser, "Tales of Sound and Fury: Observations on the Family Melodrama," in *Film Theory and Criticism: Introductory Readings*, 4th ed., ed. Gerald Mast, Marshall Cohen, and Leo Braudy (New York: Oxford University Press, 1992), 520, 529.

12. Thomas Schatz, *Hollywood Genres* (New York: Random House, 1981), 234.

13. Mark Stevens and Annalyn Swan, *De Kooning: An American Master* (New York: Alfred A. Knopf, 2004), 282 and 295.

14. On Mulvey's views, see discussion in Griselda Pollock, "Report on the Weekend School," *Screen* 18, no. 2 (Summer 1977): 105–13.

15. Thomas Schatz, *Hollywood Genres*, 243.

16. Michael Wood, *America in the Movies* (New York: Basic Books, 1975), 163.

17. Quoted in Ed Sikow, *On Sunset Boulevard: The Life and Times of Billy Wilder* (New York: Hyperion, 1998), 274.

CHAPTER 19

1. Ritt is quoted in Patrick McGilligan and Paul Buhle, *Tender Comrades: A Backstory of the Blacklist* (New York: St. Martin's Griffin, 1999), 563.

2. Polonsky is quoted in McGilligan and Buhle, *Tender Comrades*, 486.

3. Bernstein is quoted in McGilligan and Buhle, *Tender Comrades*, 48.

4. For Ceplair and Englund quote, see Larry Ceplair and Steven Englund, *The Inquisition in Hollywood: Politics in the Film Community, 1930–1960* (Berkeley: University of California Press, 1983), 377. For Navasky quote, see Victor Navasky, *Naming Names* (New York: Viking Press, 1980), 313. Scott is quoted in Navasky, *Naming Names*, 340.

5. David Thomson, *A Biographical Dictionary of Film*, 2nd ed., revised (New York: William Morrow, 1981), 301.

6. Thomson, *A Biographical Dictionary of Film*, 301.

7. Bernstein is quoted in McGilligan and Buhle, *Tender Comrades*, 49. Polonsky is quoted in McGilligan and Buhle, *Tender Comrades*, 486.

8. In Henry Burton, "Notes of Rossen's Films," *Films in Review*, June–July 1962, 336.

9. Rossen is quoted in Jane Cianfarra, "'Alexander's Band': International Troupe Films Rossen's *Alexander the Great* in Spain," *New York Times*, April 24, 1955, part 2, 5. See in Alan Casty, *The Films of Robert Rossen* (New York: Museum of Modern Art, 1969), 33.

10. Interview by Jean-Louis Noames, "Lessons Learned in Combat," *Cahiers du Cinema in English,* January 1967, 22.

11. Jean-Andre Fieschi, "The Unique Film," *Cahiers du Cinema in English,* January 1967, 32.

12. Jean Seberg, "Lilith and I," *Cahiers du Cinema in English,* January 1967, 36.

13. See discussion in Casty, *The Films of Robert Rossen,* 46–47.

14. Paul Buhle and David Wagner, *Radical Hollywood* (New York: New Press, 2002), 251, 231.

15. David Kalak, "Commentary," *Christ in Concrete,* DVD (All Day Entertainment, 2003).

16. Buhle and Wagner, *Radical Hollywood,* xv. Ceplair and Englund, *The Inquisition in Hollywood,* 426.

17. Pauline Kael, "Propaganda—*Salt of the Earth,*" in *I Lost It at the Movies* (New York: Bantam Books, 1966), 308.

CHAPTER 20

1. Richard Gid Powers, *Not Without Honor: The History of American Anticommunism* (New York: Free Press, 1995), 274, 425–27.

2. John Earl Haynes and Harvey Klehr, *In Denial: Historians, Communism & Espionage* (San Francisco: Encounter Books, 2003), 8. Their book is a valuable collection and analysis of this culture's materials.

3. Schrecker article is quoted in Haynes and Klehr, *In Denial,* 80.

4. Ellen Schrecker, *Many Are the Crimes: McCarthyism in America* (Boston: Little, Brown, 1998), x, 227; in the second edition (1999), see ix–x.

5. Schrecker, *Many Are the Crimes,* 46.

6. Haynes and Klehr, *In Denial,* 81. The article is Ethan Bronner, "Rethinking McCarthyism, If Not McCarthy," *New York Times,* October 18, 1998. See also the editorial "Revisionist McCarthyism," October 23, 1998.

7. For Markowitz and Cook, see Haynes and Klehr, *In Denial,* 50. For first Kovel quote, see Guenter Lewy, *The Cause That Failed: Communism in American Political Life* (New York: Oxford University Press, 1990), 131. For second Kovel quote, see Haynes and Klehr, *In Denial,* 52, and for Wald, 48.

8. For discussion of the photos, see Peter Collier and David Horowitz, "McCarthyism: The Last Refuge of the Left," *Commentary,* January 1988, 38.

9. On Frankfield, see Herbert Romerstein and Eric Breindel, *The Venona Secrets: Exposing Soviet Espionage and America's Traitors* (Washington, D.C.: Regnery Publishing, 2000), 451–53.

10. For quote from *Anatomy of Anti-Communism,* see Lewy, *The Cause That Failed,* 118. Caute is quoted in Lewy, *The Cause That Failed,* 127.

11. Howe is quoted in Lewy, *The Cause That Failed,* 127.

12. Wexley is quoted in McGilligan and Buhle, *Tender Comrades: A Backstory of the Blacklist* (New York: St. Martin's Griffin, 1999), 717.

13. See Haynes and Klehr, *In Denial,* 198–201.

14. Haynes and Klehr, *In Denial,* 205 (Schneirs), 97–101 (Venona), and 197 (immorality).

15. Haynes and Klehr, *In Denial*, 213 (Schrank); 197, 206–7 (Schrecker).

16. Haynes and Klehr, *In Denial*, 105–6.

17. Schrecker, *Many Are the Crimes*, 175. Ellen Schrecker, "The Spies Who Loved Us?" *The Nation*, May 24, 1999, 28–31. And see discussion of the consequences of McCarthyism in Schrecker, *Many Are the Crimes*, ch. 10, "A Good Deal of Trauma— The Impact of McCarthyism, 359–415. For the *New York Times* editorial, see Haynes and Klehr, *In Denial*, 81.

18. For Patterson, Haynes and Klehr, *In Denial*, 151. On Markowitz, see Haynes and Klehr, *In Denial*, 104. On the New York exhibit, see Haynes and Klehr, *In Denial*, 209–10.

19. Haynes and Klehr, *In Denial*, 151.

20. For discussion of Lowenthal, see Allen Weinstein, *Perjury: The Hiss-Chambers Case* (New York: Alfred A. Knopf, 1978), 364, 503–6, 522–23. For *Times* article, *New York Times*, October 29, 1992. For Lowenthal's obituary, *New York Times*, December 7, 1995. Both discussed in Romerstein and Breindel, *The Venona Secrets*, 140–41. See also Haynes and Klehr, *In Denial*, 152–54 and 165–68.

21. See Robert Conquest, *The Dragons of Expectation: Reality and Delusion in the Course of History* (New York: W.W. Norton, 2005), 155–63.

22. Haynes and Klehr, *In Denial*, 47 (Markowitz), 22–27 (Van Laue and Thurston), 331 (Adler and Patterson).

23. Schrecker, *Many Are the Crimes*, 158–59, 402.

24. Larry Ceplair and David Englund, *The Inquisition in Hollywood: Politics in the Film Community, 1930–1960* (Berkeley: University of California Press, 1983), 267. See similar passages 172, 203, and 243.

25. Ceplair and Englund, *The Inquisition in Hollywood*, 436 (responsibility) and 377 ($50,000).

26. *The Nation* quoted in Gerard Alexander, "Utopia's Victims," *Claremont Review*, Winter 2003, 21.

27. Navasky quoted in Haynes and Klehr, *In Denial*, 95. On Bentley, see Haynes and Klehr, *In Denial*, 143; on exchanges, see 195–96.

28. On Hiss, see Haynes and Klehr, *In Denial*, 95, 142–50. Navasky on *The Haunted Wood*, Haynes and Klehr, *In Denial*, 150.

29. On anti-Communists, see Navasky's "Introduction" in Ring Lardner Jr., *I'd Hate Myself in the Morning* (New York: Nation Books, 2000), x and ix.

30. Victor Navasky, *Naming Names* (New York: Viking Press, 1980), 47, 5, 131, 313, 333–34, 339, 411.

31. Navasky, *Naming Names*, 425 (degradation ceremonies) and 423 (moral exemplars).

32. Navasky, *Naming Names*, 279–80, 280–81.

33. Navasky, *Naming Names*, 425; see also 312.

34. Buhle's article is quoted in Haynes and Klehr, *In Denial*, 44.

35. Buhle's encyclopedia entry is quoted in Haynes and Klehr, *In Denial*, 70–71.

36. Buhle's encyclopedia entry is quoted in Haynes and Klehr, *In Denial*, 109–11.

37. On Schlesinger, see Paul Buhle and David Wagner, *Radical Hollywood* (New York: New Press, 2002), 441.

38. McGilligan and Buhle, *Tender Comrades*, xviii.

39. See William Pechter, "Abraham Polonsky and the Force of Evil," *Film Quarterly*, Spring 1962, 53.

40. Polonsky is quoted in Ron Henderson, ed., *The Image Maker* (Richmond, Va.: John Knox Press, 1971), 23.

41. Polonsky is quoted in McGilligan and Buhle, *Tender Comrades*, 491.

42. Quoted in McGilligan and Buhle, *Tender Comrades*, 492.

43. Walter Bernstein, *Inside Out: A Memoir of the Blacklist* (New York: Da Capo Press, 1966), 181.

44. Jarrico is quoted in McGilligan and Buhle, *Tender Comrades*, 345–46.

45. Rapf is quoted in McGilligan and Buhle, *Tender Comrades*, 538–39.

46. Wexley is quoted in McGilligan and Buhle, *Tender Comrades*, 720.

47. David Caute, *Joseph Losey: A Revenge on Life* (New York: Oxford University Press, 1994), 102.

48. Tom Milne, *Losey on Losey* (Garden City, N.Y.: Doubleday, 1968), 92.

49. Caute, *Joseph Losey*, 104.

50. Ritt is quoted in McGilligan and Buhle, *Tender Comrades*, 563.

51. Polonsky is quoted in McGilligan and Buhle, *Tender Comrades*, 493–94.

52. Stéphane Courtois et al., *The Black Book of Communism: Crimes, Terror, Repression* (Cambridge, Mass.: Harvard University Press, 1999), 11.

53. Aleksander Wat, *My Century: The Odyssey of a Polish Intellectual* (New York: W.W. Norton, 1988), 173–74.

Bibliography

Abel, Lionel. *The Intellectual Follies*. New York: W.W. Norton, 1984.

Agee, James. *Agee on Film*. N.p.: Beacon Press, 1964.

Amis, Martin. *Koba and the Dread: Laughter and the Twenty Million*. New York: Hyperion, 2002.

Andrew, Christopher, and Oleg Gordievsky. *KGB: The Inside Story of Its Foreign Operations from Lenin to Gorbachev*. New York: HarperCollins, 1990.

Andrew, Christopher, and Vasili Mitrokhin. *The Sword and the Shield: The Mitrokhin Archive and the Secret History of the KGB*. New York: Basic Books, 1999.

Antonov-Ovseyenko, Anton. *The Time of Stalin: Portrait of a Tyranny*. New York: Harper & Row, 1981.

Applebaum, Anne. *Gulag: A History*. New York: Doubleday, 2003.

Arnold, Edwin T., and Eugene L. Miller. *The Films & Career of Robert Aldrich*. Knoxville: University of Tennessee Press, 1986.

Barzman, Norma. *The Red and the Blacklist*. New York: Nation Books, 2003.

Bentley, Eric. *Thirty Years of Treason*. New York: Viking Press, 1973.

Bernstein, Barton J., ed. *Towards a New Past: Dissenting Essays in American History*. New York: Pantheon Books, 1968.

Bernstein, Walter. *Inside Out: A Memoir of the Blacklist*. New York: Da Capo Press, 1966.

Bessie, Alvah. *Inquisition in Eden*. New York: Macmillan, 1965.

Billingsley, Kenneth Lloyd. *Hollywood Party: How Communism Seduced the American Film Industry in the 1930s and 1940s*. Rocklin, Calif.: Prima Publishing, 1998.

Bosworth, Patricia. *Anything Your Little Heart Desires: An American Family Story*. New York: Simon & Schuster, 1997.

Brownstein, Ronald. *The Power and the Glitter: The Hollywood-Washington Connection*. New York: Pantheon Books, 1990.

Buhle, Paul, and Dave Wagner. *Blacklisted: The Film Lover's Guide to the Hollywood Blacklist*. New York: Palgrave Macmillan, 2003.

———. *Radical Hollywood*. New York: New Press, 2002.

———. *A Very Dangerous Citizen: Abraham Lincoln Polonsky and the Hollywood Left*. Berkeley: University of California Press, 2001.

Casty, Alan. *The Films of Robert Rossen*. New York: Museum of Modern Art, 1969.

Cate, Curtis. *Andre Malraux*. New York: Fromm International Publishing, 1998.

Caute, David. *The Great Fear: The Anti-Communist Purge under Truman and Eisenhower*. New York: Simon & Schuster, 1977.

———. *Joseph Losey: A Revenge on Life*. New York: Oxford University Press, 1994.

Ceplair, Larry, and Steven Englund. *The Inquisition in Hollywood: Politics in the Film Community, 1930–1960*. Berkeley: University of California Press, 1983.

Ciment, Michel. *Kazan on Kazan*. New York: Viking Press, 1974.

Clurman, Harold. *The Fervent Years: The Story of the Group Theatre and the Thirties*. New York: Hill & Wang, 1957.

Cogley, John. *Report on Blacklisting: 1—Movies*. New York: Fund for the Republic, 1956.

Cole, Lester. *Hollywood Red*. Palo Alto, Calif.: Ramparts Press, 1981.

Coleman, Peter. *The Liberal Conspiracy: The Congress for Cultural Freedom and the Struggle for the Mind of Postwar Europe*. New York: Free Press, 1989.

Conquest, Robert. *The Dragons of Expectation: Reality and Delusion in the Course of History*. New York: W.W. Norton, 2005.

———. *The Great Terror: A Reassessment*. New York: Oxford University Press, 1940.

———. *Harvest of Sorrow: Soviet Collectivization and the Terror-Famine*. New York: Oxford University Press, 1986.

———. "Revolutionary High Finance." In *The Dragons of Expectation: Reality and Delusion in the Course of History*, 95–99. New York: W.W. Norton, 2005.

Constable, Pamela, and Arturo Valenzuela. *A Nation of Enemies: Chile under Pinochet*. New York: W.W. Norton, 1993.

Cook, Bruce. *Dalton Trumbo*. New York: Charles Scribner's Sons, 1977.

Costello, John. *Mask of Treachery*. New York: William Morrow, 1988.

Courtois, Stéphane, et al. *The Black Book of Communism: Crimes, Terror, Repression*. Cambridge, Mass.: Harvard University Press, 1999.

Dallin, David, and Boris I. Nicolaevsky. *Forced Labor in Soviet Russia*. New Haven, Conn.: Yale University Press, 1947.

Davis, Nathaniel. *The Last Two Years of Salvador Allende*. Ithaca, N.Y.: Cornell University Press, 1985.

Dmytryk, Edward. *It's a Helluva Life but Not a Bad Living*. New York: Times Books, 1978.

———. *Odd Man Out: A Memoir of the Hollywood Ten*. Carbondale: Southern Illinois University Press, 1956.

Dunne, Philip. *Take Two: A Life in Movies and Politics*. New York: McGraw-Hill, 1990.

Durgnat, Raymond. "Ways of Melodrama." In *Imitations of Life: A Reader on Film and Television Melodrama*, ed. Marcia Landy. Detroit: Wayne University Press, 1991.

Elsaesser, Thomas. "Tales of Sound and Fury: Obsevations on the Family Melodrama." In *Film Theory and Criticism: Introductory Readings*, 4th ed., edited by Gerald Mast, Marshall Cohen, and Leo Braudy, 512–33. New York: Oxford University Press, 1992.

Fast, Howard. *Being Red*. Boston: Houghton Mifflin, 1990.

Friedrich, Otto. *City of Nets: A Portrait of Hollywood in the 1940s*. New York: Harper & Row, 1986.

Furet, Francois. *The Passing of an Illusion: The Idea of Communism in the Twentieth Century*. Chicago: University of Chicago Press, 1999.

Gabler, Neal. *An Empire of Their Own: How the Jews Invented Hollywood*. New York: Anchor Books, 1988.

Gallagher, Tag. *The Adventures of Roberto Rosselini: His Life and Films*. New York: Da Capo Press, 1998.

———. *John Ford: The Man and His Films*. Berkeley: University of California Press, 1986.

Georgakas, Dan, and Lenny Rubenstein, eds. *The Cineaste Interviews: On the Art and Politics of the Cinema*. Chicago: Lake View Press, 1983.

Gold, Mike. *A Literary Anthology*. New York: International Publishers, 1972.

Goodman, Walter. *The Committee*. New York: Farrar, Straus & Giroux, 1968.

Grobel, Lawrence. *The Hustons*. New York: Charles Scribner's Sons, 1989.

Gross, Babette. *Willi Munzenberg: A Political Biography*. East Lansing: Michigan State University Press, 1974.

Hamilton, Ian. *Writers in Hollywood*. New York: Harper & Row, 1990.

Haynes, John Earl, and Harvey Klehr. *In Denial: Historians, Communism & Espionage*. San Francisco: Encounter Books, 2003.

———. *Venona: Decoding Soviet Espionage in America*. New Haven, Conn.: Yale University Press. 1990.

Hays, Arthur Garfield. *City Lawyer*. New York: Simon & Schuster, 1942.

Healey, Dorothy. *Dorothy Healey Remembers*. New York: Oxford University Press, 1990.

Hellman, Lillian. *Scoundrel Time*. Boston: Little, Brown, 1976.

———. *An Unfinished Woman*. Boston: Little, Brown, 1970.

Hemingway, Ernest. *Selected Letters: 1917–1960*, edited by Carlos Baker. New York: Charles Scribner's Sons, 1981.

Henderson, Ron, ed. *The Image Maker*. Richmond, Va.: John Knox Press, 1971.

Hodos, George. *Show Trials: Stalinist Purges in Eastern Europe, 1948–1954*. New York: Praeger, 1987.

Hook, Sydney. *Heresy, Yes—Conspiracy, No!* New York: American Committee for Cultural Freedom, 1952.

———. *Out of Step: An Unquiet Life in the 20th Century*. New York: Harper & Row, 1987.

Howe, Irving, and Lewis Coser. *The American Communist Party: A Critical History (1919–1957)*. New York: Frederick A. Praeger, 1962.

Huston, John. *An Open Book*. New York: Alfred A. Knopf, 1980.

Jerome, V. J. *Intellectuals and the War*. New York: Workers Library Publishers, 1940.

Kael, Pauline. *I Lost It at the Movies*. New York: Bantam Books, 1960.

———. "Propaganda—*Salt of the Earth*." In *I Lost It at the Movies*. New York: Bantam Books, 1966.

Kahn, Gordon. *Hollywood on Trial: The Story of the Ten Who Were Indicted*. New York: Boni and Gaer, 1948.

Kaplan, Justin. *Lincoln Steffens*. New York: Simon & Schuster, 1974.

Kazan, Elia. *A Life*. New York: Alfred A. Knopf, 1998.

Keats, John. *You Might as Well Live: The Life and Times of Dorothy Parker*. New York: Simon & Schuster, 1970.

Kempton, Murray. *Part of Our Time: Some Monuments and Ruins of the Thirties*. New York: Simon & Schuster, 1955.

Klehr, Harvey, John Earl Haynes, and Kyrill Anderson. *The Soviet World of American Communism*. New Haven, Conn.: Yale University Press, 1998.

Klehr, Harvey, John Earl Haynes, and Fridrikh Igorevich Firsov. *The Secret World of American Communism*. New Haven, Conn.: Yale University Press, 1995.

Knight, Amy. *Beria: Stalin's First Lieutenant*. Princeton, N.J.: Princeton University Press, 1983.

Koch, Howard. *As Time Goes By*. New York: Harcourt Brace Jovanovich, 1979.

Koch, Stephen. *Double Lives: Spies and Writers in the Secret Soviet War of Ideas against the West*. New York: Free Press, 1994.

Koestler, Arthur. *The Invisible Writing: The Second Volume of an Autobiography*. New York: Macmillan, 1954.

Kolakowski, Leszek. *Main Currents of Marxism: The Founders, the Golden Age, the Breakdown*. New York: W.W. Norton, 2004.

———. *My Correct Views on Everything*. New York: St. Augustine's Press, 2004.

Kornbluth, Peter. *The Pinochet File: A Declassified Dossier on Atrocity and Acceptability*. Washington, D.C.: A National Security Archive Book, 2003.

Lamphere, Robert J., and Tom Schactman. *The FBI-KGB War: A Special Agent's Story*. New York: Random House, 1986.

Landers, Robert K. *An Honest Writer: The Life and Times of James T. Farrell*. San Francisco: Encounter Books, 2004.

Landy, Marcia, ed. *Imitations of Life: A Reader on Film and Television Melodrama*. Detroit: Wayne State University Press, 1991.

Lardner, Ring, Jr. *I'd Hate Myself in the Morning*. New York: Nation Books, 2000.

———. *The Lardners: My Family Remembered*. New York: Harper & Row, 1976.

Lawson, John Howard. *With a Reckless Preface*. New York: Farrar and Rinehart, 1934.

Lenin, V. I. *The Proletarian Revolution and the Renegade Kautsky*. Moscow: Foreign Languages Publishing House, 1952.

Leprohon, Pierre. *The Italian Cinema*. New York: Praeger Publishers, 1972.

Lewy, Guenter. *The Cause That Failed: Communism in American Political Life*. New York: Oxford University Press, 1990.

Liehm, Mira. *Passion and Defiance: Film in Italy from 1942 to the Present*. Berkeley: University of California Press, 1984.

Lobl, Eugen. *My Mind on Trial*. New York: Harcourt Brace Jovanovich, 1976.

Lottman, Herbert. *The Left Bank: Writers, Artists and Politics from the Popular Front to the Cold War*. Boston: Houghton Mifflin, 1982.

Lyons, Eugene. *The Red Decade: The Stalinist Penetration of America*. New York: Bobbs, Merrill, 1941.

Maltz, Albert. *The Citizen Writer*. New York: International Publishers, 1950.

———. "The Writer as the Conscience of the People." In *The Citizen Writer*. New York: International Publishers, 1950.

Manfull, Helen, ed. *Additional Dialogue: Letters of Dalton Trumbo, 1942–1962*. New York: Bantam Books, 1972.

McBride, Joseph. *Frank Capra: The Catastrophe of Success*. New York: Simon & Schuster, 1992.

McDonald, Dwight. *Memoirs of a Revolutionist*. New York: Farrar, Straus and Cudahy, 1957.

McGilligan, Patrick, and Paul Buhle. *Tender Comrades: A Backstory of the Blacklist*. New York: St. Martin's Griffin, 1999.

McWilliams, Carey. *The Education of Carey McWilliams*. New York: Simon & Schuster, 1979.

Meade, Marion. *Dorothy Parker: What Fresh Hell Is This?* New York: Random House, 1987.

Mellen, Joan. *Hellman and Hammett: The Legendary Passion of Lillian Hellman and Dashiell Hammett*. New York: HarperCollins, 1996.

Miller, Arthur. *Timebends: A Life*. New York: Grove Press, 1987.

Miller, Eugene L., Jr., and Edwin T. Arnold. *Robert Aldrich: Interviews*. Jackson: University Press of Mississippi, 2004.

Milne, Tom. *Losey on Losey*. Garden City, N.Y.: Doubleday, 1968.

Milosz, Czeslaw. "A Letter to Picasso." In *Voices of Dissent: A Collection of Articles from* Dissent *Magazine*, 381–84. New York: Grove Press, 1958.

Milton, Joyce. *Tramp: The Life of Charlie Chaplin*. New York: HarperCollins, 1996.

Moldea, Dan E. *Dark Victory: Ronald Reagan, MCA, and the Mob*. New York: Viking Press, 1986.

Montefiore, Simon Sebag. *Stalin: The Court of the Red Tsar*. New York: Alfred A. Knopf, 2004.

Morgan, Ted. *Reds: McCarthyism in Twentieth Century America*. New York: Random House, 2003.

Navasky, Victor. "Introduction." In Ring Lardner Jr., *I'd Hate Myself in the Morning*, by Ring Lardner Jr. New York: Nation Books, 2000.

———. *Naming Names*. New York: Viking Press, 1980.

Neve, Brian. *Film and Politics in America: A Social Tradition*. New York: Routledge, 1992.

O'Neill, William L. *A Better World: The Great Schism—Stalinism and the American Intellectuals*. New York: Simon & Schuster, 1982.

Orwell, George. *Homage to Catalonia*. London: Secker and Warburg, 1938.

Pagan, Edward Obregon. *Murder at the Sleepy Lagoon*. Chapel Hill: University of North Carolina Press, 2003.

Payne, Stanley G. *The Spanish Civil War, the Soviet Union, and Communism*. New Haven, Conn.: Yale University Press, 2004.

Powers, Richard Gid. *Not Without Honor: The History of American Anticommunism*. New York: Free Press, 1995.

Prindle, David F. *The Politics of Glamour: Ideology and Democracy in the Screen Actors Guild*. Madison: University of Wisconsin Press, 1988.

Rabkin, Gerald. *Drama and Commitment: Politics in the American Theatre of the Thirties*. Bloomington: Indiana University Press, 1964.

Radosh, Ronald. *Commies: A Journey through the Old Left, the New Left, and the Leftover Left*. San Francisco: Encounter Books, 2001.

Radosh, Ronald, Mary R. Habeck, and Grigory Sevstianov, eds. *Spain Betrayed: The Soviet Union in the Spanish Civil War*. New Haven, Conn.: Yale University Press, 2001.

Radosh, Ronald, and Joyce Milton. *The Rosenberg File: A Search for the Truth*. New York: Holt, Rinehart and Winston, 1983.

Radosh, Ronald, and Allis Radosh. *Red Star over Hollywood: The Film Colony's Long Romance with the Left*. San Francisco: Encounter Books, 2005.

Rapf, Maurice. *Back Lot: Growing Up with the Movies*. Lanham, Md.: Scarecrow Press, 1999.

Reagan, Ronald. *Where's the Rest of Me?* New York: Elsevier-Dutton, 1965.

Rollyson, Carl. *Lillian Hellman: Her Legend and Her Legacy*. New York: St. Martin's Press, 1986.

Romerstein, Herbert, and Eric Breindel. *The Venona Secrets: Exposing Soviet Espionage and America's Traitors*. Washington, D.C.: Regnery Publishing, 2000.

Schary, Dore. *Heyday: An Autobiography*. New York: Little, Brown, 1979.

Schatz, Thomas. *Holllywood Genres*. New York: Random House, 1981.

Schecter, Jerrold, and Leona Schecter. *Sacred Secrets: How Soviet Intelligence Operations Changed American History*. Washington, D.C.: Brassey's, 2002.

Schickel, Richard. *Schickel on Film*. New York: HarperCollins, 1989.

Schrecker, Ellen. *Many Are the Crimes: McCarthyism in America*. Boston: Little, Brown, 1998.

Schulberg, Budd. *Moving Pictures: Memories of a Hollywood Prince*. New York: Stein and Day, 1981.

———. *Writers in America: The Four Seasons of Success*. New York: Stein and Day, 1983.

Schwartz, Nancy Lynn. *The Hollywood Writers' Wars*. New York: McGraw-Hill, 1983.

Sikow, Ed. *On Sunset Boulevard: The Life and Times of Billy Wilder*. New York: Hyperion, 1998.

Silver, Alain, and James Ursini. *What Ever Happened to Robert Aldrich? His Life and Films*. New York: Limelight Editions, 1995.

Solzhenitsyn, Aleksandr. *The Gulag Archipelago: An Experiment in Literary Investigating, 1918–1956*. 3 vols. Boulder, Colo.: Westview Press, 1997.

Starobin, Joseph R. *American Communism in Crisis, 1943–1957*. Berkeley: University of California Press, 1975.

Starr, Kevin. *Embattled Dreams: California in War and Peace, 1940–1950*. New York: Oxford University Press, 2002.

Stephan, Alexander. *"Communazis": FBI Surveillance of German Émigré Writers*. New Haven, Conn.: Yale University Press, 2000.

Stevens, Mark, and Annalyn Swan. *De Kooning: An American Master*. New York: Alfred A. Knopf, 2004.

Stewart, Donald Ogden. *By a Stroke of Luck: An Autobiography*. New York and London: Paddington Press, 1975.

Sudoplatov, Pavel, and Anatoli Sudoplatov. *Special Tasks*. Boston: Little, Brown, 1994.

Swindell, Larry. *Body and Soul: The Story of John Garfield*. New York: William Morrow, 1975.

Taubman, William. *Khrushchev: The Man and His Era*. New York: W.W. Norton, 2003.

Taylor, John Russell. *Strangers in Paradise: The Hollywood Emigres, 1933–1950*. New York: Holt, Rinehart and Winston, 1983.

Thomas, Bob. *King Cohn: The Life and Times of Harry Cohn*. New York: G. P. Putnam's Sons, 1967.

Thomson, David. *A Biographical Dictionary of Film*, 2nd ed., revised. New York: William Morrow, 1981.

Thurston, Robert. *Life and Terror in Stalin's Russia, 1934–1941*. New Haven, Conn.: Yale University Press, 1996.

Trumbo, Dalton. "The Devil in the Book." In *The Time of the Toad: A Study of Inquisition in America*. New York: Perennial Library, Harper & Row, 1972.

———. *The Time of the Toad: A Study of Inquisition in America*. New York: Perennial Library, Harper & Row, 1972.

Tucker, Robert C. *Stalin in Power*. New York: W.W. Norton, 1990.

U.S. Congress. House Committee on Un-American Activities. *Communism in the Motion Picture Industry: Hearings before the Committee on Un-American Activities*, 1947, 1951, 1952, 1953.

———. House Committee on Un-American Activities. *Investigation of Communist Activities in the New York City Area: Hearings before the Committee on Un-American Activities*, 1952, 1953.

———. House Committee on Un-American Activities. *Report on the Communist Peace Offensive*, April 1951.

Vaughn, Robert. *Only Victims: A Study in Show Business Blacklisting*. New York: G. P. Putnam and Sons, 1972.

Viertel, Salka. *The Kindness of Strangers*. New York: Holt, Rinehart and Winston, 1969.

Volkogonov, Dimitri. *Lenin: A New Biography*. New York: Free Press, 1994.

———. *Stalin: Triumph and Tragedy*. New York: Free Press, 1990.

———. *Trotsky: The Eternal Revolutionary*. New York: Free Press, 1996.

Warren, Frank A. *Liberals and Communism: The Red Decade Revisited*. Bloomington: Indiana University Press, 1966.

Wat, Aleksander. *My Century: The Odyssey of a Polish Intellectual*. New York: W.W. Norton, 1988.

Weinstein, Allen. *Perjury: The Hiss-Chambers Case*. New York: Alfred A. Knopf, 1978.

Weinstein, Allen, and Alexander Vassiliev. *The Haunted Wood: Soviet Espionage in America—the Stalin Era*. New York: Random House, 1999.

Wexley, John. *The Judgment of Julius and Ethel Rosenberg*. New York: Cameron and Kahn, 1955.

Williams, Jay. *Stage Left*. New York: Charles Scribner's Sons, 1974.

Williams, Tony. *The Cinematic Vision of Robert Aldrich*. Lanham, Md.: Scarecrow Press, 2004.

Wilson, Edmund. *A Literary Chronicle, 1920–1950*. Garden City, N.Y.: Doubleday, 1956.

Winchester, Simon. *The Fantastic Story of the Eccentric Scientist Who Unlocked the Mysteries of the Middle Kingdom*. New York: HarperCollins, 2008.

Winter, Ella. *And Not to Yield: An Autobiography*. New York: Harcourt, Brace and World, 1963.

Wood, Michael. *America in the Movies*. New York: Basic Books, 1975.

Wright, William. *Lillian Hellman: The Image, the Woman*. New York: Simon & Schuster, 1986.

Zhdanov, Andrei. *Essays on Literature, Philosophy, and Music*. New York: International Publishers, 1950.

Zubok, Vladislav, and Constantine Pleshakov. *Inside the Kremlin's Cold War: From Stalin to Khrushchev*. Cambridge, Mass.: Harvard University Press, 1996.

Index

Woltman, Frederick, 222
Wong Howe, James, 95–96, 98–99
Wood, Michael, 264–65
Wood, Natalie, 271
Wood, Sam, 65
World Committee for the Relief of the
    Victims of German Fascism, 36, 40
World Congress of Intellectuals, 9,
    147–48
World Peace Conference, 150
World Peace Congress, 149
world situation: and filmmaking, 254–
    55, 261; postwar, 56–71
World War II, 48–52; espionage and,
    128–29; and film noir, 91–92; party
    line on, 139; Rossen and, 80–82;
    and SWG, 63
Wright, Richard, 142–43
Writers Clinic, 83
Writers Club, 57

Writers Conference, 82–84
Writers Congress, 82–83
writing: Lawson on, 60–61; Lenin on,
    10; Maltz on, 3, 5, 162; Polonsky
    and, 103; Rossen and, 75–77, 82–84
Written on the Wind, 263
Wyler, William, 172, 220, 265

Ybarra, Michael, 28
Yevtushenko, Yevgeni, 15, 18
Young, Nedrick A., 223

Zanuck, Darryl, 232–33, 272
Zarubin, Vasily. *See* Zubilin, Vasily
Zborowski, Lev, 165
Zhdanov, Andrei, 5–6, 9–10, 12, 19,
    155–56
Zinnemann, Fred, 260
Zolotow, Maurice, 139
Zubilin, Vasily, 131–32, 134

About the Author

Alan Casty received his doctorate from the University of California at Los Angeles. Now professor emeritus, he has taught film studies as well as literature and writing at UCLA and Santa Monica College. He is the author of fifteen books, including *Development of the Film: An Interpretive History*, *The Dramatic Art of the Film*, *The Films of Robert Rossen*, *Mass Media and Mass Man*, and *The Shape of Fiction*. His articles on film and drama, literature, and culture have appeared in numerous magazines and journals.

Casty has made a long, wide-ranging personal study of Communism in the world and especially in Hollywood, where he grew up and later met survivors among the Hollywood Reds while doing research on several projects.

He lives with his wife, the artist Jill Casty, in Pacific Grove, California, and Pisa, Italy.